CONTEMPORARY STRATEGY

CONTEMPORARY STRATEGY

Theories and Policies

John Baylis, Ken Booth,
John Garnett and Phil Williams

HOLMES & MEIER PUBLISHERS, INC.
New York

© 1975 John Baylis, Ken Booth, John Garrett
and Phil Williams

· Published in the United States of America 1975
by Holmes and Meier Publishers, Inc.
101 Fifth Avenue
New York, New York 10003

Printed in Great Britain

Library of Congress Cataloging in Publication Data
Main entry under title:

Contemporary strategy.

includes index.
1. Strategy.   2. Military policy.   I. Baylis, John.

U162.066 355.4'3 75-19410

ISBN 0-8419-0221-6 (Hardback)
       0-8419-0222-4 (Paperback)

CONTENTS

PREFACE

The Department of International Politics at the University College of Wales, Aberystwyth, has been heavily involved in teaching and research in strategic studies for well over ten years and for over fifty-five years in the teaching of the parent discipline, international politics. Each of the authors of this book has spent an important part of his career either as a teacher or student of strategy, or both, in the Department of International Politics. While the authors themselves are very much aware of the differences in outlook and emphasis between them, readers may be more impressed by the similarity of their outlook, and therefore see this book as a reflection of the way the subject has been developed in Aberystwyth.

The authors felt that there was a need for a scholarly and comprehensive introduction to specialized strategic studies which dealt with both the theoretical and policy aspects of the subject. This book is an attempt to fulfil that requirement. The theoretical aspects provide an analytical map so that the student of strategy can find his way around the subject without getting lost in the detail. The policy aspects sharpen the student's appreciation of the theory, and help him to comment in an informed way on the strategic issues of the day.

The contents are divided into three major parts. Part One deals with the nature and evolution of strategy and the changing role of military forces. Part Two discusses major contemporary strategic concepts while the third part describes the military policies of the major powers since 1945. The book is an introductory text in that it assumes no prior knowledge of the subject; but is hoped that the analysis is sufficiently sophisticated and the scope sufficiently comprehensive to interest the specialist as well as the beginner. Though the book should be considered as a whole, individual chapters are nevertheless meant to be self-contained

The authors would like to thank Kay Critchley, Marian Weston, Dilwen Williams, Gloria Davies and Lily Findlay who have typed successive drafts. They would also like to express their appreciation to Mike Clarke, the Research Officer in the Department of International Politics, for various forms of assistance, including helping to check footnotes. Ken Booth would like to thank Colin Gray and James King for reading and commenting upon his chapter, "The Evolution of Strategic Thinking". John Baylis likewise wishes to thank David Steeds who read the chapter on "Chinese Defence Policy" and made many valuable comments. Phil Williams would like to express his gratitude to David Greenwood for all his assistance and encouragement. Any deficiencies are of course the responsibility of the authors themselves.

PART ONE

STRATEGY AND ITS EVOLUTION

1 STRATEGIC STUDIES AND ITS ASSUMPTIONS

John Garnett

The Nature of Strategic Studies

'Strategy', as one of the contributors to this volume has remarked, 'is a deadly business'.[1] It is concerned with the darker side of human nature, in that it examines the way in which military power is used by governments in the pursuit of their interests. Now because military power refers to the capacity to kill, to maim, to coerce and destroy, it follows that it is a crude instrument. Its use determines not who is right in any dispute, but whose will is going to prevail, and its utility arises, fundamentally, out of the depressing fact that human beings, their property, and the society in which they live are easily destroyed. It is this fragility of human beings and their artefacts which is exploited by those who wield military power.

Inevitably pain, suffering, destruction and death are close to the surface of strategic analysis, though they may not figure prominently in the literature of the subject. Various writers have commented on the way in which the horrors and miseries of war are submerged in the neutral, anodyne jargon of strategic terminology. Strategists talk of 'taking out' cities, of making 'counterforce' strikes with 'collateral damage', of crossing 'thresholds', and of engaging in tactical nuclear 'exchanges'. It is easy to forget that what is being discussed in this clinical fashion is the extermination of thousands — perhaps millions — of human beings by the most dreadful weapons ever invented. There is no need to labour the point, but no student should forget the grim realities which lie behind the vocabulary of strategic studies.

For the man in the street, strategy is intimately connected with planning wars and fighting them. It is a military activity *par excellence* in which high-ranking officers plan the overall conduct of wars. This popular impression is reinforced by Clausewitz's definition of strategy as 'the employment of battle as the means towards the attainment of the object of war'.[2] But in a very important sense the man in the street has got it wrong. To be sure, strategy is about war, and the conduct of military compaigns, but it is about much more than that. Fundamentally, it is about the ways in which military power may be used to achieve political objectives — and it cannot be repeated too often that waging war is only one of the ways in which military power can be used to implement political goals. It is for this reason that strategy is much wider than the study of wars and military campaigns. The German von

Moltke described strategy as 'the practical adaptation of the means placed at a general's disposal to the attainment of the object in view',[3] and the same thought was reiterated by Liddell Hart who believed that strategy was 'the art of distributing and applying military means to fulfil the ends of policy'.[4] Both of these definitions have the advantage of releasing strategy from its traditional strait jacket – war – by acknowledging that military power can be equally purposeful in peacetime.

Indeed, in the nuclear age, when modern technology threatens to turn any war into Armageddon, to concentrate on planning wars is little short of madness. Today there is no alternative to peace, and this being so, as Liddell Hart put it, 'old concepts and old definitions of strategy have become not only obsolete but non-sensical with the development of nuclear weapons. To aim at winning a war, to take victory as your object, is no more than a state of lunacy.'[5] Given the power of modern weapons it is the prime task of strategic doctrine not to wage war but to create alternatives less catastrophic than thermonuclear holocaust.

Today, purely military definitions of strategy have virtually disappeared because they failed to convey either the flavour or the scope of a subject that straddles the spectrum of war and peace, and is as much concerned with statesmanship as with generalship. However, though strategy is more about peace than it is about war, it is generally recognised that if we fail to manage the former, then some thought must be given to surviving the latter.

Any satisfactory definition of strategy must take into account the peacetime applications of strategic thinking, and must locate the use of military force in the more general context of foreign policy-making. Robert Osgood has suggested that "military strategy must now be understood as nothing less than the overall plan for utilizing the capacity for armed coercion – in conjunction with the economic, diplomatic, and psychological instruments of power – to support foreign policy most effectively by overt, covert, and tacit means.'[6] And André Beaufre has, on occasion, spoken of the need for the West to devise an overall strategy which would incorporate and co-ordinate the political, economic and military instruments of policy.[7] As Michael Howard has said,[8] for Beaufre the whole field of international relations constituted a battlefield in which the Communist powers, thwarted in the use of force by the nuclear stalemate, were attacking the West by indirect, political manoeuvres such as infiltration and subversion. It was only natural, therefore, for our strategies to include a political component.

There is some danger that political interpretations such as these may make it impossible to distinguish strategic studies either from the study of foreign policy-making, or even the wider subject of international politics. Indeed, the distinctions are not clear-cut. If anything they reflect differences of emphasis rather than differences in subject matter.

Though he focuses his attention on the way in which military force is exploited, either by its use or non-use, the strategist must acquaint himself with the political problems which provide the context for strategic theorising. The connection between politics and strategic studies has been well expressed by Raymond Aron. 'Strategic thought draws its inspiration each century, or rather at each moment in history, from the problems which events themselves pose.'[9] Without such background knowledge, strategic analysis is almost meaningless. Today, strategic thought is so inextricably entwined with international politics that it would be misleading and dangerous to try to separate the two subjects.

Those without much understanding of politics often have too crude and simplistic a picture of state behaviour either to understand the context in which strategic problems arise, or to appreciate the analysis which deals with them. In strategic studies the ability to argue logically and to follow a piece of strategic reasoning is very important, but even more important is the elusive, almost indefinable quality of political judgement which enables a man to evaluate a piece of analysis and locate it in a wider political framework. If this intuitive feel can be taught at all, it can only be done by familiarising a student with political behaviour. That is why, throughout this book, and particularly in the chapters which describe the defence policy of the major powers, a deliberate attempt has been made to relate military policy to political events.

It follows from this that strategy is not a discipline in its own right. It is a subject with a sharp focus — the role of military power — but no clear perimeter, and it is parasitic upon arts, science and social science subjects for the ideas and concepts which its practitioners have developed. It is perhaps worth noting that Herman Kahn was originally a physicist, Thomas Schelling an economist, Albert Wohlstetter a mathematician, and Henry Kissinger a historian.

The definitions so far considered have all emphasised that strategy is fundamentally about 'means' rather than 'ends'. It has been assumed that settling political goals is the proper business of politicians, and that strategic planners are only interested in how given military resources can usefully be applied to the achievement of those goals. Their job, it has been argued, is to harness military power to the national interest; but their mandate does not extend to determining what, in a particular situation, the national interest is. The subordination of strategy to politics which is implicit in this analysis is now generally accepted. If war is to be a functional thing and not pointless violence, then the politician must be in control of it. Clausewitz's famous recommendation that war ought to be a continuation of political intercourse with an ad mixture of other means has rightly become the most famous of all strategic aphorisms.

In democratic societies few would wish to challenge either the supremacy of political direction or the view that strategic analysis should concentrate on identifying and evaluating the various choices available to states in their use of military power for ends clearly defined by political authorities; but there are certain dangers in completely prohibiting strategists from participating in high-level political planning. While it may be legitimately argued that politicians rather than their military and civil servants should decide the goals of democratically controlled foreign policy, they should not do so without consulting those, who by virtue of their specialist knowledge, are best able to think through the implication of pursuing particular policies and who, though unqualified to pass comment on their desirability, are well able to advise as to their practicability and consequences. Strategists have become government *advisers* as well as government *executives*.

To be sure, politicians must exercise ultimate control, but the decisions they arrive at ought to be moderated by the advice they receive from specialists. If, as Clemenceau is reputed to have claimed, war is much too serious to be left to the generals, it is also too serious to be left to the politicians. What is required is a continuous dialogue between political and military minds. Henry Kissinger has made a convincing plea for this dialogue.

A separation of strategy and policy can only be achieved to the detriment of both. It causes military power to become identified with the most absolute applications of power and it tempts diplomacy into an over-concern with finesse. Since the difficult problems of national policy are in the area where political, economic, psychological and military factors overlap we should give up the fiction that there is such a thing as 'purely' military advice.[10]

Kissinger looked forward to the day when, 'At every stage of formulation of strategy, doctrine would be considered as a combination of political, economic and military factors replacing the incongruity of the present system which seeks to compromise two incommensurables, "purely" military and "purely" political considerations.'[11]

At this point it may be worth emphasizing that the influence of civilian and military strategists at the highest levels of political planning is no more a threat to the democratic process than the influence of any government advisers. In fact canvassing specialist opinion is simply an indication that the government is exploiting its advisory resources properly without losing its rightful monopoly of decision-making power. However, some commentators have seen the movement of military and academic strategists into and out of government departments as part of an insidious plot to undermine the democratic process. A good deal of the literature about the American 'industrial military complex' and the 'war-peace establishment' which is part of it, has a note of hysteria about it, but a number of serious writers have identified a threat to democracy. Harold Lasswell, for example, has argued that the arena of world politics is moving towards the domination of 'specialists in violence'.[12] His famous 'garrison state hypothesis' predicts the growing and anti-democratic influence of 'specialists in violence' in the decision-making process. A proper discussion of the 'garrison state hypothesis' and the influence of the 'industrial military complex' in American decision-making is beyond the scope of this book. What must be said, however, is that in theory at least, the influence of civilian and military specialists in strategy need not threaten democratic values.

Once the meaning of strategy was widened to incorporate a political as well as a military component, and to include analysis of the peacetime uses of military power, it was inevitable that the armed services' monopoly of the subject would be broken. Since the Second World War most of the creative thinking in the field of strategic studies has not been done by serving officers in war colleges, but by civilians in research insitutes and universities. It was soon recognised that military experience was a much less important qualification for studying strategy in its new, wide sense than a trained analytical mind grounded in history or one of the social sciences. The foundations of contemporary strategic thought were laid in a handful of American universities and research institutes like the Rand Corporation. Scholars like Bernard Brodie, Albert Wohlstetter, Henry Kissinger, William Kaufmann, Herman Kahn and Thomas Schelling, have made an indelible, profound, and widely acknowledged imprint on the subject.

Around them has developed an enormous industry of specialists dealing with issues of war and peace. This intellectual community is sometimes described as the 'war-peace establishment'. It is, as Herzog comments, not an establishment in the usual sense of an institution, but 'one of ideas and theory, of scientists, seers and strategists, who have worked out the form and rationale of present American defence and foreign policy.'[13] Within this subculture are dozens of research institutions preoccupied with military doctrines, technology and foreign policy, and hundreds of academics and government officials concerned with national security. Throughout the Western world more and more scholars are taking an interest in questions of defence.

In Britain, the number of individuals professionally engaged in the study of strategic questions is still not very large, but it is growing, and there are a good many civil servants, journalists, and students of political science who are sufficiently interested in the subject to contribute to its development. In Britain there are no counterparts to research institutions like the Rand Corporation or the Hudson Institute, but the International Institute for Strategic Studies in particular, and to a lesser extent the Royal United Services Institution, have both contributed to the development of the subject and a growing public awareness of its importance. The research output, both classified and unclassified, of this international group of scholars and students is enormous, and in the English language there is now a formidable and impressive body of contemporary strategic literature.

Although scholars in the strategic studies field tend to know each other, at least by reputation, they do not always agree on how the subject should be taught, or even where its central focus lies. Divergencies of opinion and different interests account for the fact that different university departments put the emphasis in different places. In Britain, for example, university departments differ significantly in the way in which they approach the subject. At Aberdeen, particular attention is paid to defence economics; at King's College, London, a more historical treatment is favoured; at Lancaster there is an orientation towards defence planning. Here in Aberystwyth the department has concentrated on strategic theory.

Not only are there differences of opinion about the content of the subject and how it should be taught, but there are also differences of opinion as to whether 'strategic studies' is the most appropriate description of the subject matter taught in its name. Some argue that the traditional narrow military usage of the word strategy has given 'strategic studies' a military connotation which, if adopted, delimits the field of strategy far too narrowly for an age which places emphasis of non-violent responses to conflict situations. The title adopted for the subject should not preclude the possibility of examining non-violent techniques of conflict. It is for this reason that 'war studies' is equally misleading as a description for a subject which devotes at least as much time to thinking about the preservation of peace as it does to the conduct of war.

Attempts have been made to avoid the ambiguities inherent in the term 'strategic studies' by thinking up alternative titles, but some of the new titles also have their disadvantages. 'Conflict resolution', borrowed from the journal of that name, is sometimes suggested as a reasonable substitute, but this phrase is both too wide and too narrow for its purpose. It is too wide in the sense that it does not accurately specify the kind of conflict students of strategic studies are interested in, and it is too narrow in the sense that it implies that they are exclusively concerned with the problem of *resolving* conflicts. The word 'resolution' has precriptive overtones which are not entirely appropriate for an academic activity concerned primarily with *understanding* the world rather than with improving it. 'National security studies', which is another of the titles sometimes considered, suffers from the disadvantage of implying an actor-orientated study which revolves around questions of national defence. 'Strategic studies' is not so ethnocentric as that. Perhaps, in view of the difficulties involved in finding suitable alternative titles, there is something to be said for sticking to 'strategic studies' and hoping that as this title becomes more widely used, its meaning will become settled and the misleading connotations will disappear.

Some Assumptions Underlying Contemporary Strategic Thought

But in spite of these differences of interpretation and emphasis, and in spite of serious differences of opinion on particular strategic issues, it is fair to say that most contemporary strategists in the Western world belong, in an important sense, to the same intellectual tradition. Their minds are tuned to the same wavelength; they share a common set of assumptions about the nature of international political life, and the kind of reasoning which is appropriate to handling political military problems. That is why, though strategists sometimes disagree with each other, they rarely misunderstand each other.

The assumptions which underpin a good deal of contemporary strategic thought are rarely articulated, and may not even be appreciated by those who actually engage in strategic analysis. It takes real effort to identify and sort out the philosophical underpinnings of any subject, and more often than not the only consequence of this painful exercise is to undermine the intellectual confidence of those who do it. Nevertheless, just as an argument is only as strong as the premises upon which it is founded, so a body of strategic analysis is only as sound as the assumptions on which it is based. For the sake of his intellectual integrity and his peace of mind, therefore, the serious student is bound to articulate, if not to question, some of the major assumptions upon which the sophisticated edifice of post-war strategic doctrine has been laboriously built.

Realism
Perhaps the most pervasive assumptions underlying contemporary strategy are those which are associated with the theory of political behaviour known as 'realism'. This philosophical tradition, which was largely a reaction on the idealism of the 1920s and 1930s, has dominated the literature of international relations since the end of the Second World War, and it is now implicit in most writing on the subject.

It is impossible to summarise the body of ideas and attitudes normally associated with 'realism' in international politics, because even among the self-professed realists there are important differences. But the general flavour of the realist position is unmistakable. Realists tend to be conservative in their views, that is to say, they see virtue in evolutionary change which is sufficiently slow for that which is best in international society to be preserved and they are cautious both in their estimate of what can be done, and what ought to be done, to ameliorate international relationships. Realists tend to accept a world subdivided into independent sovereign states as being the normal, if not the permanent, condition of international society, and they consider *Realpolitik* an inescapable feature of the international environment. They are sceptical about the possibilities of permanent peace, and suspicious of all grandiose schemes of revolutionary change. Ideas for world government, general and comprehensive disarmament and collective security are carefully scrutinized and rejected as impractical, perhaps even undesirable, solutions to the world's ailments. As far as their contribution to peace and international security is concerned, even the activities of the United Nations and its subsidiary organs are regarded with some scepticism.

The realists, disillusioned with nineteenth-century ideas of inevitable progress in international relations, are nonetheless incapable of pointing, with any degree of confidence, in the direction in which progress lies. Many would sympathise with M. Oakeshott when he says, in that justly celebrated inaugural of his,

> in political activity then, men sail a boundless and bottomless sea; there is neither harbour for shelter nor floor for anchorage, neither starting-place nor appointed destination. The enterprise is to keep afloat on an even keel; the sea is both friend and enemy; and the seamanship consists in using the resources of a traditional manner of behaviour in order to make a friend of every hostile occasion.[14]

Perhaps the main reasons why the realists entertain minimal expectations of state behaviour are to be found in their conceptions of human nature and international society. Men are seen to be inherently destructive, selfish, competitive, and aggressive, and the international system one that is torn by conflict and full of uncertainty and disorder. R. Niebuhr, a founding father of the realist school and one of its most brilliant exponents, speaks of man's 'stubbon pride', his 'egotism', 'will to power', 'brute inheritance', and of course, his 'original sin'.[15] For the realists there is an element of tragedy in human relations. In the words of Herbert Butterfield, 'behind the great conflicts of mankind is a terrible human predicament which lies at the heart of the story.'[16] George Kennan also regarded statesmen as 'actors in a tragedy beyond their making or repair.'[17]

The realists are quick to point out the limitations of international law and to emphasise the disintegrating, anarchic influences at work in an intractable international system. It is not really surprising that Hobbes is one of the realists' favourite philosophers, since his conception of the 'state of nature' resembles their conception of international society, and they share similar views of human nature. It was Hobbes who described the human condition as 'a restless struggle for power which ceaseth only in death'.[18] The realists also emphasise the ubiquity of the power struggle, and their literature is dominated by the concepts of national power and interest. Conflict is regarded as an inescapable condition of international life. This simple assumption is the starting point of realism. World like 'harmony'and 'co-operation' do not come easily to realist lips and the realists are not much given to moralising about international politics.

In short, the realists take exception to those who put too much faith in human reason, to those idealists who refuse to recognise the world as it is, and who talk in pious platitudes about the world as it ought to be. In the words of one writer, 'Realism is a clear recognition of the limits of morality and reason in politics: the acceptance of the fact that political realities are power realities and that power must be countered with power; that self-interest is the primary datum in the action of all groups and nations.'[19]

In defence of the realists it must be admitted that they do not approve of the hard, ruthless world which they describe. They simply regard it as a given; something which must be accepted before any progress can be made. In the words of one of the founders of political realism, Hans Morgenthau, 'the world, imperfect as it is from a rational point of view, is the result of forces inherent in human nature. To improve the world one must work with these forces not against them.'[20] But a student may be forgiven for seeing pessimism, even cynicism, in realist writing, and perhaps even a detached observer would detect in it a note of quiet satisfaction at the predicament of mankind.

Most of the realists' ideas have been absorbed, either consciously or unconsciously, by contemporary strategic thinkers. Indeed, for those whose politically formative years followed the Second World War, it was impossible to escape the all-pervasive influence of this powerful school of thought. Undoubtedly one of the reasons for its widespread influence was that it fitted the grim mood and temper of international politics in the Cold War era. Those American strategists who laid the foundations of contemporary strategic thought in the late 1950s and early 1960s operated in an environment where realism was the orthodoxy, and almost without exception they swallowed its precepts. It is perfectly possible, for example, to connect the demise of general and comprehensive disarmament as a practical goal for policy-makers and the rise of arms control with the death of idealism and the rise of realism. Against a realist background, the idealist view that peace and security could best be achieved by reducing or abolishing the weapons with which men fight, had a curiously dated and impractical ring about it. Arms control, that is to say, the successful management of weapons policy, seemed to offer more practical though less ambitious prospects for peace. It is fair to say that the concept of disarmament which was developed in the inter-war years and is typified by the writings of Mr. Philip Noel Baker,[21] is now almost dead. Today we are all arms controllers, and the realists who forced us to face up to hard facts and to settle for less than perfect solutions undoubtedly had something to do with it.

It might be argued that some strategists absorbed only the most crude power-political principles of what, after all, was a very sophisticated and profound intellectual position. The realists were rarely cynical; their ideas were always tempered by a real concern for humanity and by a genuine intellectual humility. Both Niebuhr and Morgenthau, for example, agonised about the human condition and their writing was tempered by deeply-held ideas of Christian charity. But some of those who absorbed the raw aspects of realism, rejected or failed to appreciate the movement's emphasis on balance, on enlightened self-interest, and on sympathy and vision. In an interview conducted in the 1960s Hans Morgenthau commented, 'Yes, realism helped lay down the basis for deterrence in making the use of force acceptable to liberals who were squeamish about using it. But there is no doubt that realist ideas have been taken over by the military. My own ideas have been made to look harder than they are in this context.'[22]

Accepting a selective and simplistic version of a profound and humane intellectual position led some strategic writers to extol not just the virtues of power but only the virtues of military power, and to develop an almost paranoic interpretation of Soviet intentions and capabilities. The influential writings of Cold War warriors like Mr. Straus Hupé and his colleague W. A. Kinter typify this kind of distorted, cynical realism, and to capture the flavour of the so-called 'Forward Strategy School', students might care to examine 'A Forward Strategy for America' and 'American Strategy for the Nuclear Age'[23] — both of which are predicated upon fairly hair-raising, 'hawkish' analysis of Soviet behaviour, and both of which recommend exceptionally tough policies against the Russians.

Moral Neutrality

Realist writing did not concern itself very much with moralising about the way states ought to behave, though most of its proponents were sensitive to moral issues and some were acutely so. Similarly, many contemporary strategists have failed to allocate priority to the moral aspects of strategic policy, and as a result much contemporary strategic writing has an air of moral neutrality about it. The clinical, cool, unemotional way in which strategists analyse modern war, and contemplate highly destructive and dangerous policies which may result in the death of millions, outrages ordinary men of good will who cannot help feeling that those who reflect so objectively on military violence must be devoid of human sentiment and must actually approve of the grim situations they envisage. This is an understandable reaction, but it is worth stressing that research into a subject in no way implies approval of it.

It is a curious fact that when doctors study malignant carcinomas, no one assumes that they are in favour of cancer, but when political scientists examine war it is assumed all too frequently that they approve of it. In fact few of them do, and then only as a very last resort, in desperate circumstances. Hedley Bull spoke for most writers in the field when he wrote, 'war appears to me, here, now, something evil, in which any kind of acquiescence is, in some measure, morally degrading. Organised violence itself, and the habits and attitudes associated with threatening it and preparing for it are ugly and alien.'[24] And yet the accusation of moral insensitivity lingers on. Philip Green is only one of those who claim that for years most of the deterrent theorists were and some still are "egregiously guilty of avoiding the moral issue altogether, or misrepresenting it".[25]

I believe that there is a sense in which those who criticise the strategists for paying insufficient attention to moral questions are missing the point. To be sure, contemporary strategic thought does not dwell on the moral issues raised by strategic policies. However, this is not because strategists consider moral questions unimportant; indeed it is difficult to disagree with Hedley Bull's assessment that 'strategists as a class are neither any less nor any more sensitive to moral considerations than are other intelligent and educated persons in the West.'[26] If they relegate moral questions to the periphery of their subject it is either because their attention is focused elsewhere or because they recognise that their intellectual training may not have equipped them to deal with or consider the enormous moral issues involved.

Most strategic writers readily admit that 'The Moral Aspects of Military Power' is a vitally important subject, and they are delighted when theologians, philosophers, and political scientists devote their attention to it. But it is a quite separate subject from strategic studies in that it requires a quite different expertise, and it is therefore unfair to blame specialists in the latter for their lack of competence in it. No one in his right mind would blame a butcher for being unable to make bread. Nor would anyone accuse him of wilfully underestimating the importance of bread just because he did not bake it himself.

Klaus Knorr was absolutely right when, in introducing Herman Kahn's book *On Thermonuclear War*, he wrote that it 'is not a book about the moral aspects of military problems'.[27] It was, therefore, somewhat unfair of J.R. Newman in *Scientific American* to cast his criticisms in moral terms: 'this is a moral tract on mass murder, how to commit it, how to get away with it, how to justify it.'[28] The point that escaped Mr. Newman is that strategic analysis, like philosophy, leaves the world as it is. To describe the rules of the game known as 'strategic thinking' no more implies taking sides in it or making moves within it than describing the rules of golf implies playing a round of it.

Of course, to argue that strategic studies does not — and ought not — to focus on moral questions, is not to argue that there are no ethical stances implicit in strategic doctrine; there are. Philip Green has done much to expose the moral assumptions which lie behind deterrence theory.[29] The nuclear deterrers, he argues, consciously or unconsciously adhere to the ethical values held by their employers and clients. To be blunt, they assume that in certain circumstances it is justifiable to kill innocent persons. That may or may not be a morally *virtuous* stance, but it is very obviously a moral stance.

Behind most strategic policies lie moral positions on the question of whether, and in what circumstances, it is right to hurt and kill both combatants and non-combatants. And if, in certain circumstances, strategic analysts are prepared to risk war, it is not because they are insensitive to moral considerations, but because their moral values are so important to them that even war must be risked in their defence.

Peace and Security

The truth of the matter is that 'strategic studies' is riddled with 'value' assumptions of one kind or another. One has only to think for a moment of the way strategic analysts either consciously or unconsciously assume the desirability of one kind of world rather than another to see that 'value' preferences lie behind their reasoning. Almost without exception, for example, strategists share the view that 'peace' and 'security' are desirable goals, and direct their thoughts towards promoting them. Elsewhere the writer has developed the argument that many contemporary strategic doctrines are, in effect, simply different theories about how a peaceful and secure world is best pursued.[30]

Deterrence is the theory that peace and security can be promoted by threatening potential enemies with unacceptable retaliatory damage. Disarmament is the theory that peace and security can be achieved by reducing or abolishing the weapons with which men fight. Arms control is the theory that peace and security can be brought about by the skilful management of weaponry. Limited war is the theory that peace and security can be realized by controlling and limiting the amount of military force used in any conflict. Crisis management is the theory that peace and security can be promoted by developing techniques for handling international crises.

Precisely what is meant by the terms 'peace' and 'security' is, of course, open to debate, as also are questions of their compatibility and relative importance. But that some notion of these values underpins Western strategic thought is probably indisputable.

In an international society where war is a powerful instrument of change, the overall effect of attempting to preserve peace and promote security is to support the *status quo*. For that reason Western strategic thought has a very conservative flavour about it. Now the preservation of things as they are is an understandable goal for those who are satisfied with the *status quo* — and, of course, to use Lord Annan's phrase, 'the fat cats of the West' have every reason to be satisfied with it. But for millions of underprivileged in Africa and Asia, to support the *status quo* is to prop up an unjust system. Those who are desperately poor naturally accuse Western states of caring everything for peace and nothing for justice. For them, 'peace' and 'security' are undoubtedly important, but even more important perhaps is 'social justice' – and contemporary strategic thought is not much concerned with that. If for no other reason than this, Western strategic thought may not carry much weight in large areas of the world.

It is perhaps worth stressing that there is nothing wrong with normative studies. As one political scientist put it, "there is no logical reason why a social philosopher should not postulate any value he chooses provided only that he avows what he is doing."[31] In exposing the values implicit in strategic thought, students might care to consider the logical status of all values. In particular, they should ask themselves whether values reflect anything more than the personal prejudices and preferences of those who hold them, and in what sense it is possible to describe some values as 'better' than others.

The Cold War
In much the same way that political realism forms the philosophic backdrop for contemporary strategic throught, so does the Cold War pattern of international politics provide the essential model for much strategic speculation. Ideas of deterrence, arms control, limited war, flexible response, and crisis management were all elaborated by scholars and practitioners whose ideas and thoughts were decisively shaped and moulded by the intellectual climate of their time.

Fundamentally, strategic ideas and policies were designed to deal with a bi-polar world dominated by the hostile relationship of the two superpowers. The United States recognised only one enemy, the Soviet Union, and strategic policy was almost entirely orientated towards containing the Soviet threat. Deterrence theory concentrated on the strategic balance between the United States and the Soviet Union. The central questions of the day related to the problem of acquiring and maintaining effective retaliatory capability, and of perpetuating a stable balance in the face of dramatic innovation in weapon technology. Arms control negotiations were mainly American Soviet negotiations designed to control the arms race without destabilising deterrence. Whatever successes were recorded happened largely because decision-makers in Washington and Moscow were able to agree. Whatever failures occurred happened because the superpowers failed to agree. The doctrine of 'limited war' wrestled with the problem of reconciling the possibility of American-Soviet conflict with the near certainity of nuclear oblivion if neither side practiced restraint. Techniques of 'crisis management' were largely developed to deal with an American-Soviet crisis on the model of the Cuban missile crisis. Strategies of 'massive retaliation', 'pause', 'trip-wire', and 'flexible response', were similarly designed to meet the requirements of

East-West confrontation. Thus, behind almost all Western military thought and giving point to it, lay the assumptions of Cold War — Soviet intransigence, and a bi-polar world permanently divided into two armed camps led by two superpowers whose leaders were the only significant decision-makers.

In retrospect at least, the Cold War was a remarkably stable period of international politics, and it is easy to sympathise with those who came to regard it as a permanent feature of the international landscape. But in international politics nothing lasts for ever, and through the 1960s confrontation gave way to *détente* and to a softer climate of East-West relations. As the language and terminology of Cold War passed into history, the talk was of 'peaceful coexistence', of 'force reductions' and of 'security conferences'. The United States and the Soviet Union have now become, in the words of Marshal Shulman, 'limited adversaries'. They enjoy an 'adverse partnership', and no longer confront each other across the Iron Curtain. Furthermore, as the forces of 'polycentrism' undermine the unity of both NATO and the Warsaw Pact, and as other new powers rise to great and even superpower status, new and powerful centres of strategic decision-making may emerge to destroy the old bi-polar world so confidently assumed by much traditional strategic literature.

It remains to be seen how well the strategic ideas of the 1950s and 1960s translate into the very different world conditions of the late 1970s and 1980s. There are signs that the basic intellectual apparatus is standing up well to the tests of time. We may agree with Hedley Bull that 'it is difficult to escape the conclusion that even though the civilian strategists have sometimes committed errors they have served us well.'[32] But it would be surprising if no modifications were required to ideas borne in radically different international and technological circumstances. It will be interesting to see, for example, how well the idea of deterrence stands up in a world of many nuclear powers, and how far NATO strategy will have to be modified to accommodate the new international circumstances implicit in mutual force reductions and the settlement of outstanding European security problems.

Conceivably it will not be the older generation of strategic writers who will modify or rewrite the theories. Their minds may be too set in traditional patterns of thought. Some may be so used to thinking in Cold War terms that they are incapable of acquiring a new set of assumptions more relevant to changed conditions. They are suffering, not from hardening of the arteries, but from a more common and equally serious disease once aptly described by Professor Charles Manning as 'hardening of the categories'.

Rationality
On the one hand there are those who attack strategic studies because it assumes a pessimistic view of human nature and diminishes the role of

reason in the affairs of mankind, and on the other hand there are those who accuse the strategists of excessive reliance on human rationality. The latter group of critics are supported by the fact that a casual glance through the literature of strategic studies does seem to suggest that many strategic arguments are underpinned by an assumption of 'rationality'. The works of Herman Kahn, Thomas Schelling, Glenn Snyder, Albert Wohlstetter, and others, all have a scientific, *reasonable*, flavour about them, and they make constant and explicit references to the concept of rationality, to 'rational choice', to 'rational opponents', to 'rational decision-making', to 'rational behaviour'. In the words of Hedley Bull 'a great deal of argument about military strategy postulates rational action of a kind of strategic man, a man who, on further acquaintance reveals himself as a university professor of unusual intellectual subtlety.'[33]

Now the most usual concept of rationality is that it is a process of means-ends analysis. By that is meant that a man is behaving rationally when his actions are calculated to bring about the ends which he desires. Thus, according to Snyder, 'rationality may be defined as choosing to act in the manner which gives best promise of maximising one's value position on the basis of a sober calculation of potential gains and losses, and probabilities of enemy actions.'[34] Of course, theoretically rational behaviour involves more than that. It involves the selection, from among alternative possible actions, of that which, *from the point of view of an omniscient and objective observer,* is most likely to promote the value pursued. It is to be noted that, strictly speaking, rationality cannot be *subjectively* assessed. Even a lunatic may think his behaviour is rational in the sense of being calmly calculated to promote his interest, but because he has a distorted image of reality, because, to put it mildly, he is not in possession of all the relevant facts, actions conceived in the light of his image have little relevance to the real world and produce totally unforeseen consequences therein.

The international crisis which a balanced and sane statesman may find himself dealing with, and in the context of which his behaviour seems rational, may not be the *real* crisis, but simply the statesman's mental distortion of it, and for this reason his behaviour will, to an objective, omniscient observer, seem inappropriate and irrational, if not entirely inexplicable. However, in the context of strategic analysis, rational behaviour refers to behaviour in which the actors *try* to maximise their value positions, as well as to behaviour in which they *do* maximise their value positions.

It follows from the above definition that the term rational is most appropriately applied to the process of *achieving* a goal or value, rather than to the goal itself. One cannot, for example, comment on the rationality of 'suicide' or 'survival' or 'security' as human goals. One can only comment on the rationality of the means chosen to pursue those values. Perhaps the only sense in which it is possible to talk about the rationality or irrationality of *particular* human goals is in the context of a total value system. It is irrational, for example, though by no means uncommon, to hold a value system which is internally inconsistent in the sense that it implies the simultaneous pursuit of incompatible objectives.

At the time of the Abyssinian crisis, Churchill put his finger on one such inconsistency in British foreign policy. Speaking of Baldwin, he said, 'First the Prime Minister had declared that sanctions meant war; secondly, he was resolved that there must be no war; and thirdly, he decided upon sanctions.' What Churchill was pointing out was that a policy of peace at almost any price and a policy of collective security are logically incompatible, and hence that any value system which incorporated those incompatible individual values was irrational even though it might be shared by many people. And today there must be a good many voters who favour increased national security and reduced taxation without realising the dilemma inherent in trying to have one's cake and eat it. Not all men, not even all statesmen, are sufficiently clear-minded to think through the logical implications of their values in order to iron out any inconsistencies, and to arrange goals in a compatible and hierarchical order.

Not only are men incapable of neatly ordering their priorities, they are, for some of the time, incapable of making rational choices of the kind hinted at in Snyder's definition. After all, men are creatures of passion as well as reason. They are capricious; they have impulses of rage, indignation, revenge, pity and altruism — all emotions which may actually undermine their ability to choose those policies which would maximise their values. In other words, strategic decision-makers are fallible human beings, and under conditions of stress, even perhaps under normal circumstances, they may not behave in a rational, value-maximising, way. As Hedley Bull has commented:

> the decisions of governments on matters of peace and war, . . . do not always reflect a careful weighing of long-range considerations, or a mastery of the course of events: . . . governments appear to . . . stumble about, groping and half-blind, too preoccupied with surviving from day to day even to perceive the direction in which they are heading, let alone steer away from it.[35]

If strategic man is a fiction, then surely an analysis which. assumes rational behaviour in all circumstances is likely to be at best mistaken and at worst downright dangerous. However, this conclusion can only be reached by fudging the vital distinction between strategic *policy-making* and strategic *analysis*. No strategic policy-maker ever assumes that decision-makers are wholly rational all of the time; only that they are not totally irrational some of the time. Strategic policies are certainly not predicated on an assumption that statesmen are one hundred per cent rational. In deterrence, for example, the 'assured destruction' threatened by American deterrent capability is deliberately massive because the aim is to deter not just sane, reasonable men who could perhaps be deterred by the threat of minor retaliatory damage, but half-crazy, unreasonable men, who are likely to heed nothing short of massive threats. As Herman Kahn puts it, 'we should want a safety factor in deterrence systems so large as to impress even the irrational and irresponsible with the degree of their irrationality and therefore the need for caution.'[36]

In essence, rationality may boil down to two common-sense propositions. First, that it is sensible to assume that a statesman involved in a conflict will prefer strategic postures which seem to minimise damage to his country, and second, that it is sensible to believe that this preference will be shared by his opponent. The strategies of 'limited war' and 'deterrence' are certainly predicated on such assumptions, as also are the doctrines of 'controlled escalation', and 'counterforce targetting'.

Now strategic analysts — who are engaged in a very different activity from strategic decision-makers — do sometimes assume rationality. They do this, not because they believe decision-makers will always act rationally, but because, for the purposes of analysis it is very difficult to make any other assumption. In short, the value of the rationality assumption is in its *explanatory* rather than its *predictive* power. It demonstrates the logic in strategic postures, but it offers no guarantees that statesmen will abide by that logic. Failure to distinguish between the perfectly sensible assumption of rationality in strategic *analysis* and the quite foolish assumption of rationality in strategic *policy-making* has led to much confusion amongst students of strategy. What this means is that strategy is pursued at two levels. First it is pursued at the purely rational level at which attention is focused on reasonable, conscious, artful behaviour motivated by the cold calculation of interests, and second, it is pursued at a level which examines the participants in a conflict in all their complexity, that is to say, with regard to conscious and unconscious behaviour, and with regard to psychological motivations as well as logical calculations.

For the first kind of analysis it is sometimes convenient to assume a 'strategic man' who evaluates every conceivable action in terms of cost-gain analysis. 'If I do this, he will do that, and if he does that, then I must do this.' That is typical of a kind of strategic reasoning which assumes both rationality and complete knowledge of the value systems of all parties to a conflict. It is a useful exercise because it reduces a complicated world to intellectually manageable proportions, and because it highlights the logic of situations and policies. But when it comes to deciding policy, the intellectual constraint of 'strategic man' is forced to make way for a more human individual, and policies have to be designed to take account of his unreasonableness. Notwithstanding the assumptions which underlie it, strategy is an important subject if only because the successful management of military power is a prerequisite for survival in the nuclear age. Of course, there are some who are sceptical about the prospects for regulating the use of military power and who would prefer to see it abolished. It is, perhaps, debatable which group is the most optimistic — those who believe that, with luck and good judgement, military power can be effectively managed, or those who believe that, by sustained effort, the capacity for organized violence can be abolished. The following pages should make it clear that the authors belong to the former group: they believe that military power is an intrinsic part of the international system, and though they do not believe that contemporary strategists have produced any foolproof formulae for survival, they do believe that their ideas may help us to cope with a dangerous and uncertain world.

Notes

1. K. Booth, 'Teaching Strategy: An Introductory Questionnaire', *Survival*, 1974, Mar/Apr., p. 79.
2. Von Clausewitz, *On War* I (trans. J.J. Graham, 1908), reprinted London: Routledge, 1966, p. 165.
3. Quoted in B.H. Liddel Hart, *Strategy: The Indirect Approach*, London: Faber, 1967, 6th Ed., p. 334.
4. *Ibid.*, p. 335.
5. B.H Liddel Hart, *Deterrent or Defence*, London: Stevens, 1960, p. 66.
6. R.E. Osgood, *NATO: The Entangling Alliance*, Chicago: University of Chicago Press, 1962, p. 5.
7. A. Beaufré, *An Introduction to Strategy*, London: Faber, 1965; *Deterrence and Strategy*, London: Faber, 1965; *Strategy of Action*, London: Faber, 1967.
8. M. Howard, 'The Classical Strategists', in Problems of Modern Strategy I, *Adelphi Paper* 54, 1969, Feb., pp. 31-32.
9. R. Aron, 'The Evolution of Modern Strategic Thought', in Problems of Modern Strategy I, *Adelphi Paper* 54, 1969, Feb., 1969, p. 7.
10. H.A. Kissinger, *Nuclear Weapons and Foreign Policy*, New York: Harper and Row, 1957, p. 422.
11. *Ibid.*, p. 422.
12. H. Lasswell, 'The Garrison State Hypothesis Today', in S.P. Huntington, Ed., *Changing Patterns of Military Politics*, New York: Free Press, 1962, pp. 51-70.
13. A. Herzog, *The War-Peace Establishment*, New York and London: Harper and Row, 1963, p. 3.
14. M. Oakeshott, *Rationalism in Politics*, London: Methuen, 1962, p. 127.
15. See R. Niebuhr, *Moral Man and Immoral Society*, New York and London: Charles Scribner's Sons, 1932.
16. Quoted in K.W. Thompson, *Political Realism and the Crisis of World Politics*, Princeton, N.J.: Princeton University Press, 1960, p. 53.
17. G.F. Kennan, *American Diplomacy: 1900-1950*, Chicago: University of Chicago Press, 1951, p. 78.
18. T. Hobbes, *Leviathan* (Oakeshott Ed.), Oxford: Basil Blackwell, 1946, p. 64.
19. Gordon Harland, quoted in A. Herzog, *op. cit.*, p. 88.

20. H.J. Morgenthau, *Politics Among Nations,* New York: Alfred A. Knopf, 1956, 2nd Ed., p. 4.
21. See for example, P. Noel-Baker, *The Arms Race,* London: Stevens and Sons, 1958.
22. A. Herzog, *op. cit.,* p. 94.
23. R. Strausz-Hupé, *A Forward Strategy for America,* New York: Harper and Low, 1961. R. Strausz-Hupé, W.R. Kinter, J.E. Dougherty and A.J. Cottrell, *Protracted Conflict,* New York: Harper & Row, 1959.
24. H. Bull, *The Control of the Arms Race,* London: Weidenfeld and Nicolson, 1961, p. 21.
25. P. Green, *Deadly Logic,* Ohio: Ohio State University Press, 1966, p. 250.
26. H. Bull, "Strategic Studies and Its Critics", *World Politics* XX(4), 1968, Jul, p. 597.
27. H. Kahn, *On Thermonuclear War,* Princeton, N.J.: Princeton University Press, 1960, p. v.
28. J.R. Newman, Review in *Scientific American,* CCIV, 3, 1961, Mar., p. 200.
29. P. Green, *op. cit.,* ch. 6.
30. J.C. Garnett, Ed., "Introduction", *Theories of Peace and Security,* London: Macmillan, 1970.
31. G.H. Sabine, 'What is Political Theory?', *Journal of Politics* I, 1939, p. 13.
32. H. Bull, *op. cit.,* p. 605.
33. H. Bull, *The Control of the Arms Race,* London: Weidenfeld and Nicolson, 1961, p. 48.
34. G.H. Snyder, *Deterrence and Defense,* Princeton, N.J.; Princeton University Press, 1961, p. 25.
35. H. Bull, *op. cit.,* p. 49.
36. H. Kahn, *Thinking About the Unthinkable,* New York: Horizon Press Inc., 1962, pp. 111-112.

2 THE EVOLUTION OF STRATEGIC THINKING

Ken Booth

It goes without saying that there have always been wars and that men, with a curious mixture of horror and fascination, have always been interested in them. "It is a good thing war is so terrible, or we should become too fond of it" was General Robert E. Lee's first-hand observation, while Thomas Hardy was expressing a common attitude when he wrote that "War makes rattling good history but Peace is poor reading." In view of this fascination with war it is in some ways surprising that the comprehensive study of *strategy* (as opposed to the study of individual battles, campaigns, wars, leaders, or weapons) is such a relatively recent activity, in terms of the significance accorded to it, and the quantity of professional expertise invested in it. With proliferating shelves of books and journals on the subject it is sometimes difficult to realise that it is only since the mid-1950s that the subject has been thoroughly studied on a wide scale.

Before discussing the chief milestones in the evolution of strategic thinking several explanations are required. Firstly, *strategy* is used in this chapter in the sense in which it was used by Liddell Hart: "The art of distributing and applying military means to fulfil the ends of policy."[1] Secondly, *thinking* is the focus of this chapter, but it is necessary for understanding and appraisal to set this within the wider context of such phenomena as changing technology, the history of war and war plans, and the developing foreign policies of different countries. Thirdly, *evolution* does not imply qualitative improvement, in the sense of "better" strategic thinking. It simply refers to an unfolding of strategic happenings. The presence in strategic thinking over the last thirty years of more "sophisticated" thinking, and the absence of massive chaos does not prove that we have been qualitatively wiser strategic thinkers than our forefathers. In the short run, Man the Military Animal may have been rescued from disaster simply by the unprecedented enormity of the technological threat. Perhaps we have not been worse than our forefathers, but it is far too soon to proclaim that we have become markedly "better".

Pre-Napoleonic writings

There is some profit to be gained, and certainly some interest to be had, from an examination of some of the very early contributors to thinking about war and strategy. Several names are outstanding, in particular

Sun Tzu, Thucydides, and Machiavelli. Sun Tzu's *Art of War,* written in China about 500 BC has been said by Liddell Hart, Britain's most prolific writer on strategy in recent times, to outshine Clausewitz's *On War* in terms of its style and quality. Equally important it is said to have been "the source" of Mao Tse-tung's strategic theories and of the tactical doctrine of the Chinese armies.[2] Thucydides (ca. 460-404 BC) who is often thought to have been the first important writer on war, can also be recommended.[3] The writings of Machiavelli (1469-1527), although limited in terms of strategy, were informed by a long interest in military affairs, were full of military imagery, and were an exhibition of the rationality and *Realpolitik* which many students of this subject — certainly its practitioners — would regard as its starting point.[4] In addition to theoretical writings such as these, military professionals have traditionally searched the campaigns of famous commanders such as Frederick the Great and Marlborough for insights into the dynamic interplay of material and non-material factors in the prosecution of war.

Strategy in the Age of Nationalism and Industrialisation

The period of Napoleonic warfare has been generally considered to be a useful beginning for students of modern strategy. In contrast to the limited wars of manoeuvre which characterised the conflicts between the absolute monarchs of the previous century, Napoleonic warfare presaged total war, being characterised by the dynamic of escalation rather than the habit of moderation. In place of the old rules and constraints, "modern" war tended to free itself of limitations. Modern war was nourished by nationalism and ideological conviction; it became equipped with the products of the industrial revolution; and it was manned by the system of universal conscription. Although some of the old traditions of war remained for another century, the Napoleonic era was the harbinger of the fact that warfare had ceased to be another of the blood-sports of kings for dynastic trifles, and instead had become a clash between whole peoples over their very political and physical independence. In this new era of expanding force the concept of strategy grew from being the "art of the general", focusing on the battlefield conduct of affairs, to being the business of arranging a nation's whole disposition for war — a business which increasingly intruded upon peacetime affairs.

The first writer to incorporate Napoleonic warfare into what became a major treatise on strategy was the Swiss military theorist, Henri Jomini (1779-1869). His major work, the *Précis de l'art de la guerre* (first published in 1838) was very influential in the following half-century in teaching the armies of Europe and North America what he thought were the lessons of the great struggles which he had witnessed.[5] Because Jomini wrote for directly practical purposes, he had a relevance to nineteenth-century military life and thinking which is now difficult to recapture. With the declining relevance of his prescriptions, however, he was overtaken in reputation by Clausewitz. This change was widespread by about 1870, but had occurred much earlier in Germany.

Karl von Clausewitz (1780-1831) has been widely acknowledged to be "the first modern strategist". His chief work *Vom Kriege* (*On War*), which was first published in 1832, has been recognised in many countries to be a classic. It covers a wide range of subjects, from the philosophical to the minutely practical. It deals with the nature of war, the theory of war, the interplay of theory and practice, the relationship between war and politics, the object of strategy, the relationship between the civilian and military leaderships, the psychological aspects of war, battles, tactics, and is at the same time full of military history. His discussion of these subjects (with the exception of the directly practical side of battles and tactics, and the military history) is still pertinent to thinking about war and strategy today. He provides no final answers, but he is a good (if complicated) starting point for students of the subject today. He cannot be ignored.[6]

Clausewitz's importance lies largely in the fact that he has been the leading exponent of what has been called the "political philosophy of war"; this is the view that war is rational, national, and instrumental.[7] As the leading exponent of the prevailing philosophy of war in the last 150 years Clausewitz's importance has been secure. His influence has been both direct and reinforcing. His most famous adherents were a succession of German military leaders and some founders of Soviet strategic doctrine, including Lenin.

Although Clausewitz's importance has been secure, his precise reputation has not been: in fact, his reputation has fluctuated considerably, in both time and place. He has been variously identified as a strategist who recommended pushing violence to its utmost (the "Apostle of Violence"), as the man who created the climate in which decision by bloody battle became accepted by political and military leaders alike as the proper objective of a campaign and which reached its culmination in the attrition of the Great War (the "Mahdi of Mass"), as a proponent of militarism, as a writer whose ideas were betrayed by his style and the approach of his readers (the "misunderstood Metaphysician") and as one of the keenest observers of war and one of its most perceptive interpreters (the "great philosopher of war"). Much has been said and done in his name. He has been important whether he has been understood or misunderstood.Because of the contemporary significance of his concern for the relationship between ends and means (as expressed in his most famous dictum: "War is nothing more than the continuation of politics by other means") Clausewitz has been "rediscovered" in Western strategic studies in the last fifteen years. And for better or worse, contemporary strategic writing has been dominated by "neo-Clausewitzians".[8]

Clausewitz stressed the importance of the ends-means problem. In the study of means, the analysis of physical capabilities is a key consideration; increasingly, as time has gone on, this has involved the need for a sound appreciation of progressively more complex technological factors. For centuries the history of war witnessed a marked technological stability; however, strategy in the middle of the nineteenth century was marked by the advent of a phenomenon which has been a dominating consideration since the Second World War, that is, the problem of accommodating the problem of continuous technological innovation into existing strategic concepts.

The forty years before 1870 saw a series of intense technological changes. The chief developments were the growth of firepower and the increasing speed and efficiency of transport and communications. Together, these developments upturned old calculations about time, space, and destructive potential. The industrial revolution which caused the changes in the equipment of war also altered the character of Western society. In the period between 1815 and 1914 the most interesting war was the American Civil War (1861-65). As the first war fought with the new military products of industrialisation and the fervour of the age of nationalism and ideology, its most significant feature was not the action on the battlefields but the economic, industrial, and general staying power of modern socieites.

Those responsible for strategic doctrine in the chief European armies in the second half of the nineteenth century did not perceive the potential significance of the American Civil War.[9] Instead, they were much impressed by the rapid and decisive wars of the Prussian Army under the influence of Helmuth Von Moltke[10] against Denmark (1864), Austria (1866) and France (1870-71). With its superb planning, its efficient and detailed mobilisation plans, its use of the best weapons, its good training, its General Staff system, and its Clausewitzian inspiration, the Prussian Army was the model for much of Europe. As for the character of future war, the precedent was taken to be the rapid and decisive war of movement in the early days of the Franco-Prussian War, not the prolonged war of technology and attrition which had ground on a few years earlier between the Confederacy and the Union.

The Armed Peace, 1871-1914

France, the defeated power in 1870-71, was obviously the country most directly affected by the successful Prussian innovations. Hitherto, France had complacently regarded itself as the major military power on the Continent; it was now battered by the defeat into reviving interest in military affairs, as part of the effort to restore national prestige. The military system was reformed, and military theorists discovered Clausewitz and sought to rediscover the verve of Napoleon. In compensa-

25

tion for the country's material weaknesses in relation to Germany, French writers began to emphasise the non-material aspects of war. Under the influence of Ardant du Picq, General Bonnal, the future Marshal Foch, and Colonel Grandmaison in particular, successive French war plans came to be infused with the idea of *l'offensive à l'outrance*.[11] In the elaboration of the theory of the offensive questions of morale and spirit were given more careful attention than the assimilation of the implications of the further developments in firepower and communications at the end of the century. The desperate spirit which informed the theory of the offensive was personified by Foch during the disasters at the outbreak of the Great War (although his own writings were more moderate than his reputation). In a message to Joffre in September 1914 he reported: "My centre is giving way, my right is in retreat; situation excellent. I shall attack."

If French military thinking for the European battlefield was anachronistic, there was one area, doctrine for colonial warfare, in which French thinkers showed flair and an understanding which was before its time. Men who were both theorists and practitioners, notably Marshals Gallieni and Lyautey, elaborated ideas which some counter-insurgency theorists in the 1960s did (or could have) read with profit in this field where continuity of experience has been considerable.[12] Such "small wars" were even more the main employment for the British Army during the period of the "armed peace". The British had more practice than the French, but predictably they produced less theory. The chief problems facing the British Army were the result of the enormous extent and diversity of the country's colonial interests. One of the most interesting military commentators at the time summed up the army's predicament in these words:

Each new expedition demands special equipment, special methods of supply and special tactical devices, and sometimes special armament . . . Except for the defence of the United Kingdom and of India, much remains to be provided when the Cabinet declares that war is imminent.[13]

Britain's chief contribution to the development of strategy was at sea rather than on land. As the predominant naval power, and with responsibilities in a world-wide Empire, the Royal Navy faced numerous problems in maintaining at least the semblance of the *Pax Brittannica* during a period of changing international relationships and rapidly evolving maritime technology. The latter was manifest by the fascinating evolution of the architecture of warships from Nelson's *Victory* to Fisher's *Dreadnought*. As in land warfare, Britain's contribution to naval strategy was through example rather than theory. There were a number of naval writers at the turn of the century whose concern was speculative — notably the Colombs, Sir John Laughton, and Sir

Julian Corbett[14] – but the major interest of British naval circles at the time was narrowly technical. Overall, the practical contribution of Admiral Sir John Fisher, in terms of structural reorganisation, technical innovation, and strategic and tactical readjustment far outweighed the contribution of any of the theorists.[15]

The task of encapsulating current naval wisdom was left to, or was usurped by an American, Captain (later Admiral) Alfred Mahan (1840-1914). In the twenty-five years before his death Mahan wrote a series of voluminous books on sea power, with a novel emphasis on the role of navies in a country's foreign policy.[16] His work emphasised the critical interrelationship between sea power, commerce and colonies. Success in naval war was based in his view on employing a concentration of fire-power from battleships in decisive battles. Generalising as he did from the Royal Navy's experience in the age of sail, he was dismissive of other approaches to naval warfare; most notably, he minimised the potential impact of a *guerre de course* doctrine. Mahan became the most widely acclaimed naval writer of his time, and had a generally reinforcing influence in the age of imperialism; his exposition gave further impetus to existing ideas about naval strategy, big navies and the inter-relationship between commerce, colonies and sea power. However, his direct influence has probably been exaggerated: and certainly his prescriptions were quickly obsolete, as a result of his weak methodology and the rapid technological innovation of his later years, notably the development of the submarine and aeroplane.

While the strategic problems for Britain (and the United States even more so) were eased by the relative security provided by geography, geography made the strategic problems of the Continental powers, especially Germany, much more immediate and critical. These problems were also compounded by technological developments. Surrounded by potential enemies and in an environment in which warfare appeared likely to be decided by the opening moves, the framers of German strategic doctrine became psychologically encircled. At the same time, Germany's armies became increasingly efficient. This was the background to the influence and especially the war plans of Alfred von Schlieffen, Chief of the General Staff between 1891 and 1905.[17] Schlieffen's plans attempted to deal with the dilemma of a possible war on two fronts. His final solution was to concentrate first on defeating France in the west; he aimed to achieve this by a massive hook by the right wing of the German forces through neutral Belgium, thereby outflanking the French forces and pressing them against the German frontier. With this victory achieved, he then planned to turn eastwards to deal with the more slowly mobilising Russians. Schlieffen's grandiose conception, which in its altered version in 1914 came near to success, nevertheless left a great deal to chance. It also played down the political aspect of strategy. The history of the German Army in the fifty years before the First World War was personified by the contrast between the flexible approach and political intelligence of Moltke the Elder, and the military obsession of Schlieffen and the technical and psychological inflexibility of his war plans. Such was the hair-trigger mentality and sense of encirclement amongst key members of the Germany military and political leadership that German strategic doctrine meant that mobilisation not only meant war, but inevitably a major European war at that.

In a number of important ways the Schlieffen Plan epitomised strategic developments at the start of the century: The concept of strategy was expanding, with the idea that detailed advanced planning from mobilisation to victory was necessary and possible before the outbreak of war. International politics were becoming militarised in several senses: in foreign policy considerable attention was paid to the military factor as a signifier of prestige and as a major instrument of diplomatic leverage; in domestic politics military establishments, which were increasingly specialised and professional, claimed more autonomy and influence. Civil and military co-ordination was generally poor. The alliance systems and their attendant strategic doctrines promised to spread danger rather than improve stability through deterrence. The increasing complexity of war meant that organisation for it depended much more on corporate technique. The General Staff system proliferated, and war became much more bureaucratic. The complexity of war, together with the belief that the opening moves would be decisive,[18] meant that as much as possible had to be worked out in "peacetime". The bureaucratisation of war together with the conviction that to move first would dramatically increase the chances of victory, produced a rigidity and instability which was summed up in the dangerous maxim that "mobilisation means war". In such an unstable environment ideas about preventive and pre-emptive war flourished, and produced the edginess in crises which gives meaning to A.J.P. Taylor's verdict that the First World War was "imposed on the states-men of Europe by railway timetables".[19]

The increase in peacetime military planning did much to blur the distinction between war and peace. This distinction was also being significantly eroded by military practice: in particular there were frequent "small wars" in the colonial field; there was the thriving phenomenon of "gunboat diplomacy" in which the object was to threaten rather than to use force; and there were demonstrative shows of military power in the European context as a means of structuring the policies of others. The manipulation of the instruments of violence well short of the set-piece battles for which European armies had traditionally been trained was becoming an increasing feature of the foreign policies of the great powers. It was an important advance in the accelerating trend towards the mid-twentieth-century situation in which "strategy" and "policy" became almost synonymous.

The generation of Total War, 1914-1945

In the opinion of many, the four years after 1914 are the classic example of strategy, in its narrowest sense, usurping policy. "Military necessity" came to dominate other considerations. Important aspects of the running of the war were handed over to the technicians of violence, in order that they might bring about the "victory" which was the aim of the struggle. The problems caused by the uncertainity of the political as opposed to the military objectives of the war were compounded by the bloody indecisiveness of the means at hand. The massive confrontation in a limited geographical theatre of ever larger armies, ever more destructive firepower, ever quicker communications, ever more efficient industry, and ever more impassioned nationalism produced a prolonged strategic deadlock. It was beyond the wit of generalship to break it by military means, and it was beyond the wit of statesmanship to settle it by diplomatic means: technology hobbled military success on the battlefield, while the daily loss of men and treasure constrained diplomatic initiatives.

With fluctuating ends and indecisive means the so-called "Great War" is a major symbol to students of strategy. Its importance and novelty, historically, was the "remarkable disparity between the end sought, the price paid, and the results obtained."[20] As long as the verdict is rejected that a whole generation of soldiers and politicians were either stupid or mischievous or both, then 1914-1918 is a symbol of the tragic and inescapable dilemmas of war and of the delusion that acceptable solutions can always be found for military problems. At the end of it all Clemencau said: "War is too serious a matter to be left to generals." This should not be read to mean that those who are not generals can necessarily do better. Rather it should be taken as a reminder that modern war has become so complex and significant that it demands the pooling of the widest range of a society's relevant intelligence. More particularly, the specific horror of the Great War might be taken, not as an excuse for hiding away from the study of war and strategy, but as a sick invitation to think about them all the more. They will not go away.

While the emotions of the peoples of many countries after 1918 were in an anti-war direction, certain groups of military theorists were turning to two new forms of warfare which seemed to offer a hope of escaping from prolonged strategic deadlock, and restoring instead a style of warfare which might produce speedy and decisive results. Theories of mechanised warfare and air power were the most interesting features in the evolution of strategic doctrine in the inter-war years.

In theorising about mechanised warfare the pragmatic British for once took a lead. First in prominence was the unconventional J.F.C. Fuller, who finally became a Major General and who later wrote a series of interesting and idiosyncratic books on the subject of war.[21]

He was sufficiently far-sighted, even in the poorly handled tank operations of 1916-18, to see the immense potentialities of this new weapon, if organised into sufficiently large groups, and co-ordinated with mobile artillery, mechanised infantry, and integrated air power. Fuller's inspiration was enthusiastically taken up, developed, and publicised by Liddell Hart, who from the mid-1920s to the late 1960s was Britain's most well-known (if not always influential or popular) writer on military strategy.[22]

Liddell Hart's twin interests in military history and mechanised warfare converged in the late 1920s to produce *Strategy: The Indirect Approach,* which was first published in 1929, and which has presented his general theory of strategy through its various editions. In essence, the "indirect approach" involved an attempt to weaken resistance before attempting to overcome it; this was to be achieved by exploiting movement and surprise away from the line of natural expectation. The most common description of Liddell Hart is that of "prophet without honour" in his own country. Certainly, his ideas faced much military conservatism; perhaps even more important, his doctrine of mechanised warfare was not considered to be of primary relevance to an army preoccupied with world-wide imperial policing, and a strategy of limited liability for the European Continent.

There was also a group advocating mechanised warfare in France. This group, of which Charles de Gaulle was the most famous member, was having an equally frustrating time in a country whose leaders were pushing the static warfare of the First World War to its logical conclusion — the idea of the Maginot Line. However, the Maginot Line itself was not pushed to a logical conclusion. For political reasons it was not extended along the frontier with Belgium, and so left dangerously exposed the French flank which Germany had attacked thirty years earlier. Given the alliance policy pursued by the French in Eastern Europe, the projection of power made possible by mechanised warfare made it a relevant doctrine for them. However, the unwillingness of French leaderships to take war-related decisions was even greater than that of their British counterparts.

In contrast, in Germany and the Soviet Union, there was a receptive audience for ideas of mechanised warfare. In both cases military defeat and political revisionism provided the fertile ground in which the *blitzkrieg* idea could develop. To its supporters, tank warfare reached its culmination in the decisive and cheap victories by Hitler's forces between 1939 and 1941. To the sceptics, however, the subsequent tank battles of 1942-5 on the eastern front were more spectacular and significant; they indicated that although tanks had restored mobility, they did not necessarily reduce the appalling casualty lists of modern war.

The second method by which it was hoped to overcome strategic deadlock was through air power, which attracted a particularly bombastic group of advocates. The most famous air power theorists were the Italian Brigadier General Douhet (1869-1930), the Commander-in-Chief of the RAF General Sir Hugh Trenchard, and General "Billy" Mitchell in the Uniited States. These three individuals have attracted an exaggerated amount of attention.[23] The influential group from which they sprang was wide. In Britain alone, for example, attention is also due to F.W. Lanchester, Sir Frederick Sykes, the Smuts Committee, Brigadier General Groves, J.M. Spaight, Sir John Slessor, Air-Commodore Charlton, E.J. Kingston-McLoughry and Professor Haldane.[24] Although the early air power enthusiasts differed over important details, they shared many common beliefs. In particular, they believed that air power had revolutionised warfare. They argued that it would be devastating in the next war. Command of the air would make the difference between a good victory and a bad defeat. The expectations of the air power theorists were inflated by a mixture of vested interest, ignorance, and hope. Many of the assumptions upon which their theories were based were untested: the destructive power of high explosive bombs was exaggerated, the problems of target selection were minimised, the accuracy of bombing was overestimated, the impotence of air defence was considered almost axiomatic (but this belief was invalidated by radar), and the fragility of civilian populations in face of bombing was taken as an article of faith. History has shown that these assumptions are not valid in conventional war. The test of the Second World War showed the important contribution which successful air power could make to the prosecution of varied military missions, but it also showed that for the time being at least, strategic bombing could not make air power independently decisive.[25]

The promise of air power was particularly attractive to the two Anglo-Saxon powers. To the British, air power promised a capital-intensive solution to the bothersome problems of the "Continental commitment". To the United States on the other hand air power promised to be the perfect technological accompaniment to such traditional American attitudes to war as the direct approach ("there is no substitute for victory") the ideological fervour ("give me liberty or give me death") the tendency to absolutes (the opposite to war is "normalcy") and the crusading spirit ("the devil theory of war").[26] Although the ideological element in US thinking distinguishes it from that of Britain, both their attitudes to strategy were affected by the luxury of relative security, which permitted a strategy of the "long haul", and by an attitude which tended to see war and peace as separate entities and so deserving of very different postures. In contrast to the relative doctrinal consistency of Marxists and Nazis, resulting from their appreciation of politics in terms of *struggle* between massive forces, the Anglo-American approach was more incoherent, resulting from their seeing war as an "aberration", a "crusade", a "disease", or a "scourge", and their seeing so-called "peace" as "normal". The result

31

of this perception was to produce policies which Lippmann neatly summed up as "too pacific in peace: too belligerent in war".

The Clausewitzian philosophy of war fitted very comfortably into the conflict doctrine which was developed by Marx and Lenin and their supporters. Soviet military doctrine as it evolved after 1917 fitted into an overall strategy which was permissive about means: expediency was the guide to any particular usage. It was also incorporated into an overall foreign policy which was markedly pragmatic and rational, once the short-lived period of revolutionary innocence had passed. The evolution of Soviet military policy can be seen as the synthesis of two heritages, the revolutionary and the traditional,[27] within the framework set by the geopolitical opportunities and constraints of the Soviet Russian state, and the thrust of events in international relations. Given the strategic weaknesses of the Soviet Union after 1917, and its perception of "inevitable war", the objective demands were for a deterrent and defence strategy allied to a foreign policy which sought to buy time and allies, and weaken potential enemies. In such an environment it was not possible for a "revolutionary" element to intrude prominently into Soviet strategic practice – whatever the theory.[28]

In Hitler's Germany there was a comparable appreciation of the permanence of the struggle and the utility of violence. However, not only was the violence of the struggle seen to be more glorious, but also the geopolitical environment was more permissive, giving him more opportunity to play out his appointed role: and time was more pressing for Hitler than almost any Marxist. In the late 1930s Hitler showed himself to be a consummate manipulator of the techniques of bargaining backed by the threat of military force. To those leaders in Western Europe who wanted peace at almost any price his style was irresistible. As a result, up to 1939, he was able to incorporate a large amount of territory into the *Reich* at relatively little cost. The urgency of his ambition fed upon his success. When war was the only instrument, he had little hesitation in using it. In the first two years of the Second World War he proved to be as successful a military strategist as he had been an exponent of the "diplomacy of violence". By 1941 he was "master of war".[29] However, like many military adventurers his success was short-lived. His policies were badly based; they built up formidable opposition. He also made a series of strategic and political mistakes which threw away the opportunities which his earlier success had created for him. His failure in 1945 could not have been more complete.[30]

It required six years of the most total warfare in history to bring about Hitler's downfall. It was the first truly global war, extending into all continents and seas, and was the first real air war. With some reservations it was remarkably total in both ends and means: limits were fixed by expediency and capability rather than morality. It sucked in the lives of millions, by-standers and workers, as well as fighting men.

Unprecedented destructive potential was developed and displayed. Science and industry were mobilised as never before. Its economic and psychological dimensions were far-reaching. It had massive impact, in the realms of politics, science, economics, social change and culture, as well as strategically. Both on and off the battlefields, the Second World War is a fascinating subject for the student of military affairs.[31]

In terms of the evolution of strategic thinking the Second World War was most impressive in the realm of practice rather than theory. Its "lessons" are still being assimilated. On the battlefield itself the most notable feature was the return (in some campaigns) of hard-hitting mobile warfare, based on tanks and close air support organised around the *blitzkrieg* concept. In the air the tactical utility of aircraft was proved time and again, although many questions still remained about the "decisiveness" of strategic bombing, on which so many resources had been invested by the Allies. Naval warfare changed significantly, with the aircraft carrier emerging as the primary force at sea, and with the increased efficiency of the submarine. At sea the era ended where like fought like. The allied amphibious landings, which were huge feats of organisation as well as offensive spirit, were notable integrations of all arms. While there was much that was novel in this war, the ultimate importance of ground forces in order to occupy territory was again demonstrated, with the war on the Russian front having a significance which is only now being fully appreciated. On the home front there was plenty of interest in the social, psychological, and material mobilisation of whole populations. It was a war in which the strategic impact of logistics and administration was particularly important. At the theatre level it was full of fascinating case studies of "command decisions" in circumstances which were confused, but over issues which were fateful. At the governmental level all the problems of civil-military relations in modern wars between giant coalitions over widely separeted theatres were manifest. Inevitably there were the perennial problems of relating ends and means when the consequences of defeat were unthinkable. At the diplomatic level there was the relationship between alliance problems and the course of the campaigns, and the tendency for conferences to usurp the traditional primacy of the battlefield. And underlying everything there was the interplay of relative competence in integrating national strategy and tactics with developments in science and industry. In short, by studying the Second World War the student may fully appreciate the meaning of Kissinger's dictum that "strategy is the mode of survival of a society" in a most detailed way and in its manifold dimensions. Because it is within living memory, and its impact is still with us in many fields, the Second World War is also a reminder that strategy is ultimately a very practical business.[32] As Brodie has put it: "There is no other science where judgements are tested in blood and answered in the servitude of the defeated."[33]

The Nuclear Strategists

It took about a decade after the atomic bombs were dropped on Hiroshima and Nagasaki before the world entered the period of "contemporary" strategy as it is now understood. While it is tempting to impose a historical unity on the "nuclear age" as a whole, close observation soon reveals it to be a period of quickly changing strategic emphasis, frequent technological innovation, multiple "great debates" on military affairs, and complex diplomatic evolution. The strategic world with which we are now familiar is surprisingly recent. It was not until the mid-1950s that both superpowers had nuclear plenty and intercontinental delivery systems. It was not until the early 1960s that they had significant numbers of invulnerable missiles (submarine-launched, or in hardened silos) and so the potential for an assured destruction capability even when striking second. From the strategic plateau of the early 1970s the alarms, fears and scramblings of the post-war foothills are easily forgotten.

Many of the strategic writings of the early post-war period now have a rather underdeveloped tone. In the West there was a good deal of untutored technological and political speculation about the "Russian threat" and the "ultimate weapon". However, there were also a number of interesting public analyses which dealt with the challenging new situation in an interesting and restrained fashion. In the United States the work of Brodie, Viner and Bush stand out; in Britain important contributions were made by Blackett and Liddell Hart.[34] For the most part, however, few people today study the works produced in this period. Meanwhile, in the USSR, strategic thinking was ostensibly frozen by Stalin, whose public posture included a determined and prudential deprecation of the significance of nuclear weapons: in practice however, the Soviet leadership pressed ahead with a vigorous weapons policy, in an effort to end the US atomic monopoly.

In many ways strategic thinking in the first decade of the nuclear age followed traditional patterns. After initial disquiet, public interest in *the* bomb subsided: military security, as ever, was left to the experts. Official circles, dependent mainly upon military or retired military personnel, still dominated the theory of strategy. However, there were signs of change, not the least in the practice of strategy. For example, incipient revolutionary struggles were threatening the traditional picture in which "strategy" exclusively involved military interaction between the legal armed forces of formally constituted authorities. For the major military powers, business as usual was hectic: it involved the need to assimilate the "lessons" of the Second World War, accommodate the technological developments in weaponry and communications, and meet the daily military problems of the Cold War confrontation and/or imperial sunset, which in some cases (e.g. Korea, Malaya, Indo-China) involved fighting on an extensive scale. The major powers shared some common strategic problems: their attempted solutions, however, were often different, being moulded by different priorities, traditions, and perspectives. At staggered intervals each took a "new look" and for a mixture of economic, political, and military reasons adopted more osten-ostensibly nuclear strategies. As the major military powers increasingly incorporated nuclear weapons into their arsenals, the chief effect was that "total" war between them no longer appeared to be a rational instrument of policy. Little else changed, however. Neither the nature of war nor the nature of politics among nations was radically revolu-tionised by the new weaponry. International politics accommodated the so-called absolute weapon.

By the mid-1950s the gestation period of the nuclear strategists came to an end. The modern arms debate, with which we have been familiar since, finally arrived. In the United States it was induced by the arrival of the H-bomb, the Eisenhower Administration's adoption of it, and the articulation of the much criticised strategy of "Massive Retaliation". At the same time, in the Soviet Union, a defence debate of unusual open-ness was caused by an array of economic and military pressures, and was made possible by the death of Stalin. The strategic doctrine which emerged from the Soviet Union appeared undeveloped beside its US counterpart, but appearances in these matters are nor everything. Strategic sophistication, like beauty, may only be skin deep. What matters is whether strategies *work,* within the ideological, political, and economic capabilities and intentions of their framers; the proper criteria are not those of strategic fashion as set by the *haute couture* of North American think-tanks.

The strategic debate of the mid-1950s turned into what some have called the "golden age" of contemporary strategic thinking. It has been one of the pastimes of its observers in recent years to delineate its bounds. There is more agreement about its starting-point than its fini-shing point, though certainly all are agreed that the golden age has passed. The opening of the period is usually thought to have been 1956-7, with the publication of W.W. Kaufmann's influential *Military Policy and National Security* or, more eye-catchingly, Henry A. Kissinger's *Nuclear Weapons and Foreign Policy.* The latter was the first compre-hensive treatment of the subject and "the first best-seller" in the field of nuclear strategy.[35] The end of the exciting and fertile golden age has been dated at a number of points between 1961-5. The turning point is said to have been marked by G. Snyder's *Deterrence and Defence,* or R. S. McNamara's major policy statements, or Herman Kahn's *On Escalation.* However, 1966 might be offered as an alternative and more appropriate boundary. In that year were published two lucid and impor-tant works which attempted to comprehend the theory and practice of the nuclear age and assess the uses and utility of force. The works were T.C. Schelling's *Arms and Influence* and K. Knorr's *On the Uses of Military Power in the Nuclear Age.* With these works the end of the golden age was marked, as it had been begun by Kissinger, with comprehensive efforts to incorporate "strategy" within its proper intellectual, constitutional, and political home: that is, within foreign policy. In addition, 1966 also saw the publication of Philip Green's *Deadly Logic*, which was a powerful critique of the nuclear strategists, and a timely reminder that all that glitters is not gold.

What then were the chief characteristics of this decade from the mid-1950s to the mid-1960s, which was marked by such a vital "arms debate"?[36] The range of approaches, interests, methodologies and backgrounds was wide. Approaches ranged from "marginalists" to "systemists".[37] Interests ranged from the "forward strategists" through the "realists" and the "experimentalists" to the "peace movement".[38] Methodologies ranged from the "traditionalists" (historical-empirical) to a variety of "scientific strategists", whose expertise encompassed game theory, systems analysis and other novel techniques. Backgrounds included the traditional military, but increasingly the subject became heavily dominated by civilians, whose own academic backgrounds varied from history and political science to economics, mathematics and physics. Despite this apparent diversity, the archetypal nuclear strategist is not difficult to recognise. He was (is) an American; a civilian; basically an "academic", operating from a university or a well-funded research institute, but moving relatively freely between this base and government; and with a commitment to peace and stability through a combination of deterrence, arms control, and crisis management. This was the dominant group in the golden age (and since): they were the most productive, the most read, the most fashionable, and they were considered the most congenial by the policy-makers. However, having said this one must be warned against the common mistake of seeing *Modern Strategic Man* as *American Strategic Man* writ large, and of seeing different types of strategists as Americans gone wrong. Although strategy is a universal preoccupation, its meaning is always contextual, set by the problems, perceptions, traditions, and ideology of a particular nation or group.

The strategic literature of this period was heavily dominated by the contributors from the United States, writing primarily with US problems in mind and with identifiable ethnocentric positions. To the surprise of some, but not others, the policy prescriptions which were produced by the new strategists have not been considered relevant by those of other countries with different world views. Many countries, for example, still prepare to fight with what is essentially Second World War generation technology. Thus they find most relevant the practical analyses of conventional battlefield war which have been eschewed by most "academic strategists". Countries pursue national paths to strategic salvation, or it's disastrous opposite. And at both ends of the spectrum of violence there have been some distinctive national contributions to contemporary strategic thinking. Apart from the United States the major contributions have come from Britain, France, the Soviet Union and China.

By and large it is impossible to recognise a distinctive *British* school of contemporary strategic thinking. The British writers, of whom Buchan and Howard have been the most notable, have been distinctly transatlantic in some ways, although their backgrounds, abilities and approaches have enabled them to produce work which casts rather different beams on the central problems.[39] The most distinctive Western European contributions have come from France, however, where questions of alliance and deterrence strategy, the case for national ("independent") deterrents, and European regional deterrents, as well as general interpretations of strategic theory were taken up with verve by Ailleret, Aron, Beaufre, and Gallois in particular.[40]

Soviet conceptions of strategy are a further step still from American strategic theory. Not surprisingly, the volume of strategic writing which has emerged from the Soviet Union is far less than in the West. Military secretiveness, lack of vocal critics, tradition, and rigid constitutional arrangements all ensure that defence decision-making is less exposed to outside influences than in the West, and that "defence debates" are more muted. However, there have been some "debates", and some theoretical contributions which have attracted attention.[41] For the most part Soviet strategic theory has been developed in occasional writings within the military press, and its dissemination outside has depended upon the work and expertise of a relatively small number of Western specialists in the field of Soviet strategy.[42] As a result of the Soviet Union's different military and political traditions, the absence of a pluralistic society and the absence of independent civilian involvement in the strategic debate, different historical context, different geopolitical situation, and different aims and capabilities, there have been some important differences between Soviet and Anglo-American approaches to strategy in the nuclear age.[43] For example, while the primary aim of Soviety military policy has been to deter attack, strategic postures have not been dominated by the idea of *mutual* deterrence, as in the United States. As in the traditional Western military view, successful deterrence has been seen as a function of an impressive (preferably superior) war-fighting capability, and not something separate. Despite a widespread view that Soviet strategic thinking has been less sophisticated than its American counterpart, it has often made a good deal more sense than some of its culture-bound critics have assumed.[44]

Strategic thinking in China has been far removed in both tradition and environment from that of both the Soviet Union and the United States. The most notable Chinese contribution to modern military thinking has been the theory of revolutionary war as propounded by Mao Tse-tung and his disciples. A number of other notable military theorists from other countries have emerged from the anti-colonialist experience, notably Debray, Giap, and Guevara.[45] Thinking about this so-called "sub-limited" type of warfare has in fact been more of a pre-occupation for most underdeveloped countries than the nuclear problems which have attracted concern elsewhere. As far as conventional warfare is concerned, the peculiar combination of China's size, circumstances, and population invalidate the model of the north European plain as a school for strategy, while Chinese thinking about nuclear strategy has scarcely begun to be articulated in a Western sense, even since their demonstration of a nuclear explosive capability in 1964.

Important parts of the world have been preoccupied with urgent military matters for much of the post-war period. While publicity in the literature of the subject has been usurped by academic strategists in the United States, national strategic paths dominate both the theory and practice of the activity. It cannot be otherwise, while the structure of international society remains based on the nation state. "Any search for the strategic equivalent of economic man on the basis of which a grand theory of military behaviour might be erected is bound to be ephemeral and unproductive."[46]

Since the mid-1950s the areas of attention which have attracted the dominant nuclear strategists have changed with the thrust of events, but the focus of their interests has remained stable: deterrence, arms control, crisis management, and limited war (at all its hurtful levels). If for no other reason, the work of the American nuclear strategists has been notable because of the vast amount of literature which they have produced. However, much of it has been repetitious: the key statements for those who wish to understand the evolution of the subject have been few. They are, in chronological order: A. Wohlstetter, *Selection and Use of Strategic Air Bases* (1954, but not declassified until 1962), W.W. Kaufmann (ed.), *Military Policy and National Security* (1956), H.A. Kissinger, *Nuclear Weapons and Foreign Policy* (1957), R.E. Osgood, *Limited War : the Challenge to American Strategy* (1957), A. Wohlstetter, "The Delicate Balance of Terror", *Foreign Affairs*, January 1959, B. Brodie, *Strategy in the Missile Age* (1959), H. Kahn, *On Thermonuclear War* (1960), T.C. Schelling, *The Strategy of Conflict* (1960), H.A. Kissinger, *The Necessity for Choice* (1960), H. Bull, *The Control of the Arms Race* (1961), G. Snyder, *Deterrence and Defence : Toward a Theory of National Security* (1961), T.C. Schelling and M. Halperin, *Strategy and Arms Control* (1961), K. Knorr and T. Read, *Limited Strategic War* (1962), M.H. Halperin, *Limited War in the Nuclear Age* (1963), W.W. Kaufmann, *The McNamara Strategy* (1964), H.J. Morgenthau, "The Four Paradoxes of Nuclear Strategy", *American Political Science Review*, March 1964, A. Rapoport, *Strategy and Conscience* (1964), H. Kahn, *On Escalation: Metaphor and Scenarios* (1965), T.C. Schelling, *Arms and Influence* (1966), P. Green, *Deadly Logic* (1966), and K. Knorr, *On the Uses of Military Power in the Nuclear Age* (1966). The remaining chapters of this book, especially Part Two, will assess what these writers and others said about the issues of the time and about the nature of contemporary strategy.

The nuclear strategists shared a common understanding of the "real world" which they sought to analyse and, sometimes, to influence. Furthermore, despite many differences of opinion about particular issues, their general area of interest — nuclear weapons and the threat of nuclear war — was quite narrow, as was their range of prescriptions. Their common understanding of this ostensibly new strategy included elevating *mutual* deterrence to a novel doctrinal prominence, replacing the old utopian idea of disarmanent with the less grandiose but more feasible concept of arms control, [47] stressing that force was still an important factor in structuring international politics, believing that wars short of all-out nuclear war could still have political utility, as long as those wars which did occur could be kept limited, being concerned about the effectiveness of communication and the explicitness of bargaining, and being generally inspired with some of the social scientist's confidence in being able to manage affairs more rationally.

In addition to this common set of attitudes, the phenomenon of the nuclear strategists included some other interesting features. They introduced a jargon and a set of analytical concepts which gave them a novel identity. Their prescriptions were such that they had an impact which encouraged policy-makers to look to civilians rather than military officers for strategic advice. They introduced a variety of methodological techniques, most notably of a quantitative type. Because of the complexity of the issues and the range of expertise required, the study of strategy was quite a corporate activity, full of cross-pollination.[48] The absolute volume of strategic literature produced in the 1960s was unprecedented, and even those paid to keep up with it found their task increasingly difficult (and perhaps unneccessary). With the expanding literature the study of strategy grew as a university discipline, usually as part of an international politics course: from being non-existent, "strategic studies" quickly became mainstream. While attention was attracted by the published literature of non-officials, most of the practical thinking about the subject (in some ways the most important) remained hidden in the memories and secret files of governments. Some of the influential "strategists" remain quite obscure.[49] There is sometimes a glaring dichotomy in the study of strategy between what governments did and what "strategists" wrote. The literature of the subject changed rapidly as new issues arose; and these did arise frequently as technological innovation spurred on the need for change in strategy and tactics. In general, the concern of the academic civilian analysts was very much on the nuclear rather than the "conventional" aspects of the problem: to the extent attention was paid to the latter, it was in the subject of counter-insurgency. Furthermore, the background and interests of the strategists were such that they were sometimes criticised for being naive about the world of politics: in particular, for being ignorant about the value systems and politics of the countries which they fed into their analyses, and about the way decisions were actually made. [50] One notable feature of recent developments is that modern academic strategists, unlike the professional military thinkers of the past, have frequently been concerned about ends as well as means.[51] Unlike the traditional military mind, the academic mind does not necessarily take the objectives of policy as settled. For all these reasons strategy in the West at least has become civilianised, with only a small number of military officers making much of a contribution. For better or worse, Clemenceau's maxim has been put into practice in an age when war became even more serious than ever before.

The impact and contribution of the nuclear strategists has produced a mixed reaction. Some of their defenders have characterised their work as "timeless". Others, more restrained, consider that despite the buffetings which their analysis and prescriptions have taken, and recognising the limitations faced by the activity, the nuclear strategists have made a very important contribution to the study and sometimes the practice of a vitally important area of human affairs. They argue that the conceptual frameworks which were developed at the turn of the 1950s/1960s has stood up well to the test of time, and that our understanding of the strategic world has been greatly enriched by their efforts.

Other appreciations are far less complimentary. Some critics have rejected the "community" of academic strategists as "new civilian militarists", and have dismissed their much-lauded conceptual frameworks as immoral as well as misbegotten. Some of the radical critics have produced sophisticated critiques of the work of the academic strategists and their brother scholar-advisers. The attacks have been far-reaching. Academic strategists have been criticised for their methodology, especially on the grounds that they have been pseudo-scientific and/or do not understand the real world of politics. They have been criticised for their scholarly conduct (or rather their lack of it) on the ground that academic integrity is not compatible with fees from governments for advisory work, security clearances, and semi-official status. They have been criticised on moral grounds, with the argument that strategists are "hard-nosed" and leave ethical questions out of account, and that their so-called "realism" is a mixture of dehumanised cynicism and *naiveté*. Of the radical critics, the works of P. Green and A. Rapoport stand out for their pungency and insight.[52] On the whole, however, the radical critics have been "outsiders" as far as the development of modern strategic thinking is concerned: they have been largely ignored by governments, and have had only a limited impact on the dominance of the established nuclear strategists. Whether or not one agrees with the radical critics, there can be no doubt about the value of their contribution: they have confronted the purveyors of the conventional wisdoms with a series of significant and telling questions.[53]

The nuclear strategists have been criticised from both sides: from traditional military professionals on grounds of inadequate practical experience, and from the radical community on grounds of methodology and scholarly conduct. The radical criticisms show, however, that it is easier to demolish many of the approaches and prescriptions of the academic strategists than replace them with alternatives that the majority think feasible or desirable. For example, the works of Green and Rapoport are more impressive in their criticism of the old world, than in their thoughts on its replacement. It is far easier to criticise the world of force and power than replace it with something better, or even change it. For all their faults the academic strategists do involve themselves in the great issues of war and peace. They may not be paragons, but they are one of the few defences against the Praetorian state, and the complete domination of military affairs by the "specialists in violence".

Security on Spaceship Earth

It is inevitable that a golden age will be followed by a period of anti-climax. After about a decade of excitement, debate and growth there was in strategic studies from the mid-1960s onwards an apparent decline in creativity, a certain complacency about the contribution which had been made, and a tendency for inertia to take over. In the view of many, the academic strategists had done their job well, and there seemed little else to say. In addition, the world of the early 1970s seemed a much safer place than the world of the early 1960s: problems other than military ones seemed urgent and requiring the investment of special effort. Furthermore, as a result of the criticism which had been levelled against the subject on grounds of scholarship and method, and as a result of the embarrassment caused by the inability of theory to result in more effective practice (notably in and around Vietnam) there has been a certain defensiveness in recent years on the part of some of those professionally involved in strategic thinking. The "decline of strategic studies" has been an oft-heard refrain, although more at the turn of the 1960s/1970s than today. The extent of the pessimism was partly the result of academic strategists turning their training in assuming the worst inwards on their own profession.[54]

To a large extent much thinking about strategy today is along the lines of "more of the same"; a good deal of the subject involves the study, refinement, and synthesis of the conceptual frameworks and insights developed a decade earlier. Many would argue that this corpus of ideas has stood the test of time very well, and that despite some frayed edges the ideas are still serviceable. They are necessary tools for students of strategy in the contemporary world.

However necessary they might be, a feeling has been growing that these tools are no longer sufficient. The holders of this view vary in the stress which they place on the contemporary relevance of the conceptualisations developed during the era of the Cold War and the technology of Polaris and Minuteman. How important are such ideas to the different problems and different technologies of the middle 1970s and beyond? While ordinary conservatism and in some cases complacency remain strong, there has already been a response to these changes from within the profession in the West.

Gray has called this evolution the "Second Wave";[55] it involves not so much "new directions" as "some old questions revisited". As a result of this development the early 1970s have witnessed something of a revitalisation of strategic thinking, with a sceptical eye having been turned towards some of the conventional wisdoms and some interesting forays having been made into areas which, hitherto, have been little trodden or even ignored. There are several currents within the force behind the second wave. Of particular importance has been a dissatisfaction with the concept of deterrence based upon mutual assured destruction (MAD): it is considered by some that this posture is neither good ethics nor good defence. The corollary to this view is the belief that technology now allows a better "war-fighting" capability (with a counter-force strategy and more defensive emphasis) and that this is not only ethically preferable but also likely to prove a more stable deterrent. This emphasis on war-fighting as the basis for deterrence has always been the major thrust behind Soviet thinking, so that recent developments suggest more of a convergence of strategic doctrines. In addition to re-examining deterrence, the second wave has also begun to re-investigate established views about strategic stability and technological innovation, the nature of arms racing, the utility of military power in general and nuclear power in particular, the utility of formal arms control processes, the assumption of rationality, and has also branched out into improving expertise in area studies and decision-making. While the new literature which is addressing itself to these problems is far from extensive, a second wave is evident. Some of its noteworthy contributors have been Brennan, Dror, Gray, Ikle and Janowitz.[56] It still remains to be seen whether the second wave will deposit masses of intellectually sound and politically relevant strategic material, or will merely disappear into the sand.

This reformulation of ideas from within the subject is beginning to meet some of the criticisms of existing strategic thinking à la archetypal American nuclear strategist. However, such reformulations do not meet (and are not meant to meet) the criticism of those who claim that strategic studies are over-intellectualised. Furthermore, they do not meet a more substantial concern about the general trend and direction of the subject. This feeling, which is based on defining strategic studies in terms of general security rather than military security, argues that strategic studies should not be "more — if better — of the same", but rather that the concerns should be redirected. Underlying this viewpoint is the belief that recent strategic thinking is out of touch with the quickly changing international context: the view is that the *strategists* are not attuned to the changing military and other security preoccupations of present-day societies. In particular, the military security which was traditionally the primary concern of governments of nation states must now be accompanied — some would say it has been superseded — by other "security" considerations.[57] The world has changed rapidly, and the concerns and conceptualisations of the nuclear golden age seem from this viewpoint to be outdated, esoteric and culture-bound rather than timeless and universalistic.

The significant changes in the world politico-strategic environment since the early 1960s have been both manifold and complex. In the world of diplomacy the chief development has been the break-up of the bipolar world into a world of more diffused political power. The military structure of the Cold War has been replaced by the more complex manoeuvrings of an "era of negotiation". In the central relationship, between the United States and Soviet Union *détente* and a "limited adversary relationship"[58] have replaced that of "eyeball to eyeball" confrontation, for the time being at least. In the sphere of politics, despite the powerful persistence of nationalism, it makes sense also to talk about "world politics" or "world society" as an alternative to "international relations". Nation states, their boundaries and governments, remain critically important political facts, but the thickening cobweb of transactions is a growing challenge to the traditional conception of politics among nations. Economic factors have played a primary role in this development. World-wide economic conerns such as the energy crisis, the general resource problem, the strains on the international monetary system, the problems of the international trade — all are productive of a sense of both strain and interdependence. They also produce a belief in some quarters that economic security will replace military security as the primary preoccupation of governments.[59] Such feelings were intensified by the novel use of the "oil weapon" at the turn of 1973-74. All these problems have been intensified by such socio-economic problems as the booming world population and the spreading of pollution. In political, economic, and social spheres there is therefore more inter-dependence on a world-wide level than ever before. Consciousness of this — if not the will to change things — has been vastly increased by the ease and rapidity of communications.

In the military sphere the dialectic of conflict and interdependence set against a background of change is peculiarly marked. The sense of interdependence has been increased by the pervading nuclear threat, the increasing destructiveness of violent conflict anywhere, and the rise of the phenomenon of political terrorism. Other changes have affected the patterns of thinking established during the Cold War. Bipolarity has been diffused by the rise of other centres of important military power: in addition, small countries have shown a novel strength and resilience in the face of great power coercion. Meanwhile, some of the traditional assumptions about the threat of war and the utility of force have changed, certainly in the Western world. There is, for example, a strong perception in much of the world that major war is not likely, and that interstate politics is no longer primarily decided by the movement of divisions and ships. Major war between the chief military powers is ruled out on rational grounds as politically pointless. Military power has to be manipulated in peacetime rather than used in wartime.[60] The possibility of mass destruction by nuclear weapons has abolished the strategy of war between the great powers, and has replaced it with the strategy of crisis management.[61] At a lower level of danger, the utility of great power military intervention is perceived to have been reduced by its increasing costs and declining benefits, by an associated decline in the "imperialistic" self-confidence of the superpowers, and by the reborn determination of the Davids when facing the Goliaths. While technological and political changes make nuclear strategy appear increasingly esoteric, other technological innovations have significantly affected warfare at the "coventional" level, as seemed to be indicated by the war in the Middle East in October 1973.

In this changing strategic environment with its new problems — more complex if not so immediately catastrophic as the relatively simple strategic problems posed by the Cold War — some of the established books have a rather old-fashioned tone to them. New conceptualisations seem required. Furthermore, with the relative absence of traditional battlefield warfare and the rise of international political terrorism on a large scale, new skills are called for. Instead of the military science required to understand the movements of troops, the expertise of the psychologist, sociologist and political scientist is required to understand the impulses of the terrorist. For a number of countries, active politically instrumental violence is dominated in the mid-1970s not by the "military mind" but by the idealistic — some would say psycopathic — terrorist. Such changes make the tasks of those concerned with the theory and practice of military (and para-military) affairs a dynamic and complex one. In the world of writing about contemporary strategy, ten years is a very long time.

The changes mentioned above have not run their course, and their long-term implications remain to be seen. Clearly the field of strategic studies cannot be defined statistically. But there is continuity as well as change. The new concerns are additions, not replacements to traditional interests. While amongst large sections of opinion there is a belief in the declining likelihood of war and a strong feeling that strategic questions are not as urgent as they once were, it nevertheless remains true that the problem of war or peace is both critical and universal. Many familiar concerns remain: nuclear war remains possible; conventional war with tanks and aircraft is planned; military interventions are contingencies which are feasible; and revolutionary war and counterinsurgency actions have been frequent. Although strategy has moved into a "grimmer" period[62] with the rise of the terrorist, the movement and roles of legal armed forces remain dominating factors in structuring interstate relations. And although the "technological Frankenstein" has remained caged for a generation, vigilance cannot be purdently relaxed, for the monster has grown more powerful, not less, while in captivity. Furthermore, his offspring, when they sometimes slip through the bars, show that they can inflict pain and destruction with ever more efficiency. Wars still occur, and if the utility of military force has changed in some respects, it still has vital defensive utilities, it is still threatened and used for acquisitive purposes, and it remains a basic foundation of international order.[63] The basic framework of interstate politics is still set by the willingness of groups to fight if necessary in order to defend their patch of territory. While this is so, strategic studies will remain an important, dynamic, and deadly business.

Notes

1. B.H. Liddell Hart, *Strategy: The Indirect Approach* (London: Faber, 1967), p. 335.
2. S.B. Griffith, *Sun Tzu: The Art of War* (Oxford: OUP, 1963), Foreword by B.H. Liddell Hart. The latter called it "the best short introduction to the study of warfare".
3. Thomas Schelling, perhaps the most prominent (and certainly the most lucid) of modern "scientific strategists" has also attested to this: "For browsing in search of ideas, Caesar's *Conquest of Gaul* is rich reading and Thucydides' *Peloponnesian War* the best there is, whatever their historical merits − even if read as pure fiction." *Arms and Influence* (New Haven, Yale UP, 1966), vii
4. For an introduction to the military aspects of Machiavelli's writing see Felix Gilbert, "Machiavelli: The Renaissance of the Art of War", in E.M. Earle (ed.), *Makers of Modern Strategy* (Princeton: Princeton UP, first published 1941, 1966 printing), pp. 3-25.
5. His work has been reprinted recently. Baron de Jomini, *The Art of War* (Westport, Connecticut: Greenwood Press, 1971). For an introduction to his work see M. Howard, "Jomini and the Classical Tradition in Military Thought", pp. 3-20 in his *The Theory and Practice of War* (London: Cassell, 1965).
6. And is not. There have been numerous commentaries. See Paret, P., "Clausewitz. A Bibliographical Survey", *World Politics*, Vol. 17, No. 2, 1965, pp. 272-85. See also the introductions of the many editions of *On War*.
7. This formulation is by Anatol Rapoport. See his brilliant and idiosyncratic Introduction to his *Clausewitz On War* (Harmondsworth: Pelican Books, 1968).
8. Ibid., especially pp. 54-80. Rapoport, who coined the phrase, is convinced that this domination has been for the worse. Many so-called neo-Clausewitzians, however, would not feel insulted by the attribution: in fact, just the opposite would be the case.
9. This subject is interestingly and exhaustively dealt with by J. Luvaas, *The Military Legacy of the Civil War: the European Inheritance* (Chicago: Chicago University Press, 1959).
10. An introduction to Moltke's interesting contribution to strategic thinking is given by H. Holborn, "Moltke and Schlieffen: The Prussian-German School", pp. 172-205 in Earle op. cit.
11. An introduction to this doctrine is given by Liddell Hart in M. Gilbert (ed.),

A Century of Conflict 1850-1950 (London: Hamish Hamilton, 1966).
12. See J. Gottmann, "Bugeaud, Gallieni, Lyautey: The Development of French Colonial Warfare", Chapter 10 in Earle, op.cit., pp. 234-59. This is one of the most rewarding chapters in the book.
13. Colonel G.F.R. Henderson, quoted by Jay Luvaas, *The Education Of An Army. British Military Thought, 1815-1940* (London: Cassell, 1965) p.244. This book, which looks at the evolution of British military thinking through the work of eleven major writers, is the best introduction to the thinking as opposed to the action of the British Army.
14. An analysis of the work of these theorists, and others, can be found in D.M. Schurman, *The Education Of A Navy. The Development of British Naval Strategic Thought, 1867-1914* (London: Cassell, 1965).
15. The classic work on this period is the series by A.J. Marder, *From the Dreadnought to Scapa Flow* (London: OUP, 1961-71), 5 vols.
16. His main work was *The Influence of Sea Power upon History 1660-1783*, first published in 1890. It was recently reissued by University Paperbacks, Methuen, London, in 1965. For introductory analyses see M.T. Sprout, "Mahan: Evangelist of Seapower", Chapter 17 in Earle, op.cit., Chapter 4 in V. Davis, *The Admiral's Lobby* (Chapel Hill: University of North Carolina Press, 1967) and K. Booth, "History or Logic as Approaches to Strategy", *Journal of the Royal United Services Insitute for Defence Studies*, Vol. 117, No. 3, September 1972, pp. 34-41.
17. The most thorough work on the Schlieffen Plan, with a usefully critical Foreword by Liddell Hart, is G. Ritter, *The Schlieffen Plan. Critique of a Myth* (Horsham: Riband Books, n.d. First published in German in 1956).
18. Not everyone believed this. Nor did everyone believe that a future European war would be short, or even that warfare was still rational, national, and instrumental. Two critics of the prevailing view of war, widely read in "liberal" circles, were Ivan S. Bloch, *The Future of War in Its Technical, Economic, and Political Relations* (first published in 1897) which argued that war had become impossible, except at the price of suicide; and Sir N. Angell, *The Great Illusion* (first published in 1910) which also argued that wars did not pay. The beliefs of governments and military establishments prevailed however.
19. A.J.P. Taylor *The First World War. An Illustrated History* (Harmondsworth: Penguin Books, 1966), p. 20.
20. D. Thomson, *Europe Since Napoleon* (Harmondsworth: Penguin Books, 1966), p. 548.
21. Most notably his *The Conduct of War, 1789-1961* (London: Eyre and Spottiswoode, 1961).
22. Two synoptic essays on Fuller and Liddell Hart, with useful references for further study are Chapters 10 and 11 in Luvaas, op. cit.
23. Douhet in particular is said to have had an "influence" on thinking which is difficult to substantiate. For two contrasting views of his importance see B. Brodie, *Strategy in the Missile Age* (Princeton, N.J.: Princeton UP, 1959), Chapter III, which supports the idea of Douhet's heritage, and R. Higham, *The Military Intellectuals in Britain: 1918-1939* (New Brunswick, N.J.: Rutgers, UP, 1966), Appendix C, which is critical. E.M. Emme, *The Impact of Air Power* (Princeton, N.J.: Van Nostrand, 1959) provides a varied selection of readings on the general subject, and has a useful bibliography.
24. An indication of their contribution can be found in Higham, op. cit.
25. There is a vast and controversial literature on the subject of strategic bombing. For a introduction see Brodie, op. cit., Chapter 4; N. Frankland, *The Bombing Offensive* against Germany (London: Faber, 1966); and A. Verrier, *Bomber Offensive* (London: Batsford, 1968).
26. See H.A. Kissinger, *Nuclear Weapons and Foreign Policy* (London: OUP, 1957) and R.F. Weigley, *The American Way of War: a History of United*

States Military Strategy and Policy (London: Collier Macmillan, 1973).

27. This thesis is developed fully by M. Garder, *A History of the Soviet Army* (London: Pall Mall Press, 1966).
28. The evolution of Soviet military policy in the period is covered in detail and with insight by J. Erickson, *The Soviet High Command: a Military-Political History, 1918-1941* (London: Macmillan, 1962) and J.M. Mackintosh, *Juggernaut: a History of the Soviet Armed Forces* (London: Secker and Warburg, 1967). For a brief introduction see K. Booth, *The Military Instrument in Soviet Foreign Policy, 1917-1972.* London: RUSI, 1974).
29. Liddell Hart's phrase: *Strategy: The Indirect Approach* 1942 edition, p. 243.
30. A useful presentation of the various sides of the debate on Hitler's responsibility for the war can be found in E.M. Robertson, *The Origins of the Second World War* (London: Macmillan, 1971).
31. Perhaps the most useful short treatment of this war, which is probably the most researched in history, is G. Wright, *The Ordeal of Total War, 1939-45* (New York: Harper and Row, 1968).
32. Some would not see its study *in universities* in these terms. Some are content that its study in a university environment is justified solely by the presence of a substantial literature. See J.C. Garnett, *Theories of Peace and Security* (London: Macmillan, 1970), p. 20. I share this traditional view, which sees improved strategic practice as a happy by-product of academic strategic studies, rather than their *raison d'etre*.
33. Brodie, op. cit., p. 21.
34. B. Brodie, "The Atomic Bomb and American Security", Memorandum 18, Yale Institute of International Studies, November 1945, 27 pp.; see also *The Absolute Weapon: Atomic Power and World Order* (New York: Harcourt Brace, 1946); V. Bush, *Modern Arms and Free Men* (New York: Simon and Schuster, 1949); J. Viner, "The Implications of the Atomic Bomb for International Relations", *Proceedings of the American Philosophical Society,* Vol. 90, No. 1, January 1946, pp. 53-8; P.M.S. Blackett, *The Military and Political Consequences of Atomic Energy* (London: The Turnstile Press, 1948); B.H. Liddell Hart, *The Revolution in Warfare* (New Haven: Yale University Press, 1947). These early works, and some others, are assessed by J.E. King in *The New Strategy,* Prologue, Ch. 1. (forthcoming). This substantial and scholarly work is the first intellectual history of strategy in the nuclear age.
35. The characterisation is King's op. cit. Part II, Ch. I.
36. There have been few attempts to treat the spectrum of this subject comprehensively. For a consciously "social science" approach, see R.A. Levine, *The Arms Debate* (Cambridge, Mass.: Harvard University Press, 1963). For a journalist's account, see A. Herzog, *The War-Peace Establishment* (New York: Harper & Row, 1965).
37. Levine's basic categories, op. cit.
38. Some of Herzog's chapter titles. op. cit.
39. See, for example: Alistair Buchan, *War in Modern Society : an Introduction* (London : Watts, 1966), and Michael Howard, *Studies in War and Peace* (London: Temple Smith, 1970).
40. See below, Chapter XIV. Important references are: Raymond Aron, *The Great Debate. Theories of Nuclear Strategy* (New York : Anchor Books, 1965); André Beaufre, *An Introduction to Strategy* (London: Faber, 1965); Pierre M. Gallois, "U.S. Strategy and the Defence of Europe", *Orbis,* VII, No. 2., Summer 1963.
41. See below, Chapter XI. The single work which has attracted most attention in the West has been *Military Strategy,* edited by Marshal V.D. Sokolovsky (Three editions: 1962, 1963, 1968).
42. In particular see the works of J. Erickson, R.L. Garthoff, J.M. Mackintosh, and T.W. Wolfe cited in Chapter XI.

43. See below, Chapter XI.
44. This is explained below, Chapter XI.
45. See below, Chapter VII.
46. Robert E. Osgood, "The Reappraisal of Limited War", *Adelphi Papers*, No. 54., Hedley Bull was first to draw attention to this false analogy: *The Control of The Arms Race* (London: Weidenfeld and Nicolson, 1961) pp. 48-9.
47. This is the theme of Chapter V, below.
48. The dominant group of academic strategists is relatively small and distinct, as is testified by the acknowledgements pages of strategy books, lists of conference participants, and the contents pages of edited symposia.
49. Norman Moss, *Men Who Play God. The Story of the Hydrogen Bomb* (Harmondsworth: Penguin Books, 1970), p. 252 Halberstam is revealing on this: see his *The Best and the Brightest* (London: Barrie and Jenkins, 1972).
50. There has been some progress in both areas since the early 1960s. While the involvement of area studies specialists in "strategic studies" remains limited, the study of "bureaucratic politics" has been a major growth sector of political science, and one which has had important spin-off in the study of military policy.
51. See footnote 1 above.
52. See, for example, P. Green, *Deadly Logic: The Theory of Nuclear Deterrence* (Columbus, Ohio: Ohio State University Press, 1966); and A. Rapoport, *Strategy and Conscience* (New York : Harper and Row, 1965).
53. A range of the questions which strategists should face can be found in my "Teaching Strategy. An Introductory Questionnaire", *Survival,* March/April 1974, Vol. XV1, No. 2, pp. 79-85. It includes a short and selective reading list reflecting a variety of serious opinion about the value and impact of the academic strategists.
54. What else are they to do profitably in a period of *détente*?
55. Colin S. Gray, "The Second Wave : New Directions in Strategic Studies", *Journal of the Royal United Services Institute for Defence Studies,* December 1973, Vol. 118, No. 4, pp. 35-51.
56. For a sample of the new tone in some of the literature see Y. Dror, *Crazy States. A Counterconventional Strategic Problem* (Lexington, Mass.: Heath Lexington Books, 1971); C.S. Gray, "Rethinking Nuclear Strategy", *Orbis,* Vol. XV11, No. 4, Winter 1974, pp. 1145-60; Fred Charles Ikle, "Can Nuclear Deterrence Last Out The Century?" *Foreign Affairs,* January 1973; Morris Janowitz, "Toward A Redefinition of Military Strategy in International Relations", *World Politics,* Vol XXV1, No. 4, 1974, pp. 473-508; William R. Kintner and Robert L. Pfaltzgraff, (ed.) *SALT. Implications for Arms Control in the 1970s* (Pittsburgh: University of Pittsburgh Press, 1973). A useful collection of readings illustrative of the bureaucratic politics approach is provided by Morton H. Halperin and Arnold Kanter, *Readings in American Foreign Policy. A Bureaucratic Perspective* (Boston: Little, Brown and Company, 1973). The potential value of mixing strategists and area studies specialists is shown by Michael MacGwire (ed.), *Soviet Naval Developments: Capability and Context* (New York: Praeger, 1973).
57. This broadening of interest, with its implications for the discipline, is well reflected in the annual *Strategic Survey* produced by the International Institute for Strategic Studies.
58. The phrase is Marshal Shulman's. See his "Relations with the Soviet Union" in K. Gordon (ed.), *Agenda for the Nation* (Washington: Brookings Institution, 1968), p. 374.
59. See, for example, Richard Rosecrance, *International Relations. Peace or War?* (New York: McGraw-Hill, 1973) p. 320.
60. This view has been most lucidly expressed by Schelling, op. cit., *passim.*
61. The idea is McNamara's: "There is no strategy any more − only crisis

management." Quoted by Michael Howard, "The Transformation of Strategy", *Brassey's Annual 1972* (London: William Clowes and Sons Ltd, 1972), p. 8.

62. Ibid., p. 9.

63. This argument is well expressed by Michael Howard, "Military Power And International Order", *International Affairs,* Vol. XL, July 1964, pp. 397-408.

3. THE ROLE OF MILITARY POWER

John Garnett

At its simplest, the term military power refers to the capacity to kill, maim, coerce and destroy, and although occasionally this power may be possessed by individuals within the state — as the feudal barons possessed it during the Middle Ages and as the IRA possesses it today — nowadays military power tends to be monopolised by states and used primarily by *governments* to protect their countries from external aggression and internal subversion. Military power, therefore, is the legally sanctioned instrument of violence which governments use in their relations with each other, and, when necessary, in an internal security role.

Underlying the above definition is the assumption that military power is a purposive, functional thing — one of the many instruments in the orchestra of power which states use at an appropriate moment in the pursuit of their respective national interests. Since Clausewitz it has been fashionable to regard military power as but one of the many techniques of statecraft, taking its place alongside diplomacy, economic sanctions, propaganda and so on. But of course even Clausewitz recognised that war is not always an instrument of policy, a purposive political act. Sometimes war is a kind of madness, an explosion of violence which erupts not as a result of political decisions but in spite of them. Herman Rauschning, in his analysis of the Nazi phenomenon, claimed that the Second World War was inevitable, not because of any particular political decisions but simply because of the nature of National Socialism.[1] The National Socialist movement, was, he thought, impelled towards a war of destruction by its own inherent madness. Now this book is concerned only with the conscious exploitation of military power as a rational technique for the pursuit of foreign policy objectives. But although it is not concerned with irrational or pointless violence, the authors recognise that wars are not always a result of calculated self-interest. Sometimes they are a consequence of human frailty and passion, and once started, they can develop a frightening momentum in which political goals become submerged in senseless violence.

The authors also recognise that military power may be used for purposes not directly related either to defence or foreign policy. For example, in many new states the army is regarded as part of the essential paraphernalia of statehood without which recognition by the international community would either be denied or incomplete. As W.

Gutteridge has pointed out, military power is a symbol of national prestige which no self-respecting state can do without. "The army joins the flag, the national anthem and other symbols, and in some cases is itself joined by national air and shipping lines, as the outward sign of independence and progress."[2] The ceremonial and symbolic functions of military power are not unimportant, but they are not the concern of this book.

Nor are the authors interested in the 'nation-building' role of military power, though they recognise that in many newly emergent states the armed services are a powerful instrument of national unity and may be consciously used for that purpose. In Israel, for example, the importance of compulsory national service in instilling a sense of purpose and unity to citizens from diverse backgrounds cannot be overstated. The army has been deliberately used by the government to weld the Jewish people to national purposes. And in numerous African countries, the discipline and cohesion which is implied by military training has been used by central governments to erode tribal and racial differences which might disrupt the stability of emergent states. Gutteridge has stressed the importance of the armed forces as a social and political institution in recently independent states. He says that armed forces

> may have a direct educational role in society; they certainly
> have an indirect use. In some cases they are the channels
> through which modern technology penetrates a traditional
> community. They are generally on the side of 'modernization',
> even though politically they are as often conservative as they
> are radical or progressive.[3]

Clearly, military power does not come into being by accident. It cannot be acquired without enormous effort in terms of manpower and industrial resources, and its very existence is a source of worry for the governments which control it. Democratically elected governments feel uneasy about military power for at least two reasons. First, because it is so incredibly expensive that its acquisition is bound to be unpopular with the electorate, particularly during a period of prolonged peace. In modern, welfare-orientated societies there is a tendency to see the acquisition of military power as a misallocation of resources. President Eisenhower spelt out the 'opportunity cost' of modern weapons very clearly when he said, "the cost of one modern bomber is this: a modern brick school in more than thirty cities. It is two electric power plants each serving a town of 60,000 population. It is two fine, fully equipped hospitals. It is some fifty miles of concrete highway."[4] In short, military power is regarded by many not as a means to economic well-being, but as an alternative to it.

Japan is sometimes cited as the new model of how materialistic, growth-orientated states can achieve prosperity without military strength. The example begs many questions, but the fact of public hostility to military expenditure is undoubted. Any government which spends too much money on defence runs the risk of losing the next election — as Baldwin saw in 1936.[5] Inevitably, therefore, because politicians seek first and foremost to acquire and retain power, they are very susceptible to pressures to reduce military expenditure.

But there is an even more fundamental reason why democratic societies feel uneasy about the existence of large amounts of military power in their midst. Their unease stems from a real dilemma; while it is widely acknowledged that military power is necessary to protect democratic states from aggression and subversion, it is also recognised that the mere existence of this power in the hands of a few represents an inherent threat to the very democratic values it is supposed to protect. The problem of reconciling or striking a balance between the need to concentrate military power in the hands of a few and the need to preserve democratic values is a fundamental one for any democratic state. The political control of the military is almost taken for granted in the United Kingdom where there is a long tradition of political neutrality in the armed services, and where the threat of military rule is quite unreal. But not all states are as fortunate in their constitutional arrangements. In post-war years, even the United States has experienced growing tension between its large military establishment and its liberal democratic principles. The 'Industrial Military complex', as President Eisenhower called it, is a very real symptom of this problem. Once 'Big Business' and 'the Military' became inextricably entwined, an enormous and frightening pressure group was created which, according to some critics, is now so powerful that it dominates large areas of American life and is beyond democratic civilian control.[6]

If military power is electorally unpopular and inherently difficult to control, one is tempted to ask why governments do not abolish it. And the answer, of course, is that the serious worries which are caused by the acquisition of military strength are quite dwarfed by the worries of trying to manage without it. Given the kind of world in which we live, military power is regarded by most statesmen as a prerequisite for national survival. Even neutral states, with no great ambitions, have found it necessary to remain armed, and many states have found that, over the years, their prosperity and influence has been directly related to their military power. In a world of independent sovereign states which, by definition, acknowledge no authority higher than themselves, and which are in constant and unceasing compeition for scarce resources, military power has been an indispensable instrument of the national interest. Life in international society has been likened to life in Hobbes' 'state of nature'.[7] To survive in that tough, ruthless, ungoverned environment is a difficult business, and military power has proved a useful weapon. Its use frequently determines not who is right, but who is going to prevail in the constant jockeying for prosperity, prestige and security. Its acquisition represents an attempt by statesmen to control as far as possible the dangerous and unpredictable environment in which they have to make their way, and it is difficult to imagine what international politics would be like in its absence. It is perfectly true that there are groupings of states within which war is unthinkable — the Common Market is one such 'security community'[8] — but it is dangerous to assume either that relations between Common Market countries are unaffected by military power or that such relations could ever be extended to the world as a whole.

Michael Howard has suggested that "the capacity of states to defend themselves, and their evident willingness to do so, provides the basic framework within which the business of international negotiations is carried on." Military power is an intrinsic part of the rather fragile international order associated with the international system, and as Howard says, "it is not easy to see how international relations could be conducted and international order maintained, if it were totally absent."[9] Until the world is radically transformed and the system of sovereign states replaced by a quite different international order, military power, and the capacity for violence which it implies, are bound to play a significant part in international politics.

Because military power is an intrinsic part of a world of sovereign states, there is a sense in which criticism of it is irrelevant. Of course it would be nice if the world was ordered differently; but it is not, and schemes to change it invariably founder on grounds of practicality. Over the years there have been many proposals to rid the world of armed power, to disarm and to build a better organised world community, but none of them have been practical politics. Henry IV's reputed comment on one such scheme is still appropriate 'It is perfect', the king said, 'perfect. I see no single flaw in it save one, namely, that no earthly prince would ever agree to it. Hedley Bull has rightly condemned such solutions as "a corruption of thinking about international relations and a distraction from its proper concerns."[10] Constructive criticism accepts military power as a fact of life. It seeks not to abolish that which cannot be abolished; but to manage it successfully so that wars, both inter-state and internal, become less rather than more frequent occurrences in international politics.

Traditionally, of course, neither statesmen nor political theorists have queried the utility of military power, and even today its value is self-evident in many parts of the world. It is very doubtful, for example, whether the Israelis or the Arabs or the Indians or the Chinese hold any illusions about the continuing importance of military power. Nor are there many signs of Soviet disenchantment. Many statesmen would consider it preposterous to question the value of military power given the dangerous world in which we all live and given the historical record of violence in the twentieth century. The authors of the recent volume of the *Cambridge Modern History* dealing with the twentieth century entitled it 'The Age of Violence', and this grim description is perhaps some sort of indication of the importance of military power in contemporary international politics.

Nevertheless, a number of American commentators — not all of them left-wing radicals — have in recent years questioned the importance of military power. One of the reasons that they have been able to do this with any degree of plausibility at all is that from the perspective of the United States and Western Europe, the international environment seems less dangerous than at any time since the Second World War. After all, the USA has managed to extricate herself from Vietnam, the politics of Cold War have given way to the easier atmosphere of *détente*, there have been *rapprochements* with China, and the crises which threatened world peace throughout the 1950s and early 1960s have melted into history. All this has produced, in L.W. Martin's words, "a diffused feeling of greater safety" in which military force seems less necessary and, hence, less useful. As Martin puts it, "For many Western taxpayers, the military are on the way to becoming latter-day remittance men, given a small slice of the family income on condition that they go off and pursue their unsavoury activities quietly where they will not embarrass decent folk."[11]

It remains to be seen, however, whether these optimistic features of the international environment reflect long-term changes in state behaviour or whether they reflect a much more transient and fortuitous juxtaposition of circumstances. It is possible to speculate that if the world economic crisis deepens and the competition for energy, raw materials and markets intensifies, then states may once again find it expedient to pursue their interests by the age-old techniques of intimidation, war and conquest.

Many of the critics of military power have emphasised the uselessness of weapons of mass destruction for all practical purposes. American writers, soured by their country's experience in Vietnam, have noted that those who are the most militarily powerful are not always the most politically successful. Military preponderance cannot always be translated into political victory. The United States, for example, was not able to capitalize her virtual nuclear monopoly in the late 1940s and early 1950s by 'winning' the Cold War, and the Vietnam War must be the classic case of a superpower capable of destroying the entire world finding itself unable to defeat a guerrilla movement in what one writer described as a "rice-based, bicycle-powered, economy".

However, it is worth pointing out that it is dangerous to deduce from the American experience in Vietnam any general propositions about the utility or otherwise of military power. It may be that the American failure in Vietnam can be attributed to the incompetent way in which military power was used rather than any inherent defect in the military instrument itself. Hanson Baldwin, for example, has suggested that lack of success was a result not of using military power, but of not using enough of it early enough.[12] In other words, so his argument runs, rapid escalation might have induced the enemy to give up by presenting him with intolerable costs. The mistake the Americans made was not fighting the war in the first place, but fighting it at a level which the enemy found tolerable, rather than escalating to a point where the North Vietnamese would find it unbearable.

Nevertheless, the critics of military power undoubtedly have a point. The relationship between military strength and political influence is certainly not the proportional one implied by Mao Tse-tung's famous dictum that 'political power grows out of the barrel of a gun'; but although it is not a straightforward connection, few would dispute that in general terms there is a relationship between military strength and political power. On the whole, those who wield the most military power tend to be the most influential; their wishes the most respected; their diplomacy the most heeded. Of all the great powers, only Japan appears to disprove the connection between military and political strength. As Ian Smart says, "Japan is allegedly intent upon that alchemist's 'grand experiment'; the transmutation of great economic into great political power without the use of any military catalyst."[13] Whether she will succeed is highly problematic, and the fact that she is trying is not so much because she is confident of success as because she has no real alternative.

The connection between military strength and political power was clearly perceived by R. Chaput, when, commenting on the relative decline of British military strength in the 1930s, he wrote, "The weight of Great Britain in diplomatic bargaining is, in the last resort, proportionate to the strength of her armaments, and her influence for peace is measurable in terms of the force she can muster to prevent the overthrow of the political equilibrium by armed force."[14] It is undoubtedly a serious mistake to assume that political influence is proportional to military strength; but it is an even more serious error to deny any connection between the two.

A second arrow in the quiver of those who query the utility of military power in the modern world is the argument that in ideological quarrels military power is an inappropriate weapon because ideas cannot be defeated by force of arms. It is sometimes claimed, for example, that the notion of a 'united Ireland' which gives point to IRA activity in Ulster cannot be defeated by the British military presence, and, therefore, that a political solution must be found to the problems of that troubled province. It is also sometimes claimed that in so far as the West is engaged in an ideological struggle with Communism, its concentration on military confrontation means that it is planning to fight the wrong war. It is, of course, debatable whether the IRA is much interested in a United Ireland or whether the East-West struggle is predominantly ideological, but even if they are, the proposition that ideas cannot be defeated by military force cannot be accepted without serious qualification.

It is perfectly true that ideas cannot be eradicated without destroying all the books where they are written down and killing all the people who have ever heard of them. In that sense the proposition that ideas cannot be destroyed by military force is probably true; but even though it may be impossible to *eliminate* ideas, it is certainly possible to render them politically ineffective by the use of military force. The ideas of Hitler and Mussolini live on in their writings which are accessible to all, but the military defeat of the Axis powers in 1945 went a long way towards relegating Fascism to the periphery of practical politics. Similarly, in Ireland one may speculate that the ruthless use of military power could make the idea of a United Ireland politically irrelevant for the foreseeable future. The word 'ruthless' is important. If the Kremlin had the problem of Ulster to deal with, it is easy to believe that within a period of weeks rather than months, the IRA would have been systematically destroyed, their sympathizers incarcerated and the entire province subjected to military discipline. In other words, criticism about the way in which the Briitish Government has used its military power in Ireland are not criticisms about the effectiveness of the military instrument *per se*; they are only criticisms about the half-hearted, squeamish way in which successive British Governments, rightly or wrongly, have used it.

The argument that military power cannot defeat political ideas is only part of a more general argument which queries the appropriateness of military power as an instrument of modern statescraft. Today, it is argued, the real stakes of international politics are quite unrelated to such traditional uses of military power as the acquisition of territory and empire. In the modern world, the goals of states are much more intangible, like, for example, improving trade relations, securing markets, gaining political friends, winning the favour of world opinion. And in the pursuit of these objectives, military power is at best irrelevant and at worst counterproductive.

There is a good deal of sense in this view. Certainly there is plenty of evidence that the use of military power for territorial conquest is much less popular than it used to be — at least amongst advanced industrial states. The appetite for conquest has probably become jaded partly because the military, moral and political costs of unprovoked aggression have risen sharply, and partly because the expected value of conquest to advanced industrial states has fallen sharply. It has become increasingly clear that an industrial state bent on improving the material prosperity and standard of living of its citizens would be better advised to use its resources for increasing industrial investment and technological research rather than expending them in wars of conquest. The world contains many examples of states which have become wealthy and prosperous without military power. Japan and West Germany both spring to mind and there are many who see a direct connection between their impressive growth rates and their low military expenditure.

And it is not just outright conquest which has become unfashionable. Enthusiasm for the use of military power to pursue interests in the Third World has also cooled. Over the years, both East and West have invested a great deal of money in attempts to project their influence in uncommitted areas of the world, but it has become clear that the use of the military instrument in this context can easily backfire by provoking the very hostility it was designed to avoid. Anyway, the benefits of access to these uncommitted countries seem much less important and more problematic these days. There is, therefore, a growing tendency to look for 'local' balances of power, and to argue that when it comes to providing stability, intervention is counter-productive. To use Professor Martin's phrase, 'the era of competitive meddling' is over,[15] but it would be dangerous to conclude from this that all military intervention in foreign states is a thing of the past. There are powerful reasons why states may involve themselves, for example, in local wars in spite of the risks and costs involved. First because intervention in local conflicts provides the superpowers with an opportunity to pursue national and ideological goals without running the risks of mutual destruction which are implicit in more direct confrontations. Second, because internal wars cause anxiety even in states not immediately affected. Internal wars constitute a form of social change which is fundamentally unpredictable and "no situation is more threatening to nations than one whose outcome has become so uncertain as to have moved beyond their control."[16] In particular, civil violence is a contagious phenomenon, and what is not controlled in one country may, it is feared, spread to others. And the third reason why states may become militarily involved in the internal affairs of others is that few of them are immune from the moral pressure to throw their power behind a just cause even when so doing contravenes the principle of sovereign independence.

And though it is unfashionable to say so, the possibility that powerful states will find it necessary to intervene militarily in order to protect their interests cannot be ruled out.

The declining utility of military power in its traditional functions may reflect the manifestly diminished interest which western states have in foreign affairs generally. Numerous commentators have detected a tendency for advanced industrial countries to turn inwards on themselves and to display only a minimum interest in the world around them. External involvements, particularly military involvements, are seen as expensive distractions from the proper concerns of government. Thus, the United States is increasingly reluctant to play a global role, and the energies of her statesmen are increasingly absorbed by domestic problems. In Western Europe, many formally imperialistic states — including our own — have relinquished their overseas possessions and become introspective or 'euro-centric'. Not without some reason do critics of the Common Market see it as a rich man's club, self-centred and disinterested in the wider world. Undoubtedly one of the effects of this shift of emphasis away from foreign affairs to domestic matters has been a further downgrading in the perceived utility of military power.

One of the most common – though not the most intelligent – arguments against the continuing usefulness of military power is implied by the assertion that modern weapons, particularly nuclear and thermonuclear weapons, are so destructive of life and property that they cannot reasonably be regarded as a usable instrument of policy. There are, so it is argued, no conceivable political objectives in the pursuit of which these devastating weapons could justifiably be used. In the public mind, at least, there is a widespread belief that any use of nuclear weapons is synonymous with Armaggedon. It is claimed, therefore, that we are in the incredible situation of spending vast amounts of money on a kind of armament which cannot be used rationally and which is therefore useless. Walter Millis has put the case very well.

The great military establishments which exist are not practically usable in the conduct of international relations, and in general are not being so used today; and if it were possible to rid ourselves of the whole apparatus – the military establishments, and the war system they embody – international relations could be conducted far more safely, more efficiently, and more creatively in face of the staggering real problems facing humankind than is now the case.[17]

Though the argument is superficially attractive, it contains several serious flaws. First, and most obvious, it assumes that military power can only be useful if it is used physically, and it ignores the fact that a good deal of modern military power is most useful when it is not being used. Indeed, the most powerful weapons in the arsenals of the superpowers have been specifically acquired in order not to be used. The strategy of deterrence, which has come to dominate East-West relations and which provides the backdrop against which all East-West negotiations take place, is built on the assumption that it is the possession, not the use, of thermonuclear weapons which is sufficient to deter attack. Today, strategic power is designed to promote peace and security by preventing wars rather than by winning them. Not surprisingly, Strategic Air Command has adopted the motto 'Peace is our Profession', and should it ever be necessary to launch American bombers and missiles in a retaliatory strike, it is fair comment to argue that their usefulness is virtually over. In other words, it is quite unfair for critics of military power to imply that enormously destructive weapons are useless because they cannot be used physically for any conceivable political objective. The truth of the matter is that they are useful precisely because they cannot be so used.

In this context it may be helpful to make the distinction between military power and military force. Military power may depend to a large extent on the availability of military force, but conceptually it is quite different; it emphasizes a political relationship between potential adversaries rather than a catalogue of military capabilities. In a nutshell, the difference between the exercise of military force and military power is the difference between taking what you want and persuading someone to give it to you. In a sense, therefore, the use of military force represents the breakdown of military power. The physical use of deterrent power shows not how strong a country is but how impotent it has become.

One of the changes which has occurred since the Second World War is the increasing sophistication with which military power is exploited without military force being used. This is the age of 'brinkmanship', 'crisis management', 'deterrence' and 'signalling'. All of these phenomena support the thesis that modern military force tends to be threatened and manipulated in peacetime rather than used in war. An example may reinforce the point. Think, for a moment, of the political attitude of Finland towards the Soviet Union. Though the sovereign independence of their state is not in question, the gross disparity in power between the two countries has forced the Finns into a relationship of reluctant deference towards the Soviet Union which the latter must find very reassuring. Now 'Finlandization' as it is sometimes called, was brought about neither by Soviet threats nor any physical use of Soviet military power against Finland. It was simply an inevitable consequence of Soviet military preponderance in the area; an almost automatic payoff from the possession of powerful military forces.

Some observers believe that the Russians would like to 'Finlandize' the whole of Western Europe. Certainly it would be a less expensive and less risky policy than military conquest, and in terms of the security which it would provide, the results would not be less satisfactory. M. Mackintosh believes that the Soviet leaders seek "to alter the balance of power in Europe to the advantage of the Soviet Union without endangering Soviet security by what Communist terminology calls 'adventurist' policies."[18] With this in mind, the Soviet Army is an important instrument in any political offensive which the Soviets may undertake in Europe. Its mere existence as the strongest military force in the European theatre ensures that West European states treat the Soviet Union with respect if not deference.

The fact of the matter is that military power forms the backdrop against which all diplomatic activity takes place, and whether the Soviets are negotiating in the forum of the European Security Conference or the Mutual Balanced Force Reduction talks, their military strength is an ever-present reality which colours the attitude of all who know about it even when no explicit references are made to it. The same point can be made in a slightly different way. If, in an argument between a big man and a small man, the latter concedes the point, the fact that his opponent is bigger than he is may have had something to do with it even though the fact was never mentioned in the argument. Military power does not have to be used to be useful, and, indeed, it may not have to be mentioned. The critics of military power sometimes need reminding of that fact.

The second major flaw in the Millis thesis is that it is quite illogical to argue from the fact that using the most powerful military weapons is likely to be mutually destructive, that the use of *all* kinds of military force is equally pointless. At the moment of writing only six states have acquired any kind of nuclear capability at all, and although one may reasonably expect nuclear proliferation to continue, it seems clear that in the foreseeable future the vast majority of the world's states will not be able to avail themselves of this peculiarly destructive power, and in their relations with each other are not likely to be much troubled by its terrible potential.

And, of course, it is also worth pointing out that even the nuclear powers have not renounced the physical use of all military power, not even all nuclear military power. Limited wars, that is to say, wars in which the belligerents exercise restraint in their use of military force, still make good political sense to nuclear powers. Indeed, it is not always recognised that limited wars are feasible precisely because total wars are not. The major incentive to keep limited wars limited is the fear that they may become total, and it follows, therefore, that the same terrible innovations in weapon technology which have taken total war out of the spectrum of rational options available to nuclear states, have encouraged them to develop strategies of limited and sub-limited war rather than give up the idea of war altogether. In short, though the advent of nuclear and thermonuclear weapons may have imposed new restraints upon those who control them, there is no evidence that they have seriously undermined the utility of military power.

What has happened is that states have developed strategies which emphasize the political uses of military power even in war itself. It was never true that diplomacy ended when the shooting started, but in the pre-nuclear age there did seem some sense in the view that war was an *alternative* to diplomacy. But today the distinction is so fudged and blurred as to be almost meaningless. T.C. Schelling's definition of war as a 'bargaining process' or a sort of 'tough negotiation', and his telling phrase 'the diplomacy of violence' all suggest that war, far from signifying the end of diplomacy, has become part of diplomacy itself.

Schelling has invented the terms 'coercive warfare' and 'compellance' to describe the use of military force for goals which are not strictly military at all and where "the object is to make the enemy behave",[19] rather than to weaken or defeat him. The chief instrument of this 'vicious diplomacy' and 'dirty bargaining' is the power to hurt, to cause pain and suffering. Now all wars involve pain and suffering, and modern wars more than most, but traditionally the anguish caused by war has been no more than an incidental, almost regrettable, by-product of military action. What is being emphasized now is the strategy of using the power to hurt in a deliberate and conscious way to intimidate, demoralize, blackmail and bargain to a position of advantage.

The use of nuclear weapons on Japan at the end of the Second World War is an interesting example of this technique. Though literally dropped on Hiroshima and Nagasaki, there is a sense in which these two atomic bombs were not really aimed at those cities at all. Their target was the decision-makers in Tokyo, and the object of the exercise was not the military one of destroying the war-making capability of Japan, but the political one of inducing her leaders to surrender. In Schelling's words, "The effect of the bombs and their purpose were not mainly the military destruction they accomplished but the pain and the shock and the promise of more."[20] Military power, the power to hurt, was being used physically to intimidate an enemy and make him 'behave'.

Similarly, in Vietnam, American bombing has been used not only to disrupt supply lines to the Vietcong and to damage their war industries, but also to induce in the North Vietnamese a degree of compliance with American wishes. The United States was certainly engaged in a normal military campaign against North Vietnamese and Vietcong forces, but she was also engaged in a *coercive* campaign against the Government of North Vietnam designed to force its government to sue for peace on reasonable terms. In December 1972, for example, after the prolonged peace talks in Paris had once again become deadlocked, President Nixon ordered the resumption of the full-scale bombing of North Vietnam. Between 18 December and the end of the month the bombing continued with unprecedented intensity. The point of the exercise was not military; it was political and diplomatic to put the North Vietnamese delegation in Paris in a negotiating frame of mind. Military power, though physically used, was designed to convey the will and determination of the United States Government, and it is probably significant that within a month of the bombing, a cease-fire was agreed in Paris.

According to Lasswell and Kaplan, "an arena is *military* when the expectation of violence is high; *civic* when the expectation is low."[21] For hundreds of years it has been customary to regard the international system as a military arena in which inter-state war is a more or less normal phenomenon, and the internal structure of states as a civic arena characterized by stability and order and a low expectation of violence. Today, however, there are signs that this situation is being reversed; that is to say, that inter-state violence is becoming comparatively rare, and domestic violence comparatively common. It would, of course, be going too far to describe the modern international system as a civil arena and the modern state as a military arena, but strategic stability at the super-power level combined with political instability in many Afro-Asian states has undoubtedly contributed to the shift of emphasis away from inter-state violence towards intra-state violence.

S. Huntington has pointed out that between 1961 and 1968, 114 of the world's 121 major political units endured some significant form of violent civil conflict.[22] And in 1966 Mr. R. McNamara claimed that in the previous eight years, out of 164 internationally significant outbreaks of violence, only fifteen were military conflicts between two states.[23] The statistics may be queried in detail if only because of the ambiguity surrounding the terms, but the overall picture is clear. In many parts of the world, particularly in Southern Asia, Latin America, Africa and the Middle East, intra-state violence in which a non-governmental body attempts to overthrow and replace an established government, has become a common if not normal pattern of political change. Internal wars, described by Eckstein as "any resort to violence within a political order to change its constitution, government or politics",[24] have become commonplace in the wake of decolonization, modernization, westernization and rapid economic development. In periods of rapid social, political and economic change many governments were unable to control the tensions which simmered beneath the surface of political life before finally erupting in revolutionary violence. The reasons for this upsurge of revolutionary warfare and the strategies of insurgency and counter-insurgency which it gave birth to are examined in greater detail in Chapter VII. Here it is sufficient to note this new dimension of military activity, and the impact which it has had on the use of military power. The theory of revolutionary warfare is now a well-articulated and sophisticated body of doctrine, and the writings of Mao, Giap, Guevara *et alia* are standard works which no serious student of modern military power can ignore. The ideas which underpin all military activity in large areas of the undeveloped world have brought about significant changes in the way in which military power is used.

Whether these doctrines are relevant to advanced industrial states is more debatable. Fidel Castro expressed the orthodox scepticism on this point with his comment that "the city is the graveyard of revolutionaries and resources",[25] but the fact of urban guerrilla warfare cannot be questioned. In Latin America there is plenty of evidence of urban violence, and even British has experienced a whiff of urban guerilla violence in Northern Ireland and in those English cities selected for terror bombings by the IRA. It is too early to estimate the effectiveness of the urban guerilla, but in conditions of political and economic instability, governments may be forced to devote increasing quantities of their military effort to maintain law and order. Though this kind of soldiering is unpopular in many armies, it may become an accepted part of the military routine.

It has been estimated that since the Second World War there have been 84[26] armed conflicts. Without confusing the continued use of military force with its usefulness, it is reasonable to believe that most of the states which engaged in those wars regarded the use of military power as an appropriate and reasoned response to the international situation in which they found themselves. The frequency and persistence of military violence around the world provides *prima facie* evidence that large numbers of people continue to think that military power is a useful, perhaps even indispensable, instrument of policy. The various qualifications which have to be made to the fashionable thesis that military power has lost its utility go a long way towards undermining it completely.

In fact few objective observers dispute the utility of military power in a variety of fields. Anyone who knows anything about Northern Ireland, for example, cannot dispute the useful role which the army performs in keeping an uneasy peace between two hostile communities. Anyone who understands the role and record of the North Atlantic Alliance cannot dispute the defensive role of military power in the European theatre. Anyone familiar with the strategic stalemate between the two superpowers will not need convincing that the 'balance of terror' depends very much on the existence of enormous military power in the arsenals of both the United States and the Soviet Union. Anyone cogniscent of the political and social instability which disrupts so many countries of the world cannot doubt the usefulness of military power both for insurgents and those who seek to counter them. The world around us is full of examples of military power being more or less effectively used. We live in a military age and there are few signs that either our children or grandchildren will experience anything else.

Notes

1. H. Rauschning, *Germany's Revolution of Destruction,* trans. E.W. Dickes (London : Heinemann, 1939).
2. W. Gutteridge, *Military Institutions and Power in the New States* (London : Pall Mall Press, 1964), pp. 40-41.
3. *Ibid.,* p.176.
4. Quoted by C. Hitch, *The Economies of Defence in the Nuclear Age* (Cambridge, Mass : Harvard University Press, 1961), p. 4.
5. Michael Howard, *The Continental Commitment* (London : Penguin Books, 1974), pp. 78-9.
6. See for example, C.W. Mills, *The Power Elite,* (London : Oxford University Press, 1956).
7. T. Hobbes, *Leviathan* (Oakeshott Ed.) (Oxford: Basil Blackwell, 1946).
8. See K. Deutsch, *Political Community and the North Atlantic Area* (Princeton, N.J.: Princeton University Press, 1957).
9. M. Howard, "Military Power and International Order", *International Affairs,* Vol. XL, No. 3, July 1964, p. 405.

10. H. Bull, *The Control of the Arms Race* (London : Weidenfeld and Nicolson, 1961), pp. 26-7.
11. L.W. Martin, "The Utility of Military Force" in 'Force in Modern Societies: Its Place in International Politics', *Adelphi Paper* No. 102 (London : International Institute for Strategic Studies, 1973), p. 14.
12. H. Baldwin, "The Case for Escalation", *New York Times Magazine,* 22.2.1966, pp. 22-82.
13. I. Smart, "Committee Discussions on the Utility of Military Force in Modern Societies: Report to the Conference", in 'Force in Modern Societies: Its Place in International Politics', *Adelphi Paper* No. 102, (London : International Institute for Strategic Studies, 1973), p. 22.
14. R. Chaput, *Disarmament in British Foreign Policy,* (London : George Allen and Unwin, 1935), p. 372
15. L.W. Martin, *op. cit.,* p. 19.
16. J.N. Rosenau, "International War as an International Event", in J.N. Rosenau (ed.), *International Aspects of Civil Strife* (Princeton : 1964), p. 57.
17. W. Millis, "The Uselessness of Military Power" in R.A. Goldwin (ed.), *America Armed* (Chicago: Rand McNally, 1961), p. 38.
18. M. Mackintosh, "Future Soviet Policy towards Western Europe", in J.C. Garnett (ed.), *The Defence of Western Europe* (London : Macmillan, 1974), pp. 43-4.
19. T.C. Schelling, *Arms and Influence* (New Haven and London : Yale University Press, 1966), p. 173.
20. *Ibid,* p.18.
21. H.D. Lasswell and M.A. Kaplan, *Power and Society* (New Haven : 1950), p. 252.
22. S.P. Huntington, "Civil Violence and the Process of Development", in 'Civil Violence and the International System', *Adelphi Paper* No. 83 (London : International Institute for Strategic Studies, 1971), p. 1.
23. Quoted by D. Wood, "Conflict in the Twentieth Century", *Adelphi Paper* No. 48 (London : International Institute for Strategic Studies, 1968), p. 1.
24. Quoted by R. Falk in *Legal Order in a Violent World* (Princeton, N.J. : Princeton University Press, 1968), p. 132 n.
25. Quoted by L.W. Martin, *Arms and Strategy* (London : Weidenfeld and Nicolson, 1973), p. 153.
26. Based on a definition of conflict as involving "the use of regular forces on at least one side and the use of weapons of war with intent to kill or wound over a period of at least one hour", see A. Wilson, *The Observer Atlas of World Affairs* (London : George Philip & Son, 1971), pp. 24-5.

PART TWO

STRATEGIC CONCEPTS

4 DETERRENCE

Phil Williams

I   The Development of the Concept

During the period since 1945 nuclear deterrence has gradually become the mainstay of international peace and security, although not without arousing considerable disquiet about its moral basis and acute anxiety over its dangers. Indeed, the concept of deterrence has been elaborated, analyzed, dissected, and criticized in innumerable discussions and arguments. The literature on nuclear deterrence has become voluminous and ranged from the work of those who see in its operation the prospect of minimizing, if not abolishing, international violence, to the analyses of those critics who condemn any posture that rests ultimately upon an ability and willingness to commit mass slaughter of innocent civilians.[1] Furthermore, theories of arms control and limited war have been developed as adjuncts to deterrence, the former being concerned with stabilizing, and the latter with strengthening it.[2] The question arises, however, of why deterrence has attained such pre-eminence in the post-war era when it has, after all, been a characteristic feature of inter-state relations throughout history.

Any answer to this question must obviously emphasize the existence of nuclear weaponry. The development of weapons of mass destruction, coupled with an ever-increasing ability to deliver them quickly and efficiently, has ensured that defeating an enemy on the field of battle is no longer a prerequisite for inflicting enormous casualties on his civilian population, disrupting the administrative apparatus of his state, or destroying his industrial wealth. The vulnerability of the modern state to nuclear attack has added a new dimension to the range of tasks facing military establishments. War prevention has, by and large, superseded victory during hostilities as the main objective of the nuclear powers.

This is not the whole of the answer however. Even if the means of mass destruction had not multiplied so quickly, deterrence would still have had a central role in the post-war world. The original conception of the Western Alliance, for example, was of a traditional guarantee pact in which the strength of the United States was added to that of the much-weakened West European nations to offset the power of the Soviet Union. The rationale underlying the North Atlantic Treaty of 1949 was that any Soviet move against Western Europe could most surely be prevented by making clear that it would inevitably involve hostilities with the United States, whose massive war potential had already been clearly demonstrated in the struggle against Germany and Japan. 'The guarantee was not, as is commonly assumed, an essentially nuclear one, for it antedated the full dawn of the nuclear age, preceding as it did the invention of the thermonuclear weapon and the emergence of nuclear plenty.'[3]

One of the major reasons for this early emphasis on deterrence was the experience of conciliation and appeasement in the inter-war years.[4] The Western democracies had pursued a policy of appeasement towards Nazi Germany in the 1930s which, far from placating Hitler, directly encouraged his expansionist designs and therefore failed in its primary objective of avoiding war. Thus it is not surprising that in the aftermath of World War Two, conciliation of potential enemies was eschewed, any hint of weakness under pressure scrupulously avoided. Appeasement had fallen into complete disrepute: there were to be no 'Munichs' in the post-war world.[5] With such a sentiment firmly entrenched among Western governments it was perhaps inevitable that, as East-West relations deteriorated and an open schism developed between the superpowers, the United States adopted a deterrent posture *vis-à-vis* the Soviet Union. Deterrence was developed as a means of protecting vital security interests and upholding international order while simultaneously preventing war. At times it seems to have been regarded almost as a panacea, as the answer to most of the West's security problems in the struggle against the Communist states. Indeed, the notion of deterrence was nurtured and developed almost entirely within an intellectual context dominated by the problems of the Cold War and the bipolar relationship between the superpowers. The problems demanding attention throughout the 1950s centred around Washington's ability to prevent Soviet aggression against either the United States homeland itself, or that of America's allies in Europe and Asia. The academic literature on deterrence fully reflected this preoccupation with immediate security problems.

Despite the time and attention devoted to the mechanics of deterrence as part of the superpower relationship, however, it should not be forgotten that it has far wider application. The principles and practices of deterrence are neither unique to international politics nor to the post-war era. Deterrence is a mode of behaviour common to many walks of life – both human and animal – and one with a long history. Furthermore, it is present in areas rarely associated with it, such as parent-child and husband-wife relationships, and is perhaps ultimately as important in domestic politics as it is in international affairs. The functioning of deterrence is essential to civilized society since it forms one of the main bases of law enforcement. Although habitual obedience and a strong sense of obligation to the community are crucially important considerations in ensuring adherence to the law, in very few societies can the element of deterrence be completely disregarded. In some cases deterrence is likely to be the most significant factor promoting obedience: unpopular laws will be observed merely because the citizens fear the consequence of breaking them. By acknowledging the wide ramifications of deterrence, it becomes clear that it is not the exclusive prerogative of statesmen and soldiers, to be explained solely in terms of the esoteric language of the 'defence intellectuals' or 'nuclear strategists'. Rather does it intrude into everyday life and personal relationships to such an extent that it can be understood without resort to highly abstract speculation or elaborate scenarios depicting the horrors of nuclear war. Thus it seems useful and appropriate to analyse deterrence, initially at least, in very broad and general terms, particularly as this facilitates an understanding of the basic principles involved in its operation.

II The Concept of Deterrence

In its simplest form, deterrence can be seen as a particular type of social or political relationship in which one party tries to influence the behaviour of another in desired directions. Influence can, of course, be wielded in many different ways and for many different purposes. Deterrence, however, involves a particularly distinctive type of influence that rests directly and openly upon threats of sanctions or deprivations. It is basically an attempt by party A to prevent party B from undertaking a course of action which A regards as undesirable, by threatening to inflict unacceptable costs upon B in the event that the action is taken.[6] Although this is a crude rough and awkward definition, it nevertheless captures the essence of the concept. Furthermore, it is possible by elucidating or elaborating it, to highlight the various characteristics inherent in any situation where deterrence is operative.

It is obvious from the definition that deterrence is an attempt by party A to influence the intentions, and consequently the actual behaviour, of party B in a particular direction — that of inaction. Moreover, this attempt at exerting influence is very much a psychological phenomenon. It does not involve physically obstructing a certain course of action, but making that action appear costly and unattractive. Thus the strategy of deterrence attempts to influence B's perceptions or structure his image of the situation in such a way that he decides not to undertake the move he might have been contemplating.[7] In other words, B is prevented from doing something by being made to believe that to refrain from the action is in his best interests. Deterrence, therefore, makes certain options or courses of action which are available to B, and possibly appear highly attractive and tempting, to look most unattractive. Any potential gains to be made must be outweighed by the costs which B believes would be inflicted upon him in the event of the specified option being chosen or the prohibited action taken.

The other side of the coin is that by refraining from the action, party B will not suffer any costs. Deterrence involves the threat rather than the application of sanctions, and the threat is contingent. It will be carried out and the costs actually inflicted in the event – and only in the event – that the undesired action takes place.[8] This gives the party being deterred every incentive to refrain from the prohibited behaviour. In other words, deterrence posits a close inter-relationship between the behaviour of the deterrer and that of his adversary. More specifically, the former's behaviour is highly dependent upon the actions of the latter. Once the deterrence situation has been clearly established, A will act so as to inflict costs only in response to B's initiatives.

Because of this responsive element in deterrence, the fulfilment of the threat often seems to take the form of retaliation, of punishment after a transgression has occurred. But this is not invariably the case, however, as becomes clear from the following example. The commander of an attacking force laying siege to a defensive position may realize that he could successfully storm the fortifications, although only at the expense of exorbitant losses among his men. Such costs would obviously be suffered during the hostilities themselves rather than incurred as retaliatory punishment after the event but nevertheless might be sufficient to deter an attack. In this situation the defenders could successfully avoid combat by convincing the opponent that the pain and suffering involved would be too high to make an attack worthwhile, even though it would ultimately succeed in its objective of overrunning the position. The problem is how to do this, how to demonstrate clearly that the costs attendant upon an offensive would be prohibitive.

To assess the extent of this problem it is necessary to look at the requirements of deterrence in greater detail. So far the concept of deterrence has been analyzed in its simplest and most rudimentary form in order to discern clearly the major principles involved in its operation. The way deterrence functions in practice must now be examined and an attempt made to describe more fully the prerequisites of an effective deterrence posture. The complexities and difficulties of successfully implementing such a strategy contrast starkly with the basic simplicity of the notion itself, calling to mind the remark by Carl von Clausewitz that 'in strategy everything is very simple, but not on that account very easy'.[9] If deterrence is not to fail dismally, therefore, it must meet fairly stringent requirements.

III The Requirements of Deterrence – Communication, Capability and Credibility

1. Communication

The first requirement of an effective deterrent posture is that the adversary be made aware of precisely what range of actions is prohibited, and what is likely to happen if he disregards the prohibition. Clear and careful communication is therefore a necessity. Many examples of such communication occur in the animal kingdom. A grizzly bear, for example, demarcates certain territory as his own particular province by making claw marks as high as he can reach on tree trunks around the periphery of his chosen area. This has a dual function of communicating to would-be interlopers in the bear kingdom not only that it is private property, but also that trespassers will be prosecuted. In the world of international politics, of course, communication is in some respects more difficult and the room for error and misinterpretation much greater. The prospects for states with differing cultures and value systems, divergent historical traditions and beliefs, and alien political structures, to readily achieve understanding of, and sympathy for, each other's position, problems and objectives, are not considerable. Understanding can be achieved, but perhaps not without making full use of a variety of channels and methods of communication. Public statements, private messages and demonstrative actions may all have to be used to convey accurately and successfully a particular message to a rival state. The Berlin airlift in 1948, for example, combined with public statements and private messages, communicated clearly to the Soviet Union that West Berlin was irrevocably within the United States' sphere of interest and that any direct attempt to take it by force would set off a disastrous and perhaps uncontrollable chain of consequences.

One of the advantages for the West in this instance was that a clear dividing line had already been drawn. Even before the blockade was initiated by the Soviet Union there had been a *de facto* division of the city into the Eastern zone under Soviet control and the Western zones of Britain, France and the United States. With Western occupation troops permanently stationed in the city, the Soviet leaders could have little doubt about where their jurisdiction ended and that of the West began.[10] The same has been true for the European situation as a whole during most of the post-war era. The line between East and West, with the possible exception of Yugoslavia, has been clearly and unequivocally demarcated. In his discussions of limited war, Thomas Schelling emphasized that prominent geographical landmarks or salient 'focal points', as he called them, could facilitate tacit agreement on the territorial limitation of hostilities.[11] This notion has equal, if not more, relevance to preventing the initiation of hostilities in the first place. The clearer, more salient, and less ambiguous the line a potential aggressor must not cross, the more successful is deterrence likely to be. Unfortunately, not all situations are so clear cut: many lines do *not* stand out in such bold relief. In these situations there will be serious difficulties in communication. An inevitable result of this is the existence of 'grey areas' where there is ambiguity about the line itself or the extent to which a particular action is prohibited, and further uncertainty about the deterrer's intention, ability and willingness to act if the line is crossed.

There is likely to be an irreducible minimum of such uncertainty in many relationships among states. Governments face numerous problems and have limited time and resources to cope with them. As a result they are unable to communicate clearly their likely response to all possible contingencies. Circumstances may arise which a government did not foresee and for which it has not made prior plans or pronouncements. Moreover, a government may be unable to communicate its likely response to an opponent's actions in advance purely because it is uncertain of its own intentions and likely behaviour. The transmission of messages is further complicated by the fact that governments are not monolithic actors rationally determining their interests and planning out their future actions to accord with these.[12] It is easy to imagine a situation where, for example, there are profound and irreconcilable differences among policy-makers on the question of whether or not the state should offer protection and help to a small nation in danger of attack by a larger neighbour. The degree of support for this nation will vary considerably. Some officials and agencies will be militant in their support, others lukewarm, and yet others indifferent if not openly hostile to any idea of a guarantee. The result may be a series of bureaucratic manoeuvres, in which a variety of different messages and 'signals' emanate from particular elements within the bureaucracy as part of the attempt to strengthen political bargaining positions. This will increase dramatically if the issue becomes a matter of public debate and controversy. Policy-makers in the state contemplating a move against the small nation may find this all very confusing. Trying to guage the likely reaction to such a move, they will find it enormously difficult to make sense of the varied and contradictory 'signals' they are receiving. The dangers of miscalculation, therefore, are considerable to say the least.

But the problems of communication do not all lie with the deterrer. The reception, analysis, and interpretation of 'signals' is probably fraught with even more difficulties than their transmission.[13] Thus, even if a government manages to decide upon its future intentions, and openly and clearly declares them, there is no guarantee that they will be received or understood correctly by a putative aggressor. 'Signals' transmitted by one government have to be processed as incoming information by the recipient states. In some cases this may require that the communications run the whole gamut of the bureaucracy. Bureaucratic organizations are the 'eyes' and 'ears' of governments. But although completely indispensable they are not without serious deficiencies and defects. These may have significant and far-reaching implications for the interpretation of information.[14] When information is passed up the organizational hierarchy it almost inevitably goes through a process of selection and distortion which, at its worst, can render the final assessment given to the decision-makers a complete travesty of the original 'signal'. Psychological preconceptions may also adversely affect the interpretation and evaluation of another state's behaviour.[15] If policy-makers have a preconceived belief (stemming from past experience, the traditional image of the other state, or merely intuition) as to a rival power's unwillingness to take a strong stand on an issue, then most communications and 'signals' to the contrary will make little impression. Public statements will be regarded as meaningless unless, or until, they are backed up by firm actions communicating an unequivocal declaration of intent. But by then it could be too late: deterrence may have failed and an attempt already been made to overturn the *status quo*.

Thus preconceived beliefs may result in the acceptance only of ideas and facts confirming those beliefs and rejection of anything contradicting them. The consequences of this are sometimes incalculable. 'Misperceptions among nations may have disastrous effects on policy decisions.'[16] During the Korean War, for example, the Chinese tried to convey to the United States just how seriously they regarded the advance into North Korea. Washington, however, disregarded the signals and continued its chosen course of action until it provoked a Chinese intervention that took the United States completely by surprise. Communist China's attempt at deterrence failed partly because its threats were not transmitted clearly and explicitly enough. At least equally important, however, was the firm United States belief that 'the Chinese Communists neither would nor could intervene in Korea', particularly with American and United Nations forces so near 'victory'[17] Despite such occurrences, the problems surrounding communication in a deterrence relationship have been given little attention by academic strategists. The difficulties of assimilating and evaluating information have been analyzed in somewhat greater depth by foreign policy analysts, but the implications of these difficulties for the functioning of deterrence remain to be examined. This is an area demanding much further thought and research. What can be said with some certainty, however, is that a government trying to deter rival states from actions it deems undesirable should endeavour to make as clear as possible what the prohibited actions are, as well as indicating the possible penalties for non-compliance with its wishes.[18] Whether or not the state has the ability or capacity to inflict these penalties, and whether they in turn will be a sufficient threat to deter are matters for separate discussion. It is to these questions that attention must now be given.

2. Capability
The capability requirements of deterrence cannot be seen exclusively in terms of a physical capacity to inflict harm or deprivation upon another party. This is an essential part of deterrence, of course. The deterrer, unless he is bluffing, requires the capacity for imposing unacceptable costs relative to any possible gain his opponent could hope to make. But such a capacity will not suffice if the challenger is unable to assess properly the likely relationship of gains and losses attendant upon any move he might make. In other words, deterrence assumes at least a minimum degree of rationality in the thought and behaviour of the party being deterred. It requires that he is able to make cold and sober calculations, weighing and balancing the potential costs and gains of any action. If the adversary recognizes that the costs likely to be incurred

from his initiative will outweigh the possible gains, if he is rational, he will refrain from moving. Thus, a successful deterrence posture must aim to ensure that the threatened costs are sufficiently high to convince a potential challenger that action would not be worthwhile.

The assumption of rationality contained in this analysis is in no sense an absolute one. Although it presumes that cost-gain calculations will be made, it recognizes that the outcome of these deliberations depends ultimately on the adversary's value system and his incentives for action. Indeed, it is the opponent's values which determine the relative weight he puts on the gains he stands to make and the costs to be incurred. The greater the incentive or propensity for action, the higher must be the level of costs threatened. If a mother threatens to smack her young son for eating sweets before dinner, this may be so unattractive that the child will forgo the sweets. But if he has had no breakfast and has a particularly 'sweet tooth', the threat of a smack may not be a sufficient deterrent. In these circumstances the boy may be prepared to incur the wrath of an outraged parent. Deterrence can be restored however, if the mother increases the potential costs by threatening to smack the child *and* confine him to bed.

Simple as this example is, it indicates that the cost-gain calculation is a subjective mental process by the challenger. Consequently, the deterrer must try to influence his opponent's perceptions, to make it patently obvious that the costs he can inflict far outweigh the gains in terms of the opponent's values and incentives for action. A failure of empathy, an inability to put oneself in the shoes of others and understand how the situation looks to them, may result in the deterrer not posing a sufficiently high penalty — and being taken by surprise when deterrence fails.[19] In other words, it is not so much the physical capability of the deterrer which matters, as the way it is perceived and evaluated by potential adversaries.

The importance of such perceptions was clearly demonstrated in the operation of deterrence prior to the nuclear age. During an era when war was regarded with far less abhorrence than it is at present, deterrence could only be achieved through the maintenance of large military forces capable of defeating the enemy's armies in the field and ensuring that any gains he made were transient and far outweighed by his eventual losses. Thus an obvious and overwhelming military preponderance was essential. In many circumstances, however, assessments of relative military capabilities were problematical at best. There was considerable room for miscalculations and mistakes, and ample opportunity for rival states to initiate hostilities, each with a firm expectation of victory.[20] Since the actual ratio of gains to costs could only be discovered through war itself, deterrence was rather fragile and subject to frequent breakdowns. With the growth of air power and the advent of nuclear weapons the situation changed dramatically. The costs of a nuclear war would almost certainly exceed any gains that could hope to be made thereby. Indeed, so destructive have weapons become that threats to use them are not readily believable. Yet if deterrence is to succeed, it must meet the third requirement — credibility.

3. Credibility

Any analysis that focuses exclusively on the mere possession of a capability to inflict unacceptable costs on opponents is inevitably somewhat artificial. For a deterrent strategy to work it must make any potential challenger aware not only that the costs of taking prohibited action *could* exceed the gains to be made, but also that they *would* do so. In other words, it is necessary to influence the adversary's expectations in such a way that he believes the deterrent threat would actually be implemented and that he would certainly incur the specified penalty in the event of any transgression. To revert to the parent-child example, it is obvious that if the boy does not believe he will be punished, the attempt at deterrence will fail and he will eat the sweets. Not only must the threat of sanctions be communicated clearly, therefore, but it must be made believable. Herein lies much of the art of deterrence.

The difficulty of this task, however, varies considerably from one situation to another. Some threats are inherently credible; others have to be made so. A prime example of the first type can be seen in the animal kingdom, in the way in which a lioness protects her cubs from intruders. She will communicate her intentions by roaring and demonstrate her capability by showing her fangs. Consequently it will be immediately obvious to intruders that they will be harmed if they venture too near the cubs. The inherent credibility of the threat stems largely from the fact that the lioness has a lot at stake and is protecting something she values highly. It is also a result of the fact that the deterrence relationship is essentially one-sided or unilateral. Credibility is more difficult to achieve where both sides are able to inflict harm upon each other, since the implementation of a threat may then require that the deterrer himself is prepared to make certain sacrifices. A man with a knife is more likely to protect a friend from an unarmed thug than from one also armed with a knife. But even where the relationship is not one of mutual deterrence the problems of credibility are not absent. A potential criminal, for example, may feel that even though the maximum penalty for a particular offence is severe, he is not certain of being caught, and even if he is, will be dealt with fairly leniently. It was perhaps to counter such feelings that the Great Train Robbers were given long prison sentences. To create such a precedent could only give the threat of punishment much greater credibility in the future.

Thus it is apparent that an optimum deterrent would be one where the recipient of a threat is absolutely *certain* that in the event of his taking action, wholly unacceptable costs *would* be inflicted upon him almost automatically. Such would be the situation facing a potential

criminal in a state which retained the death penalty, had a harsh judiciary and a super-efficient police force. On the other hand, deterrence would be certain to fail where there is not only serious doubt about the willingness of the deterrer to carry out his threat, but also a willingness to accept the level of costs he is able to inflict. This seems to have been the case with the British guarantee to Poland in 1939. Hitler probably felt that, under pressure, Chamberlain would renege on his commitment.[21] But even if he did not, Hitler was nevertheless prepared to accept the losses which he felt Britain could inflict upon Germany in a war. Not surprisingly, therefore, the British guarantee to Poland had little impact on Hitler's behaviour, doing nothing to halt his expansionist policy.

It is the intermediate area between these two extremes, however, which is of most interest, and stimulates greatest debate and controversy. How does a threat to inflict high losses, for example, compare with a more believable threat to impose lesser costs? Is a small possibility of disaster a more effective deterrent than a significant probability of moderate losses? Such dilemmas have been at the heart of many of the problems facing statesmen in the nuclear era, and must now be examined further.

IV   Nuclear Deterrence

In order to highlight some of the general principles of deterrence the concept has been analyzed in very broad terms. This process can lose its value, however, if taken too far. To understand deterrence fully it must also be examined in specific and carefully delineated contexts. In fact, much of the academic literature on deterrence in the West has been concerned with the best way of preventing either a Soviet nuclear attack on the United States itself, or conventional and nuclear attacks on America's allies. The problems involved in these two tasks are in some ways rather different. For America to deter an attack upon its homeland, for example, does not involve serious problems of credibility. It is almost axiomatic that the US would retaliate for an attack upon its own territory so long as it retained the wherewithal to do so.[22] In the second case, however, the deterrent threat has to be projected and made credible. This has led to an important distinction between active or extended deterrence on the one hand, and passive deterrence on the other. The latter has been defined as deterrence of a direct offensive assault upon one's own nation; the former as deterrence of military aggression against allies and other powers.[23] Since passive deterrence is in certain respects the simplest of the two this can be discussed first.

1. Passive Deterrence
Throughout the 1950s it was assumed by many people that an attack upon the United States by the Soviet Union could be deterred merely

by the possession of large stockpiles of nuclear weapons and delivery vehicles. Albert Wohlstetter of the Rand Corporation spent much of the decade trying to demonstrate to both civilian and military officials that the capability requirements of deterrence were much more stringent than this. His thesis was presented in a series of articles, briefings and reports ranging from the famous study of SAC's overseas bases policy in 1954 to the even more well-known 'The Delicate Balance of Terror' published in the January 1959 issue of *Foreign Affairs*.[24] Claiming that deterrence was far from automatic, Wohlstetter's argument rested on two fundamental assumptions: that deterrence capabilities were both relative and dynamic.

Wohlstetter's first assumption was that the level of capabilities relative to those of the opponent was more significant than the absolute level. This was not a matter of numerical equality however. He recognized that a deterrent force could also be a tempting target. Thus it was the residual capability of that force, that part of it which could survive a surprise nuclear attack and strike back at the attacker, which was really crucial. In other words, if the deterrent was to deter rather than merely provoke or invite a first strike attack by the Soviet Union it had to have the capacity to ride out such an attack and inflict unacceptable retaliatory damage. This would ensure that there was no incentive for the Soviet Union to strike first, since even by doing so it would not be able to avoid enormous damage to its population and industrial centres. Later, attempts were made by US Secretary of Defence McNamara to quantify the amount of damage thought necessary to perpetuate deterrence. These calculations were enshrined in the notion of an 'assured destruction' capability which, in McNamara's formulation, was the capacity to destroy one-fifth to one-quarter of the Soviet population and one-half of its industrial capacity even after absorbing a first strike against American strategic forces.[25]

Partly as a result of Wohlstetter's analysis great emphasis was placed on making the American nuclear force invulnerable. During the early 1960s missiles were placed in hardened silos and dispersed in Polaris submarines. Difficulties remained, however, because the 'assured destruction' capability had to be maintained within the context of a volatile and rapidly advancing technology. Thus, although it appeared that a plateau of strategic stability and mutual deterrence had been reached when the Soviet Union also created an invulnerable missile force in the mid-'sixties, fears that the situation might soon be destabilized were not long in emerging.

Part of the problem arose from the widely divergent approaches to deterrence followed by the two superpowers. Washington recognized only very slowly and reluctantly that an 'assured destruction' capability did not provide the only feasible basis for nuclear deterrence, and that the Soviet posture rested on an entirely different rationale. Indeed, the Soviet Union emphasized nuclear war-fighting to a far greater extent than did her rival. At the heart of Soviet strategy has been the belief that the best way of deterring a nuclear attack upon the USSR is by being supremely prepared to fight, survive, and possibly even win a nuclear war. This has required an offensive-defensive mix of weapons that is perhaps unique to the Soviet Union. In discussing the evaluation of the Kremlin's military posture under Khrushchev's successors one eminent analyst of Soviet affairs has observed that 'provision for the strategic defence has been a major feature of the Soviet build-up: protection of the Soviet "homeland" enjoys first priority and is to be effected through a combination of "deterrence", air defence systems, ABMs and counter-launch strikes (peacetime surveillance as on the high seas and immediate pre-launch destruction in war, a form of nuclear Kamikazes).'[26] In other words, the Soviet Union sees no incompatibility between deterrence and defence and gives equal prominence to limiting damage to herself as to inflicting it upon the enemy.

A situation in which one side emphasized assured destruction and the other paid more attention to damage limitation rendered a further spiral in the arms race highly likely since 'the two elements were reciprocal and the success of one power in damage limitation must imply a reduction in the capacity of the other side to achieve assured destruction.'[27] The improvements in the deterrent force of either side tended to be regarded by the opponent as a potential threat. The problem was exacerbated by the technological developments of the later 'sixties and early 'seventies.[28] Not only were there limited deployments of ballistic missile defences or ABMs, but the accuracy of intercontinental ballistic missiles was improved dramatically and coincided with an increasingly sophisticated technology that made possible the installation of multiple warheads in single delivery vehicles. Since accuracy is the most important determinant of the ability to destroy hardened missile silos, this provoked anxieties about the vulnerability of land-based missile systems.[29] The desire to offset any possible gains that might accrue to the opponent made a new and highly expensive round of the arms race difficult to avoid. Each of the superpowers seems to have felt that it had to forge ahead to ensure that it was not left behind.

It was perhaps a growing realisation of the futility of this competition coupled with its exorbitant costs that provided a major incentive for the negotiations on limiting strategic armaments. As a result of the SALT talks, the deployment of ABMs has been strictly limited and a ceiling, albeit a fairly high one, established on offensive missile systems. But probably even more important than the formal agreements have been the informal exchanges that have given the United States the Soviet Governments greater awareness and understanding of each other's deterrent posture.

Such interchanges perhaps help to explain why the United States has gradually moved from excessive reliance on an assured destruction capability to a posture which preserves options other than the large-scale destruction of cities. This change, however, also represents a reaction against a strategy that had as the concomitant of assured destruction of the opponent, assured vulnerability of oneself. Indeed, the acceptance by Secretary of Defence Robert McNamara of a situation of mutual assured destruction helped create a more profound awareness of the ethical problems attendant upon nuclear deterrence. Although these questions tended to be discounted in much strategic analysis of the 1950s and 1960s, there is a range of moral issues that the proponents of nuclear deterrence would do well to ponder. Is it ever legitimate to retaliate against civilian populations for the acts of their governments? Can the mass killing of those who are so obviously non-combatants be justifiable even as part of a retaliatory strike? Is there any significant difference between a conditional intention to kill the innocent and the act itself, between the threat of nuclear punishment and the implementation of that threat?[30] Since the prevalent doctrine seemed oblivious to such questions a number of analysts were prompted into advocating alternative strategies that more easily accommodated ethical considerations. Among the more notable proposals were suggestions for a targeting strategy which deliberately sets out to avoid population areas and keep collateral damage to a minimum.[31]

The strategy elaborated by Secretary of Defence, James Schlesinger, in various statements throughout 1974 goes at least some way towards this with its emphasis on counterforce and options other than city destruction. It would be misleading, though, to suggest that the rationale underlying the move away from sole reliance on 'assured destruction' was primarily moral. Political and military considerations were far more important, with the new posture designed to ensure that no American President would be paralyzed into inaction in the event of a nuclear war by a choice between a massive strike against Soviet cities or nothing at all. Indeed, the counterforce options have not replaced the assured destruction capability but merely been added to it. It is the knowledge that each side can destroy the other as an organized society that would provide the incentive to keep a war limited even after nuclear weapons were introduced. The Schlesinger doctrine in fact lays considerable emphasis on the operation of intra-war deterrence, resting upon the assumption that a stable nuclear deterrent makes fairly intense, but limited, hostilities possible. It also suggests that stability at the highest levels of deterrence could encourage instability at lower levels. This is no novel concern, however, and strategic analysts have long been afraid that nuclear stalemate would enable the Soviet Union to attack America's allies with relative impunity, a fear that goes far to explain why so much attention has been devoted to the requirements of active or extended deterrence.

2. Active Deterrence

Attempting to deter aggression against one's allies is somewhat different from deterring attacks upon oneself. The major problems centre on the psychological dimension of deterrence rather than its physical aspects. There is often no doubt that the deterrer can inflict unacceptable costs on an aggressor; the question is whether or not he would actually do so. The main focus of attention must be the extent to which a deterrent threat made in order to protect a third party is believed, and those factors which establish that belief in the mind of a potential aggressor.

It must be remembered, however, that the credibility of an extended deterrent is not entirely independent of a state's capability *vis-à-vis* its opponent. If one superpower has a disarming first strike capability then it can extend its deterrent by nuclear means.[32] Its commitment can be honoured without it having to incur inordinate costs. In the early 1950s, for example, the United States was able to extend its nuclear umbrella over Western Europe and credibly threaten to retaliate massively against the Soviet Union in the event of conventional aggression. The United States would have suffered little or no devastation in return. But with the growth of Soviet nuclear capabilities the superpower relationship was transformed from one of unilateral to mutual deterrence. It has already been suggested that with the attainment of invulnerable retaliatory forces by both superpowers, stability of passive deterrence was achieved. Beneficial as this may have been in terms of the overall strategic context, it had significant implications for active nuclear deterrence. It eroded the credibility of the American nuclear guarantee to its NATO allies. The option of a first nuclear strike against the Soviet Union — which had been the basis of massive retaliation — could now result only in the destruction of the United States as a civilized society. With the active nuclear deterrent no longer credible, other ways had to be found of protecting allies.

The French response to this predicament was to emphasize the value of their own nuclear force. Developed partly for reasons of prestige and diplomatic leverage, the French 'deterrent' seemed to acquire a new significance with the erosion of the American nuclear guarantee. The intellectual rationale for the 'force de frappe' which was provided by Pierre Gallois certainly highlighted this fact. The Gallois thesis was essentially that the vulnerability of the American homeland had rendered the NATO Alliance obsolete since the US could no longer be relied upon. 'If resort to force no longer merely implies risking the loss of an expeditionary army but hazards the very substance of national life, it is clear that such a risk can be taken for oneself — and not for others including even close allies.'[33] The corollary of the inability of a nuclear state to extend its deterrent umbrella was that any state with a substantial nuclear force of its own was automatically converted into an 'inviolable sanctuary'.[34] It could even deter the great nuclear powers from launching an attack against it, since any gains the attacker could hope to make would be more than nullified by the losses it could expect from retaliation against its own cities. Thus he argued that nuclear weapons were the 'great equalizer', bringing a new stability into the relationship of those states possessing them. Although the British were never so brutally explicit as the French, the UK nuclear capability was at times similarly regarded as good insurance in the event that America would not sacrifice New York for one or more of the European cities.

The American response to the 'credibility gap' was rather different. Discouraging the development of European nuclear forces, Washington replaced the strategy of 'massive retaliation' by one of 'flexible response'. Even before America's vulnerability to a Soviet counter-attack had finally undermined massive retaliation, the strategy had been severely criticized as an inappropriate, and therefore incredible, response to a wide range of contingencies. An American nuclear attack on Soviet cities seemed an inordinately militant reply to local and limited aggression — particularly if this should occur in areas relatively peripheral to America's interest. William Kaufmann, in an early but effective critique of massive retaliation, compared it to going on a sparrow hunt with a cannon.[35] It was argued that the strategy was no deterrent to small-scale attacks and encouraged the adoption of 'salami tactics' by the Soviet Union — even in Western Europe, which was central to America's concerns.[36] The critics also suggested that the likelihood of US involvement in a European conflict would be considerably increased if the scale of the United States response was tailored more closely to the Soviet initiative. This became even more urgent with the loss of American immunity to attack. To inflict large-scale nuclear punishment on the Soviet Union would necessitate enormous sacrifices by the United States. The price for carrying out the deterrent threat would have been too high.

'Flexible response' avoided this problem. The new emphasis was on proportionality, on meeting the enemy at the same level as his initial attack occurred. A conventional attack would elicit a conventional response which, if it was not able to secure victory should at least force a stalemate. This would minimize the potential gains for the enemy while simultaneously inflicting some costs upon him. Its supreme advantage, however, was that it made the potential costs for the deterrer worth incurring, and spared him the difficult choice between 'humiliation and holocaust'. Thus the problems of establishing a credible response were overcome. But this alternative was not without its difficulties. It downgraded the punitive element in deterrence in favour of denial violence. Although the idea that a strong and viable defence makes the best deterrent was popular

81

among US officials, it inevitably emphasized war-fighting rather than war prevention. This was anathema to most Western European governments since such a war would almost certainly be fought on their territory. Furthermore, they felt that it reduced the prospective costs of aggression to so low a level that the Soviet Union might no longer be deterred from a more adventurist policy.

The European preference -- and the strategy which NATO formally adopted in 1967, under the rubric of 'flexible response' -- tended more towards a strategy of risk-manipulation.[37] This promised to maintain the credibility of a strong response while also posing the prospect of high costs for aggression. It rested upon the assumption that it is not necessary to threaten, very coolly and rationally, to initiate nuclear war. Where this means deliberately committing suicide, it would have little effect. But the costs and risks for an aggressor can still be made unacceptably high by demonstrating both an ability and a willingness to start events moving in such a way that nuclear war might be the eventual outcome. The adversary can be made to refrain from action not by coldly threatening total violence but by raising the possibility that events might get so out of control that the level of violence would escalate disastrously. This requires that the deterrer be prepared to enter and pursue vigorously the 'competition in risk-taking' should a challenge arise. In this competition there is a premium on bargaining tactics such as escalation and brinkmanship, burning one's bridges, and seeming to act in a irrational manner. It may not be necessary to pursue such tactics to their ultimate and most dangerous level, however, if the adversary can be convinced that the issue or area at stake is of greater importance for the deterrer than it is for him. If this can be successfully achieved, it seems unlikely that a challenge will arise. If unsuccessful, it is possible for a vigorous response to restore the credibility of the threat and convince the challenger that the risk of disaster is just not worth taking.

Thus it is important to demonstrate the depth of one's commitment: the strength and clarity of the commitment are important variables in deterring or inviting challenges. What has the deterrer said he would do in the event of an attempt to overturn the *status quo?* How long has the commitment been in operation? Have the public and private pronouncements of the deterrer put the nation being protected well within his 'sphere of interest' or have they left an area of ambiguity? If the commitment has been in existence a long time, remains strongly supported, and is formally expressed in a legal or public contract, there is probably little likelihood of it being challenged. The main function of the North Atlantic Treaty, signed in 1949, was that of indicating very clearly the fundamental American commitment to Western Europe. George Kennan has argued that since this commitment was already clearly apparent its enshrinement in a treaty was merely a manifestation of the 'legalistic-moralist tradition' in American foreign policy.[38]

It can equally well be argued, however, that the framers of the treaty were masters of *Realpolitik*. They almost certainly conveyed to the Soviet Union more clearly than hitherto that Western Europe was irrevocably within the American sphere of interest and that any attempt to establish Soviet domination over the area would therefore have dire consequences.

It is sometimes suggested that in international politics words are cheap while the actions they require are enormously expensive. But words themselves can frequently have considerable impact. The clearer and better-publicized a commitment, for example, the more it would damage the state's prestige and reputation to renege on it. This is not to suggest that words are always sufficient: they obviously take on a much greater impact to the extent that they are backed by physical force. Thus the deterrent effect of the North Atlantic Treaty was considerably reinforced in the early 1950s with the development of a semi-integrated military organization and the stationing of an increased number of American troops in Europe. These forces are still regarded as the visible token of America's commitment, and to some extent as a hostage to ensure American involvement in hostilities. In terms of the present strategy, they are particularly crucial in demonstrating a willingness to get on the escalator. If the risk-manipulation strategy is to work, an 'assured response' is vital.[39] This is guaranteed by the physical presence of US troops since without them it would be almost impossible to raise the prospect of events getting out of hand and leading to direct nuclear hostilities between the superpowers.

Yet another variable to be considered when discussing the credibility of deterrent threats and the reliability of commitments is the deterrer's reputation. A potential aggressor is much more likely to be deterred by a state which has honoured its commitments in the past than by one which has not. If a government has shown a willingness to make sacrifices, incur costs, and run risks in order to meet its commitments, then this will add substantially to its credibility since 'precedents create expectations'[40]. (The main exception to this occurs if there is an obvious 'backlash' effect where a government having been 'once bitten' is expected to fight shy of similar situations in the future.) Similarly, it is recognized that to some extent at least 'commitments are inter-dependent'.[41] What a government does in support of its position in one area determines what others expect of it elsewhere. If it starts to falter in one situation this may be taken as a signal for probes against it in unrelated areas. It was for this reason that Berlin took on such importance for the West during the years of intense Cold War. It was regarded as a symbol of American determination to take a firm stand against the Soviet Union and therefore added a great deal to the validity of America's deterrent threats in other contexts and contingencies.

If the credibility of a state's deterrent threats are unequivocally established, then it is unlikely to be confronted with serious challenges. If, on the other hand, there are doubts about the willingness of a government to carry out its threats or fulfil its commitments, it is much more likely to be tested. Such doubts could arise through an adversary's belief that the public is not united in support of the government, or that the particular individuals holding office are willing to offer concessions rather than run substantial risks. In such circumstances it might be necessary for the deterrer nation to become involved in a crisis or limited hostilities in order to restore its reputation and the credibility of its guarantees. The Cuban missile crisis, for example, served to demonstrate to Khrushchev that Kennedy was prepared to adopt a relatively uncompromising position on certain issues and would not readily be coerced. Indeed, although the relationship between the two superpowers has been punctuated by periodic crises, they have on the whole developed and maintained a high degree of understanding about what acts are prohibited and just what freedom of manoeuvre each retains. Even when misperceptions, failures of communication, and miscalculations of the other's determination have led to direct confrontations, the problems and errors of judgement have been rectified during the crises themselves. The superpowers have also reached some accommodation on the limitation of strategic arms. But what of the prospects for deterrence in the future? Can it be as successful in the next thirty years as it has been in the last thirty? To answer such questions the stability of deterrence as it presently exists and the extent to which it can be perpetuated in the face of certain disquieting trends and developments must be assessed. Particularly central is the question of whether or not the stability attendant upon the superpower balance can be reproduced in relationships among smaller nuclear powers.

V The Future Prospects for Deterrence

The situation of mutual deterrence between the superpowers is characterized by a relatively high degree of restraint and understanding. At the level of capabilities, both sides have invulnerable forces and the SALT agreements suggest that for the moment they are containing 'the problem of continuous innovation' in weapons technology.[42] On the political and psychological levels too the prospects are similarly optimistic. The *status quo* has, on the whole, been clearly demarcated and 'grey areas' with all their ambiguities kept to a minimum. Each superpower acknowledges the legitimate self-interests of the opponent, while both are fully aware of their common interest in the avoidance of nuclear war. The acquisition of substantial nuclear capabilities by Britain, France and China has not, so far at least, detracted from the stability of the central strategic balance.

The entry of India to the nuclear club, however, indicates that far from being an exclusive 'institution' open only to a select few, it could be a rapidly expanding circle in which well-established rules and procedures would have to make way for new modes of behaviour. Thus, although it is not possible in the present chapter to deal fully with questions of pace, scope, and potential consequences of nuclear proliferation, some of the problems likely to surround the operation of deterrence in a multipolar nuclear world must be briefly discussed.[43] Can deterrence really be expected to work as successfully in a world of twelve to twenty nuclear powers as it did in a world of only five nuclear states? For a number of reasons, the answer to this question must be in the negative.

In the first place it is conceivable that governments which are much less responsible than the present nuclear powers could develop weapons of mass destruction. States with oversimplified but extremely militant ideologies, states profoundly dissatisfied with the *status quo*, and states with 'underdeveloped political systems in which decisions can be made by a relatively small number of disorganized and romantic individuals', might well regard the acquisition of nuclear weapons as an attractive option.[44] It is possible, of course, that the mere possession of these weapons could induce their owners to become less revolutionary, less fanatical, and more moderate in their objectives. Equally plausible, however, is that such states would adopt high-risk policies, thereby demonstrating their willingness to live dangerously. In this event, they would be difficult to deter.

If the deterrer is a moderate, *status quo*-oriented government it could lack all understanding of the values of the state it is trying to influence. The threats it poses — which under other circumstances would be highly credible — might be ineffectual against a 'crazy state' or a government with a 'give me victory or give me death' philosophy.[45] 'Deterrence through threatening punishments directed at values and targets which seem important to the deterring country may be quite irrelevant for the crazy state.'[46] Thus the requirements of credibility would be far more difficult to assess than in the present international system. As a consequence the opportunities for miscalculation would be considerable, particularly as the problem of communication among states with such alien values would be even more formidable than in the present international system. A world of many nuclear states could so easily degenerate into a world of fluctuating and temporary alliances in which demarcation lines become blurred and challenges to the prevailing constellation of power a frequent occurrence. Confrontations and crises would be endemic in such a system.

Nor would the instabilities be lessened by the technology available to the smaller states. Responsibility is not solely a function of political considerations. Local and regional conflicts will almost certainly stimulate a series of arms races among the hostile powers. The danger is that those involved will lack the resources for establishing control and safety measures similar to those introduced by the superpowers into the central arms race. They may find it impossible to render their weapons invulnerable, a problem which could result in all sorts of 'pre-emptive instabilities'.[47] During crises in which the protagonists possess vulnerable nuclear weapons, for example, there would be a 'premium on haste', a felt need to jump the gun, to strike first in order to prevent the opponent from doing so. Thus, conflicts normally settled peacefully could lead inexorably towards war. Even without crises, 'the reciprocal fear of surprise attack' invites the adoption of 'launch on warning' postures. In this situation a false alarm could precipitate a nuclear war. the scope for the accidental or unauthorized firing of nuclear weapons is also much greater. Yet further instabilities could arise from the temptation of established nuclear powers to prevent — or expel — new entries to 'the club' either through intimidation or the physical destruction of weapons and production facilities.

In a world of many nuclear powers, therefore, the operation of deterrence would probably be far less satisfactory than it is at present. Whether the problems outlined above would undermine the stability of the central strategic balance is difficult to foresee. If the large nuclear powers had attained a higher level of mutual trust than at present it would be virtually impossible for a smaller power to spark off a 'catalytic war' among them. But even the superpowers might have to face the problem of anonymous nuclear attacks, not knowing against whom to retaliate. Thus the picture is not a pleasant one, particularly when it is remembered that one breakdown of nuclear deterrence could spark off a disaster without precedent. Yet so long as international politics retains its rudimentary structure, deterrence will have a crucial role in the maintenance of international order. Perhaps the most tragic paradox of the nuclear age, therefore, is that nuclear deterrence, which has provided a relatively high measure of peace and stability, is based upon foundations that are becoming increasingly fragile.

Notes

1. The most useful work on deterrence probably remains that by G.H. Snyder, *Deterrence and Defense* (Princeton: Princeton University Press, 1961), while a trenchant critique of deterrence theory can be found in P. Green, *Deadly Logic* (Columbus: Ohio State University Press, 1966). A useful debate between the deterrence theorists and their critics which raises important methodological and moral questions can be found in M. Kaplan (ed.), *Strategic Thinking and Its Moral Implications* (Chicago: Chicago University Press, 1973).
2. See, for example, H. Bull, *Control of the Arms Race* (London: Weidenfeld & Nicolson, 1961) and R.E. Osgood, *Limited War: The Challenge to American Strategy* (Chicago: Chicago University Press, 1957).
3. L.W. Martin, "The Nixon Doctrine and Europe", in J. Garnett (ed.), *The Defence of Western Europe.* (London: Macmillan, 1974) p.1.

4. The two types of strategies are discussed in E. Luard, "Conciliation and Deterrence", *World Politics,* Vol. 19, No. 2, January 1967.
5. The importance of this emerges very clearly in E.R. May, *Lessons of the Past: The Use and Misuse of History in American Foreign Policy* (New York: Oxford University Press, 1973), Chapter 2 and 3 in particular.
6. This definition and the arguments that follow are based upon the analyses found in Snyder, op. cit.; T.C. Schelling, *The Strategy of Conflict* (New York: Oxford University Press, 1963); B. Brodie, *Strategy in the Missile Age* (Princeton: Princeton University Press, 1959); and T.C. Schelling, *Arms and Influence* (New Haven and London: Yale University Press, 1966).
7. The problem of projecting a particular image to others is superbly dealt with in R. Jervis, *The Logic of Images in International Relations* (Princeton: Princeton University Press, 1970).
8. Schelling, *The Strategy of Conflict,* p. 123.
9. Carl von Clausewitz, *On War* (London: Penguin Books, 1968), p. 243.
10. A useful account of the conflict over Berlin is to be found in J.E. Smith, *The Defense of Berlin* (Baltimore: The Johns Hopkins Press, 1963).
11. See Schelling, *The Strategy of Conflict,* pp. 67-77.
12. This thesis is developed further in the 'bureaucratic politics' model of decision-making presented by G.T. Allison, *The Essence of Decision* (Boston: Little Brown, 1971). See also M. Halperin, *Bureaucratic Politics and Foreign Policy* (Washington: The Brookings Institution, 1974).
13. See R. Wohlstetter, "Cuba and Pearl Harbour: Hindsight and Foresight", *Foreign Affairs,* Vol. 43, No. 4, July 1965, and R. Jervis, "Hypotheses on Misperception", in J. Rosenau (ed.), *International Politics and Foreign Policy,* revised edition (New York: Free Press, 1969).
14. This theme is superbly developed in H.L. Wilensky, *Organizational Intelligence* (New York: Merrill, 1968).
15. See J. de Rivera, *The Psychological Dimension of Foreign Policy* (Columbus, Ohio: Merrill, 1968).
16. J. Stoessinger, *Nations in Darkness* (New York: Random House, 1971) p. 4.
17. Ibid., p. 52. The Chinese intervention is discussed at greater length in A. Whiting, *China Crosses the Yaln* (New York: Macmillan, 1960).
18. The need to maintain freedom of choice will on occasions militate against the need for clarity. A government may also have sound political reasons for being somewhat ambiguous in its threats and commitments.
19. A good example of this seems to be the Japanese attack on Pearl Harbour which took the United States by surprise. See B.M. Russett, *Power and Community in World Politics* (San Francisco: Freeman, 1974), Ch. 13: "Pearl Harbour: Deterrence Theory and Decision Theory".
20. See J.G. Stoessinger, *Why Nations Go to War* (New York: St. Martin's Press, 1974) and G. Blainey, *The Causes of War* (London: Macmillan, 1973).
21. This was the result of the appeasement policy, the dangers of which are carefully elaborated in J.L. Payne, *The American Threat: The Fear of War as an Instrument of Foreign Policy* (Chicago: Markham, 1971).
22. The form of that retaliation would obviously depend upon the scale of the Soviet attack and whether it was directed at American cities or military installations.
23. See R.E. Osgood, *NATO: The Entangling Alliance* (Chicago: Chicago University Press, 1962), p. 136, and the same author's "Stabilizing the Military Environment", *American Political Science Review,* Vol. 55, No. 1, March 1961.
24. A good account of the development of the overseas bases study can be found in Bruce L.R. Smith, *The RAND Corporation* (Cambridge, Mass.: Harvard University Press, 1966), Ch. 6. See also A. Wohlstetter, "The Delicate Balance of Terror", *Foreign Affairs,* Vol. 32, No. 2, January, 1959.

25. At different times the Secretary quantified this in different ways. This particular formulation can be found in R. McNamara, *The Essence of Security* (London: Hodder and Stoughton, 1968) p. 76.
26. J. Erickson, *Soviet Military Power* (London: Royal United Services Institute for Defence Studies, 1971), p. 47. An excellent account of the nuclear doctrine and capabilities of the Soviet Union can be found in Chapter 3 of this work.
27. L.W. Martin, "Ballistic Missile Defence and the Strategic Balance", in J. Garnett (ed.), *Theories of Peace and Security* (London: Macmillan, 1970) p. 114.
28. These are dealt with in an extremely lucid manner in L.W. Martin, *Arms and Strategy* (London: Weidenfeld and Nicolson, 1973).
29. See A. Wohlstetter, "The Case for Strategic Force Defense", in J.J. Holst and W. Schneider Jr., *Why ABM?* (New York: Pergamon Press, 1969).
30. Many of these issues are dealt with in Kaplan, op. cit.
31. See B.M. Russett, op. cit., Ch. 14, "A Countercombatant Deterrent? Feasibility, Morality, and Arms Control", and A.L. Burns, 'Ethics and Deterrence: A Nuclear Balance without Hostage Cities'. Adelphi Paper No. 69 (London: Institute for Strategic Studies, July 1970).
32. This is what H. Kahn calls Type II Deterrence. See his *Thinking About the Unthinkable* (London: Weidenfeld, 1963).
33. P. Gallòis, "United States Strategy and the Defence of Europe", in H.A. Kissinger, *Problems of National Strategy* (New York: Praeger, 1965), p. 295.
34. Ibid, p. 292.
35. See W.W. Kaufmann, *Military Power and National Security* (Princeton: Princeton University Press, 1956), Ch. I: "The Requirements of Deterrence".
36. See, for example, H.A. Kissinger, *Nuclear Weapons and Foreign Policy* (New York: Harper and Row, 1957).
37. This strategy is elaborated upon in Schelling, *Arms and Influence*, Ch. 3.
38. G.F. Kennan, *Memoirs* 1925-1950 (London: Hutchinson, 1968), pp. 407-9.
39. The term 'assured response' was used by T.W. Stanley, "NATO's Strategic Doctrine", *Survival*, Vol. II, No. 11, November 1969, reprinted from *Orbis*, Spring 1969.
40. Schelling, *Arms and Influence*, p. 135.
41. Ibid., pp. 55-9. Important qualifications to this notion are made in G.H. Snyder, "Crisis Bargaining" in C.F. Hermann (ed.), *International Crises: Insights from Behavioural Research* (New York: Free Press, 1972).
42. This problem is elaborated upon in H. Kahn, "The Arms Race and World Order", in M.A. Kaplan (ed.), *The Revolution in World Politics* (New York: John Wiley, 1962).
43. These issues are discussed at greater length in R. Rosecrance (ed.), *The Future of the International Strategic System* (San Francisco: Chandler, 1972).
44. M.A. Kaplan, "The Unit-Veto System Reconsidered", in ibid., p. 53.
45. This problem is examined in Y. Dror, *Crazy States: A Counterconventional Strategic Problem* (Lexington: D.C. Heath, 1971).
46. Ibid., p. 81.
47. These problems are superbly dealt with in Schelling's *Arms and Influence*, Ch. 6, "The Dynamics of Mutual Alarm". This paragraph rests heavily on this chapter which takes its examples from a variety of situations including the Sarajevo crisis of 1914. Indeed, there is nothing peculiar to a nuclear world about such problems.

5 DISARMAMENT AND ARMS CONTROL

Ken Booth

Disarmament is a continuation of politics by a reduction of military means. Arms control is a continuation of politics by a mutual restraint on military means. These amendations of Clausewitz's famous dictum underline what has become the prevailing view about disarmament and always was the prevailing view of arms control, namely that disarmament and arms control are to be properly understood as strategies in the activity of politics among nations, rather than as ideals or imperatives on which to build the structure of international peace.

On first sight disarmament and arms control appear straightforward approaches to the problem of peace and security; however, it can be quickly seen that they are highly complex, reflecting and having implications for some of the profoundest problems of the international system. In the age of nuclear weapons disarmament and arms control have been seen by many to have increased urgency, but their difficulties have been compounded rather than eased by the very military developments which have focused attention upon them. The subject of disarmament and arms control has been an arena for much of the compelling interplay of optimism and pessimism, realism and utopianism, naïveté and sophisticatican, and fascination and frustration which has characterised thinking about peace and security in the nuclear age.

Definitions, and the Relationship between Disarmament and Arms Control

The most widely used definitions of the two concepts are those of Hedley Bull.[1] According to him, *disarmament* is "the reduction or abolition of armaments. It may be unilateral or multilateral; general or local; comprehensive or partial; controlled or uncontrolled." *Arms control* on the other hand is "restraint internationally exercised upon armaments policy, whether in respect of the level of armaments, their character, deployment or use." These by no means exhaust the definitions which have been offered, but they do reflect prevailing usage.

The terms "disarmament" and "arms control" are sometimes used synonymously. However, although they are clearly related, there is value in preserving a distinction between them, based on the difference between *reduction* and *restraint*. Whereas disarmament always refers to a reduction, therefore, arms control can refer to an increase in the level of armaments. The critical consideration will be whether or not the increase is consciously restrained.

Because of this distinction, some have thought of an arms control policy as being an alternative to a disarmament policy. This was largely the case within the US Administration after the early 1960s for example, when it became accepted that mutual reduction was not a feasible objective. Disarmament was largely rejected, except for propaganda purposes. In its place arms control ("restraint internationally exercised") became the dominant theme. As guides to policy they were almost antithetical: instead of being thought of as disarmament *and* arms control, they became thought of as disarmament *versus* arms control. This distinction could be seen clearly in the negotiations about ABM systems in the SALT I talks. Neither side appeared intent on abolishing ABMs: instead, they were discussing the possibility of agreeing to restrict numbers rather than have an uncontrolled quantitative race, and the possibility of agreeing to limit deployment to certain sites rather than have uncontrolled deployment. Eventually the arms control agreement of May 1972 allowed an increase in the level of ABMs for both parties: restraint was agreed, however, in their numbers, character, and deployment.

In addition, there can be both arms control and disarmament without formal agreement. Disarmament which is unilateral and unconditional is an example of this. This would have been the case had the "Ban the Bomb" movement in Britain at the turn of the 1950s/1960s succeeded in translating its objectives into government policy. It was the case in the massive disarmament by all the powers at the end of the Second World War. Furthermore in a sense "arms control" is always being practised, unilaterally, tacitly or informally.

The concepts of disarmament and arms control are not identical therefore. Sometimes they are alternative strategies: sometimes they overlap. In approach disarmament has been classified as "systemic", while that of arms control has been classified as "marginalist".[2] In a narrower sense, though, arms control has been seen as encompassing a wider range of issues than the reduction of armaments. In terms of feasibility, disarmament appears to have declined, while that of arms control remains viable. Another difference is that disarmament is the older, and arms control the newer approach. It is therefore appropriate to begin with the theory and practice of the former.

The Theory of Disarmament, and its Critics.

Disarmament theory is a time-honoured and straightforward approach to the problem of war. In its most extreme form it simply aims to abolish war by stripping states of the weapons with which they fight. Eliminate weapons: eliminate war.

Despite numerous disarmament conferences in the last seventy years, the nations have utterly failed to beat their spears into pruning hooks, and their swords into ploughshares. In fact, the opposite has been the case: there has been an unprecedented accretion of absolute destructive power. Although disarmament has been unsuccessful, and is generally dismissed by the strategic *cognoscente,* it nonetheless remains a popular idea.

The reasons for its continuing popularity are not difficult to discover. First, there are various ethical arguments. These range from the ideas of those who are uneasy about relying on war as a means of settling international disputes to those of pacifists who argue that war and the preparation for war are morally indefensible.

Second, there are a range of social objections. These include a traditional suspicion of the corrupting and militarising influence of standing armies and the fear of the political threat represented by "the man on horseback". These fears have been shared by both Liberal and Marxist societies.

Third, there are a number of economic arguments;[3] these have made disarmament policies particularly attractive to countries with chronic economic problems such as Britain. Particular resentment has often been expressed about the use of taxes, which are always begrudgingly given, for the purpose of amassing weapons, which in a direct sense are economically unproductive. Unlike pruning hooks and ploughshares, howitzers and tanks do not directly contribute to the wealth of nations. Furthermore, such weapons are also increasingly costly. Critics of armaments have argued that money saved on weapons could be spent on "better" things, such as schools or hospitals, or simply left in the pockets of the citizenry. If disarmament were arranged carefully and gradually, it is argued that the run-down in the armaments industries should cause no problem in the way of unemployment.

Fourth, the supporters of disarmament argue that the universal stockpiling of weapons is a primary cause of international tension and war. Armaments become not only an instrument of policy, but also an end in themselves, and a director of policy. As one writer has put it: "The most serious wars are fought in order to make one's own country militarily stronger or, more often, to prevent another country from becoming militarily stronger, so that there is much justification for the epigram that 'the principal cause of war is war itself".[4] In addition, it is obvious that the more powerful the weapons, the more destructive is likely to be any war in which they are used. At the least, therefore, armaments exacerbate suspicions between governments by contributing to the "action-reaction" phenomenon. Furthermore there is a well-established belief that armaments shape the will to use them.[5] To find some evidence to support this belief it is not necessary to look beyond some episodes in US foreign policy in the 1960s.[6] On ethical, social, economic, military and political grounds therefore, the case for disarmament appears to be a powerful one.

On the other hand, the critics of disarmament theory believe that their case is much stronger. History certainly shows that the critical viewpoint has been more congenial to almost all governments in the world. First, the critics argue that the ethical case is by no means clear. It is contended that the pacifist can decide to renounce the use of force himself, but he cannot do so on behalf of those with different values; and the fact has been that pacifists have always been in a minority. The majority of people in the world have usually relied on the idea of the lesser evil; that is, the idea that while war is always evil, it is not necessarily the worse evil in any particular situation. War will certainly result in pain: military impotence might also result in pain. The disarmament which resulted in British military weakness in the face of Hitler's growing power is the classic lesson for the opponents of disarmament. Such critics would stress the positive utility of armaments: they contend that armaments are the most dependable producers of security in a dangerous world. It is argued that the international system is predicated upon an expectation of violence which is almost entirely constrained by the willingness and ability of societies to defend their patch of territory, by confronting potential aggressors with a threat of unacceptable costs. Rather than armaments being immoral, therefore, they are the best (if imperfect) instruments of peace in a very imperfect world.[7] Second, the critics of disarmament do not accept the arguments about the threat represented by the institution of armed forces. Instead military virtues may be admired, supporting ideas such as "a few years in the army will make a man of you." Third, a variety of criticisms have been levelled against the economic case for disarmament. It is claimed that disarmament might not save money. For example, inspection systems to monitor agreements, especially if they are general and comprehensive, might entail a veritable army of controllers and expensive hardware. Furthermore, even if money was freed as a result of disarmament, there can be no assurance that it would be "better" spent. In addition, the critics also argue that disarmament might slow down technological and scientific progress (as a result of losing the spin-off effect of weapons production) and might also cause large-scale unemployment in certain localities. Perhaps the strongest criticism of the economic case for disarmament states that to argue that armaments are unproductive in a commercial sense is to miss the point: armaments are productive of a community value of inestimable worth, namely security. Fourthly, the view that armaments cause war is countered by the argument that weapons are essentially a symptom rather than a cause of the mistrust between states, which fundamentally arises out of their political, economic, and ideological conflicts. From this viewpoint stripping states of their modern weapons would not produce trust: it would merely mean that they would fight with substitutes — sticks and fists in the absence of anything more full of hurt. Opponents of disarmament admit that armaments do sometimes exacerbate mistrust, but they stress that the fundamental problem is the underlying political competition between states. Finally, the critics of disarmament argue that not only is disarmament undesirable, it is also not feasible on a massive scale: contemplation of it is therefore considered to be a futile activity. They argue that the idea of a totally disarmed world is inconceivable. Police systems will presumably be necessary against criminals, and the "internal security" apparatus of some countries packs a mighty military punch. Potential instruments of violence will always exist. Stones cannot be abolished, or kitchen utensils. Technological innocence can never be recaptured. If man's potential for violence cannot be abolished, the basic problem becomes not one of disarmament, but of controlling the uses to which the instruments of violence are put.

If massive disarmament is not feasible, there are also considerable problems which militate against more limited agreements. The difficulties of devising satisfactory inspection, verification and enforcement systems are primary. Furthermore, it is often pointed out that no treaty can contain weapons which have not been invented, and that disarmament treaties only inhibit a part of an arms race. Arms limitation treaties are often seen as channelling competition into other areas of the arms race. The most cited example is the Washington Naval Treaty of 1922, which placed qualitative and quantitative limits on capital ships, and so encouraged naval competition in cruiser-building. More recently the SALT I agreements, which placed quantitative limitations on strategic weapon procurement, probably intensified competition in the qualitative improvement of warheads.

Whatever weight is put on these various arguments in the disarmament debate, one point should be clear: as long as one's individual conscience does not place non-violence as the highest of all principles, the case for disarmament on political, economic, military and even ethical grounds is not obvious. In practice disarmament theory has not been productive. On a massive scale it has been seen as too ambitious; it is contrary to the alleged nature of states. Thus the opponents of disarmament have been far stronger than the supporters. Over the past seventy years in particular there have been numerous disarmament conferences, but very little concrete achievement.

The Record of Disarmament Negotiations

Disarmament negotiations have been a perennial aspect of the foreign policies of some major states. The literature on the subject inevitably concentrates upon formal agreements, but it should always be remembered that most disarmament has been an informal, unilateral, and uncontrolled affair. The traditional retrenchement of Britain and the United States in the aftermath of war — "the return to normalcy" — is a characteristic feature of such disarmament.

It is not easy to find early examples of formal disarmament. There was a case recorded amongst the states of the Yangtze Valley in about

600 BC, when a disarmament league was formed, but the earliest of the pertinent examples did not occur until much later. This was the Rush-Bagot Agreement of 1817 between the United Kingdom and United States which resulted in the US-Canadian border becoming the largest demiliterized border in the world. The pace of thinking about disarmament quickened in the second half of the nineteenth century. Little was achieved, but there was a spread of liberal ideas about the economic waste and political insecurity which resulted from armaments, and which therefore pointed to disarmament as a solution. Diplomatic progress was manifest with the Hague Conference of 1899 and 1907, initially called by Tsar Nicholas II to limit armaments. Popular sentiment was high, and so was international suspicion, for it was well-known that Russian finances were feeling the strain of armaments production. A Permanent Court of Arbitration was established as a result of the Conferences, but there was little progress in the limitation of armaments. There were, however, a series of conventions to limit the horrors of war. Even after three decades without a major European war, the most notable feature of the Hague conferences was the pervading suspicion amongst each delegation about the unilateral advantages being sought by others.

It took the horror of the First World War, and the wound left by it, to inspire greater efforts in the cause of disarmament. The Treaty of Versailles forcibly limited German armaments, and the League of Nations Covenant recommended its members to reduce their forces also. The mood of the period was reflected in the Geneva Protocol of 1924 for the Pacific Settlement of International Disputes, and the Kellogg-Briand Pact of 1928 in which 65 states renounced war as an instrument of national policy. In addition, in 1925 the League Council had appointed a Preparatory Commission for a World Disarmament Conference. Despite this activity, actual progress in formal disarmament was slow in the 1920s: it hardly seemed urgent in the relatively peaceful atmosphere of the time, with its widespread unilateral disarmament. The only important formal progress was in naval limitation. The Washington Naval Treaty of 1922 was a remarkable achievement, in which a series of treaties resulted in a complex bargain, primarily between the UK, USA and Japan. It was hoped to balance the quality and quantity of naval armaments (including bases) between them, and to cement the agreements with various political guarantees. The Washington "system" caused great enthusiasm, but attempts to build upon it at Rome in 1924, Geneva in 1927 and London in 1930 and 1936 were unsuccessful. At the end of 1934 Japan gave the necessary two years' notice of withdrawal from the Treaty, and the system collapsed. Its foundations had always been more tenous and its implications more risky than its enthusiastic supporters had claimed.

Progress elsewhere had been limited. The Geneva Protocol did something to prohibit the use of chemical and biological weapons, though many states did not bind themselves to it, and inhibitions were moral and expediential rather than legal. Meanwhile, the League of Nations was becoming the forum for more wide-ranging efforts. A notable episode was the call in 1927 by the Soviet representative, Litvinov, for the total abolition of all armed forces and weapons, and all their supporting systems. Some considered it to be simple propaganda: others believed that it made good strategic sense for a Soviet Union which was isolated and relatively weak. For almost all delegates, however, such a far-reaching proposal was altogether too revolutionary to contemplate. If simple calls for disarmament proved to be unproductive, detailed preparation proved no more conducive to international agreement. The World Conference on the Reduction and Limitation of Armaments which was finally convened at Geneva in 1932 totally failed in its ostensible objective. In a world in which military force was again coming to the fore as an instrument of national policy, it proved impossible to reach agreed ratios of military strength amongst the sixty states represented. Rearmament, not disarmament, was increasingly the theme of "Devil's Decade" leading up to the Second World War.

Unlike the First World War, the end of the Second World War did not produce a massive clamour for disarmament, although there was retrenchement in all countrues. Certainly disarmament was still popularly regarded as a desirable objective, but it was not regarded as a priority by governments. The maxim which they had learned from the 1930s was that of Vegetius rather than President Wilson.[8]

Nonetheless, partly under the aegis of the United Nations there has been a series of disarmament negotiations since 1945, in which the aim has sometimes been thought to have been the reduction of armaments.[9] The negotiations have progressed through several stages, in which it is possible to record progress in the growth of the understanding of the problems, if not in the growth of actual formal agreements.[10]

In the first stage, 1945-50, progress was negligible. Discussion focussed almost entirely on the control of atomic energy, of which the United States had a monopoly. There was little discussion of conventional armaments, in which the Soviet Union had a marked superiority. The most interesting proposal of the period was the Baruch Plan, proposed on behalf of the US Government in 1946. On face value the Baruch Plan was enlightened and generous. It's proposals included a supervised abolition of atomic weapons, an international monopoly of nuclear research, and nuclear production for civilian purposes. The process was to be controlled by an International Atomic Development Authority (IADA). Subsequently, the generosity of the US Government has been seriously questioned. It has been suggested that the US Government must have considered the possibility of Soviet acceptance to have been low: consequently, the Baruch Plan must be seen to have been a propaganda exercise to discredit and isolate the Soviet Union, while attracting accolades for US altruism. If, against expectations, the Soviet leadership had accepted the proposal, they would have been committing themselves to a nuclear world on US terms: the US possessed nuclear knowledge, it would have advantages at all stages in the disarmament process, it would dominate IADA, and it would have an automatic majority on the veto-free IADA to impose sanctions against violators. There is therefore room for considerable doubt about US motives.[11] Certainly the Soviet leadership felt it had a strong grounds for suspicion. Consequently it rejected the Bartuch Plan, and instead presented a counterproposal; this called for a ban on the use or manufacture of nuclear weapons and the destruction of existing stockpiles, but without any serious system of inspection. Deadlock ensued. The details of Soviet and US proposals on conventional and nuclear disarmament have led one writer to conclude that:

> Disarmament proposals could thus be written to eliminate
> some category of weaponry from power calculations if one felt
> behind, or to freeze one's superiority when one was ahead.[12]

The "parallel monologue" was thus enjoined.[13] Disarmament negotiations were frequent, but they failed to produce agreements. It was in any case naive to assume that agreements were necessarily the objective behind negotiations. It seemed that the proposals were invariably directed more at the public opinion of the allies and the proposing country, rather than at the other participants. The first half of the 1950s saw a number of multi-stage disarmament plans. Discussions largely focused on the relative priority of conventional and nuclear disarmament, with each side demanding priority for disarmament in the field in which it was inferior. In the background the nuclear power of both superpowers proceeded to grow apace, while Western defence became consolidated on the foundation of NATO.

Between 1955 and 1958 there was a change, resulting from a growing recognition of the difficulty of reaching a comprehensive disarmament agreement. Nuclear plenty annually increased the problems of verification. Thus the idea of nuclear disarmament became more remote. The Soviet Union, for example, which was increasingly strong in nuclear terms, now proposed nuclear disarmament at a later stage in its proposals. For its part the United States had made proposals to obstruct the advance of Soviet nuclear power. As a result discussion focused on "partial measures". The chief proposals of this period, in the background of which were fears of accidental war, surprise attack, and nuclear proliferation, were: aerial inspection or control posts to minimise the possibility of surprise attack (Eisenhower's "open skies" proposal of 1955 and the Soviet plan of March 1957); a nuclear test ban, either partial or complete; the disengagement or reduction of forces in certain zones, especially Central Europe (e.g. the Rapacki Plan of 1957); proposals for the creation of "atom-free zones" in Europe and the Far East; and the liquidation of military bases on foreign territory. At Geneva there were conferences on the discontinuance of nuclear weapons tests and on surprise attack (1958). The move to partial measures was not marked by success, but it did reflect a certain flexibility and a recognition of possible mutual interests even within the still harsh climate of the Cold War.

The new realism which was emerging in the age of the "delicate balance of terror" did not preclude consideration of GCD. In fact, it is almost a feature of international life that GCD plans are periodically taken out of the files of the great powers, dusted down and revived. Mr Khrushchev set the pace this time, when he presented a "total disarmament" proposal to the UN General Assembly in September 1959. President Kennedy was susceptible to those who pressed him to respond positively. The McCloy-Zorin talks of 1961 resulted in "Agreed Principles", and in 1962 both governments presented draft GCD plans to the UN's Eighteen Nation Disarmament Committee in Geneva. While no concrete agreement was ever near, the "sustained intellectual attention" given to the subject in the West between 1961-64 resulted not only in more sophisticated US plans, but also a "less frivolous" set of plans on the Soviet side. Nevertheless, there was no agreement. Since 1965 the discussion of GCD has become, in Bull's phrase, a "perfunctory affair".[14]

The demise of GCD did not encourage formal disarmament efforts in more limited fields. Activity since the mid-1960s has been rather restricted. In 1964 the United States and the Soviet Union announced a cut-back in the production of fissionable materials. This commitment was followed by further reductions by the US Government, but no announced reciprocation by the Soviet Union. In 1964, and on subsequent occasions (the last being in 1973) the Soviet Union proposed the reduction of budgetary allocations as a means of reducing military power. The other powers have not responded positively, because of their scepticism at this approach, and especially the problems of comparability and verification. Belatedly, the only formal disarmament agreement in these years was the Convention on the Prohibition of Biological Warfare and of the Production of Biological Weapons, which was opened for signature in April 1972. It called for the destruction of stocks meant for military purposes (but not research) and the prohibition of all uses, including defensive use. At the end of 1973 talks on Mutual and Balanced Force Reductions in Europe began. Although they are likely to be difficult and protracted they nevertheless have the potential of becoming the most significant talks on actual reduction in recent years. The talks quickly confronted all the historic problems of defining "balance" and "equal security" amongst a diversity of countries, with differing military systems, size, location, responsibilities and so on. Differences and difficulties were faced over such matters as the proper phasing of reductions, the types of weapons to be reduced, the scale of reduction, and the verification of reduction. None of these difficulties have so far been resolved.

Approaches to Agreement

The history of disarmament suggests a variety of approaches to the problem amongst those who see some merit in it. These can be classified in terms of point of departure and type of agreement.

As far as point of departure is concerned, J. David Singer has distinguished three approaches.[15] He calls the first the "tensions-first approach". This is the UNESCO approach of attempting to ameliorate conflict through education and understanding, by working on the "minds of men". It is argued that changing attitudes will be reflected in decreasing intergovernmental tensions, and so a diminishing need for armaments. Singer sees little merit in this. The "political-settlement approach" is somewhat similar, and is reflected in the writings of Morgenthau, Kennan, de Madriaga and Lippmann. This is the view that the way to break into the arms-tension circle is by attacking the underlying political problems: as Lippmann has put it, "the powers will not and cannot disarm while they are in conflict on vital issues." Singer sees little merit in this approach, mainly because it ignores the role of weapons in threat perception. The third approach is the "armaments-first approach", which Singer favours. This approach is based on the idea that tensions can only begin to be reduced and political conflicts resolved when the disarmament process begins.

The armaments-first school itself falls into two broad types, on the basis of the preferred type of agreement. The first approach might be called the gradualist school, in which Singer himself belongs. They argue that by eliminating the weapons of war, carefully and in a controlled manner, an atmosphere of trust will be generated between the countries involved. As the process progresses, there will be a spiral of trust and disarmament. It will be a veritable arms race in reverse. The most notable schemes have been the GRIT scheme (Graduated Reciprocation In Tension Reduction) of Charles E. Osgood and the Zones scheme of L.B. Sohn.[16]

Such gradualist approaches have been rejected by other proponents of the armaments-first school; these critics share the Litvinov conception that "the way to disarm is to disarm". They base their hopes in a single multilateral treaty. If states are serious they should act decisively, when the environment is ready. Noel-Baker has been the foremost proponent of this view.[17]

Problems of Inspection, Verification and Enforcement

Whatever approach one favours (if any) to cut into the vicious circle of arms and tension there are a series of complicated practical problems in addition to the perennial political problems. As long as states share a degree of mutual mistrust, they are not likely to enter a serious disarmament agreement which does not contain some form of inspection and enforcement system. Much thought has therefore gone into these problems.[18]

In the disarmament negotiations since the war the breakdown has frequently been focused on the inspection issue, since this is a sensitive barometer of mutual mistrust. The phasing and order of inspection has caused much disagreement (how much inspection is necessary when? and what first?). The US Government has insisted on "inspection before disarmament", while the Soviet Union has generally insisted upon disarmament first. The United States would not weaken itself without inspection: the Soviet Union would not allow what it considered to be industrial and military spies inspecting its military system. Some technological developments (e.g. reconnaissance satellites) have solved some of the problems of inspection, by making national verification more reliable. Other developments however (e.g. "mirving") have created new problems, entailing very intrusive inspection in order to ascertain the number of warheads at the point of a missile. Essentially, only weapons which can be comprehensively photographed from space can be seriously considered for negotiation at present.

Certainly, any far-reaching agreement would involve rather intrusive inspection, to an extent that governments would probably not consider it compatible with sovereignty and independence.[19]

The character of inspection systems can vary greatly. The means can be on-site control posts, or remote observation platforms or monitoring systems; it can be done by people at first hand or essentially by machines (satellites and seismographs); it can be carried out by international agencies specially created or national means. The target of the inspection system will vary according to the agreement: it might be deployed weaponry, testing facilities, budgets, or the whole complex of facilities and human resources which make up a country's military system. It is to the regret of the supporters of disarmament that the one historical case study of a large-scale inspection was not really successful. The Inter-Allied Control Commission which was set up to supervise the dismemberment of Germany's war potential after the First World War could not prevent evasions. It inhibited large-scale rearmament but was not able to contain the many evasions which helped maintain the nucleus around which rearmament eventually grew.[20]

To make sense, an inspection system must be associated with some form of sanctions or enforcement action against violators or suspected violators.[21] If there is verified evasion, the ultimate response must either be in the form of unilateral national abrogation and consequent rearmament, or the threat of punishment by an international agency. To some an international police force is a 1984-ish prospect: to others such an agency must be an integral part of a disarmament system which is not to break down quickly into national mistrust and arms competition. Whether individual nations maintain hidden stocks to hedge their bets, or international agencies are given punishment powers, we must return to the old dilemma: "Is there any means of enforcing a disarmament agreement short of war itself?"[22] The answer would appear to be negative. Madriaga's perceptive observation is thus underlined: "the problem of disarmament is not the problem of disarmament. It really is the problem of the organisation of the World-Community."[23]

The Theory of Arms Control

Out of the impasse which had developed in post-war disarmament negotiations there emerged, at the end of the 1950s, an approach which has been called the "new thinking".[24] It was not as new as was thought at the time, but it nevertheless provided the stimulus for the development of "arms control" as it is now understood. Bull has described the central ideas of the "new thinking" as follows: a concern about the dangers of nuclear war, and a dissatisfaction with existing policies; a suspicion of the goal of a negotiated general and comprehensive disarmament agreement; an insistence upon the unity of strategy and arms control; a broadening of the scope of the subject and a perception of the links between varieties of military activity hitherto thought separate; a criticism of the assumption that disarmament (arms reduction) should be the objective of arms control policy; and a determination to destroy the illusions of disarmament discussion while remaining optimistic about the contribution of the social sciences to improving the prospects of peace and security. Out of this emerging school developed the theory of arms control, and a major stimulus for its practice.

The best-known description of the theory of arms control is perhaps that of Schelling and Halperin. At the start of their important book on the subject they stated that:

> We mean to include all the forms of military cooperation between potential enemies in the interest of reducing the likelihood of war, its scope and violence if it occurs, and the political and economic costs of being prepared for it. The essential feature of arms control is the recognition of the common interest, of the possibility of the reciprocation and cooperation even between potential enemies with respect to their military establishments. Whether the most promising areas of arms control involve reductions in certain kinds of military force, increases in certain kinds of military force, qualitative changes in weaponry, different modes of deployment, or arrangements superimposed on existing military systems, we prefer to treat as an open question.[25]

The "national interest" as the crux of the negotiation and effectiveness of arms control agreements has been stressed by most writers, as has the importance of recognising that there is the possibility of mutual interest and therefore joint action even between potential adversaries.[26]

100

Arms control agreements may be drawn up when the participants in an arms race agree that it would be economically wasteful, or strategically self-defeating to develop or keep developing a particular weapon system, or when they perceive a measure to reduce the risk of war (e.g. by improving communications). Unlike large-scale disarmament, arms control does not require the same degree of mutual trust. This is because an arms control agreement will usually affect only a small sector of a nation's armoury, and secondly because it is usually possible to avoid some of the more difficult inspection problems. While some form of inspection is thought necessary, it is usually possible by national and remote means, thereby by passing the objections to international or on-site systems. The Partial Test Ban Treaty of 1963 was able to avoid the inspection issue because developments in reconnaissance satellites and seismology enabled the satisfactory checking of tests by remote national means.[27]

In addition to formal arms control agreements, the importance of informal measures, either tacit or unilateral, should not be underestimated. In a sense conscious restraint along the lines of the "new thinking" has been constantly taking place. Informal arms control, in fact, has been a frequent and unheralded aspect of the subject. Among the many examples, it is possible to include the development of "fail-safe" devices, the French assurance that they would behave as if they had been signatories of the Non-Proliferation Treaty although they were not willing to sign it, and the fact that China has not transmitted either nuclear knowledge or equipment.

Although the minimum requirements of arms control are less exacting than disarmament, and the implications are more limited, the idea of arms control still does present states with considerable problems. The armaments and security nexus is such a sensitive one that governments have not been predisposed to move quickly. Despite its eminent sense to "arms controllers" the theory has not been free from criticism.

The Arms Control Debate

The arms control debate overlaps with the disarmament debate, but lacks the wide ideological gulf that separates supporters and critics of the latter. It is argument about degree rather than kind. Puchala has identified six major themes in it.[28]

The critical position states that: (1) Advocating arms control is putting the cart before the horse, because arms are a reflection of political mistrust, not the cause. (2) Arms control is unrealistic, because security follows from maintaining military superiority. (3) Arms control agreements are worthless because those who respect them might be penalized by those who are tempted to cheat. (4) The paucity and insignificance of the agreements reached demonstrates the sham of the undertaking. (5) Arms control (if it leads to reduction) would bring economic recession. (6) Military power brings status (deference and respect) in the world.

Against these criticisms, the supporters of arms control have argued that: (1) Arms control should be pursued regardless of underlying political tensions (it might "buy time", build mutual confidence, eliminate a source of international tension, and reduce the destructiveness of wars). (2) The idea of trying to achieve military "superiority" is meaningless in the age of overkill, while striving for it might provoke dangerous arms racing. (3) The only effective arms control agreements are based upon mutual self-interest. (4) The record of arms control agreements, even if slow and uneven, have been cumulative, so that the prospects are for further progress. (5) With planning, economic difficulties can be overcome, while the vast resources released could be put to more productive use. (6) Arms control is good propaganda, and brings status (deference and respect) in the world.

In contrast to the supporters of disarmament, the supporters of arms control have had much more success in overcoming their critics, and in translating their hopes into practice. As a much less ambitious theory than disarmament, and consequently a more feasible proposition, arms control has been pursued by governments with more seriousness and more success.

The Record of Formal Arms Control Agreements

The history of arms control is much shorter than that of disarmament but more successful, certainly in terms of formal agreements. The agreements concluded so far can be divided into three categories: those concerned with prohibiting the deployment of particular weaponry in hitherto non-used areas; those broadly concerned with the management of crises; and those concerned with restraining the growth in the quantitative and qualitative aspects of nuclear weaponry, both vertically (among existing nuclear powers) and horizontally (dissemination to additional countries).

To date, there have been four examples of what might be called preventive arms control agreements. In December 1959 the Antarctica Treaty was signed, prohibiting all military activities in the region. In January 1967 The Treaty on the Exploration and Use of Outer Space was signed; it prohibited the deployment of weapons there, but not military communication and intelligence satellites. In February 1967, after five years of hard negotiating, the Latin American Nuclear Free Zone Treaty was signed; it prohibited all activities concerned with the manufacture and use of nuclear weapons, but not the peaceful uses of nuclear energy.[29] In February 1971 the Treaty on the Prohibition of the Emplacement of Nuclear Weapons and Other Weapons of Mass Destruction on the Seabed and Ocean Floor and Subsoil Thereof (the "Seabed Treaty") was signed; it banned any facilities related to weapons of mass destruction in or on the seabed beyond a 12-mile limit from land. Critics have argued that these agreements are not substantial, largely because the military rationale for the deployment of the particular weapons in the particular zones was not powerful. On the other hand, the treaties do add extra constraints if pressure for deployment arises in future; they do help signal intentions and so add reassurance; and they take large areas out of the arena of arms competition. Some of these areas, notably the seabed, will become increasingly important in years to come.

Although not actually concerned with restraint on weaponry, the crisis management agreements are usually considered to be a part of a liberal definition of arms control, and were certainly an offshoot of the "new thinking". The earliest and best-known crisis management agreement was the "hot line" of June 1963, which arose out of contemporary fears of accidental war. Its aim was to provide an instant and secure channel for communication in crisis between the superpowers. Its first operational use was in June 1967, when it was used to provide reassurances about Middle Eastern policy.[30] Several other less noted crisis management agreements have occurred more recently, largely in the wake of the SALT talks and Soviet-American *détente*. They were the Agreement on Measures to Reduce the Risk of Outbreak of Nuclear War (September 1971), the Agreement on the Prevention of Naval Incidents (May 1972) and the Agreement on the Prevention of Nuclear War (June 1973) in which they agreed to enter into "urgent consultations" if there were any risk of nuclear conflict.

Without doubt the most important arms control negotiations have concerned the question of restraint on nuclear weaponry. The first major agreement in this respect was the treaty banning nuclear weapon tests in the atmosphere, in outer space, and under water (the "Partial Test Ban Treaty") in August 1963; it prohibited test detonations of nuclear devices except underground. An escape clause allows the resumption of testing after three months notice, in order to protect the parties against the possibility of a technological breakthrough. Inspection is by remote national means. Numerous underground tests have taken place since that time, while atmospheric tests have been carried out by the primary non-signatories, France and China. In the light of this continuing testing, sorrowful[31] or cynical observers have merely dismissed the agreement as a "clean-air bill". In addition to this worthy environmental objective, it was chiefly hoped that the treaty would inhibit nuclear proliferation and improve the state of relations between nuclear powers. In the next five years much time and effort was spent, by the superpowers in particular, in trying to draw up an agreement to prevent the further horizontal proliferation of nuclear weapons, which some but by no means all observers considered to a major threat to international stability.[32] The superpowers have a particular mutual interest in preventing the rise of further independent centres of nuclear power. Eventually, the Non Proliferation Treaty (NPT) was signed in July 1968, but China and France took no part in it, and several key non-nuclear states failed to sign or ratify it. While the intention of the treaty was generally welcomed, it has had to face much criticism. The text can be criticised for being weak. Guarantees for non-nuclear states are unsatisfactory. The question of the "peaceful" uses of nuclear energy present problems and create suspicion. Provision for verification is inadequate. There are no means for enforcement. On the other hand, it is doubtful if there would have been any agreement at all if the text had been stronger. At the minimum the NPT is an extra constraint against proliferation, and assists the parties in their assessment of the nuclear intentions of others. In particular, it was also a symbol of positive US-Soviet co-operation at a difficult time, and was a token of a more general desire to arrest the increase in the number and potential of nuclear weapons in the world. The future of the Treaty is more problematical than any of the earlier arms control agreements. In 1972, at the Tenth Anniversary of the Conference Committee on Disarmament in Geneva Mrs. Myrdal described the NPT as existing in a "twilight zone", because of the refusal of some near-nuclear states to sign or ratify. Her fears have been justified. In May 1974 the Government of India announced a nuclear explosion; even though this was accompanied by protestations of peaceful intentions and an explicit rejection of a military path, it nevertheless raised increased doubts in the minds of many about the future of the NPT when it comes up for renegotiation in 1975. In addition, the premium on nuclear energy and the spread of nuclear reactors encouraged both by political motives and the energy crisis have added uncertainty to the NPT. Together these developments have raised the problem of proliferation with a renewed urgency.

In 1969 the Strategic Arms Limitation Talks began between the United States and the Soviet Union. As the first formal bilateral arms control negotiations between the superpowers, and with the focus on their most destructive weapons, SALT has attracted more attention and speculation than any other set of arms control negotiations. The negotiations have always been complex and difficult: the issues are sensitive, the significance of the talks is uncertain, the technical aspects are involved, the changing world outside cannot be completely excluded, the participants are naturally cautious, and they have provided themselves with appropriate bargaining chips to strengthen their positions.

In May 1972 a bundle of agreements was reached. The most important were the strategic arms limitation accords themselves. These consisted of a treaty limiting anti-ballistic missile systems (of unlimited duration, but subject to five-yearly reviews) an interim agreement limiting offensive strategic missiles (up to five years) and a protocol defining the effect of the latter upon submarine-launched missiles. A variety of additional agreements was also reached, and there was a declaration of the "Basic Principles of Relations". Almost all observers accept the significance of SALT, but not the precise nature of that significance. The agreements of SALT I were of apparent consequence, but it will be some time before the full consequences are apparent.

In the meantime the SALT I agreements were the subject of much debate, especially in the United States.[33] A variety of interpretations of the significance of the agreements have been put forward. The US Administration and some but not all "arms controllers" claimed the agreements to be a portentous achievement, because of the alleged implications for Soviet-American relations and the future control of the arms race. Conservative critics of the Administration rejected the agreements, because they saw them chiefly in terms of the freezing of Soviet numerical superiorities while areas of qualitative US superiority were left open for competition, Less confident anti-Soviet observers in the United States believed that the agreements were worthwhile, arguing that in their absence the Soviet Union might have pressed ahead in the arms race towards "superiority". Some observers have been highly critical on international rather than national strategic grounds; those favouring more "defensive emphasis" in strategic postures, for example, were disappointed that the agreements crystallised the strategy of Mutual Assured Destruction, which they had already christened MAD. Finally, there was a widespread viewpoint, a suspicion which also moderated some of the foregoing arguments, that the achievements of SALT I were exaggerated; certainly the continuing arms build-up by both countries gave this view some support, with the development of *Trident* by the United States and its *Delta* class counterpart in the Soviet Union, the B1 Bomber and MARVS by the United States and the unexpectedly rapid development of MIRVS by the Soviet Union. Even if progress occurs, it will take the prolonged friction of much SALT to retard the wheels of military innovation.

At the end of 1972 SALT II began in Geneva. Nobody imagined the negotiations would be easy. In fact, there was every reason to think the opposite. The subjects which had been most amenable to agreement had been dealt with; domestic and negotiating pressures had resulted in more innovation and somewhat stiffer positions; and the qualitative aspects of arms control are always significantly more difficult areas upon which to find agreement. Many issues were open for inclusion on the agenda, but the main thrust, as identified by a Nixon-Brezhnev agreement in Washington in June 1973, was a commitment to work out an agreement on offensive arms in 1974.

Progress on the control of offensive arms proved to be very difficult. As the negotiations developed, the expectations of outsiders focused on MIRVs. The comments of insiders, however, hinted that the development of MIRVs had gone too far, and that the most which might be achieved in SALT II would be a further meeting of minds. In the background the problem of symmetry was being seriously exacerbated by the continuing innovation of strategic weaponry. In particular, the balance of 1972 seemed to be challenged by the unexpectedly rapid development of MIRVs by the USSR and, from the Soviet viewpoint, by the strategic conucopia and the new targeting philosophy of the United States, In view of the complexity and significance of the problems, including the Watergate issue, the modest consolidation of SALT apparent in the Nixon-Brezhnev summit in Moscow in July 1974 could be represented as a minor success.

The agreements reached in July 1974 were very limited. The Treaty on the Limitation of Underground Nuclear Weapons Tests established a threshold of 150 kilotons for testing after March 1976. An ABM Protocol, limiting deployment to one site only, merely ratified the *status quo*. The communiqué affirmed the determination of both countries to continue the development of their bilateral relations, especially in trying to control the arms race; there was a specific commitment to consider an agreement to limit strategic arms up to 1985. In addition, there was a series of secondary agreements, including a verbal agreement to station observers from either side to monitor underground "peaceful" explosions.

The verdict on SALT II must await whatever further agreements emerge. For the time being MAD was enshrined the *detenté* consolidated. For the rest, the significance of SALT II was in the realm of wait-and-see. Kissinger talked impressively of the frankness which had been exhibited: he said it "might have been considered to violate intelligence codes a few years ago". There was apparently progress in strategic understanding, and a commitment to attempt to deal with the next generation of MIRVs, if not the present one. Whether the closer philosophy of approach can be translanted into concrete terms quickly enough to affect the next generation of weaponry, let alone the review of the NPT, still remains to be seen. Frankness and promises are significant, but they may not be enough.

In the short run the augury is satisfactory. The first Brezhnev-Ford summit meeting at the end of November 1974 in Vladivostok gave some cause for confidence, even if it was not the "breakthrough" its participants claimed. The Vladivostok agreement reaffirmed the joint commitment to strategic arms limitation, and reaffirmed their intention of concluding, hopefully in 1975, a new agreement on strategic offensive arms which would incorporate the interim agreement of May 1972 and would last until 1985. The most specific agreement was on ceilings of strategic delivery vehicles and MIRVs to guide their discussions. If the Vladivostok guidelines were translated into a treaty, there would be further negotiations no later than 1980-81 to discuss further limitations and possibly reductions.

Even if the ceilings were high (2400 delivery vehicles, of which 1320 could be "mirved") they nevertheless depended upon concessions by both sides. It may well be, as Kissinger has claimed, that the fact that a specific agreement was possible is much more important than the actual numbers agreed. It suggests some progress towards defining "equal security". Many obstacles naturally remain, from internal critics to verification difficulties, but the guidelines are further evidence that both leaderships want to regulate the arms race, if they cannot end it or win it. If a new agreement emerges it is unlikely to put "a cap" on the arms race, for building and qualitative improvement will continue. However, a ten-year treaty should inhibit innovation and add reassurance. Either of these results would produce a safer and less costly arms race.

Whether or not SALT II, III, IV, etc. produces further agreements, three general points should be made about the general exercise. Firstly, it is unfortunate that the process did not begin a few years earlier, before the genie of technology released ABMs, MIRVs and other deadly complicating factors: with the best will in the world, the SALT negotiations have a complex and esoteric task. Secondly, while progress has been slow, it has apparently been affected to a relatively small degree by outside events. However, there are a number of major instabilities which could undermine the process: in particular, the Chinese factor, a major US-Soviet confrontation in a local dispute, the enhanced significance of "hawks" in the decision-making processes of the participants, runaway technology, or further nuclear proliferation. Finally, while SALT might be too late, it does exemplify a novel attempt to grapple with the problem of continuous weapon innovation at the highest level. Criticisms can be levelled against the participants, who are certainly guided entirely by national interests, but the mathematics and theology of modern strategy are simply too complicated to permit any spectacular progress. The world may still be in the realm of arms control promise rather than substantial achievement, but after comparing the frankness of the present efforts to grapple with strategic arms limitation with the "parallel monologue" of twenty years earlier, it is difficult to disagree with Elizabeth Young that: "The mouse may be small, but it is not ridiculous."[34]

Some observers of the SALT talks have contributed to a distortion of one important aspect of the problem of arms control, namely too narrow a focus on strictly formal agreements. It must be emphasized that the value of such negotiations may not primarily be in any formal accords, but will rather be in terms of developing strategic communication[35] and sounding out tacit restraints. Indeed there has generally been much more "arms control" in recent years as a result of unilateral or tacit decisions than is usually given credit by those who concentrate only on the more theatrical international events. By their behaviour in crises, by their military postures, and by their restraint, all the major powers show a clear awareness of the desirability of controlling military power carefully. A formal treaty is to arms control what marriage is to love: it dramatizes, formalizes, constrains and solidifies a relationship, but is by no means necessary for its essential realization.

In assessing the arms control record in the light of the goals selected by the "new thinking" Bull has noted a paradox. On the one hand he notes that the world is a "great deal safer", at least against the danger of major nuclear war, but on the other hand he feels that the progress of arms control has been "slight" and the contribution which it has made to the strengthening of international security is "problematical". In his view the chief importance of arms control agreements "lies not in their intrinsic effects upon the military policies they are designed to restrict, but in their symbolic effect." A stable balance of terror has been created unaided by formal agreements, but "unilateral arms control" measures "have undoubtedly played an important part, although it is difficult to estimate whether the dimension of arms control thinking was essential to the taking of them."[36]

Why Negotiate?

The achievements in the fields of disarmament and arms control have been limited: on the other hand, the governments of many major and minor powers have spent much time and effort in the activity. In examining their motives there is plenty of evidence to justify a good deal of cynicism.

States pursue arms control and disarmament policies for very direct gains: it is the "national interest" which is being pursued, and only coincidentally the international interest. This becomes very clear after a detailed examination of various proposals. In fact, such negotiations are a fascinating field for the study of international "gamesmanship". The tactical nature of such negotiations was brilliantly demonstrated by Spanier and Nogee in their book *The Politics of Disarmament.*[37] Although the thesis which they presented has been criticised on the grounds of exaggerating the tactical element in negotiations and underestimating the genuine conviction which might sometimes be involved,[38] it nonetheless remains an indispensable warning against considering negotiations at face value.

Despite the difficulties of reaching agreement, the reasons for the frequency of negotiations are not difficult to find. The participants may have a genuine interest in controlling the arms race, which may be a cause of unacceptable international tension. Useful strategic communication might be possible. The arms race is expensive for all involved: it is always desirable to save money, if it can be done without impairing security. National security might be enhanced as a result of a mistake on the part of one side, or the recognition of mutual interests. In some cases disarmament negotiations are part of the arms race.[39] The negotiations might be a useful tactic in a cold war, either to intensify it (e.g. the Baruch Plan) or to reduce tension (the Partial Test Ban). Negotiations might be manipulated in order to strengthen or weaken various alliance systems. Public opinion in all countries favours the activity, and therefore governments feel the need to respond: governments cannot afford to ignore the propaganda value of these negotiations. Disarmament negotiations give ample opportunity to blacken the reputation of an opponent while consolidating support for oneself. This has been done by the formulation of a package of proposals to give the impression to third-party onlookers of a serious interest in disarmament: however, on the other hand what Spanier and Nogee call a "joker" has been inserted, that is a proposal which is known will be unacceptable to the other side and therefore a cause for the rejection of the whole package.[40] For both superpowers, the inspection issue has always been the most effective joker. Other side-effects (i.e. objectives not concerning actual agreement) may be sought. In addition to propaganda, the most important have been to maintain contact (as a substitute for violent action), intelligence, and deception.[41]

There is plenty of justification for cynicism about motives as far as GCD negotiations have been concerned. With the exception of some British governments in the 1920s genuine idealism can be discounted. Thus one meets many cynical comments about disarmament policy. "When disarmament is possible it is unnecessary." "In the race to disarm the aim of every runner is to remain conspicuously in the lead. . . and come in last." And as it was wittily summed up by a French negotiator in the 1930s: "The verb 'to disarm' is an imperfect verb: it contains no first person single."

In considering the reasons why states have involved themselves so frequently in such negotiations, it seems justifiable to draw the conclusion that while national policies have differed greatly, the range of underlying national attitudes is narrow. In particular, all governments have been justifiably conservative: when far-reaching proposals have been put forward their "seriousness" can be questioned. Idealism has not been the motive. Few governments have accepted the view that disarmament is a good thing in itself: their position has been that it is desirable only in so far as it contributes to national security. National interest is the key: if the position of one's own country can be improved, militarily, economically or politically by a disarmament policy then it will be pursued. The tactical nature of declaratory policy, definitions (e.g. what is "offensive" and "defensive") and proposals (e.g. "jokers") will always be high. For one reason or another it is a subject which governments cannot ignore, except at some cost in international prestige (as has been the case to some extent with France and China). But even if formal agreements are not achieved, the desirability of tacit and informal arms control in its widest sense is appreciated by almost all in a world in which the risks and costs of the uncontrol of national arms has become inflated beyond reason.

Issues and Prospects

At the present time there are four areas in which the proponents of arms control are hoping for progress. Firstly, they hope for a comprehensive test ban, to close the "loophole" of the 1963 treaty. While technical improvements greatly improve the prospects for remote inspection, the political and strategic opposition of the superpowers is likely to remain stubborn. Secondly, they hope to tighten the Non-Proliferation Treaty and increase its adherents. Here again the prospects are not good, and will depend greatly on the restraint, guarantees and regional policies offered by the superpowers. Thirdly, they hope that the SALT might produce restraint in both the qualitative and quantitative aspects of the superpower arms race, by a variety of controls such as limiting or banning the testing of delivery vehicles, at least freezing numbers, and perhaps attempting to freeze system design. However, the difficulties facing qualitative agreements remain considerable. Fourthly, they hope that the talks on the military balance in Europe, renamed the Negotiations on the Mutual Reduction of Forces and Armaments and Associated Measures in Central Europe will contribute to stabilising the situation in that heavily armed region at a lower level of military power. Here again the problem of defining symmetry is perplexing; furthermore the domestic pressures for reduction are so much greater on the NATO side that time favours the Warsaw Pact, which has a limited stake in agreement. In addition to these four major areas, there are pressures for the control of chemical weapons and the arms trade. Running through the subject there is a hope for continued tacit and informal arms control, in ways which will contribute to international security.

Amongst those who speculate about the immediate future in this subject there is a range of pessimism and optimism. Few believe that much energy will be expended on the pursuit of GCD. This has been regretted by some,[42] but seen as eminently practical by others.[43] Many hope that arms control will be practised increasingly, in an effort to stabilize the balance of terror, but those who look for substantive agreements are already disappointed.[44] On the other hand those who accept that "unilateral action" and "tacit agreements" are most important, and that progress can only be piecemeal, are moderately confident that something is being done to make safer an imperfect world.[45]

Armaments play a major role in international order. The changes which would be required by massive disarmament rule it out as a feasible policy for governments: they prefer the devil they know. However, while the desirability and practicality of massive disarmament can be doubted, and while the impact of arms control has been limited, this is not to dismiss them. Limiting or restraining weaponry is not a panacea for the problem of international violence, but it is an approach which cannot be ignored by those who wish to ease the mistrust which exists between states.[46]

Notes

1. H. Bull, *The Control of the Arms Race, Disarmament and Arms Control in the*

Missile Age (London: Weidenfeld and Nicolson for the ISS, 1961), ix.

2. R.A. Levine, *The Arms Debate* (Cambridge, Mass.: Harvard University Press, 1963), pp 28-30, 235.

3. There is a large literature on the difficult question of the economics of disarmament. For an introduction see S. Melman, (ed.). *Disarmament: Its Politics and Economics* (Boston, Mass.: The American Academy of Arts and Sciences, 1962). Many reports have been published by the US Arms Control and Disarmament Agency. For a limited study see The Economist Intelligence Unit, *The Economics of Disarmament* (London, 1962).

4. R.G. Hawtrey, *Economic Aspects of Sovereignty*, p, 105, quoted by E.H. Carr, *The 20 Years' Crisis 1919-1939* (London: Macmillan, 1966) p. 111.

5. See I.L. Claude, *Swords Into Ploughshares. The Problems and Progress of International Organisation* (London: University of London Press, 1966) pp. 262-3. Chapter 13 of this book is an excellent general introduction to the subject of disarmament.

6. In the *Pueblo* episode and Vietnam. For a critique of the former see R. Fisher, *Basic Negotiating Strategy* (London: Allen Lane, 1971), pp. 89-94; for the latter see D. Halberstam, *The Best and the Brightest* (London: Barrie and Jenkins, 1972), *passim*.

7. Thus the motto of the Strategic Air Command: "Peace is our Profession." Depending upon one's sympathies, this motto is an object of extreme pride or extreme derision.

8. Vegetius had advised his emperor: "If you want peace, prepare for war." President Wilson had advised the world (his fourth point) to reduce national armaments "to the lowest point consistent with domestic safety."

9. The other reasons why governments participate in disarmament negotiations are discussed more fully below.

10. Details of various negotiations and proposals can be found in Keesing's Research Report, *Disarmament Negotiations and Treaties 1946-1971* (Charles Scribner's Sons, NY, 1972); and B.G. Bechhoefer, *Postwar Negotiations for Arms Control* (Washington: Brookings, 1961). Since 1969 the Stockholm International Peace Research Institute has worked on an annual *Yearbook,* which has become an invaluable source of material in this subject. The periods in the section below are based upon Chapter I in E. Luard, (ed.), *First Steps to Disarmament* (London: Thames and Hudson, 1965).

11. This critique of US motives, arguing that the plan was a "deliberate fraud", has been put most persuasively by J.W. Spanier and J.L. Nogee, *The Politics of Disarmament: A Study In Soviet-American Gamesmanship* (New York: Praeger, 1962), pp. 56-75. They describe the plan as a "superb tool of psychological warfare".

12. G.H. Quester, *Nuclear Diplomacy. The First Twenty-Five Years* (New York: Dunellen, 1970), p. 23.

13. The phrase was used by a UN delegate about the period 1946-1954: quoted by R.J. Barnet, *Who Wants Disarmament?* (Boston: Beacon Press, 1960), p. 21 ff.

14. H. Bull, "Arms Control: A Stocktaking and Prospectus", *Adelphi Papers* No. 55, March 1969, pp. 15-16.

15. J.D. Singer, *Deterrence, Arms Control and Disarmament: Towards a Synthesis in National Security Policy* (Columbus: Ohio State University Press, 1962), Chapter 7.

16. C.E. Osgood, *An Alternative to War Or Surrender* (Urbana: University of Illinois Press, 1962); L.B. Sohn, "Zonal Disarmament and Inspection: Variations on a Theme", *Bulletin of the Atomic Scientists,* Vol. 18, September 1962.

17. P. Noel-Baker, *The Arms Race. A Programme for World Disarmament* (London: Atlantic Books, 1958).

18. The literature on this subject is large: see R.H. Cory, "International Inspection: From Proposals to Realization", *International Organization*, Vol. 13, October 1959, pp. 495-504; S. Melman (ed.), *Inspection for Disarmament* (New York: Columbia UP, 1958); D.G. Brennan (ed.), *Arms Control and Disarmament* (London: Cape, 1961), Chapters 16-19; Ted Greenwood, "Reconnaissance, Surveillance and Arms Control", *Adelphi Papers*, No. 88, June 1972.

19. The visit of President Nixon to Moscow in July 1974 resulted in the first sign of some progress in the inspection problem for many years in terms of human as opposed to technical means of verification. While it is too early to say whether the idea will develop very far, many observers saw the most interesting point to emerge from the talks to be an "unwritten but firm understanding" to allow on-site inspection of nuclear tests for "peaceful purposes". This was potentially a major development in Soviet policy. *The Times,* 4 July 1974.

20. E.J. Gumbel, "Disarmament and Clandestine Rearmament Under the Weimar Republic", pp. 203-19 in Melman, op. cit.

21. See, e.g., F.C. Ikle, "After Detection — What?" *Foreign Affairs,* Vol. 39, January 1961, pp. 208-20.

22. Barnet, op. cit., p. 94. Barnet sees enforcement as "the central problem of the disarmament riddle".

23. S. De Madriaga, *Disarmament* (London: OUP, 1929) p. 48.

24. H. Bull, "Arms Control: A Stocktaking and Prospectus", p. 11.

25. T.C. Schelling and M.H. Halperin, *Strategy and Arms Control* (New York: Twentieth Century Fund, 1961), p. 2.

26. For an elaboration of these arguments see R.R. Bowie, "Basic Requirements of Arms Control", pp. 43-55 in D.G. Brennan, op. cit.

27. Underground testing has proceeded apace. Between 1963 and 1970 the USA carried out 539 tests, the USSR 242 tests, and Britain 25 tests. In the meantime France had carried out 38 tests in the atmosphere, and China 11.

28. D.J. Puchala, *International Politics Today* (New York: Dodd, Mead and Co., 1971), pp. 294-6.

29. Interestingly, both France and China overcame their objections to arms control treaties, and in 1973 signed Protocol Two of the Treaty, under which nuclear powers agree not to introduce nuclear weapons into Latin America. In 1974 there was apparent progress in Latin America on the control of conventional armaments also. *Guardian,* 24 December 1974.

30. While it makes eminent sense, it should not be forgotten that the hot line, like all channels of communication, can be used on the side of the devil, as well as on the side of the angels.

31. E.g. Elizabeth Young, *A Farewell to Arms Control?* (Harmondsworth: Penguin Books, 1972) pp. 17, 86.

32. The literature on proliferation, mainly clustered in the early and middle 1960s, has been massive. An introduction is provided by L. Beaton, *Must the Bomb Spread?* (Harmondsworth: Penguin Books, 1966); A. Buchan, *A World of Nuclear Powers?* (Englewood Cliffs, N.J. : Prentice-Hall, 1966); P.M. Gallois, "U.S. Strategy and the Defense of Europe", Orbis, VII, No. 2, Summer 1963; F.C. Ikle, "Nth Countries and Disarmament", *Bulletin of the Atomic Scientists,* December 1960, pp. 391-4; G.H. Quester, *The Politics of Nuclear Proliferation* (Baltimore: The Johns Hopkins Press, 1973).

33. Sceptical analyses of SALT I can be found in C.S. Gray, "Of bargaining chips and building blocks: arms control and defence policy", *International Journal,* Spring 1973, pp. 266-90; and W.R. Kintner, and R.L. Pfaltzgraff, "Assessing the Moscow SALT Agreements", *Orbis,* XVI, Summer 1972, pp. 341-60. For an orthodox view, see J. Newhouse, *Cold Dawn: The Story of SALT* (New York: Holt, Rhinehart and Winston, 1973).

34. Young, op. cit., p. 236.

35. This is very important, but also very difficult: see J.J. Stone, *Strategic*

Persuasion: Arms Limitation Through Dialogue (New York: Columbia University Press, 1967). The "conceptual breakthrough" which Mr. Kissinger failed to achieve during the SALT II talks in Moscow, March 1974, was ample proof of this.
36. H. Bull, "Arms control: A Stocktaking and Prospectus", pp. 13-17.
37. See note 11 above.
38. R.E. Osgood, and R.W. Tucker, *Force, Order and Justice.* (Baltimore: The Johns Hopkins Press, 1967), p. 182. Spanier and Nogee might also be criticised for seeing armaments entirely as symptoms of mistrust, and not sometimes as a major cause (e.g. op. cit., pp. 13-15).
39. Spanier and Nogee, op. cit., pp. 13-15, 176-81.
40. Ibid, pp. 5, 47, ff.
41. F.C. Ikle, *How Nations Negotiate* (London: Harper, 1964), Chapter 4: "Negotiating for side-effects".
42. E.g. R.R. Neild, *What Has Happened to Disarmament?* Annual Memorial Lecture, David Davis Memorial Institute of International Studies (London, 1968).
43. E.g. H. Bull, "Arms Control: A Stocktaking and Prospectus".
44. Young, op. cit.
45. E.g. H. Bull, "Arms Control: A Stocktaking and Prospectus", p. 18; L.W. Martin, *Arms and Strategy* (London: Weidenfeld and Nicholson, 1973), p. 243.
46. Claude, op. cit., *passim.*

6 LIMITED WAR

John Garnett

1 The Evolution of Limited War Thinking

Not even the most enthusiastic proponent of the strategy of deterrence would claim it was infallible although, during the 1950s, many people anaesthetized themselves to the possibility of its failure. Much of our faith in that strategy may be justified, but few would maintain that its adoption by the superpowers provides an absolute guarantee of perpetual peace. There are a number of reasons for this. First, it is generally recognised that threats, even threats of severe punishment, are not always successful in deterring. Potential murderers in our society are threatened with life imprisonment as they used to be threatened with death; neither threat abolished the phenomenon of murder. Adolf Hitler was threatened with war if he invaded Poland and it was quite obvious from his subsequent behaviour that he found that threat quite unimpressive. Certainly he was not deterred,

The second reason why deterrence cannot guarantee peace is that it is directed towards affecting the conscious, calculating behaviour of *reasonable* statesmen. The strategy of deterrence is founded upon the assumption that in deciding whether or not to be deterred policy-makers will react to threats by making very rational cost/gain calculations. "If I do this, they will do that. At the end of the day will I be better off or worse off?" That is the kind of analysis which deterrent theorists assume threatened statesmen will make, and to be successful the deterrent must be of such proportions that the statesman invariably decides that the cost of aggression clearly outweighs the potential gains.

The critical question of course is whether it is sensible to make this implicit assumption that all policy-makers in all circumstances will react with such sweet reasonableness. To the extent that men are creatures of passion with impulses of rage, frustration, aggression and even blind revenge, they are not likely to count the costs of their behaviour in the calm and rational way so beloved by the deterrent theorists. When directed against 'strategic man' the policy of deterrence looks foolproof, but against flesh and blood statesmen with all their human weaknesses it seems rather more fallible. In short, while most of us would agree that the strategy of deterrence has made war less likely, only a rationalist or an optimist could believe that it has made war impossible.

And of course, because the strategy of deterrence is directed towards affecting the conscious choices of enemy politicians, it makes no contribution at all to the avoidance of those accidental wars which have their origin not in malevolent human intentions, but in technological failures of one kind or another. Wheeler and Burdick, in their gripping novel *Fail Safe*,[1] describe a situation whereby as a result of the failure of a minute electronic component in a communications system, a wing of nuclear-armed SAC bombers fails to turn back at the 'fail safe' point and continues towards the Soviet Union with devastating consequences. And in the real world there was the famous instance in the 1950s when on US radars a flight of geese crossing the Arctic was misinterpreted as a squadron of Soviet 'Bear' aircraft heading towards the United States. One does not need much imagination to see how as a result of the mechanical failure of some weapons system, or as a result of misinterpreting radar information, or as a result of a failure in the command and control arrangements of nuclear weapons, the two superpowers could find themselves in a war which neither intended and which the strategy of deterrence was powerless to prevent. Needless to say a good deal of money and energy has been devoted to eliminating the possibility of accidental war, but it is probably true that no level of effort can reduce that possibility to zero.[2]

A further major weakness in the strategy of deterrence began to be perceived and articulated during the 1950s. When the United States nuclear monopoly was broken and the Soviet Union acquired a significant nuclear armoury and the capacity to retaliate against the United States homeland, very real doubts were voiced about the ability of the United States to deter the Soviet Union from *all* kinds of aggressive behaviour. Though there seemed little doubt that a direct attack on the United States could be deterred by a threat of massive retaliatory damage, the capacity of such a threat to deter lesser provocations seemed much more questionable. The Korean War had already demonstrated that the nuclear superiority of the United States was incapable of deterring the Soviet Union from major adventurism in the Far East, and several commentators were questioning whether the doctrine of massive retaliation could deter minor aggressions in Europe. In the mid-1950s B. Brodie and W. Kaufmann were suggesting that in the face of minor and perhaps ambiguous aggressions, the enormity of a massive nuclear response was out of all proportion to the challenge.[3] This gross disparity between ends and means inevitably paralysed the political will of those required to implement the deterrent threat, and the entire deterrent posture began to take on the characteristics of a gigantic bluff.

Inevitably, as the nuclear capability of the Soviet Union grew more formidable, questions began to be asked about the credibility of the United States' guarantee to Western Europe. So long as the United States was invulnerable to a retaliatory strike, the Europeans could feel confident of the protection provided by their major ally's threat of massive retaliation. When standing by her allies involved the United States in no risk her help could reasonably be regarded as reliable. But when the Soviet Union acquired the capability to "take out" Washington and New York, it seemed that the United States might have to pay dearly for the protection which they had so freely promised to their European friends. Putting it crudely, threatening the Soviet Union with massive retaliation even for a relatively minor aggression in Europe lacked all credibility when the consequences of implementing the threat were likely to result in the complete destruction of the American way of life. How could any European have faith in the United States' guarantee when even the Americans themselves freely admitted that "the decision to use nuclear weapons is so awesome that most alternatives look better at the time — if they exist; and they usually do"?[4] General Gallois neatly summed up the situation with his dry comment that "no nation can be expected to commit suicide for the sake of another."

The logic was clear and unanswerable. The weakness of massive retaliation as a deterrent to all aggressions short of an attack on US territory was exposed. Unless deterrence could be supplemented by some new policy, the Western alliance could fall victim to Soviet 'salami' tactics — a series of hostile acts which, considered individually, were not sufficiently serious to justify massive retaliation and against which NATO could muster no appropriate lesser response, but which collectively might tip the balance of power in favour of the Soviet camp. This fear of being eaten piecemeal, or 'nibbled to death' as President Kennedy put it, was a powerful incentive for developing a limited war capability which would add to the deterrent by providing the means to fight a war in a way which did not automatically involve suicide.

The gist of the argument so far has been to suggest that in spite of the strategy of deterrence, war, even nuclear war, remained a very real if unquantifiable possibility. And it is worth adding that if war did break out, then given the quality and quantity of weaponry which had been accumulated on both sides, it was likely to be mutually disastrous if not suicidal for the belligerents. On that, at least, the theorists were agreed.

Now these two points, that war is both possible, and, should it occur, likely to be disastrous to both parties, form the starting point for nearly all the theorizing which has gone on about limited war. In the late 1950s strategists came to agree that if a war threatening the entire human race was possible, then a certain amount of attention should be directed towards the problem of controlling and limiting wars in such a way that their occurrence would not inevitably be disastrous. It was further agreed that the acquisition of limited war capability might actually plug the gaps in a 'minimum' deterrent strategy, by enabling the United States to pose a more credible threat than massive retaliation to less than massive aggressions.

It is interesting to note that limited war strategies were advanced as a response to two quite different pressures. First, they developed because if deterrence failed men wanted an alternative to anrihilation, and second, they developed because many believed that the ability to wage limited war enhanced deterrence. Most limited war theorizing has, therefore, to be considered from two distinct perspectives; that of those who are interested in waging wars in a controlled fashion, and that of those who wish to avoid war altogether.

It is perhaps worth saying that thinking about the problem of controlling and limiting war represented something of a revolution in contemporary strategic thought. Until that moment strategists had devoted almost all their intellectual energy towards the problem of either avoiding war or winning it. Current thinking was all about deterrence, massive retaliation and disarmament, and as B. Brodie has pointed out, this amounted to an 'all or nothing' attitude to the use of force: "one either did not fight at all, or one fought with all one had or could lay hands on."[5] In this intellectual environment — which prevailed long after the Korean War ought to have undermined it — it was very unfashionable to think about the conduct of war and about what would happen if deterrence failed and the Western world got itself into a fight. Herman Kahn's massive *On Thermonuclear War,* published in 1960, was the first and most formidable attempt to grapple with the possibility and consequences of modern war.[6] Kahn's pseudo-scientific analysis led him to two main conclusions; first, that contrary to the views of laymen reared on novels like *On the Beach* by Nevil Shute,[7] nuclear war was in fact survivable, and second, that the United States should acquire the limited war capability which would enable it to survive. Kahn's views were widely condemned[8] but his writing helped prepare the ground for many of the limited war ideas which dominated the strategic literature of the early 1960s.

II Criticism of Limited War

The shift of emphasis away from deterrence towards limited war was not welcomed by everyone. Those who opposed the new thinking which concerned itself with the problem of fighting wars in a limited and controlled way had at least three very good arguments.

The first argument claimed that ideas of limited war undermined the strategy of deterrence which the two superpowers were pursuing. It was suggested that the main reason why, in spite of bitter 'cold war' hostility, no hot war had broken out in post-war years, was that the potential aggressors were terrified by the prospect of global destruction. If people now began to think that this global destruction was not an inevitable consequence of war, that perhaps wars could be controlled and managed, then statesmen would not be so reluctant to wage them. That was the essence of the argument that ideas of limited war are dangerous because they undermine rather than complement the strategy of deterrence.

The second and related argument advanced by those who opposed ideas of limited war was that ideas about limited war brought war back into the realms of political practicability. K. von Clausewitz made a reputation for himself largely by arguing that "War is nothing but a continuation of political intercourse, with a mixture of other means," but the nuclear age seemed to disprove his point. War could no longer sensibly be regarded as an instrument of any political policy if it meant mutual annihilation. But if the limited war theorists were right and war could be controlled so that it did not inevitably lead to Armaggedon, then Clausewitz's doctrine was instantly rehabilitated. Once more war would be regarded as a political phenomenon, an instrument of policy to be used by statesmen whenever they thought it appropriate. The feeling that by implication at least the new strategists were trying to make war a usable technique again caused widespread hostility to ideas of limited war.

The third argument put forward in opposition to ideas of limited war was that the whole body of reasoning implied a level of rationality on the part of decision-takers which was quite unrealistic, and a degree of control over the battlefield which was technically impossible. Statesmen are perhaps more responsible than ordinary men but they are no less susceptible to human frailty. For that reason alone it is highly dangerous to assume that they could conduct a war as rationally and coolly as they could play a game of chess. And in situations where considerable power has to be delegated to soldiers operating thousands of miles away and surrounded by the 'fog of war', it is difficult if not impossible for statesmen to exercise the kind of control which is required if a limited war is to remain limited.

Not all those who opposed ideas of limited war queried the practicability of controlling it. Some certainly did, but others, more sophisticated perhaps, argued that even if it could be shown that limited wars were a feasible proposition, this did not make them any the less undesirable. Ideas of limited war still undermined the strategy of deterrence, and so long as this remained the cornerstone of Western defence nothing should be done to diminish its credibility. In effect, the argument was that even though it was true that wars could be limited, this fact should be suppressed in favour of the popular proposition that modern war meant mutual suicide. Whereas the latter myth perpetuated deterrence, the former truth undermined it, and in that situation it was imperative that governments should promote convenient myths rather than dangerous truths.

III   The McNamara Strategy

In spite of very articulate opposition, limited war theorizing gained ground in the United States, particularly during the time when Mr. R. McNamara was Secretary for Defence. Mr. McNamara believed very strongly that if war was a possibility then we ought to try and get away from the notion that it would inevitably be spasm war — a war where each belligerent let fly at its enemy with all the power at its disposal. Such a conception of war made neither military, political nor moral sense, and it was ludicrous that a superpower like the United States should rely solely upon a military doctrine which, if it ever had to be implemented, was tantamount to suicide. President Kennedy himself was well aware of the danger inherent in the United States military posture.

> We have been driving ourselves into a corner where the only choice is all or nothing at all, world devasation or submission — a choice that necessarily causes us to hesitate on the brink and leaves the initiative in the hands of the enemy.[9]

Because they had been interested almost entirely in avoiding war, American strategists had stopped short of considering, except in the most general terms, how precisely to use the enormous military power they had acquired if it ever became necessary to do so. In effect the United States had built a military force which had no coherent operational strategy. That was why their leaders were confronted with such an impossible choice. More recently President Nixon has reflected on the same problem. "Should a President, in the event of a nuclear attack, be left with the single option of ordering the mass destruction of enemy civilians, in the face of the certainty that it would be followed by the mass slaughter of Americans?"[10] It is ironic that the same worry which led President Kennedy to direct his Secretary of Defence to provide him with a wider choice than "humiliation or all-out nuclear war", has led President Nixon, through Mr. Schlesinger, to announce, in 1974, that the United States proposed to weld on to its established 'assured destruction' doctrine, a new targetting philosophy which bears startling resemblances to the old 'counterforce' strategy of Mr. McNamara.[11]

The 1960s witnessed a sophisticated elaboration of limited war doctrine. Mr. McNamara in particular erected an elegant and intellectually satisfying strategic doctrine which embraced both deterrence and limited war. 'The McNamara strategy', as it was called, was a formidable attempt to reshape US defence policy along realistic lines. In an attempt to avoid the cataclysm implicit in 'spasm' war, Mr. McNamara developed the distinction between counterforce and counter-value targets, and sought to maximise the options available to the United States in conducting a limited, albeit nuclear, war. City avoidance strategies and counterforce targetting became important priorities for forces which were designed to limit civilian damage in the hope that the Soviets would reciprocate in kind. The flavour of his policy is accurately conveyed by this extract from his testimony before the House Armed Services Committee in 1963.

> What we are proposing is a capability to strike back after absorbing the first blow. This means we have to build and main-

tain a second strike force. Such a force should have sufficient flexibility to permit a choice of strategies, particularly an ability to: (1) strike back decisively at the entire Soviet target system simultaneously, or (2) strike back first at the Soviet bomber bases, missile sites and other military installations associated with their long-range nuclear forces to reduce the power of any follow-on-attack-and then, if necessary, strike back at the Soviet urban and industrial complex in a controlled and deliberate way.

. . .By building into our forces a flexible capability, we at least eliminate the prospect that we could strike back in only one way, namely, against the entire Soviet target system including their cities. Such a prospect would give the Soviet Union no incentive to withhold attack against our cities in a first strike. We want to give them a better alternative. Whether they would accept it in the crisis of a global nuclear war, no one can say. Considering what is at stake, we believe it is worth the additional effort on our part to have this option.[12]

Mr. McNamara was interested in avoiding the stark alternatives of annihilation or surrender. But he was also interested in bolstering the strategy of deterrence by improving the conventional war capability of the United States and NATO. His strategy of 'flexible response' envisaged a considerable build-up of non-nuclear limited war capability. The aim was to replace the increasingly incredible threat of 'massive retaliation' with a much more credible threat to meet the enemy at a lesser and more appropriate level of violence. In a famous speech at Ann Arbor, Michigan, Mr. McNamara called upon NATO

"to strengthen further their non-nuclear forces, and to improve the quality of these forces. These achievements will complement our deterrent strength. With improvements in Alliance ground force strength and staying power, improved non-nuclear air capabilities, and better equipped and trained reserve forces, we can be assumed that no deficiency exists in the NATO defense of this vital region, and that no aggression, small or large, can succeed.[13]

There were some who argued that the conventional limited war capability which Mr. McNamara favoured seriously undermined the credibility of strategic deterrence by suggesting to the Soviet Union that the United States was reluctant to implement its nuclear threat. The Russians, it was argued, would confuse the capability to fight below the nuclear threshold with a reluctance to fight above it. Freed from the fear of escalation beyond the nuclear threshold, they would feel few inhibitions about waging conventional war in Europe. Instead of discouraging war, the doctrine of flexible response actually made its occurrence more likely.

Mr. McNamara defended himself quite simply by arguing that a deterrent threat, to be credible, has to be a rational instrument of policy. As he repeatedly emphasised, "One cannot fashion a credible deterrent out of an incredible action." Except in the direst circumstances massive retaliation was an incredible response and therefore a poor deterrent, whereas limited war, because it was a credible response, was a much more effective deterrent. To those who argued that the risks posed to the enemy by his strategy of flexible response were less than those implicit in the threat of massive retaliation, Mr. McNamara countered by claiming that this disadvantage was more than compensated for by the increased likelihood of the threat being implemented. In other words, his new strategy, far from undermining deterrence, actually enhanced it.

The McNamara doctrine crystallized many of the limited war ideas which circulated in defence circles in the United States during the 1950s By abandoning massive retaliation in favour of a strategy of options and a doctrine of limited war, the American Secretary of Defence had succeeded in putting the politics back into war, or, as M. Howard put it, in "reintegrating military power with foreign policy".[14] It was a formidable achievement by any standards, and though modified and refined by subsequent administrations, his ideas are still at the heart of American defence thinking.

IV   The Meaning of Limited War

As the idea of limited war gained currency in defence thinking, it became clear that what had seemed a fairly precise term denoting an alternative to 'massive retaliation', was in fact a highly ambiguous bundle of ideas which, in the interests of conceptual clarity, needed to be separated out. Exclusive definitions of limited war were impossible because different writers used the term in different ways. Indeed, there seemed to be some danger that the phrase 'limited war' would be emptied of all meaning by the diversity of its applications. Now that the dust has settled a little it is possible to identify four major ways in which the term is used in contemporary strategic literature.

First, it is sometimes used to describe wars which are limited geographically; that is to say, limited war is a term which is applied to wars which are fought in, and confined to, restricted areas of the world's surface. In this sense of the term the Indo-Pakistan War of 1968 was a limited war, as also was the Korean War, the Vietnam War and the Yom Kippur War of 1973. By contrast, the Second World War was an unlimited war in the sense that the belligerents were in conflict on a global scale in many continents. The main analytical difficulty with this geographical criteria is that it lumps together such diverse conflicts as, for example, Korea and the Indo-Pakistan War. In short, it does not discriminate between those wars in which the superpowers are involved on opposite sides, even if only by proxy, and those in which neither of the two superpowers is directly or indirectly involved. This ambiguity may be disappearing because there is some evidence that usage of the term 'limited' is now beginning to be confined to the former kind of war, that is to say, wars in which the superpowers are involved. Other geographically restricted wars are more usefully described as 'local' rather than 'limited' wars.[15]

The second way in which the term limited war is used as a description of wars fought for limited objectives. The idea is that limited wars are to be distinguished from unlimited wars according to the war aims or objectives for which the war is fought. The Second World War was an unlimited war because the Allies had an unlimited objective — 'unconditional surrender'. In contrast, Vietnam was a limited war because the United States neither sought to defeat the North Vietnamese totally nor to impose 'unconditional surrender' terms on them. She simply aimed to perpetuate the existence of South Vietnam as an independent sovereign state — a limited objective if ever there was one. It remains a moot point whether the criteria of limited objectives is met when a war is fought for limited objectives by one belligerent and unlimited objectives by the other. Vietnam is a case in point because however limited United States objectives may have been, few would dispute that by seeking to destroy South Vietnam as an independent state, the North Vietnamese were pursuing unlimited objectives. For that reason it is not entirely satisfactory to regard the Vietnam War as one fought for limited objectives. The same problem of asymmetry in objectives occurs in the case of the Korean War.

The third usage of the term 'limited war' is to describe wars fought with limited means, that is to say, wars in which restraint is practised by the belligerents in respect to the quantity and quality of the weaponry used in the conduct of the war. Wars are limited, not because our ends permit it, but because our means compel it. According to this definition the Korean War was a limited war because although both sides had access to nuclear weapons neither side used them. Each belligerent deliberately shackled its available military power. Again it is not entirely clear whether this restraint has to be practised by both sides for the war in which they are engaged to qualify for the description 'limited', or whether unilateral restraint by one belligerent is a sufficient requirement. In Korea the restraint was mutual but in Vietnam it might be argued that although United States troops refrained from using many of the weapons in their arsenal, the North Vietnamese threw all they had into the conflict.

Neither the Indo-Pakistan War nor the recent Arab-Israeli wars meet this 'limited means' criteria of limited war. None of the participants in those wars practised much restraint; in fact, all the evidence suggests that each used all the military power at its disposal to achieve its object-ives. It is perfectly true that the violence was confined to the conventional variety, but this was not a result of restraint on the part of the belligerents. It was simply a consequence of the fact that none of them had the capability to escalate to the nuclear level. A war which is limited simply because neither side has the capacity to make it total is not really a limited war at all. Only conflicts which contain the potentiality for becoming total can be described as limited.

The difficulty of defining limited wars simply according to whether or not the combatants practise restraint in the use of available weaponry is that the degree of restraint can vary enormously from conflict to conflict. The Second World War, for example, is usually regarded as a total war in the sense that both the Allies and the Axis powers used all the weapons at their disposal in order to win. And yet a degree of restraint was present. Neither side, for example, used poison gas though this was readily available to both. Does this relatively small degree of restraint make it possible for us to regard the Second World War as a limited war? And in the present nuclear environment is it possible to regard even a nuclear war as a limited war provided the participants restrained themselves by not expending all of their nuclear weapons? Mr. McNamara was not alone in believing in the possibility, if not the desirability, of limited strategic exchanges in which each superpower made selective nuclear strikes against the other. As early as 1955 the American nuclear physicist Leo Szillard had outlined a frightening scenario of how such a war might be executed.[16] Professor Szillard suggested that the United States should work out in advance a set of exchange values for possible objects of Soviet aggression. Thus, if the Soviets attacked Iran, for example, the United States would destroy a previously announced number of Soviet cities whose value was deemed to be equal to that of Iran. Some years later similar ideas were developed by other writers.[17] Amongst them, Herman Kahn contemplated the possibility of 'tit-for-tat' nuclear exchanges in which the two super-powers destroyed each other's cities on a one-for-one basis until some sort of political accommodation was reached.[18] The question which must be asked is whether these bizarre and terrifying acts of violence fit the category of limited wars just because they fall short of 'spasm' war? Does it really make sense to describe a war in which cities are destroyed and millions of people killed as a limited war just because, with less restraint on the part of the belligerents, the consequences might have been even worse?

Common sense suggests that it is nonsense to regard such large-scale violence as a limited war, and this feeling has prompted a number of writers to argue that if a war is to qualify for the description 'limited', then the restraint which is practised must be *massive*. In other words it is not enough to deliberately refrain from using a relatively unimportant weapons system like poison gas, nor is it sufficient to refrain from using *some* nuclear weapons. In 1959 B. Brodie was tempted to write, 'One basic restraint has always to be present if the term "limited war" is to have any meaning at all: strategic bombing of cities with nuclear weapons must be avoided.'[19]

A fourth use of the term limited war which is common in the literature of the subject is as a description of wars in which restraint is practised not in the quantity or quality of weaponry used, but in the targets selected for attack. According to this usage of the term, limited wars are wars which involve restraint on targetting. In essence this was the point of Mr. McNamara's 'counterforce' strategy which sought to discriminate between military and civilian targets. Mr. McNamara hoped that if war came, it would be limited in the sense that the belligerents avoided destroying urban centres. An equally unpalatable kind of restraint on targetting was envisaged by General de Gaulle when he speculated about the possibility of nuclear war in Europe. The General envisaged a war in which the two superpowers, while battling it out with nuclear weapons in Europe, agreed to restrain themselves from striking each other's homelands. This kind of targetting restraint might be attractive to the superpowers, but it would have little to recommend it to the Europeans whose continent was destroyed in a war which, from their point of view at least, was total.

It should be clear from the foregoing that the term 'limited war' is difficult to define precisely partly because the limits involved are matters of degree, and partly because they are matters of perspective. A war that is limited for one *party* may be total from the point of view of the state on whose territory it is being waged. For those who insist upon a short, general definition, the most satisfactory is by R. Osgood:

> A limited war is generally conceived to be a war fought for ends far short of the complete subordination of one state's will to another's and by means involving far less than the total military resources of the belligerents, leaving the civilian life and the armed forces of the belligerents largely intact and leading to a bargained termination.[20]

V Problems of Waging Limited War

Sovereign states do not find it easy either to settle for limited objectives in a war, or to fight with limited means. It is interesting to speculate about why this should be so. Some have suggested that belief in the righteousness of their cause makes it virtually impossible for statesmen to settle for compromise solutions which fall far short of unconditional surrender. Their argument is that if statesmen regard their cause as a just one, then the war becomes a moral and emotional crusade which cannot be compromised by settlements which stop short of destroying the evil against which it is waged. In the First and Second World Wars once the Kaiser and Hitler were cast in the role of the Devil, compromise became unthinkable. Unconditional surrender was the only honourable objective, and anyone suggesting anything less ran the risk of being castigated as an immoral traitor. Belief in their cause has meant that statesmen are sometimes reluctant to pull out on terms which fall short of unconditional surrender. A.J.P. Taylor once made the very pertinent observation that "Bismarck fought necessary wars and killed thousands; the idealists of the twentieth century fight just wars and kill millions."[21] If, in the future, we are to avoid annihilation, statesmen may have to jettison some of their moral and emotional commitment to just causes. Belligerents may have to adopt a much more rational and functional attitude to war which enables them to accept solutions which, though unsatisfactory to each, are nonetheless tolerable to both.

Perhaps it is because we find limited objectives and compromise solutions so psychologically unpalatable that we also find difficulty in restraining ourselves in the conduct of war. On his dismissal from command during the Korean War, General Douglas Macarthur is reputed to have said, 'There is no substitute for victory.' As B. Brodie has commented, this remark "reflects an attitude endemic in all the armed services, one which works strongly against any restraint upon the use of force during wartime."[22]

Certainly Macarthur himself found it very difficult to adjust to the idea of deliberately refraining from using readily available means to win the war. At one stage, when American casualties were very high because of air attacks from bases in Southern China, Macarthur wanted to destroy the bases. He had the power to do it, and doing it would have saved many lives. But President Truman was adamant. It would have been a serious escalation of the war and would have had profound and incalculable international implications. Macarthur never really appreciated that — and in the end he had to go. From his point of view, his own government was deliberately condemning to death American soldiers whose lives could have been saved. He never grasped the fundamental point about limited war — that it is a *political* process conducted by military means, a sort of tough bargaining in which the aim is not to win but rather not to lose, and to fight in such a way that the enemy will settle for a compromise peace.

Soldiers in a limited war need a quite different and much more sophisticated attitude of mind than those engaged in a straightforward, unlimited clash or arms, and the actual conduct of a limited war imposes new rules on the combatants. When an adversary has the power to make a war total, great care must be taken not to push him too far. For example, in an ordinary battle, if one side achieves a breakthrough it will probably pursue the retreating forces ruthlessly in order to destroy them or prevent them from regrouping. Having got the enemy on the run, a military commander would be sorely tempted to follow up his advantage. But in a limited war this would be a very dangerous thing to do because pursuing the enemy may push him into a corner and make him more desperate. A point may come when he is so desperate that rather than be pushed further, he would prefer to escalate the war to a new, higher and more dangerous level.

In other words, the greater the transformation the winning side seeks, the more plausible is the enemy's threat to escalate. And, therefore, the winning side, instead of becoming more enthusiastic about its advance, becomes increasingly reluctant to press on for fear of provoking an escalation which will destroy it. Curiously enough, in this situation the psychological advantage lies with the losing rather than the winning army. In limited war 'winning' is an inappropriate and dangerous goal, and a state which finds itself close to it should immediately begin to practise restraint.

VI   The Idea of Escalation

Because sovereign states do not find it easy to practise restraint in either objectives or means, and because the tactics of waging limited war are so complicated, there is always a possibility that limited wars will degenerate into total wars. The term which is used to describe the process by which limited wars become more violent and less restrained is 'escalation'.

Not so very long ago, strategists almost invariably talked about the dangers of escalation. They thought of it as a tragedy, a disaster which sometimes occurred in spite of efforts to prevent it. It was widely believed that the most likely way for escalation to occur was as a result of an accident or miscalculation in 'the fog of war'. Whatever its causes escalation was deplored by all right-thinking people. Now that idea of escalation as a deplorable, if inadvertent, calamity is still prevalent, but a new idea has grown up alongside it — namely the view that escalation can be a deliberate, planned, purposive strategy which states use in the pursuit of their interests.

Escalation began to be thought of in this new way because it soon became evident that certain advantages could accrue to those who, in a limited war, were prepared to deliberately increase the level of violence. For instance, a state might reasonably hope to make its enemy 'back down' by a sudden and intense show of force. It might hope to undermine the morale of an adversary by making him think that continuing the war was no longer worth the effort involved. The assumption underlying this ploy is that a state may believe that a war is worth fighting up to a particular level of violence, but not beyond it. Once the level of violence has escalated beyond this critical point, an enemy may be persuaded to terminate the war.

Obviously the policy of deliberate escalation is a dangerous one. H. Kahn has pointed out some illuminating parallels between 'escalation' and the 'chicken game' which is reputedly played by wayward teenagers in the United States.[23] 'Chicken' is played by two drivers on a straight road with a white line down the middle. The cars, straddling the white line and facing each other at opposite ends of the road, are driven towards each other at top speed. The first driver to lose his nerve and swerve to his own side of the road 'chickens out' and loses the game. The object of the exercise is to swerve last, and as Kahn notes the strategy employed may be very interesting.

> The 'skilful' player may get into the car quite drunk, throwing whisky bottles out of the window to make it clear to everybody just how drunk he is. He wears very dark glasses so that it is obvious that he cannot see much, if anything. As soon as the car reaches high speed, he takes the steering wheel and throws it out of the window. If his opponent is watching, he has won. If his opponent is not watching he has a problem; likewise if both players try this strategy.[24]

This highly dangerous game has the same logical structure as competitive escalation in a limited war. In each case success comes to the player who shows the greatest willingness to run enormous risks and the strongest determination to win at all costs. In limited war such qualitites may be demonstrated by a reckless use of force, or a deliberate loss of control, and a 'couldn't care less' attitude about the consequences. T.C. Schelling, in a quite brilliant analysis, has perceptively described this technique as 'the threat that leaves something to chance', and it is dangerous precisely because it does leave something to chance.[25] Risky behaviour, whether in motor cars or wars, is certainly dangerous, but since it may achieve its object it can scarcely be described as irrational behaviour. Quite rightly, Schelling has stressed the essential rationality of behaviour which on the face of it appears to be dangerously insane.

In a way, the technique of escalation is a bit like driving aggressively in traffic, nudging forward into traffic lanes, behaving unreasonably, even dangerously, because it is this sort of behaviour which makes other drivers give way. The trouble of course, is that just as some drivers are not intimidated by the dangerous behaviour of others, so some enemies are not intimidated by escalation. It is quite likely that the enemy has read his Kahn and Schelling as throughly as we have and is also using escalation as a deliberate strategy. That is why limited wars may develop into competitions in risk-taking, where each side tries to outbid the other in intimidation behaviour. No wonder the game is a dangerous one.

But although escalation is a dangerous tactic, the employment of which could cause a limited war to degenerate into a total war, this is by no means inevitable. In fact, paradoxical as it may seem, it is possible that the escalation of a limited war may be a necessary prerequisite for its termination. The thought underlying this view is that a limited war only continues because both sides find it more or less tolerable. What is required to bring it to an end, therefore, is a sharp escalation in the level of violence to a point where one or both sides find it intolerable and are prepared to sue for peace. In other words, escalation may be regarded as a device for terminating wars as well as for making them more violent.

The usual metaphor for thinking about escalation is that of a ladder. Now a ladder is a linear arrangement of equally spaced steps each of which represents an increasing level of violence. An escalation ladder suggests a progression of steps through an ascending order of intensity of warfare. H. Kahn has devised a formidable 44-rung escalation ladder which encompasses not just war, but the entire spectrum of international conflict (see Figure I, p. 130). His ladder leads in progressive steps from Cold War at the bottom to the 'aftermath' of 'spasm' or 'insensate' war at the top. Each rung represents a particular, indentifiable level of violence, and the ladder takes us step by step through mild crises, intense crises, limited conventional wars, limited tactical nuclear wars, limited strategic wars in which some targets are spared, to strategic wars in which no one is spared.

Between some of the rungs of the ladder are barriers or psychological breakpoints which are known as 'thresholds', and crossing a threshold is always a significant escalation. One important threshold in a war may be described as the 'Nuclear war is unthinkable' threshold. Below it, though the fighting may be fierce, there is no real prospect of nuclear exchanges. Above it, nuclear war is a more likely possibility in the sense that the adversaries have started to think and worry about it. Since the dawn of the nuclear age there have been very few occasions when the 'nuclear war is unthinkable' threshold has been crossed. The last occurred at the time of the Cuban missile crisis when the possibility of nuclear war seemed very real.

Perhaps the most important threshold of all is the 'no nuclear use' threshold. As Kahn has pointed out, "once war has started, no other line of demarcation is at once so clear . . . so easily defined, and understood as the line between not using and using nuclear weapons."[26] Crossing this threshold is a most serious escalating step because it involves an obvious qualitative change in the intensity of military operations. But it is interesting to note that it occurs less than halfway up Kahn's ladder. Beyond it lie, first, the 'Central Sanctuary' threshold above which the homelands of the superpowers are attacked if only by exemplary nuclear strikes; second, the 'Central War' threshold, above which nuclear exchanges become more widespread and 'counter-force' targets are destroyed; and third, the 'city targetting' threshold beyond which cities are targetted and the war approaches an all-out, total conflict.

Apart from the fact that an escalation ladder provides us with a very useful framework for thinking about different kinds of limited war, an escalation ladder can be regarded as a set of sophisticated rules for those who wish to engage in such a war. It represents an attempt to build artificial, but psychologically important, limitations into a conflict so that the belligerents can more easily keep to particular levels of violence. If both sides are aware of the idea of an escalation ladder, then during a war, instead of responding wildly and dangerously to each other's initiatives they can make calculated and appropriate responses which do not unwittingly violate thresholds.

Obviously for the rules to be of any use they have to be appreciated by both sides. It is all very well for Herman Kahn to try and put the stops into warfare by devising an escalation ladder, but what is obviously critical is what the Soviets think about it. It takes two to play a game, and if one side neither acknowledges nor approves of the rules, then a game is out of the question. So far the Soviets have been sceptical about ideas of controlling limited wars, and they have been particularly scornful about the possibility of controlling wars in which the nuclear threshold has been crossed.

Many Western strategists share these Soviet doubts. They point out that military force is a blunt, crude instrument, better compared with the woodcutter's axe than the surgeon's scalpel. Inevitably, therefore, war is not usually a nicely calculated, precisely controlled, business. More frequently it is a bloody, messy, painful and savage affair which, because it inflames the passions, provides an emotionally charged environment in which miscalculations and misperceptions flourish. The theory of controlled escalation ignores the crudity of the military instrument, and seriously underplays the psychological pressure on each belligerent to misread his enemy's moves and to misjudge his own.

The reluctance of Soviet strategists to accept the idea of an escalation ladder suggests that it may be difficult to contain a limited war in which they are directly involved, but as Kahn has pointed out, just because they say they will not play does not mean that they will not play. If the likely alternative is a mutually disastrous global war, the Soviet leadership may feel a powerful incentive to see virtues in even the most distasteful rules.

The ladder concept is an illuminating one, but in so far as it suggests equally spaced and well-separated rungs which can only be climbed by deliberate effort, it may be a dangerous one. Arguably, warfare is not the sort of activity which lends itself to the rather precise classifications implied by a 'ladder'. Perhaps a more appropriate metaphor is that of a *slide*. Certainly there are many defence analysts who would argue that once the nuclear threshold is crossed, it is a very slippery slope from tactual nuclear to strategic nuclear war.

Limited war, particularly limited nuclear war, does not have much to recommend it. The best that can be said for it is that it is better than its alternative, total war, and for that reason alone we must prepare for it. But everyone should realise that to engage in limited war is to unleash dangerous and inherently unmanageable forces against which even the most sophisticated escalation strategies are but flimsy barriers. Though it is primarily a heuristic rather than operational concept, escalation may encourage the myth that war is a more manageable process than it really is. If we take it seriously — and we must — it is because the illusion of manageability is better than the assumption of uncontrollability; in truth, very much better.

FIGURE 1

AN ESCALATION LADDER

A Generalized (or Abstract) Scenario

——————————————— AFTERMATHS ———————————————

CIVILIAN CENTRAL WARS
- 44. Spasm or Insensate War
- 43. Some Other Kinds of Controlled General War
- 42. Civilian Devastation Attack
- 41. Augmented Disarming Attack
- 40. Countervalue Salvo
- 39. Slow-Motion Countercity War

(CITY TARGETING THRESHOLD)

MILITARY CENTRAL WARS
- 38. Unmodified Counterforce Attack
- 37. Counterforce-with-Avoidance Attack
- 36. Constrained Disarming Attack
- 35. Constrained Force-Reduction Salvo
- 34. Slow-Motion Counterforce War
- 33. Slow-Motion Counter-"Property" War
- 32. Formal Declaration of "General" War

(CENTRAL WAR THRESHOLD)

EXEMPLARY CENTRAL ATTACKS
- 31. Reciprocal Reprisals
- 30. Complete Evacuation (Approximately 95 per cent)
- 29. Exemplary Attacks on Population
- 28. Exemplary Attacks Against Property
- 27. Exemplary Attack on Military
- 26. Demonstration Attack on Zone of Interior

(CENTRAL SANCTUARY THRESHOLD)

BIZARRE CRISES
- 25. Evacuation (Approximately 70 per cent)
- 24. Unusual, Provocative and Significant Countermeasures
- 23. Local Nuclear War — Military
- 22. Declaration of Limited Nuclear War
- 21. Local Nuclear War — Exemplary

(NO NUCLEAR USE THRESHOLD)

INTENSE CRISES
- 20. "Peaceful" World-Wide Embargo or Blockade
- 19. "Justifiable" Counterforce Attack
- 18. Spectacular Show or Demonstration of Force
- 17. Limited Evacuation (Approximately 20 per cent)
- 16. Nuclear "Ultimatums"
- 15. Barely Nuclear War
- 14. Declaration of Limited Conventional War
- 13. Large Compound Escalation
- 12. Large Conventional War (or Actions)
- 11. Super-Ready Status
- 10. Provocative Breaking Off of Diplomatic Relations

(NUCLEAR WAR IS UNTHINKABLE THRESHOLD)

TRADITIONAL CRISES
- 9. Dramatic Military Confrontations
- 8. Harassing Acts of Violence
- 7. "Legal" Harassment — Retortions
- 6. Significant Mobilization
- 5. Show of Force
- 4. Hardening of Positions — Confrontation of Wills

(DON'T ROCK THE BOAT THRESHOLD)

SUBCRISIS MANEUVERING
- 3. Solemn and Formal Declarations
- 2. Political, Economic, and Diplomatic Gestures
- 1. Ostensible Crisis

——————————— DISAGREEMENT — COLD WAR ———————————

Reprinted by permission of the publishers from H. Kahn, *On Escalation*, (London: Pall Mall Press, 1965; New York: F.A. Praeger).

Notes

1. Burdick, Eugene L., and Wheeler, J., *Fail-safe,* (London: Hutchinson, 1963).
2. For an imaginative treatment of these problems, see Peter Bryant, *Red Alert* (London: Ace Books, 1958). This is an exciting novel about a sick and disturbed SAC general who decides to wage his own private war on the Soviet Union.
3. See B. Brodie, "Unlimited Weapons and Limited War", *The Reporter,* 18 November 1954, and W.W. Kaufmann (ed)., *Military Policy and National Security* (Princeton, N.Jn: Princeton University Press, 1956), pp. 28, 38.
4. W.W. Kaufmann, *The McNamara Strategy* (New York: Harper and Row, 1964), p.131.
5. B. Brodie, *Strategy in the Missile Age* (Princeton, N.J.: Princeton University Press, 1959), p.307.
6. H. Kahn. *On Thermonuclear War* (London: Oxford University Press, 1960).
7. N. Shute, *On The Beach* (London: Heinemann, 1966). This gripping story described how, after a major strategic exchange, radioactive fall-out spread throughout the world, poisoning and killing the entire human race.
8. See, for example, the devastating review by Newman, J.R. review of *On Thermonuclear War, Scientific American* CCIV 3 (Mar. 1961) p.200.
9. Nevins, A., ed. *Strategy of Peace. John F. Kennedy* (London: Hamish Hamilton, 1960) p.184.
10. Nixon, Richard M. "U.S. Foreign Policy for the 1970's: A New Strategy for Peace", *The Department of State Bulletin,* 9.3.1970, p.319.
11. See Schlesinger, J., "Flexible Strategic Options and Deterrence", *Survival* XVI 2, (Mar/Apr 1974) pp. 86-90.
12. R.S. McNamara, Testimony before the House Armed Services Committee, 30 January 1963.
13. R.S. McNamara, Address at the Commencement Exercises, University of Michigan, Ann Arbor, June 16, 1962.
14. Howard, M. "The classical Strategists", 'Problems of Modern Strategy I', *Adelphi Paper* 54 (London: International Institute for Strategic Studies, 1969), p.25.
15. For a brief discussion of this point, see F.E. Osgood, "The Reappraisal of Limited War", in 'Problems of Modern Strategy', Part I, *Adelphi Paper,* No. 54 (London: International Institute for Strategic Studies, 1969), p.41.
16. Leo Szillard, "Disarmament and the Problem of Peace", *Bulletin of the Atomic Scientists* XI, October 1955, pp.297-307.
17. See K. Knorr and T. Read (eds). *Limited Strategic War* (London: Pall Mall Press, 1962).
18. *Ibid.,* pp.32-66.
19. B. Brodie, *op. cit.* p.310.
20. R.E. Osgood, *op. cit.,* p.41.
21. A.J.P. Taylor, *Europe: Grandeur and Decline* (London: Pelican Books, 1967), p.94.
22. B. Brodie, *op. cit.,* p.315.
23. *On Escalation,* (London: Pall Mall Press, 1965) pp. 10-15.
24. *Ibid.* p.11.
25. T.C. Schelling, *The Strategy of Conflict* (Cambridge, Mass: Harvard University Press, 1960), pp.186-201.
26. H. Kahn, *op. cit.* p.95.

7 REVOLUTIONARY WARFARE

John Baylis

Despite the controversy in the literature on strategic studies over the utility or obsolescence of military power as an instrument of state policy in international relations, most contemporary writers agree that as far as intra-state conflict is concerned, the phenomenon of revolutionary warfare would seem to be proliferating and is seen (by many dissident groups) as an effective way of obtaining their objectives. Even Walter Millis, one of the strongest proponents of the view that military power no longer performs its traditional functions, explicitly excludes revolutionary warfare from the category of obsolescence, arguing that the very abolition of the traditional "war system" which he expects, is likely in fact to give larger scope to guerrilla warfare and civil disorders.[1] Similarly, Hannah Arendt, writing in 1963, argued that with the emergence of the Cold War and nuclear stalemate between the superpowers and their alliances, revolutionary warfare was about to replace inter-state wars "which had become obsolete because of the threat of total annihilation which they posed."[2]

Whether the view that the incidence of this "new form of war" is in fact increasing in the contemporary world is true or not is difficult to determine with any precision. Numerous attempts have been made to support the contention that it is, by quantitative methods.[3] In a statement before the Senate Foreign Relations Committee in May 1966, for example, the United States Secretary of Defence, Robert McNamara, claimed that

> in the last eight years alone there have been no less than 164 internationally significant outbreaks of violence . . . and the trend of such conflicts is growing rather than diminishing. At the beginning of 1958 there were 23 prolonged insurgencies going on about the world. As of February 1966 there were 40. Further, the total number of outbreaks of violence has increased each year: in 1958, there were 34, in 1965 there were 58.[4]

Despite the statistics such as these which suggest that revolutionary wars are increasing in the contemporary world, looked at in historical terms, judgements are more difficult to make.

The major difficulty of the analyst arises from what Laurence Martin calls the problem of "commensurability"; that is, of comparing modern insurgency with guerrilla wars of the past.[5] Certainly many features of insurgency as we know it today owe a great deal to past experience, particularly in terms of the irregular military operations employed.[6]

The harassing and hit-and-run tactics of guerrilla warfare have been used throughout history as the instrument of the weak against the strong. Such techniques were used, for example, by Emperor Hang of the Han dynasty against the Miao dynasty under the leadership of Tsi Yao in about 3,600 BC. They were used in the Peloponnesian wars between 431 and 404 BC and were later perceptively analysed in some depth in the sixth century BC by the Chinese tactician and military historian Sun Tzu in his study of *The Art of War*.[7] The term 'guerrilla' or small war, however, was first coined by the Spanish during the Peninsula War from 1808 to 1814, when the defeated Spanish forces broke up into small units to harass the Napoleonic armies as they attempted to expel the English from the Iberian Peninsula.

Although after the Peninsula War similar irregular tactics were used by the Greeks against the Ottoman Empire (1821-27), in the Mexican City compaign (1847), in the American Civil War (1861-65) and in the Boer War (1898-1902) as well as in numerous other campaigns, the next milestone in the evolution of guerrilla warfare came with T.E. Lawrence's campaigns against the Turks in the First World War. Although such writers as Sun Tzu, Carl von Clausewitz and Lenin had written about guerrilla warfare before him, Lawrence was the first man to reduce guerrilla warfare to a set of principles and to articulate clearly the nature of the tactics he used in his campaigns. In *The Seven Pillars of Wisdom* he prosaically describes guerrilla warfare in terms of "an influence, an idea, a thing intangible, invulnerable, without front or back, drifting about like a gas."[8] Lawrence saw the problem of his war in terms of three categories of related variables, "the algebraical element of things, a biological element of lives, and psychological element of ideas."[9] In so doing he was moving away from the traditional notion of guerrilla warfare as a purely military phenomenon and, like Clausewitz before him, laying more stress on the political dimensions of such conflict. To Lawrence only a third of war was a military problem and the nature even of this "technical" aspect depended fundamentally on the political two-thirds.

Whether consciously or not, these ideas of Lawrence were developed in a great deal more depth and sophistication by Mao Tse-tung on the basis of his experience against Chiang Kai-shek and the invading Japanese armies. In his writings in the 1930s, in particular, Mao blended the teachings of past theorists including Clausewitz and Sun Tzu together with his own experience and Marxist-Leninist beliefs into a relatively coherent body of politico-military theory. It is this strategy for revolution which has become the basis of the writings of most contemporary revolutionary leaders from Vo Nguyen Giap to Che

Guevara and Carlos Marighella.

Although the resultant doctrine owes a great debt to the long history and development of guerrilla warfare, the fusion of political and military activity into a distinctive revolutionary strategy distinguishes it qualitatively from the purely military techniques of guerrilla warfare of the past. Any attempt therefore to compare modern revolutionary warfare with guerrilla wars in history is inevitably very difficult.

The problem of "commensurability" which this change in the essence of the phenomenon has brought is not made any easier either by the frequent use of the term guerrilla warfare to refer to revolutionary conflicts which combine both political and military dimensions. Very often in the literature on the subject,[10] guerrilla warfare is used interchangeably with insurgency and revolutionary warfare as though they were synonymous. It may therefore be useful at this stage to define these terms more precisely.

Definitions

To Chalmers Johnson, revolution involves "a sweeping, fundamental change in political organisation, social structure, economic property control, and the predominant myth of social order, thus indicating a major break in the continuity of development."[11] 'Revolution' used in this sense therefore is a generic term encompassing all of those different means by which non-governmental groups within a state attempt to capture power and establish new political, social and economic structures. The terms 'insurgency' and 'revolutionary warfare' refer to one form of revolutionary activity.[12] They are used to describe a particular variety of revolutionary action which involves a protracted struggle in which irregular military tactics are combined with psychological and political operations to produce a new ideological system or political structure. 'Guerrilla warfare' on the other hand has a narrower meaning. It refers to a particular kind of military or para-military operation performed by irregular, predominantly indigenous forces, which can, but need not necessarily, be used to achieve the revolutionary objective.[13]

Strictly speaking therefore, the terms 'insurgency' and 'revolutionary warfare' are not as all-embracing in their meaning as the term 'revolution' nor as restricted in their meaning as the term 'guerrilla warfare'. The terms refer to one of a number of techniques used to achieve revolutionary change which is characterized by guerrilla military tactics which are employed in conjunction with other political, social, economic and psychological instruments.

Insurgency therefore, is a multi-faceted activity in which conflict takes place on different planes very often simultaneously. One writer on the subject has coined the phrase the 'fourth dimension' of warfare to distinguish the fundamental differences between conventional war and revoltuionary war.[14] Conventional war focuses its attention on military considerations in terms of land, sea and air operations. Revolutionary warfare on the other hand is concerned much more with the fourth-dimensional qualities of a political, social, economic and cultural nature which in many ways weigh more heavily in the scales of victory than material quantities.[15]

This view of insurgency is a particularly suggestive and useful one because it highlights the different planes on which conflict takes place and demonstrates the essential qualitative difference between conventional military operations and revolutionary insurgent activity. Extending this interpretation a little further it is possible to identify a number of different battlefronts of revolutionary warfare, each of which is supplementary to the others and each designed to contribute to the achievement of the over-riding revolutionary objective. These battlefronts include the political, socio-economic, cultural and ideological, psychological and international planes, on which the struggle for power between the revolutionary forces and those of the authorities and its supporters takes place.[16]

The Political Dimension

Echoing Clausewitz, Mao emphasizes in his writings the essential relationship between politics and war, a relationship in which military operations must be subordinated to political direction. "War cannot for a single moment be separated from politics, says Mao, ". . . politics is war without bloodshed, while war is politics with bloodshed".[17] All operations undertaken by the revolutionary forces, and particularly those in the military field, must be designed, Mao argues, to meet distinctly political objectives. This emphasis which Mao puts on the fundamental importance of political control is shared by most other writers and is a dominant theme running through revolutionary theory.

For Mao, as for some of the other revolutionary thinkers, the essential need for political control necessitates, in organizational terms, the subordination of the military to the political infrastructure. Both Mao and Giap emphasize in their writings the need for a dual structure in which the cell system will provide the vital political direction of the guerrilla movement.[18] In practice also the experience of successful revolutions tend to indicate that in most circumstances, guerrilla forces require the active support of a political organisation outside their own ranks but still dedicated to their cause. Most rural guerrilla movements therefore in the initial stages of their revolutionary development attempt to establish an urban arm capable of providing them, either by legal or illicit means, with the assistance they require, "from the placing of bombs to defending accused revolutionaries in the courts of law".[19] Both the history of the NLF in Vietnam and the Min Yuen organisation in Malaya would seem to demonstrate the value of such a

135

political structure.[20]

The notion of a dual organisation in which the political structure is separated from, and superior to, the military structure is not, however, shared by all revolutionary theorists, particularly those with experience in Latin America. Although Regis Debray in his study of *Revolution in the Revolution* does not advocate military autonomy from politics as some have alleged, he does nevertheless emphasize the essential fusion of political and military authority. "Under certain circumstances", Debray argues, "the political and military are not separate but form one organic whole consisting of the people's army, whose nucleus is the guerrilla army."[21] He, like Guevara, even goes as far as to suggest that the principal stress in any revolutionary campaign must be laid on the development of guerrilla warfare and not on the strengthening of existing parties. Instead of the dual authority therefore represented by Mao and Chu Teh in China and Ho Chi Minh and Giap in Vietnam therefore, Cuban experience pointed to the importance of a fusion of political and military authority in one man — Fidel Castro.

Whatever the relationship between political and military organisation, however, for most theorists and practitioners of revolutionary warfare, the major political objective of the insurgent movement is to gain popular support; to win over the population to the side of the revolutionary forces. The population is seen as the key to the entire struggle. Without the consent and active support of the people, the guerrilla would be little more than a bandit and as such would be unlikely to survive for very long. As one writer puts it, "the defeat of the military enemy, the overthrow of the government are secondary tasks, in the sense that they come later. The primary effort of the guerrilla is to mobilize the population, without whose consent no government can stand for a day."[22]

From the insurgents' point of view, the objective is both to alienate the population from the government and more positively to win popular support for the revolutionary cause. Through popular sympathy the guerrilla forces can get the intelligence, the shelter, supplies and recruits so essential for the successful development of their campaign. In this sense the primacy of gaining civilian support dictates all aspects of the revolutionary struggle. In Mao's often — quoted phrase, "the guerrilla must be to the population as little fishes in the water." For the fish to survive the temperature of the water has to be right. Similarly for the guerrillas, to operate successfully the sympathy of the masses has to be secured. Largely because of the importance of this objective Mao, like other theorists, lays great stress on the correct behaviour of the insurgent forces towards the people. In his 'Rules of Discipline' and 'Eight points of Attention' he exhorts his forces amongst other things to pay for what they buy, not to damage crops, not to take liberties with the local women, and to help the population with their local problems.[23]

The method of gaining the confidence and support of the population by helping them and behaving correctly towards them is not, however, the only means of securing civilian loyalty to the revolutionary movement. Terror also under certain circumstances performs this function. Although, perhaps for obvious reasons, there is little discussion of the use of terror in the prescriptive literature on revolutionary warfare, in practice there would seem to be little doubt that both coercive and disruptive terror campaigns are often part of the repertoire of insurgent movements.[24] Intimidation and terrorism are used not only to publicize the movement, to demoralize the government, and to polarize society but also at times to ensure that people have no alternative but compliance, unless and until the government is able to protect them. On occasions such campaigns backfire, as they did during the Greek Civil War when the widespread use of terror by some Greek guerrilla leaders finally drove over half a million of what should have been their strongest supporters into the cities. One of the major reasons for the eventual defeat of the Communist forces was the alienation of large sections of the population caused by the terrorist campaign.

What discussion there is in the literature written by those who advocate revolutionary warfare tends to stress the utility of selective terrorism against alleged traitors to the movement. As two writers on revolutionary warfare have put it, "in order to be effective, terror must be regarded by the people as an extra-governmental effort to dispense justice long overdue, and it must have the effect of freeing the local communities from the felt restraints of coercive authority."[25] This sort of campaign would seem to be as popular in Northern Ireland in the early 1970s as it was in Vietnam in the late fifties and sixties. In Vietnam, about 13,000 local officials, landlords and informers are said to have been killed between 1957 and 1961 on the grounds that they were appointees of Diem and consequently "enemies of the people."[26] Similarly in Northern Ireland, over 200 people were assassinated between 1971 and 1973.[27]

Linked closely with the struggle for civilian loyalty in the multitude of forms that this takes, the revolutionary movement also engages in competition in the political arena with the authorities in as many ways as possible. One of the most important areas in which this conflict takes place is over the legitimacy of the governmental institutions. Most insurgent movements waste little time in establishing not only a local administrative network but also parallel governmental institutions which act as a focal point in the battle for the loyalty of the public. Such organs help both to provide a degree of legitimacy for the revolutionary forces and to break the monopoly of legitimacy held by the government. During the Chinese Civil War, for example, Mao attempted to create a state within a state in his liberated zones. As Lin Piao recalled in 1965, "our base areas were in fact a state in miniature . . . a grand rehearsal in preparation for a nationwide victory."[28] The revolutionary political organs were carefully fashioned in China to establish an alternative apparatus of power to challenge Chiang Kai-shek's government. Similarly in the IRA campaign in Ireland in 1919, the Sinn Fein party's legislative assembly, the Dail Eireann, was put forward as a "parallel hierarchy" of administration which would compete for legitimacy with the British Government.[29]

The Military Dimension

Conflict on the political front particularly in terms of the struggle for public support is of primary importance in dictating the military strategy and tactics of the revolutionary movement. As Peter Paret points out, "military power plays essentially a secondary role; the decisive factor is the population, which is both the strongest force in the struggle as well as its primary object."[30] Paret correctly assesses that military action is both designed to achieve population support and its very nature is largely determined by such support. Intelligence, mobility, logistic freedom and surprise are all important features of guerrilla warfare and all are largely dependent on the degree of public sympathy and support the insurgent can secure.

Through his political infrastructure which binds the insurgent to the population he is able to obtain the vital information which he needs. Knowledge of what the enemy is doing or planning to do at all times enables the guerrilla forces to fight at moments of their own choosing; it guarantees them superiority at the moment of attack; and it enables them to fade away before superior counter-insurgent forces can be brought against them. As the late Bernard Fall points out, in the first Indo-China war nearly all French troop movements in Vietnam took place in a "fish bowl".[31] Because of the difficulty of moving forces at night, even the smallest movement of troops, tanks and aircraft by day was immediately noticed by the population and brought to the notice of the Viet Minh agents.[32]

As well as intelligence, popular support also provides the insurgent with food, shelter, communications, stretcher bearers and labour for various tasks, all of which go to make up "that ubiquitous word of guerrilla catechisms : mobility."[33] Knowledge of the terrain, light weapons and the advantages deriving from the public sympathy enable the insurgent to out-manoeuvre cumbersome conventional forces. Like a flea, the guerrilla "bites, hops and bites again, nimbly avoiding the foot that would crush him."[34] It is this important attribute of mobility in conjunction with good intelligence which provides the guerrilla with his vital advantage of surprise over the regular forces of his opponent. Using his attributes the guerrilla can initiate a lightning attack at times and places of his own choosing and then just as quickly disperse before the government forces can locate him and bring the weight of their forces against him.

Summing up these characteristic features, Giap defines guerrilla warfare as

> a form of fighting by the masses of a weak and badly equipped country against an aggressive army with better equipment and techniques. This is the way of fighting a revolution. Guerrillas rely on heroic spirit to triumph over modern weapons, avoiding the enemy when he is stronger and attacking him when he is weaker, now scattering, now regrouping, now wearing out, now exterminating the enemy, they are determined to fight everywhere so that wherever the enemy goes he is submerged in a sea of armed people who hit back at him, thus undermining his spirit and exhausting his forces.[35]

Because guerrilla warfare is the war of the weak, an essential feature of guerrilla strategy must be an emphasis on the protracted nature of the struggle. Revolutionary wars are generally, of necessity, wars of long duration. They are wars of attrition. The seeds of revolution take a long time to germinate and the roots and tendrils spread silently underground long before there are any overt signs of the new plant. "Then, suddenly one day, like new wheat springing up in a cultivated field, there is a blaze of colour, an overnight growth: the rebels are there and everywhere."[36]

If the guerrilla forces are to be successful they have to avoid extermination. The problem is not to get the war over with but rather to keep it going. The object, particularly in the early days of the conflict, is how to avoid a military decision. The emphasis is on hit-and-run tactics in order to live to fight another day. For Mao, the problem was how to organize space to yield time.[37]

Using the vast territory of China, Mao established liberated or base areas initially in the more inaccessible regions to avoid detection. Then, as time went on, and the strength of his forces increased, the base areas were expanded like ink blots in the rural areas to surround the towns.

A similar attempt to organize space to yield time was made by Castro and Guevara in Cuba. Here, however, because of the difference in size and terrain between Cuba and China, less emphasis was placed on permanent bases and greater attention was given to mobility. The Fidelistas developed the *foco* idea, which stressed the importance of strategic mobile forces constantly changing their location to avoid detection and surprise the enemy. The destruction of Guevara's fixed base in the Hombrito valley in October 1957 taught the Cubans, early in the war, that elaborate permanent bases, even in inaccessible regions, were vulnerable to detection by Batista's forces. The lesson was that the guerrilla forces should take with them everything they needed. According to the *foco* concept, therefore, the guerrilla base was the territory within which the guerrilla happened to be moving; "it goes where he goes. In the initial stage, the base of support is in the guerrilla fighter's knapsack."[38] It was only during the later stages of the war that the Cuban revolutionaries established fixed security zones in the centre of the Sierra Maestra from which to operate against Batista's forces.

More recently the *foco* idea has been taken up by urban guerrilla theorists like Carlos Marighella. For Marighella the city is not 'the graveyard of the guerrilla', as Castro described it.[39] Through the *foco* operating in the back streets and tenements of the cities, the insurgent movement is able to survive and fight a war of attrition against the authorities similar to that fought by guerrillas operating in rural areas.

Whatever the environment of conflict or the method of development, according to most of the revolutionary theorists, protracted war is split into a number of, (usually three), "strategic stages". In the first, the "strategic defensive" or conspiracy phase, the insurgent builds the foundations of revolutionary movement by establishing and expanding his political infrastructure, building up popular support and through small-scale raids capturing weapons to conduct the conflict. In the second phase, the "strategic stalemate" or equilibrium stage, the insurgent continues to expand his cell structure in ink-blot-like fashion and concentrates on guerrilla tactics to wear the enemy down and redress the balance of forces. Once the process of consolidation and the building up of revolutionary forces has taken place, the stage of the "strategic counter-offensive" is reached, when the focus of insurgent operations changes to mobile warfare and the enemy is defeated in conventional pitched battles.

Although in theory the three-stage developmental model has been accepted by most revolutionary movements, the Chinese Civil War and the second Indo China War, which ended in Communist victory in 1975, are the only conflicts to have gone through the three phases. Even Giap's victory in 1954 at Dien Bien Phu, however effective psychologically, only eliminated a small proportion of total French armed strength. It was not the third phase in the strict sense in which Mao meant it. Likewise in Algeria, Cyprus and Palestine, insurgent 'victory' was achieved, not through the military defeat of the enemy but by making the territories too unprofitable and politically difficult for the colonial forces to remain.[40]

Although guerrilla actions therefore will have certain obvious military objectives such as those to obtain weapons, to inflict casualties and to force the enemy to over-extend his lines so that his communications may be disrupted, the military role, while vital, is only incidental to the political mission. Although guerrilla tactics are the most overt symbol of revolutionary war, conflict on other planes often has as great or even greater, an impact, than military operations on the final outcome of the struggle.[41]

The Socio-Economic Dimension

The object of gaining popular support and at the same time creating what Carlos Marighella, the Brazilian revolutionary leader,[42] calls a "climate of collapse" is further augmented by the simultaneous struggle between the rival social and economic systems. The insurgent movement invariably emphasizes the injustices and corruption of the prevailing system and sets up in the areas under its control new alternative economic and social institutions representing the values of the revolutionary forces. The struggle, as on other planes, takes both a negative and positive form.

On the negative side and insurgents attempt to gain popular support through the exploitation of various causes, very often emanating from particular social and economic grievances. Most theorists agree that if the revolution is to be successful such grievances have to exist, making the state "ripe for revolution". Once again, however, differences of opinion exist in revolutionary theory between those, like Mao, who believe that the "objective conditions" must exist so that all that is needed is a nucleus to organise revolutionary activity; and those who believe, like Guevara, that "it is not necessary to wait until all the conditions for revolution are fulfilled; the insurrection can create them."[43] The difference is essentially one of emphasis, as Guevara himself explains. "Naturally, it is not to be thought that all the conditions for revolution are going to be created through the impulse given to them by guerrilla activity. It must always be kept in mind that there is a necessary minimum without which the establishment and consolidation of the first centre (of rebellion) is not practicable."[44]

Whether or not the country has to be on the verge of revolution or whether this situation can be created by the careful manipulation of the necessary "minimum conditions" which exist, there is general agreement that the first task in the preparation of the revolutionary campaign is the detailed appraisal of the society in which the conflict is to take place. Mao and Giap give particular attention in their writings to the need to analyse the social and economic as well as the political structure of the community. Both emphasize the need to understand the social and economic fabric of society in order to shape revolutionary activity to exploit the contradictions which exist. A particularly good illustration of the importance of such a detailed social survey in Syria is given by T.E. Lawrence in *The Seven Pillars of Wisdom* when he says:

> . . . nature had so divided the country in zones. Man, elaborating nature, had given to her compartments an additional complexity. Each of these main . . . divisions was crossed and walled off artifically into communities at odds. We had to gather them into our hands for offensive action against the Turks. Feisal's opportunities and difficulties lay in these political complications of Syria which we mentally arranged

in order like a social map. . . . During two years Feisal so
laboured daily, putting together and arranging in their natural
order the innumerable tiny pieces which made up Arabian
society and combining them into this one design of war against
the Turks.[45]

Besides the exploitation of the contradictions which analyses of this
sort provide, the insurgents more positively also compete with the
government through the economic and social infrastructure created in
their liberated areas which act as an alternative to those of the authorities. By smashing the power of the landlord class in particular both Mao
and Ho Chi Minh attempted to build up in the areas under their control what they believed to be a more egalitarian society and a more
centralized system of economic organization in line with the values of
their ideological beliefs. Great stress was constantly laid in their
propoganda on the inherent advantages of such a communist social
and economic system over that of their opponents.

Parallel to this objective of providing a competing socio-economic
structure is also the vital need to establish an economic base to support
the war effort.[46] During the Cuban revolution Castro, for example
managed to secure control over the entire coffee crop in Northern
Oriente, worth sixty million dollars, which he allowed to go to market
and then subsequently collected taxes on the crop for the benefit of
the guerrilla movement.

Besides building up their own economy insurgent movements
often have as one of their main targets those institutions which provide
the economic strength of their adversaries.[47] Attacks on oil refineries,
ports and communication facilities, and on institutions closely related
to the commercial life of the state generally, are all designed to create
economic chaos, discourage investment and make the economic burden
of the war intolerable. Although largely unsuccessful, this was the aim
of the terrorists in Malaya who attempted to disrupt the economy
through attacks on the rubber plantations so vital for the economic
stability and prosperity of the state.

The Cultural and Ideological Dimension

Linked very closely with the conflict on the political, social and
economic planes is the struggle for cultural supremacy; the struggle
between the existing value system of society and the values of the new
order.[48]

The insurgent often attempts to undermine the governing authorities and its supporters by emphasizing the worst features of the prevailing system. the NLF in Vietnam concentrated much of their energies on highlighting the corruption, the exploitation, the torture, the
black-marketeering, the prostitution and the inequality characteristic of

South Vietnamese society.[49] At the same time they portrayed their own movement in terms of the values of honesty, purity, selflessness and self-sacrifice, poverty and discipline. Douglas Pike, in an analysis of the Viet Cong, argues that the NLF attempted to characterize their own movement as one of "great moralism".

> Virtue was the golden word. The cause consisted of moral duties based on moral absolutes, guided by moral imperatives; duty itself, under a virtuous leadership, was the highest value. Preoccupation with law and legality was not simply an effort to establish legitimacy but a justification of the moral correctness of the cause. Because he was virtuous, the NLF supporter was morally superior to the enemy and hence politically and militarily superior. The moralism manifested itself in a spirit of sincerity; the NLF surrounded its words and actions with an aura of sincerity.[50]

A similar campaign was waged by Castro and Guevara in Cuba. During the revolution they highlighted the repression and tyrany of the Batista regime in their writings, broadcasts and interviews and in contrast stressed the justice and virtue of their own cause.

The Psychological Dimension

A large part of the struggle on the political, military, socio-economic and cultural planes is linked closely with the "battle for the minds of the population". Great stress is placed in both revolutionary theory and practice on the importance of using propaganda techniques to win over popular support and to discredit the government. The importance of this component of revolutionary activity is demonstrated in Mao's emphasis on time, space and will.[51] The insurgent, he argues, must trade space for time, and time must be used to produce will.

The need for an effective strategy to fight the psychological war is spelled out as much in the writings on urban guerrilla warfare as it is on rural guerrilla campaigns. Carlos Marighella sees the main object of the terrorist operations as being the creation of a "climate of collapse" in which the morale of both the civilian and military elements of the government slowly disintegrates leaving a paralysis which the revolutionary movement can exploit.[52] This was precisely the object of the proselytising programme known as *binh van,* used with some success by the NLF in Vietnam against the ARVN and GVN civil servants.[53] As an NLF document captured in 1961 points out, the purpose of *binh van* was "to disorganize the enemy forces and build up support within the enemy's ranks and to undermine the last leg on which it stands."[54]

In one sense everything that the insurgent does is designed to have a psychological impact. Military actions in particular are viewed as being more important in psychological, and therefore political terms, than they are in purely military terms. For this reason Robert Taber sees the guerrilla fighter as "primarily a propogandist, an agitator, a disseminator of the revolutionary idea, who uses the struggle itself − the actual physical conflict − as an instrument of agitation."[55] The military struggle is the catalyst. Through what Marighella calls the "strategy of militarization", the insurgents attempt to raise the level of revolutionary anticipation and popular participation to create the right psychological environment for the revolutionary movement to flourish and for the final destruction of the government. In this sense, each battle is a lesson designed to demonstrate the impotence of the army and to discredit the government that employs it. Each military campaign is a text, intended to raise the level of revolutionary awareness.

The International Dimension

Quite apart from the psychological conflict for allegiance domestically, the insurgent also often utilizes the international stage to gain support for his cause. The propaganda war thus is frequently waged outside the borders of the country to mobilize support in order to bring pressure on the indigenous government, and those of the supporting states. The rebel casts himself in the role of David and portrays his enemy as Goliath in order to play on the sympathies and sense of justice of spectators of the conflict in other countries. The aim is to create the picture of a courageous people fighting for independence against the "monstrous forces of tyranny and oppression."

Perhaps the most successful proponent of the struggle on the international plane has been Vo Nguyen Giap. In *People's War, People's Army* he explains the technique of mobilizing world support which proved to be so vital against the French and the Americans. "In our foreign policy," he says, "efforts had to be made to win over the support of progressive people throughout the world" and particularly to influence public opinion in the enemy's country.[56] Although it is difficult to assess precisely how successful Giap's campaigns were, it seems likely that they did play some part in helping to mobilize international support for Vietnam and perhaps also had an impact on domestic opinion in France and the United States. In both cases the North Vietnamese campaign directed at the populations of both states may not have played a significant part in arousing large-scale support for the North Vietnamese. It would seem, however, that it did help to encourage a questioning of the war and a degree of demoralization with the war, which was in the last resort decisive in forcing both countries to withdraw from Vietnam.

In both cases victory for the insurgents was achieved because the war became unpopular, expensive and damaging to the prestige of the state.

In both cases, Giap successfully achieved his objective of making the war too great a political embarrassment to be sustained either domestically or on the world stage.

Although Mao emphasizes the importance of self-reliance, outside support, both moral and material, particularly from neighbouring states is often of great importance to struggling revolutionary movements. The support given to Vietnamese Communist forces in the first and second Indo-Chinese wars by the Soviet Union and China obviously played a great part in sustaining the revolutionary forces in their campaigns against the French and Americans. The sanctuary and supply lines afforded by Cambodia and Laos were also a significant advantage to the Vietnamese insurgents. In contrast the failure of Communist forces in Malaya was, in part at least, due to their failure to get large-scale outside aid and the geographical isolation of the country. Similarly, once outside support through Yugoslavia to the Greek Communist forces was cut off in 1948 following the dispute between Tito and Stalin, the fortunes of the Greek insurgents also declined dramatically.

Counter-insurgency

In the same way that revolutionary experience has spawned a vast literature of books and articles on the theory of insurgency so also the experience of operations against guerrilla forces has resulted in attempts to build up the general principles of counter-revolutionary warfare.

On the basis of their understanding, particularly of operations in the Philippines and Malaya writers such as McCuen, Thompson, Galula, Paret and Shy have established similar theories based, like the theories of insurgency, on the orchestration of political and military operations designed to win back or win over and secure, the allegiance of the population.[57]

To these writers President Magsaysay's civil–military strategy in the Philippines and Templer's strategy built on the foundation of the Brigg's Plan in Malaya demonstrated clearly the multi-dimensional nature and different battlefronts not only of revolutionary warfare but also of counter-insurgency operations as well. In each case success for the counter-revolutionary forces was achieved through the utilization of unified over-all strategic framework which dealt with each of the different dimensions of the conflict. To John J. McCuen in particular, such experience demonstrated that "the conduct of conter-revolutionary warfare is a highly complex operation, requiring the unification of diverse agencies, interests and concepts."[58]

Most theorists agree that, like insurgency, the central objective must be civilian loyalty which can only be secured by an interlocking system of actions on different planes which "drains the water from the fish", which isolates the insurgents from the population, and which secures the allegiance of the people. This is the central theme of much of Sir Robert Thompson's writing on counter-insurgency warfare.[59] Writing on the basis of his experience of the Malayan emergency, Thompson, a committed counter-revolutionary, established a unified strategy contained in his famous five principles designed as a guide to be followed by counter-insurgent forces in other theatres. According to this general framework Thompson prescribes that: the government should have a clear political aim; it should function in accordance with law; it should have an overall plan containing not only the military measures but also the political, social, economic, administrative, police and other measures needed; it must give priority to defeating political subversion, not the guerrillas; and in the guerrilla phase of an insurgency, it must secure its base areas first.[60]

Despite the importance or dominance of political considerations and the emphasis on the unification of the diverse strands of counter-insurgent operations, perhaps the most important characteristic of Thompson's writing in his recognition of the vital relationship between theory and practice. Thompson, like Mao, acknowledges that to be successful theory has to be carefully applied and adjusted to meet the particular conditions of individual states. Despite the attempt by Lin Piao and others to transfer Mao's concept of 'people's war' to the international stage and to proclaim its universal applicability, Mao himself stresses the need for flexibility and the vital importance of the application of general principles to the special circumstances of particular situations. As Mao explains,

> the difference in circumstances determines the difference in guiding laws of war; the difference of time, place and character. The laws of war in each historical stage have their characteristics and cannot be mechanically applied in a different age. All guiding laws of war develop as history develops and as war develops; nothing remains changeless".[61]

Regardless of the propaganda claims made for their own theories much of the success in practice of Giap and Castro stemmed from the way they modified and adapted Mao's theories to their own revolutions.[62]

Robert Thompson, particularly in his writings about American experience in Vietnam, recognises that the same is true of counter-revolutionary theory and practice.[63] He claims, with some justification, that many of the problems faced by the Americans in Vietnam stemmed from their attempts to introduce a number of the ideas and techniques, which had proved useful in the Philippines and Malaya, to Vietnam without taking into account the fundamental differences of the countries. Differences such as those of political culture and political control; of history; of terrain and geography; and of racial and religious

146

composition. The Strategic Hamlet programme in particular, introduced by Diem, was a direct attempt to isolate the guerrillas from the population and win their confidence on the lines of the Briggs Plan used in Malaya. Like other aspects of American and South Vietnamese strategy, however, the Strategic Hamlet Programme, particularly in its initial operation, was not geared to the realities of Vietnamese life. One of the earliest campaigns, Operation Sunrise, was established in Binh Duong Province in March 1966, a relatively isolated area with a small population which was controlled by the Viet Cong. Largely because of the traditional affinity of the Vietnamese peasant with his land, two-thirds of the population moved to the Strategic Hamlet had to be moved by force thus alienating them even further rather than gaining their support.

Another criticism made of American strategy in Vietnam is the retention of a largely conventional philosophy of war and the failure to weave together the different dimensions of their operations into an overall plan.[64] This is perhaps best illustrated by the communiqué issued by President Johnson and Prime Minister Ky after the Honolulu Conference in February 1966. In this communiqué both men agreed to give priority to the pacification programme, the "other war" as it was called, as though it was separate from the military conflict taking place. In this sense, although attempts were being made to deal with the other dimensions of the conflict there was a failure to integrate the various elements into a coherent unified strategy in line with the theoretical prescriptions of writers like Robert Thompson.

It is sometimes claimed, with perhaps less justification than in Vietnam, that there was a similar failure to adapt counter-insurgency strategy to meet the special circumstances of the conflict in Cyprus. General Grivas, the leader of the ENOSIS movement, was himself very critical of the way the British attempted to apply experience gained in Malaya and Kenya to the different conditions of Cyprus. "I laughed", Grivas claims, "when I read that General A or Brigadier B had come to Cyprus to put into operation the methods that had won him fame elsewhere. They could not understand that the Cyprus struggle was unique in motive, psychology and circumstances, and involved not a handful of insurrectionists but the whole people."[65] This may be so, but Grivas, of course, still failed to achieve his over-riding objective of securing union with Greece.

Although it is easy to prescribe, however, that counter-insurgent policy should adapt general principles to specific circumstances and should incorporate political measures which will isolate the guerrillas and restore strategic initiative to the defenders, it is less easy in practice to put such measures into operation. The application of theory to practice is obviously the hardest part. Northern Ireland clearly demonstrates the dilemmas of a government attempting to make political concessions to one faction of the population which results in the alienation of another antagonistic group in the community. The inherent hostility between the Catholic and Protestant communities makes the correct balance between the various components of the government's policy a particularly difficult one to achieve. The British Government in such a situation has had to engage in a delicate balancing act with the prospect of satisfying neither faction.

Relative Success and Future Prospects

A strong argument is often made that the very feature of counter-revolutionary warfare of introducing reforms and making concessions to disaffected groups to win popular support is in part at least the very thing the insurgents are seeking. Violence in this sense is seen to be successful in forcing the government to change its policies and give opponents what they want. Any assessment of the success of insurgent movements therefore in the post-war period perhaps ought to take into account not only situations in which the revolutionary forces have achieved their primary objective of overthrowing the government but also situations in which guerrilla operations have forced modification of government policies in line with some of the demands made by the insurgents. In Malaya, the Philippines and Cyprus, for example, the insurgents may not have achieved their main aims but there is little doubt that in each case substantial changes occurred largely because of the insurgent campaign. In Malaya and Cyprus, the British Government announced the independence of the respective colonies as part of their counter-insurgent programme and in the Philippines, the Magsaysay Government initiated a number of social and economic reforms, including land reform, which had been one of the main grievances of the Huk movement.

It would perhaps be wrong to conclude from this, however, that insurgency is the wave of the future suggested by some. In general each of the examples mentioned were relatively more successful from a counter-insurgent viewpoint than from the perspective of the insurgents themselves. Similarly there are many other examples, such as Greece, Kenya, Peru, Guatemala, Venezuela and Bolivia to demonstrate the relative failures of revolutionary warfare to offset the successes of China, Indo-China, Algeria and Cuba. It would nevertheless seem to be true that the heavy price in money, lives and prestige which governments have to invest and the compromises they often have to make in an attempt to alleviate the threat created by revolutionary forces, makes insurgency an attractive instrument for change in the eyes of many dissident groups.

This impression together with the continuing existence of political, social and economic grievances, favourable terrain, and the availability of outside support, is likely to mean that revolutionary warfare will continue to be an important feature of intra- and inter-state activity for the foreseeable future. The process of imitation which has spawned the new urban variety of insurgency would seem to suggest that for many groups, in both rich and poor, urban and rural countries, this form of military power is, and is likely to remain, a potent instrument by which they can force changes in their particular societies.

Notes

1. Walter Millis, *A World Without War* (New York: Washington Square Press, 1961).
2. Hannah Arendt, *On Revolution* (New York: Viking Press, 1963).
3. The *New York Times*, for example, from 1946 to 1959 reported on over 1200 "internal wars". Another study suggests that there were 31 major insurgencies between 1948 and 1967. See L.W. Martin, *Arms and Strategy* (London: Weidenfeld and Nicolson, 1973), p. 146.
4. Quoted in ibid.
5. Ibid.
6. See A.M. Scott, *Insurgency* (Chapel Hill: The University of North Carolina Press, 1970).
7. S.B. Griffith, *Sun Tzu* (Oxford: Clarendon Press, 1963).
8. T.E. Lawrence, *Seven Pillars of Wisdom* (London: Penguin Modern Classics, 1962), p. 198.
9. Ibid., p. 197. See also D. Garnett (ed.), *The Essential T.E. Lawrence* (London: Jonathan Cape, 1951), p.99.
10. Many writers also use the terms 'people's war', 'partisan war', 'irregular war', 'unconventional war' as well as 'guerrilla warfare' to refer to conflicts which have political and military dimensions.
11. Chalmers Johnson, *Revolution and the Social System* (Hoover Institution: Stanford University, 1964). See also M. Osanka, *Modern Guerrilla Warfare* (Glencoe: Free Press, 1962). For a fuller analysis of the term Revolution see M. Rejai, *The Strategy of Political Revolution.* (New York: Anchor Press. 1973), Chapter One.
12. The terms 'insurgency' and 'revolutionary warfare' are seen by this writer as being largely interchangeable.
13. Guerrilla warfare can be resorted to after regular forces have been defeated; before they have been created; or where they are unable to operate. For a fuller explanation of the differences between revolutionary warfare and guerrilla warfare see Huntington's introduction in Osanka, ibid.
14. M. Elliott-Bateman (ed.), *The Fourth Dimension of Warfare* (Manchester: Manchester UP, 1970).
15. For an interesting discussion of the differences between conventional war and revolutionary warfare, see P. Paret, "The French Army and La Guerre Revolutionaire', *Journal of the Royal United Service Institution* (JRUSI), CIV, February 1959, p. 59. This is not to say that conventional warfare is not supplemented by conflict on other planes. The argument is that conventional war, like guerrilla war, is essentially a military activity.
16. The recognition of the different battlefronts of insurgency is seen very clearly by Vo Nguyen Giap in *People's War, People's Army,* (New York: Praeger, 1962), pp. 97-8.
17. Mao Tse-tung, *Selected Military Writings* (Peking: Foreign Language Press, 1963), pp. 97-8.
18. For a discussion of Mao's ideas of the dual political and military structure of revolutionary movements, see R. Thompson, *Defeating Communist Insurgency*, (London: Chatto and Wind, 1966), p. 32. See also D. Pike, *Viet Cong* (Massachusetts: MIT Press, 1966).

19. R. Taber, *The War of the Flea* (Paladin, 1970), p. 32.
20. See D. Pike, op. cit., and R. Thompson, op. cit.
21. See R. Debray, *Revolution in the Revolution* (London, Penguin, 1967), p.. 64-90.
22. R. Taber, op. cit., p. 19.
23. See Mao Tse-Tung, op. cit., p. 341.
24. Coercive terrorism is designed to demoralize the population and weaken its confidence in the central authorities as well as to make an example of selected victims. Disruptive terrorism is designed to discredit the government, advertise the movement and provoke the authorities into taking harsh repressive counter-measures.
25. Paret and Shy, *Guerrillas in the 1960s* (New York: Praeger, 1962), p. 34.
26. Eric Wolf, "Peasant Problems and Revolutionary Warfare" (Paper presented to the Third Annual SSC, New York, 10 September 1967). Quoted in Sullivan and Sattler (ed.), *Revolutionary War: Western Response* (New York: Columbia UP, 1971), p. 9.
27. See M. Dillon and D. Lehane, *Political Murder in Northern Ireland* (London, Penguin Special, 1973).
28. Quoted in J.L.S. Girling, *People's War* (London: Allen and Unwin, 1969), p. 74.
29. See R. Taber, op. cit., p. 93.
30. P. Paret, "The French Army and La Guerre Revolutionnaire", op. cit., p. 59.
31. B. Fall, *Street without Joy: Indochina at War 1946-54,* (Harrisburg, 1961), p.73.
32. Similarly during the Cuban revolution, Fidel Castro claimed that the moves of Batista's forces were constantly reported by the friendly population. "We always know where the soldiers are,"he is reported to have said, "but they never know where we are."
33. See Chalmers Johnson, "Civilian Loyalties and Guerrilla Conflict", *World Politics,* July 1962.
34. R. Taber, op. cit., pp. 29 and 53. "Analogically, the guerrilla fights the war of the flea," Taber argues, "and his military enemy suffers the dog's disadvantages: too much to defend: too small, ubiquitous and agile an enemy to come to grips with."
35. Vo Nguyen Giap, *People's War, People's Army,* op. cit., p. 48.
36. R. Taber, op. cit., p. 45.
37. See E.L. Katzenbach Jr., "Time, Space and Will: The Politics and Military Views of Mao Tse-tung", in Col. T.N. Greene (ed.), *The Guerrilla – and How to Fight him* (New York: Praeger, 1962).
38. See R. Debray, op. cit., p. 65, and also J. Gerassi, *Towards Revolution*, Vol. I (London, Weidenfeld and Nicolson, 1971), p. 17.
39. Carlos Marighella, "Justification of a Thesis", in *Carlos Marighella* (Havana: Camilo Cienfuegos Press, 1970).
40. What Robert Taber says of Algeria is true of the others as well. "A clear-cut military decision was impossible for the FLN . . . the aim was to create a drain on French manpower and the French treasury too great to be sustained . . . given the domestic political dissension on the Algerian question." Taber, op. cit., p. 104.
41. Most revolutionary thinkers agree that local military successes are unlikely to have any value if the guerrilla campaign does not weaken the morale of the government and its forces, strain the financial resources of the régime and increase political pressure on it by creating widespread dissatisfaction with the progress of a war in which there is no end in sight.
42. Marighella was the leader of the 'Action for National Liberation' (ALN) movement.
43. Che Guevara, *Guerrilla Warfare* (London: Penguin, 1969), p. 13.

44. Ibid., pp. 13-14.
45. T.E. Lawrence, op. cit., p. 337.
46. See Mao Tse-tung, op. cit., p. 307.
47. See Vo Nguyen Giap, op. cit., pp. 97-8.
48. Ibid.
49. There was probably truth in some of the criticisms made by the North Vietnamese but they were undoubtedly exaggerated to support their position.
50. D. Pike, op. cit., p. 379.
51. See Katzenbach, op. cit.
52. The main focus of attention in urban guerrilla campaigns would seem to be terrorism designed to achieve this "climate of collapse". Marighella argues that "it is necessary to turn the political crisis into armed conflict by performing violent actions that will force those in power to transform the political situation in the country into a military situation. This will alienate the masses, who from then on will revolt against the army and police and blame them for this state of things." (Carlos Marighella, "Minimanual of the Urban Guerrilla"). See *Survival,* March 1971.
53. See D. Pike, op. cit., p. 253.
54. Quoted in D. Pike, ibid., p. 254.
55. R. Taber, op. cit., p. 23.
56. Vo Nguyen Giap, op. cit., pp. 97-8.
57. See J. McCuen, *The Art of Counter-Revolutionary Warfare* (London: Faber, 1966); R. Thompson, *Defeating Communist Insurgency,* op. cit.; D. Galula, *Counter-Insurgency Warfare* (New York: Praeger, 1964); Paret and Shy, *Guerrillas in the 1960s,* op. cit.
58. J. McCuen, op. cit., p. 77.
59. See R. Thompson, *Revolutionary Warfare and World Strategy* (London: Secker and Warburg, 1970), and *No Exit from Vietnam* (London: Chatto and Windus, 1969).
60. R. Thompson, *Defeating Communist Insurgency,* op. cit., pp. 50-57.
61. Mao Tse-tung, op. cit., p. 76.
62. The same can perhaps also be said of Amilcar Cabral who adapted the Chinese model to the circumstances of Portuguese Guinea. See J. Gerassi, op. cit., pp. 14-15.
63. R. Thompson, *No Exit from Vietnam,* op. cit., p. 145.
64. The same can be said of French operations in Algeria.
65. Quoted in R. Taber, op. cit., p. 119.

8 CRISIS MANAGEMENT

Phil Williams

I Introduction: The Importance of International Crises

"We create and enjoy crises . . . Why I don't know. I wish I knew. But all of us like them. I know I enjoy them. There is a sense of elation that comes with crises." Although this statement made by an unidentified American diplomat is rather chilling in its implications, it does express what may be a more widespread attitude than is generally realized.[1] The way that crises are seized upon and dramatized by the media, for example, indicates the interest and excitement that a confrontation between states arouses in a public that is otherwise largely uninterested in foreign affairs. But it also seems likely that crises have a similar macabre fascination for policy-makers themselves. For the diplomat or statesman the confrontation with rival governments is the ultimate moment of truth, the time when his will, ability, wisdom and leadership qualities are all stretched to the utmost. If he comes through it successfully he knows that his personal prestige and stature will be enormously enhanced both within his own state and in the eyes of other governments. The sense of pride with which statesmen in their memoirs highlight their decisions and actions during periods of acute tension or crisis is symptomatic of the importance they attach to these situations.

The attractions of crises for students of international politics and strategic studies are also considerable. The academic strategist is concerned with the potential as well as the actual use of force and international crises therefore provide an obvious area of interest and attention. It is in these situations that perhaps the most vigorous and explicit attempts are made by decision-makers to influence the behaviour of their opponents in desired directions. Tactics such as escalation and brinkmanship are carefully employed to this end. Indeed, techniques of coercive diplomacy and the "manipulation of the shared risk of war" lie at the heart of the tough bargaining process that is an integral feature of crisis interaction.[2] One of the main tasks of the analyst is to disentangle this bargaining process and attempt to assess the impact and utility of the various techniques that are used by the participants. Furthermore, crises provide an essential testing ground in which the more abstract theories of escalation, together with ideas about the coercive value of commitments and threats can be balanced against the considerations that actually motivate policy-makers involved in conflict situations short of war.[3]

At the same time it has to be recognized that crises lie at the crucial juncture between peace and war. Crisis interactions can result either in the outbreak of war between the protagonists or in the peaceful resolution of the crisis on terms that are at least sufficiently satisfactory to the participants as to make the option of the resorting to force seem unattractive. It is a matter of prime importance to determine the reasons for the first type of outcome as opposed to the second. An attempt must be made to isolate those tendencies that render war more likely on the one hand, and those considerations and techniques that facilitate a non-violent solution to the conflict on the other. If this were successful it would have considerable practical import and provide a useful point of contact for the practitioner and the analyst of international affairs. It would also go at least some way towards meeting the demands of those who argue the need for "policy-relevant theory".[4]

As well as providing insights into the ways in which war might be precipitated, and the manner in which states employ what has been described as the "diplomacy of violence", the study of crises is important for yet other reasons. Not only do crises offer insights into patterns of interaction between states but also into the decision-making processes within the governments involved.[5] Crises are in a sense discrete events in which the whole process of evaluating an initiative of the opponent, deciding on an appropriate response and implementing that response can be seen very clearly. Thus it is possible to focus on the way policy is made during crises and to examine the manner in which decision-makers handle information, formulate alternative courses of actions and cope with the high level of stress that is an inevitable accompaniment of crisis situations.[6]

Against all this it could be argued that crisis studies are redundant now that the superpowers have entered an era of détente. This suggestion seems rather foolhardy, however, since it rests on the assumption that all the potential conflicts of interest remaining in the superpower relationship will be eliminated. While there might in fact be a gradual movement from crisis management to crisis prevention considerations, there is no guarantee that superpower crises can be avoided in the future. It is possible that the Soviet attainment of nuclear parity heralds a greater willingness of the Kremlin to take high risks in its dealings with the United States. Even if this does not materialize, however, current trends in international affairs militate against the total absence of crises. Nuclear proliferation, for example, increases the likelihood of dangerous and destabilizing confrontations between states which hitherto have been regarded as relatively minor powers whose conflicts could easily be contained or localized. The energy problem and the resulting competition for scarce resources could provoke serious divisions and rivalries among the advanced industrialized states that have hitherto enjoyed a relatively tranquil and cordial relationship. Alternatively, one or two of these governments could decide that the only way to have regular energy supplies at reasonable economic cost is through military action against the oil-producing states. This would almost certainly precipitate a major crisis. Although such possibilities may be rather remote, they should not be ruled out altogether. Furthermore, the rise of China and the gradual emergence of Japan to great power status will add even more uncertainties to the future and widen the range of possible conflicts or confrontations that could have global implications. It seems reasonable to argue, therefore, that so long as international politics remain in a state of anarchy, periodic crises are inevitable. The changing constellations of power and alignment merely make it more difficult to predict where, and in what circumstances, the major problems and issues are likely to arise. It may also be the case that the changing context of crises will add to the difficulties of resolving them without resort to war.

Thus we may be moving into an era which is far more dangerous than the Cold War years and the relatively straightforward bipolar conflict between the superpowers. Indeed, in the period since 1945 the Soviet Union and the United States have developed certain techniques and codes of conduct that facilitate the control and regulation of international crises. So successful have they been that some commentators suggest, not only that superpower crises have become a substitute for war, but that their crisis behaviour itself becomes a form of stylistic or ritualized conflict. This point has been superbly summed up by Glenn Snyder:

> A hypothesis which presently enjoys considerable support is that crises perform a surrogate function in the nuclear age — they take the place of war in the resolution of conflict, between great powers at least, when war has become too costly and risky. This notion casts crises in a role somewhat similar to the eighteenth-century quadrilles of marching and manoeuvre which produced settlements from superiority of position rather than brute superiority in violence.[7]

Thus there exists a rather paradoxical situation in which crises, at the same time as they heighten the possibility of war, in a curious sense act as a substitute for it.

II Crisis Management in the Nuclear Age

The nuclear superpowers are motivated not only by the traditional desire for victory or the perpetual need to protect the state's interests, but also by a new concern that their actions do not precipitate nuclear war. Their behaviour is influenced by what can most appropriately be described as a basic duality of purpose. The nature of the policy-maker's task, and indeed of his dilemma, has been succinctly summarized by William Kaufmann. According to Kaufmann, the major problem of the nuclear age is how to "manage affairs skilfully enough to avoid the more terrible weapons and still uphold essential interests".[8] Most of the concepts and theories about the use of force that have been developed since 1945 have been attempts to solve this problem. So too have the strategies adopted by the superpowers. Deterrence, for example, is concerned with the "skilful non-use" of force.[9] To the extent that it is successful it serves both to maintain the peace and protect vital interests. In the event that deterrence of lesser provocations fails, states still resort to force. But there is great incentive to keep the force limited. Thus the nuclear age has also become the age of limited war.

Crisis management is a measure that in many respects parallels limited war. It involves both the "positive" or traditional aim of securing national objectives, and the "negative" aim of ensuring that the situation does not get out of hand and lead to war or escalation. This duality suggests a major difference between nuclear crises and those that occurred prior to the nuclear age. In the past states could readily resort to war if they did not achieve their aims and objectives in the crisis itself. But the dangers involved in even a limited war fought directly between the superpowers are prohibitive. Until the First World War, the major states in the international system believed that they would gain more than they would lose by going to war.[10] Thus the diplomatic gains that were possible in the crisis of July 1914 were not sufficient to make war seem an unattractive alternative, especially as the key decision-makers in all the important European capitals felt that the prospects for victory were very good.[11] As a result there was no perception of a common interest in avoiding hostilities and settling the crisis peacefully. In the 1930s the situation was somewhat different, representing a transitional period between the age when war was usually regarded as a profitable activity and the nuclear era in which general war is so obviously abhorrent to all. Different states regarded war in very different ways. The prevalent attitudes in Nazi Germany harked back to the years before 1914. At the other extreme, the attitudes of British and French leaders were decisively influenced by the carnage of the Great War. The resulting asymmetry of motives and perceptions had a profound influence on the outcome of the crises of the later 1930s. In a situation where one of the protagonists is prepared to resort to war unless he achieves his objectives, and the other is concerned solely with avoiding war, the only possible settlement of a crisis can be on the terms dictated by the former. Thus the Munich crisis, for example, was not resolved peacefully because of a shared perception of an overriding common interest in avoiding war, but because British and French policy-makers capitulated and conceded to Hitler's demands.

The crucial point is that in pre-nuclear crises there was not the same mixture of common and conflicting interests that has characterized the period since 1945. The change can be seen in crises between the super-powers that arise either out of miscalculation of each other's intentions and determination or out of an unavoidable and unequivocal conflict of interests. Even where a crisis erupts from a direct challenge of one superpower by the other, the overriding interest in avoiding a nuclear holocaust remains central to their calculations. The superpowers are concerned with preventing war and obviously want to reach a peaceful settlement of their differences. At the same time the importance of these differences must not be underestimated. They can lead to tough and dangerous bargaining over the exact nature and terms of a settle-ment. Whereas pre-nuclear crises could be regarded as almost pure com-petition in which the interests and motives of the participants over-lapped only to a minor extent, if at all, in a nuclear crisis the motives of the antagonists are likely to be far more mixed. The latter type of confrontation involves

> a curious mixture of co-operation and conflict — co-operation
> in that both parties with a certain range of possible solutions,
> will be better off with a solution, that is, a bargain, than
> without one, and conflict in that, within the range of possible
> solutions, the distribution of the total benefit, between the
> two parties depends on the particular solution adopted.[12]

This analysis goes far towards explaining the cross-pressures at work on the superpowers in a crisis. If statesmen regard their objectives as sufficiently important, they will be prepared to run considerable risks in order to achieve them — even in the nuclear age. At the same time they will strive to keep the risks of war within tolerable bounds.[13] Provocative actions tend to be combined with restraint, risk-exploitation mellowed by the need for risk-reduction.[14] This is summed up in Stanley Hoffman's argument that although the superpowers still play the traditional game of chicken, throughout the game they tend to keep their foot either on or very near the brake pedal.[15] The somewhat bizarre nature of this situation is heightened by a dichotomy inherent in the nature of crises themselves, for crises are simultaneously both periods of opportunity and times of danger.[16]

Not surprisingly, therefore, crisis management has a kind of schizophrenic quality about it. It is a curious blend of "bilateral competition" on the one hand and "shared danger" on the other.[17] Statesmen attempting to manage a crisis in the nuclear age will take risks in order to achieve their objectives while simultaneously trying to avoid the outbreak of escalation of hostilities. This latter concern leads to restriction of risk-taking behaviour and the avoidance of certain actions that might have uncontrollable or unintended consequences. As Snyder has put it: "an important constraint on the use of coercive tactics is disaster avoidance."[18] These two aspects will usually coexist side by side in superpower confrontations: the task for policy-makers in the management of these crises is to reconcile or balance them with each other. Thus crisis management is concerned on the one hand with the procedure for controlling and regulating a crisis so that it does not get out of hand (either through miscalculations and mistakes by the participants, or because events take on a logic and momentum of their own) and lead to war, and on the other with ensuring that the crisis is resolved on a satisfactory basis in which the vital interests of the state are secured and protected. The second aspect will almost invariably necessitate vigorous actions carrying substantial risks. One task of crisis management, therefore, is to temper these risks, to keep them as low and as controllable as possible, while the other is to ensure that the coercive diplomacy and risk-taking tactics are as effective as possible in gaining concessions from the adversary and maintaining one's own position relatively intact.

This poses a serious dilemma for policy-makers in that some of the coercive bargaining moves which are most attractive in bringing forth concessions from the opponent are also the most dangerous and destabilizing from the perspective of control.[19] There are certain actions — such as delegating the decision to use nuclear weapons to front-line commanders rather than keeping it tightly in the hands of the top civilian policy-makers — that would significantly enhance and strengthen the credibility of one's threats, but would render the situation potentially so much more explosive and less controllable that, in past superpower crises, they have been deliberately eschewed. Even if the more volatile tactics of this type are avoided, however, coercive bargaining is still extremely dangerous. Furthermore, crises involve not only the deliberate creation of risk, but what has perhaps most appropriately been described as an autonomous element of danger and uncertainty.[20] It is quite conceivable that a crisis could erupt into violence, not as a result of deliberate decisions, positive actions, or conscious choices, but through such occurrences as a breakdown of information or a loss of control over events.

The dangers of war, therefore, stem from three distinct aspects of crises and crisis behaviour. There are first of all the dangers that arise out of the bargaining process itself. Secondly, there are those dangers that are intrinsic to crisis situations, and encompass risks and uncertainties that are neither intended nor entirely controlled by the participants. Finally there are dangers arising from possible defects and deficiencies in the decision-making processes of the governments involved. Obviously these dangers are not unrelated to one another. Since decisions in crises have to be made amidst considerable uncertainty and on the basis of very limited or fragmentary information, for example, misperception of the opponent's strength or determination is always possible. This in turn might lead one of the participants to adopt a bargaining position that it would have regarded as intolerable or too provocative if its perception of the opponent was more accurate. For analytical purposes, however, it seems useful to make such distinctions, especially as they help provide the framework within which the rest of the argument is developed.[21]

III   Crisis Bargaining

International crises typically involve tests of will between the protagonists. Throughout periods of high tension or confrontation, attempts are constantly made both to assess the intentions and to influence the determination of the opponent. It is possible to wield such influence successfully by manipulating the opponent's perception of one's own determination and resolve. Indeed, a state's image of its adversary will have a significant effect on its own behaviour, and do much to determine whether it will adopt coercive bargaining tactics and exhibit a relatively high propensity for taking risks or tend toward accommodation and a significantly lower level of risk-taking. Much of the art of crisis bargaining lies in influencing this image in desired directions. Probably the vital key to successful bargaining is the ability of party A to convince party B that A possesses the greater resolve and consequently is prepared to tolerate a much higher level of risks in the crisis than is B. In other words, crisis bargaining is, in large part at least, a "competition in risk-taking",[22] This competition as indicated in an earlier chapter, has been discussed by some academic strategists in terms of the chicken game in which two teenagers in cars drive towards each other at speed, and the first to swerve aside is the loser.[23] Although the competition that occurs in international crises is much more complex, the analogy is both highly striking and extremely useful, and is taken up and developed slightly in the following discussion.

The central problem for each of the major participants in a crisis or chicken game is to establish the credibility of his threats and make clear to the opponent the strength of his will or resolve. Neither wants the game to result in a head-on collision since that would almost certainly be fatal for both. The aim, therefore, becomes one of convincing the opponent that he must be the party to move aside or back down if disaster is to be avoided. Since both sides know that the other would prefer a peaceful outcome to collision, however, each will attempt to convince the opponent of his unwillingness to give way. There are various strategies and tactics that can readily be exploited to this end, since they are designed specifically to promote an image of oneself as an inveterate risk-taker determined to compete successfully. Such strategies must now be outlined, albeit fairly briefly.

Superficially, at least, one of the most attractive and effective coercive bargaining moves is to "burn one's bridges".[24] When it does not seem to be in the interests of one of the protagonists to carry out a particular threat, the opponent will almost certainly doubt the credibility of that threat. These doubts are likely to disappear, however, if it is made clear to him that the threatened action will, in certain specified circumstances, be carried out automatically. In other words, the credibility of a threat is enormously enhanced when it involves an "irrevocable commitment". By cutting off the line of retreat and locking oneself into a particular position, disaster can only be avoided if the opponent is prepared to stop or swerve aside. The adversary is made to realize that you cannot fail to act or react in the manner suggested if he perseveres with the prohibited course of action. By destroying one's own path of possible retreat, the only options left open are those available to the opponent. It is he – and he alone – who has the "last clear choice" to avoid a collision. Attractive as such a bold commitment move might be in terms of winning the game, however, it demands an excessively high level of nerve and skill.

An alternative means of strengthening a commitment, but one that does not cut off irretrievably all possible means of retreat and manoeuvre, is to publicize it. While a public pledge, an open treaty of alliance, or an explicit and formal guarantee pact, does not bind a state finally and irrevocably, it does substantially increase the costs of not meeting the commitment. A threat that is made to the opponent in public, therefore, is likely to have greater impact and be more credible than the same threat made privately and through secret communication channels, since the costs of not fulfilling the latter are considerably lower.[25] To revoke a public commitment while under duress, to renege on a universally recognized guarantee, or to fail to implement an explicit and well-publicized threat can do considerable harm to the state's reputation and prestige, and invite further challenges not only from the current adversary but also from other governments. The state's behaviour in this situation will influence the expectations of others about its likely behaviour in the future. Similarly it is possible to "couple" the immediate issue with other matters in dispute and suggest that it is impossible to concede victory to the opponent on this occasion as this would lead him to expect a similar type of accommodation on other occasions and over these other disputes.[26] This is not to overemphasize the interdependence of commitments but is merely to highlight the advantages to be gained from linking issues in this way. It tends both to strengthen the credibility of one's threats and make concessions less likely and less necessary.

Yet another way of establishing credibility of one's threats – even when it is obvious that to implement them would be suicidal – is to convey the impression of being irrational. Indeed, what has been described as "the rationality of irrationality" strategy is an explicit recognition that significant advantages may accrue to one of the participants in the bargaining process if his opponent believes that he is not entirely rational and not completely in command of his senses or in control of his actions.[27] The skill is to convince the opponent that one is oblivious to the risks of a collision, which once again puts the onus on him to avoid it. A variant of this tactic is for one of the parties to play down or dismiss the costs of collision to himself relative to the costs to the opponent. The skill here is not in seeming oblivious to the costs and dangers involved — in fact it is probably to emphasize them — but to suggest that they will be more severe for the opponent than for oneself.

Another coercive bargaining tactic is to increase both the likelihood and the potential magnitude of the disaster. This can be done by escalatory tactics such as the dramatic crossing of a threshold or the flouting of conventions that have hitherto been observed. Such actions leave the opponent with the next move and have therefore been described as "initiatives that force the opponent to initiate."[28] The opponent has three broad choices available to him in such a situation: he can match the escalatory move by a similar or even greater one of his own; he can carry on with his present course of action; or he can be more accommodating and concede the game. The first alternative would suggest that he is prepared to take equal or even greater risks than the initiator of the escalation. The second would suggest that he is not prepared to match the escalation and therefore that with a bit more pressure he might be persuaded to desist from further action. The third alternative signifies that the escalatory move has been completely successful.

IV The Dangers of Crises

The above discussion of coercive bargaining tactics is designed to be illustrative rather than exhaustive, and to convey the flavour of the process rather than all its subtleties and nuances. It is also suggestive, however, of the very significant dangers that are involved in the competition in risk-taking. Perhaps the most important of these stem from the fact that it *is* competitive. Both participants will be adopting one or more of these tactics in an attempt to make the other back down. Furthermore, each will know that the other is trying to frighten him into submission and will treat his moves with scepticism and incredulity. The potential for disaster, therefore, is far from negligible even in this relatively straightforward game. Most of the tactics described depend for their success on unilateral use. If both of the protagonists make strong public commitments, both adopt rationality of irrationality tactics, or if both are prepared to escalate, the likelihood of disaster is enormously increased. The danger is essentially one of miscalculating the opponent's willingness to stand firm and can be seen most clearly if we revert to the discussion of perhaps the most dangerous move of all, the irrevocable commitment.

Throwing the steering wheel out of the window in the context of the chicken game is a valuable tactic so long as a number of conditions are met. The first is that the opponent does not do the same thing at the same time, in which event both cars would be inevitably locked on to a collision course. The second condition is that the opponent realizes what has happened and is aware that only he can now prevent the disaster which neither really wants: he must see the steering wheel being thrown out and assess the implications of this quickly enough to be able to swerve aside before the two cars meet head on. Thirdly, the opponent must be convinced that the steering wheel is genuine and that the action is really a firm commitment rather than merely a bluff. In other words, the competition can end in disaster through the simultaneous establishment of irreversible commitments, a failure of communication, or an unwillingness to recognize that the opponent is not bluffing. As Herman Kahn has put it: 'neither side is willing to back down precisely because it believes or hopes it can achieve its objective, without war. It may be willing to run some risk of war to achieve its objective, but it feels that the other side will back down or compromise before the risk becomes very large.'[29] Should these beliefs, hopes, or feelings be mistaken then war becomes much more likely: strong commitments by both sides or a miscalculation of intent can all too easily lead to disaster. Such dangers have been discussed here in relation to the "irrevocable commitment" since it is in this context that they emerge most clearly, but they are only slightly less relevant to the other tactics outlined above.

Indeed the simple chicken-game analogy that has been alluded to suffers from a number of important defects. Most importantly, it minimizes the dangers and risks associated with the "competition in risk-taking" as it could develop in international politics. It seems appropriate, therefore, to suggest a modified analogy that is perhaps more akin to the reality of interstate crises. Rather than seeing the cars moving towards each other on a straight road which gives them very clear vision, it seems more fruitful to regard them as heading towards one another from the opposite ends of a very long winding lane and being connected by a radio telephone which is subject to interference and distortion, and for some of the time at least is barely audible above the sound of the car engines. Neither driver is able to see what is around the next bend and cannot be aware how fast the other is going, or how far apart they are at any point in time. Furthermore, the cars are badly maintained and subject to possible mechanical faults such as brake failure. The drivers may not be particularly skilled and it is not inconceivable that they might lose control of their vehicles at a crucial juncture in the proceedings. Described in this way the chicken game bears greater resemblance to the confrontations that actually occur in world politics, mainly because it incorporates the element of unintended risk and the possibility of errors in decision-making.

The autonomous risk that is inherent in crisis situations has been explicitly and fully acknowledged by Thomas Schelling. At the same time though, he has suggested that this can be exploited by "making threats that leave something to chance".[30] The gambit here is not coolly and calmly to threaten to inflict unacceptable costs on the opponent, particularly if this invites a similar level of pain and damage to oneself. Rather is it to start events moving in such a way that mutual disaster becomes a distinct possibility even though neither side really wants it. In fact, it can be argued that such threats are implicit, if not explicit, in many coercive moves that are made during crises, especially if it is accepted that "the essence of a crisis lies in its unpredictability", and the fact that "the participants are not fully in control of events" but have to "take steps and make decisions in the realm of risk and uncertainty."[31]

The dangers in crises, therefore, stem not only from the bargaining process, but are also a consequence of the characteristics generally attendant upon crisis situations. A crisis is by nature extremely volatile and explosive, full of ambiguities and intangibles. Thus there are various ways in which the situation might get out of hand and lead to war despite prodigious efforts by the protagonists to prevent such an occurrence. These possibilities must now be examined.

A major problem in these situations is the danger of a violent flare-up. Incidents that are accidental and wholly unintended rather than the result of deliberate provocation can nevertheless initiate a rapid escalation that neither of the parties really wants. An outbreak of violence, even though it might have its origins in a riot or the actions of an over-zealous military commander, for example, will be difficult to contain, particularly in a situation where suspicion and hostility are rife. Indeed, it has been argued that if violence occurs directly between the forces of the two superpowers it could all too easily culminate in large-scale hostilities involving the use of nuclear weapons. "Violent interactions acquire a momentum of their own" and may precipitate an ever-deepening conflict from which both sides find it increasingly difficult to withdraw without undue loss of pride, prestige, and self-confidence.[32] To some extent, of course, this is part of a more general problem that is probably best enshrined in the notion of events getting out of hand and developing their own logic instead of remaining susceptible to government directions and control.

Such incidents can never be ruled out completely, because decision-makers are not totally in control of the implementation of their policies. The need to delegate authority and the inevitable reliance on large-scale bureaucratic organizations that function according to their own standard operating procedures sets limits to the extent to which the state's actions can be regulated and controlled by the top officials.[33] As a result, the local military commanders who may well be in close proximity to enemy forces have a certain discretionary freedom.

Although it is unlikely that hostilities would be initiated against explicit commands to the contrary, the possibility of unauthorized actions or a misinterpretation of orders cannot be ruled out entirely. Problems could also arise from differences of perspective between the policy-makers in the capitals who are aware both of the wider issues and the dangers of conflagration, and the military commanders at the heart of the crisis who are acutely conscious of local needs and the demands of the imme-diate military situation.[34] It is almost inevitable, therefore, that attempts to maintain control and ensure restraint will flounder against military resentment at what is regarded as a blatant intrusion into an area firmly within the military sphere of competence. Even without such friction, policy-makers may find their freedom of action severely curtailed by the range of contingencies for which the armed services have prepared. Unanticipated options may be difficult to execute at short notice with the result that reliance can only be placed on prelaid plans or the tradi-tional modes of action of the military organizations. Such problems can cause considerable loss of flexibility in the decisions and actions of the participants in a crisis.[35]

A somewhat similar danger is that policy-makers might feel compelled to move in a particular way, or find themselves much more deeply entan-gled than they intended, because of the behaviour of their allies.[36] With an apparently much diminished freedom of choice, decision-makers may take actions or follow policies that involve a level of risks that would be regarded as intolerable in other circumstances. A possible consequence of this is that the protagonists become locked on to a collision course as in the bargaining game. There is a crucial difference, however, in that this now occurs not through conscious choice and the calculation of advantages, but because of the limited control that each party exerts over the situation.

Another way in which events might get out of hand is through impe-tuous actions or reactions. An escalatory move by one side, for example, might lead to an automatic reaction by the opponent. The possibility of this occuring is heightened by the problems that beset the decision-making process during crises. Not the least of these is that policy-makers have to act under considerable stress. The short time available for formu-lating a response, the element of surprise, and the high level of tension all contribute to this. So does the fatigue that is inevitable if the crisis continues for any length of time. Although there is some doubt over the precise effects of stress and whether it is likely to prove a hindrance or a stimulus to effective decision-making, it has been argued very persua-sively that although "a moderate level of variety can be beneficial at higher levels it disrupts decision processes."[37] Indeed, "as the intensity of a crisis increases it makes creative policy-making both more impor-tant and less likely."[38] The search for alternatives becomes less thorough and more cursory, and the implications of each proposed action may not be thoroughly assessed. Such consequences are exacerbated by problems attendant upon group decision-making. Perhaps the main danger here is what has been described as "group think" or the "deterioration of mental efficiency, reality testing and moral judgement that results from in-group pressures."[39] The need to conform with other members of a group might silence disagreement about the implications of the opponent's actions or mute the doubts of individual group members about the damaging consequences of the chosen response.

Such possibilities are all the more dangerous because it is during crises that policy-makers need to be at their most efficient. They often have to make decisions on the basis of incomplete or fragmentary information and evaluate correctly words and deeds that are inherently ambiguous and subject to widely divergent interpretations. Indeed, the results of a misinterpretation of information or of a failure to perceive properly the signals emanating from the opponent can be disastrous. But these are not the only problems of crisis decision-making: emotional and political considerations may intrude forcefully into the process. Fear, anger, or pride, for example, might influence the choice of an alternative that renders the interaction far less amenable to control. Similarly, policy-makers might adopt an uncompromising attitude not because they feel national security demands it, but because a failure to do so would cause irreparable harm to their standing in domestic politics.[40] Although political factors of this kind are extraneous to the issue at stake, they may nevertheless have a substantial influence on the course of the crisis.

As was suggested earlier, these dangers and difficulties, far from being completely separable from one another, are mutually reinforcing. The dangers of coercive bargaining are heightened by possible inadequacies in decision-making and the prospect that events might inadvertently get out of control. Perhaps what is most surprising, therefore, is that superpower crises since 1945 have been resolved peacefully. Furthermore, many of the dangers alluded to above have been avoided, perhaps because they were explicitly recognized from the early years of the Cold War. Thus the pattern of superpower confrontations must now be analyzed and an attempt made to examine the procedures and conventions of crisis control.

V The Control of Crises

While the superpowers have taken steps to promote their security or protect their interests during international crises, they have also made deliberate moves to counter or control the risks of war. Not surprisingly, therefore, careful restrictions have been placed on the bargaining process. At the same time vigorous efforts have been made to ensure that events remained under control and did not take on their own momentum, and that decisions were made in as rational and calculating a manner as possible.

The dangers attendant upon bargaining have been moderated in a number of ways. In the first place it has to be recognized that the bargaining process is not isolated from its context or the overall setting within which it occurs. Certain structural features of international crises will tend to have a decisive impact both on the process itself and its outcome.[41] Perhaps most importantly, the willingness of the superpowers to pursue ruthlessly the "competition in risk-taking" has been determined above all by their perceptions of what is at stake in the crisis.[42] Indeed, "the comparative resolve to use force" or the "relative risk-taking propensities of the two sides" has been dependent upon the "balance of interests" between them.[43] As Robert Jervis has put it: "Often the decisive factor in bargaining, because it makes the cost of retreating and the gains from standing firm much higher, is the unequal value the states place on the issue at stake."[44]

In the major crises of the post-war period, there has eventually been an explicit recognition by both sides of just what the stakes were. This certainly occurred during the Cuban missile crisis of October 1962, with important consequences. Robert Kennedy perhaps best summed up the reasons for Soviet withdrawal of the missiles when he wrote: "The missiles in Cuba, we felt, vitally concerned our national security, but not that of the Soviet Union. This fact was ultimately recognized by Khrushchev, and this recognition, I believe, brought about this change in what, up to that time, had been a very adamant position."[45] The Kremlin was confronted with a United States government that was prepared to run a higher risk of war to remove the Soviet missiles from Cuba than was the USSR to keep them there. Something similar occurred during the Berlin crisis of 1961. Although there had been a long and sometimes bitter debate over whether or not the West should have allowed the barricades — and later, the Wall — dividing the city to remain intact, the inaction of the United States demonstrated its recognition that the Soviet move of 13 August was vital to Soviet security and designed primarily to maintain the integrity of the German Democratic Republic.[46] The United States was prepared to take considerable risks for West Berlin itself, but not for the city as a whole. The Soviet Union too ultimately recognized that American inaction would not be repeated in the event of a major move against the Western sectors of the city, and when its probes met firm resistance they were discontinued.

In other words, these situational factors have significantly influenced the outcome of superpower confrontations, probably to a far greater extent than is generally acknowledged. Although some of the academic strategists have elaborated at great length on the utility of coercive bargaining tactics, it is suggested here that these tactics are only likely to work to the extent that they support or emphasize the basic structure of the crisis. At the same time, the possibility cannot be dismissed that each of the participants will try to structure the situation so that it appears the opponent has less at stake and can afford to back down. Nevertheless, in the crises that have occurred, sooner or later there has been a mutual recognition of the asymmetry of interests and consequently of the relative willingness of each of the participants to run risks. By a mixture of good fortune and good judgement, a crisis in which both sides have absolutely vital interests at stake has been avoided. Indeed, such a crisis could be disastrous since both sides would probably be prepared to escalate the conflict to an enormously high level before sacrificing these interests.

One of the major tenets of crisis management, therefore, is the importance of limiting one's objectives. It is essential not to demand too much of an opponent since the more he is asked to concede the more intransigent he is likely to become.[47] Conversely, the more he can claim to have achieved or gained in the crisis the readier he will be to accept a peaceful solution. This suggests a second way in which the bargaining process in crisis tends to be moderated: The superpowers have used inducements and rewards, as well as threats of costs and deprivations, in their relationship with one another. Both have adopted a "carrot and stick" approach rather than coercive diplomacy alone. The Cuban missile crisis demonstrated this very clearly. Although Kennedy demonstrated his willingness to escalate the conflict if necessary, he also made it easier for the Soviet Union to withdraw its missiles by guaranteeing in return not to invade the island. This made it possible for Khrushchev to claim that his adventure had resulted in tangible gains. In other words, the superpowers have tried to resolve crises on terms that are reasonably satisfactory to both, thus avoiding, as far as is possible, the notion of "winner" and "loser".[48]

A third way in which coercive bargaining has been moderated is by avoidance of the more dangerous techniques. Both superpowers have been eminently cautious and have not taken steps likely to make the crisis uncontrollable or that would leave them with little or no freedom of choice. The Soviet blockade of Berlin in 1948, for example, was implemented only very gradually and under the pretext of "technical difficulties" with the access routes. Perhaps the most dramatic manifestation of the concern with retaining freedom of choice, however, is the meticulous way in which the superpowers have avoided the deliberate initiation of violence.[49] Resort to violence has been regarded as an irrevocable commitment likely to precipitate an escalatory process that might be impossible to control. Seen in this light the blockade of Cuba in 1962 had many advantages for the United States. It demonstrated American resolve to the Soviet Union, but did so in a "prudent" manner and without violating the threshold between coercion and overt violence. Indeed, the blockade left open the option of either intensifying or defusing the crisis, as the situation demanded.

The "quarantine", as it was called, is illustrative of yet another way in which the dangers of the bargaining process have been contained or moderated in superpower crises. The move was designed to communicate to the Kremlin that the installation of missiles in Cuba would not be tolerated and that America would take all action necessary to remove them. In some respects it finds a distinct parallel in the Berlin airlift of 1948 since this was intended not only to prevent the city from being starved into submission, but also to demonstrate the determination of the Western powers not to acquiesce in a Soviet take-over. Such communication by deeds as well as words has been a marked feature of international crises in the post-war era and has enabled both superpowers to clarify the depth of their commitment and their willingness to stand firm on some issues, together with their willingness to be more accommodating in other situations.[50]

Indeed it was the need for actions to reinforce and amplify traditional diplomatic communications that probably explains the dramatic military alert by the Americans during the Yom Kippur War — a move that has been the subject of endless debate and controversy. Although the alert of 25 October 1973 has often been regarded as a gross over-reaction motivated primarily by Nixon's domestic problems, it was far less dangerous and destabilizing than its critics suggest. The American action, like the Soviet behaviour that inspired it, was little more than a very elaborate signalling device. The Soviet Union, disturbed by Israel's advances after the initial cease-fire of 22 October and appalled by the prospect of Egypt suffering a humiliating defeat worse than that of 1967, communicated to Washington that it was prepared to accede to President Sadat's request for joint intervention by the superpowers to make Israel relinquish the gains made since the formal cessation of hostilities. It added that if the United States was not willing to co-operate then the Soviet Union would have to act "unilaterally". "At the same time the Soviet High Command made visible various rather ostentatious preparations which conveyed the possibility that they might be intending an airlift of combat forces to Egypt."[51] The American reply consisted of a similar mixture of words and actions. Declining the offer of co-operative intervention, the United States also made clear that it would not passively accept a unilateral Soviet intervention against Israel. The concern with which it viewed the impending Soviet action was conveyed by the "precautionary alert" of military bases and nuclear forces. The ultimate result of all this was greater Israeli restraint and the introduction into the area of a UN peacekeeping force in which the major powers did not participate. Egypt was relieved from an untenable military position, and direct superpower intervention in the conflict was avoided. Thus both the Soviet and American actions achieved their purpose.

Dramatic as it was, the behaviour of the two superpowers was not potentially dangerous. The preparatory actions of the USSR and the alert procedures of the United States both fit into the category of what Glenn Snyder has termed "communication moves". These "are not action choices", and therefore do not "change the basic alternatives available to the parties" or undermine their freedom of action in any way.[52] Rather are they intended almost exclusively to convey a clear message to the opponent. Indeed, the situation would have been far more precarious had the Soviet Union attempted a *fait accompli* and the US responded with a similar deployment of combat troops into the area. "Brutal" as the diplomatic messages may have been, the actions of both sides were eminently cautious.

Thus the importance of communication as a substitute for more dangerous bargaining tactics and as a means of avoiding miscalculation can be discerned clearly. The Middle East episode, however, also demonstrates the concern of the superpowers lest events pass outside their control. The introduction of superpower forces into the area, even in a peacekeeping role, would have substantially increased the likelihood of an inadvertent clash. The reluctance of both sides to intercede directly demonstrates their awareness of this. Yet, once again, the concern was neither novel nor unprecedented. In all their confrontations the superpowers have been preoccupied with avoiding moves that threaten the accidental outbreak of violence. This was one of the major considerations that led President Truman to opt for an airlift rather than send a tank convoy through the blockade. It may have been decisive too in Stalin's decision not to attempt large-scale interference with the airlift.[53] Similar fears about the unintended outbreak of violence were also prevalent in the Cuban missile crisis and help explain why the President and his Secretary of Defence were so intent on controlling and monitoring the way the blockade was conducted. Their aim was to minimize the likelihood of sinking a Soviet ship and thereby inadvertently forcing the Kremlin into a position where it felt compelled to react violently.[54]

If civilian control over military operations has been a crucial aspect of crisis management, control over allies has been almost equally important. Neither superpower has allowed its allies or client states much freedom of action. Not only have they tried to maintain strict control over the actions of their allies during crises, but they have also on occasion sacrificed the interests of their allies to the needs of crisis mangement and the demands of conflict regulation. It seems probable, for example, that the 22,000 Soviet troops in Cuba in October 1962 were directed more against Castro than Kennedy, and that their presence was intended primarily to ensure that the missiles remained very firmly under Soviet authority.[55] During the crisis itself Khrushchev communicated to the US that there was no chance of an accidental missile launch as the "volatile Cubans" were not in possession or control of these weapons.[56] Another example of superpower-induced restraint can be found in the Yom Kippur War, and Coral Bell has argued very persuasively that the US nuclear alert was such a loud signal partly because "it had to startle the Israelis, to convey the dangers of uninhibited military success even to characters like General Sharon or General Dayan."[57]

Because the governments of both superpowers have been acutely aware of the dangers involved in their confrontations, they have attempted to make decisions in as rational and detached a manner as possible. Although it would be exaggerating to suggest that the elements of non-rational decision-making have been entirely eliminated, at least the worst excesses of "group think" have been avoided. Decision-making groups, on the whole, have been "sufficiently large and diverse in outlook to ensure that the available information" was "subjected to vigorous probing from multiple perspectives, not merely from the view of the prevailing conventional wisdom."[58] They have also explored fully the available alternatives and tried to assess the likely impact of each one on the opponent's position. Indeed, Robert Kennedy has claimed that during the Cuban missile crisis the President "spent more time trying to determine the effect of a particular course of action on Krushchev or the Russians than on any other phase of what he was doing."[59] Nor was this atypical. Both superpowers have dismissed those options that would put the adversary in a position where the only recourse was a violent response. They have also tried to ensure that the opponent has sufficient time for a considered response rather than having to make an immediate, and perhaps highly emotional, decision. As a result, crisis-induced stress has been kept down to tolerable levels, and creative decision-making and problem-solving activities carried out extremely efficiently.

VI Conclusion

Thus the overall picture is one of considerable skill in controlling the risks of war. At the same time the impression must not be given that the sole preoccupation has been with the peaceful resolution of crises or that control considerations invariably outweigh the demands of coercive diplomacy. The need to control risks is only one facet of crisis management; the attractions of risk manipulation are often equally significant. As suggested above, crisis management is a strange mixture of ruthlessness and moderation, determination and prudence, intransigence and accommodation. What is perhaps most remarkable, therefore, is the way in which the superpowers have managed to achieve and maintain such a judicious blend of these qualities in their confrontations. Whether they will be able to continue to do so in the future is of course debatable. So too is the question of whether other states will become equally adept in the art of crisis management. What is certain, however, is that so long as the international system remains in its rudimentary form, the art will be indispensable.

Notes

1. The diplomat is quoted in O.R. Olsti, *Crisis, Escalation, War* (Montreal and London: McGill — Queen's University Press, 1972).

2. See T.C. Schelling, *Arms and Influence* (New Haven and London: Yale University Press, 1066), especially Ch. 3.
3. This has been done superbly in O.R. Young, *The Politics of Force: Bargaining during Superpower Crises* (Princeton: Princeton University Press, 1968), which is an important pioneering work on international crises and the way they are handled.
4. The question of 'policy-relevant theory' is discussed at length in A.L. George, D.K. Hall, and W.E. Simons, *The Limits of Coercive Diplomacy: Laos, Cuba, Vietnam* (Boston: Little, Brown, 1971).
5. See C.F. Hermann (ed.), *International Crises: Insights from Behavioral Research* (New York: Free Press, 1972).
6. These questions are dealt with in Olsti, op. cit.
7. G.H. Snyder, "Crisis Bargaining", in Herman, op. cit., p. 220.
8. W.W. Kaufmann, *Military Policy and National Security* (Princeton: Princeton University Press, 1956), p. 262.
9. See T.C. Schelling, *The Strategy of Conflict* (New York: Oxford University Press, 1963), p. 9.
10. An excellent account of attitudes towards war prior to 1914 can be found in I.F. Clarke, *Voices Prophesying War* (London: Oxford University Press, 1966).
11. See B. Tuchman, *August 1914* (London: Constable, 1962). More specifically on Germany see L.L. Farrar Jr., *The Short-War Illusion* (Oxford: ABC-CLIO Inc., 1973).
12. K. Boulding, *Conflict and Defence* (New York: Harper, 1962), p. 314.
13. These cross-pressures are analyzed in greater depth in Young, op. cit.
14. Some of the ways in which risks involved in the superpower conflict have been reduced are explored in M.D. Shulman, *Beyond The Cold War* (New Haven and London: Yale University Press, 1966), especially Ch. 5.
15. S. Hoffmann, *The State of War: Essays on the Theory and Practice of International Politics* (London: Pall Mall, 1965), p. 142.
16. See F.L. Schuman, *The Cold War: Retrospect and Prospect* (Baton Rouge: Louisiana State University Press, 1967), p. 72.
17. Schelling *Arms and Influence*, op. cit., p. 120.
18. Snyder, op. cit., p. 240.
19. This dilemma is dealt with at some length by G. Snyder, op. cit., pp. 240-55.
20. Snyder, op. cit., pp. 241-2, notes an extremely useful distinction between "autonomous" risks or the danger that the parties will "lose control of events" and the risks of miscalculation "inherent in the bargaining process". See also Schelling, *Arms and Influence*, op. cit., p. 97.
21. The following discussion of the dangers of crises has benefited considerably through the reading of an unpublished paper by Hannes Adomeit entitled "Risk and Crisis: Concepts and Processes". The paper is an elaboration of some of the ideas in the same author's 'Soviet Risk-Taking and Crisis Behaviour', *Adelphi Paper, No. 101* (London: International Institute for Strategic Studies, 1973).
22. This is one of the major themes in H. Kahn, *On Escalation: Metaphors and Scenarios* (New York: Praeger, 1965).
23. See ibid. Schelling, *Arms and Influence*, op. cit., pp. 116-25, also has a stimulating analysis of this point.
24. This paragraph rests heavily on the analysis contained in Schelling, *Arms and Influence*, op. cit., pp. 43-4. See also the critical analysis contained in Young, op. cit., Ch. 9, "Freedom of Choice".
25. See Snyder, op. cit., p. 237.
26. The tactic of "coupling" is dealt with superbly in R. Jervis, *The Logic of Images in International Relations* (Princeton: Princeton University Press, 1970).
27. Schelling, *Arms and Influence*, op. cit., pp. 36-43, contains an excellent discussion of this theme. See also the same author's *The Strategy of Conflict*, op. cit., pp. 16-20.

28. See Young, op. cit., Ch. 14, "The Role of the Initiative".
29. H. Kahn, op. cit., p. 12.
30. Schelling, *The Strategy of Conflict,* op. cit., Ch. 8.
31. Schelling, *Arms and Influence,* op. cit., p. 97.
32. Ibid., p. 93.
33. This emerges very clearly in G.T. Allison, *Essence of Decision* (Boston: Little, Brown, 1971).
34. J.E. Smith, *The Defense of Berlin* (Baltimore: Johns Hopkins Press, 1963), brings this out very clearly. See Ch. 14 in particular.
35. These issues are discussed more fully in Young, op. cit., Ch. 9, "Freedom of Choice".
36. Ibid.
37. Olsti, op. cit., p. 12.
38. Ibid., p. 17.
39. I.L. Janis, *Victims of Groupthink: A Psychological Study of Foreign Policy Decisions and Fiascoes* (Boston: Houghton Mifflin, 1972), p. 9.
40. A sophisticated version of this argument is in T. Halper, *Foreign Policy Crises: Appearance and Reality in Decision-Making* (Columbus, Ohio: Merrill, 1971).
41. Useful discussions of the importance of the 'bargaining setting' are contained in Young, op. cit., Ch. 3 and Snyder, op. cit., pp. 219-21.
42. See S. Maxwell, 'Rationality in Deterrence', *Adelphi Paper,* No. 50 (London: Institute for Strategic Studies, 1968).
43. R.E. Osgood and R.W. Tucker, *Force, Order and Justice* (Baltimore: Johns Hopkins, 1967), p. 148.
44. R. Jervis, "Bargaining and Bargaining Tactics", in J.R. Pennock and J.W. Chapman, *Coercion* (Chicago: Aldine, Atterton Inc., 1972), p. 281.
45. R.F. Kennedy, *Thirteen Days* (London, Pan Books, 1969), p. 124.
46. The argument that the barriers separating the city could have been destroyed with relative impunity can be found in J. Mander, *Berlin: Hostage for the West* (London: Penguin Books, 1962), p. 13. For an alternative, and more balanced view, see J.L. Richardson, *Germany and the Atlantic Alliance* (Cambridge, Mass.: Harvard University Press, 1966), p. 286.
47. This emerges very clearly from H. Cleveland, "Crisis Diplomacy" in *Foreign Affairs,* Vol. 41, No. 4, July 1963.
48. The question of whether either superpower can 'win' in a crisis is a difficult problem and I have benefited from several discussions of it with Mr. David Greenwood and Dr. Jean Houbert, both of Aberdeen University.
49. The distinction between coercion and violence is superbly made in Young, op. cit., especially Ch. 13.
50. See Young, op. cit., Ch. 6.
51. C. Bell, "The October Middle East War: A Case Study in Crisis Management During *Détente",* *International Affairs,* Vol. 50, No. 4, October 1974, p. 536.
52. Snyder, op. cit., p. 222.
53. See W. Phillips Davison, *The Berlin Blockade: A Study in Cold War Politics* (Princeton: Princeton University Press, 1958), p. 68.
54. E. Abel, *The Missiles of October* (London: MacGibbon and Kee, 1969), pp. 141-5.
55. A. & R. Wohlstetter, 'Controlling the Risks in Cuba', *Adelphi Paper, No. 17* (London: Institute for Strategic Studies, April 1965), p. 8.
56. Ibid.
57. Bell, op. cit., p. 538.
58. The need for this type of decision-making is emphasized in Olsti, op. cit., p. 207.
59. Kennedy, op. cit., pp. 121-2.

9 ALLIANCES

Ken Booth

Alliance is one of the major concepts of international politics. Indeed, because of the pervasiveness of alliances in both the theory of the subject and in the practice of foreign policy, it is easy to understand why, in looking at them, "we sometimes lose sight of alliances and seem to take the whole of international relations in our stride."[1]

Writings on alliances have been notably varied in attitude and conclusion. Out of the numerous studies there has emerged a profusion of sometimes overlapping, sometimes contradictory propositions, maxims, aphorisms, and explanations concerning almost every facet of alliances. Usefully, one recent book has gathered together 417 of these propositions.[2] Would-be practitioners of alliance diplomacy might derive much benefit from perusing this distillation of academic effort. They would not discover *the* truth about alliances, but they would surely find some support for any and every theory or opinion which they might come to hold: they would find "authorities" to strengthen any position in their discussions with their bureaucratic colleagues. Significantly, the recent study of alliances has exhibited an increasing realisation of the obstacles in the face of valid generalisations, and certainly in the way of any "grand theory".[3]

Technically, an *alliance* has two distinguishing features: the formality of the relationship (marked by an open or secret treaty) and the military focus of the mutual effort. It is "*a formal agreement between two or more nations to collaborate on national security issues.*"[4] Alliances are therefore one of the means whereby national military power is augmented in order to help achieve the objectives set by policy. Characteristic obligations include agreements about the deployment and training of forces in peacetime, consultation in time of crisis, and co-ordination of strategy in war.

The word "alliance" is sometimes applied to relationships which, technically speaking, do not conform to the definition. However, such usage can be illuminating. One writer, for example, has used the phrase "tacit alliance" to describe the relationship between France and Israel from the mid-1950s to the late 1960s. Military support was at the core of the relationship, but there was no express commitment or structure.[5] Another writer, in similar vein, has used the phrase "*de facto* alliance", for a relationship where no formal agreement was reached, but where states acted as if military promises had been made by their governments.[6] Other writers have described as "alliances" the informal relationships existing between governmental and non-governmental actors: for example, between the Chinese People's Republic and the Viet Cong, or between the Allies and resistance movements in the Second World War.[7]

The technical meaning of alliance has also been muddied by tactical and propagandistic usage by politicians. Advantages have sometimes been seen in using the concept of "alliance", with its implied dynamism and cohesion, for rather loose agreements for co-operation. Thus the US assistance programme to Latin America was dubbed the "Alliance for Progress."[8] Politicians have done even more to debase the technical concept of "collective security". In fact, "verbal politics" is rife in the practice of alliance policy: one man's Treaty of Friendship and Co-operation is likely to be another man's Treaty of Enslavement.

The Evolution of Alliances

Agreements on military co-operation are as old as relations between sovereign political units. Early writings have described the changing alliance policies of societies as far apart in space and time as ancient China after 800 BC, ancient India around 300 BC, the Greek city states, the Italian city states, and the early modern states system in Western Europe.[9] These systems, which might be loosely called "international", exhibited many of the characteristic features of more recent times, namely, bi-polarity, multipolarity, attempts at preponderance, counter-availing efforts to achieve equilibrium, and the complications to a balance of power situation caused by power differentials, geography, and value systems. Within these settings alliances played a major regulating role, performing "their several functions through movement as much as through being".[10]

The processes of formal military co-ordination were an integral part of the so-called "classical" modern state system, which existed from the mid-seventeenth century to the First World War.[11] The search for allies was a central objective of the foreign policies of the major powers. During the 1815-1939 period 112 alliance commitments were made; although there was clustering, no decade was without a new alliance, and the *average* figure was almost one alliance a year.[12] Alliances were formed for both acquisitive and defensive purposes, by adding to a nation's own power, by withholding the power of other nations from the adversary, and by restraining an ally by limiting its political options. Typical commitments included subsidies to support the forces of an ally, guarantees to fight alongside an ally under stated circumstances, pledges of non-intervention or mutual abstention in the event that one or both allies should become involved in a war with third parties, and agreements about sharing the fruits of victory.[13] Sometimes the would-be conquerors were deterred: on other occasions war was the outcome. Whether or not the kaleidoscope of international politics was immediately shaken, it was certain to be in the longer run. Alliances, nationalism and war changed the pieces and the patterns, but the processes of inter-state relations remained the same.

Britain was a key actor during the classical balance of power period. A characteristic feature of British behaviour was the manipulation by governments of its alliance potential in order to ensure that no one state predominated over Europe. From its position of "splendid isolation" it was able to be the "holder" of the European balance, forming the heart of alliances against such aspiring hegemonial powers as Spain, France, and Germany. Britain's shifting — some would say shifty — position over this long period gave ample demonstration of the maxim that "politics makes strange bedfellows." Indeed even at the height of the religious wars it had been possible for countries to set aside their religious differences for a period, and to act together to further limited interests. Similarly, conflicting value systems did not necessarily prevent mutually beneficial collaboration between countries in the age of ideology. Given Britain's traditional role it is not accidental that some of the most telling statements on alliances have been made by British statesmen. Outstanding amongst these were Palmerston's observation that nations have neither permanent enemies nor permanent allies, only permanent interests, and the comment of Churchill, the arch anti-Bolshevik, in support of British aid to the Soviet Union:

> I have only one purpose, the destruction of Hitler, and my life is much simplified thereby. If Hitler invaded Hell I would make at least a favourable reference to the Devil in the House of Commons.[14]

Such statements represent the pith of alliance *Realpolitik*.

World War One discredited the old system of alliances and balance of power in the minds of many people. Between 1914 and 1918 'symmetry of power, which is duly appreciated can breed restraint, led, perhaps because of miscalculation, to excess.'[15] Equilibrium did not deter violence, as it was supposed to, but instead pushed it to its utmost. Largely as a result of this experience, the League of Nations and its system of so-called "collective security" was established as an alternative. Needless to say, the League failed to achieve the impossible dream of its most idealistic supporters. Not only did it fail to prevent major war, but it also failed to eradicate alliances and the other manifestations of the discredited system. In the end, the outbreak of the Second World War discredited the League more than alliances, for the lesson which many learnt was that a peaceful deterrent alliance "was essential to peace and order."[16]

The United Nations system which emerged in 1945 was a mixture of "collective security" (ideologically, and on relatively minor matters) and "balance of power" (in practical application and in matters of major importance to international peace).[17] From some perspectives the UN experiment may be judged a modest success as far as peace and security is concerned, but as Claude has argued, this is more the consequence of the "prudential pacifism" engendered by technological and other changes since 1945 than the impact of the UN.[18]

1914 stands as the symbol of the failure of the old system, but statesmen have shown by their actions in the intervening sixty years that they remain more satisfied with the old system than with any alternatives which might be devised. Four times more peacetime alliances were formed during the twenty years of the "new world" after 1919 than had been formed during the last twenty years of the "old world": in fact, there were appreciably more alliances in the twenty years after 1919 (seventy-one) than there had been in the previous century (fifty-nine).[19] *Plus ca change. . . .*

In a useful essay on the subject, Dinerstein has noted that contemporary alliances differ from "traditional" (i.e. pre-1914) alliances in three important respects.[20] Firstly, "political" goals have superseded "military" goals. This has been the result of the determination of the major powers to avoid war. However, as the superpower relationship has been conducted increasingly on the assumption that outstanding issues would be resolved only by political means, the secondary members of their alliances have been able to pursue their goals in the confidence that there would not be a world war. In contrast with earlier times, therefore, conflicts with the "hegemonic power" within each alliance involves only political and economic costs, not fear of isolation or abandonment in war. The result has been that secondary powers, "while less influential in alliance military arrangements, enjoy more freedom of action within the alliance." Secondly, the relative power and number of participant states has altered significantly. The main change has been that the disparity in power between the largest state in each alliance and the next largest is greater than ever before. One consequence of this is that the superpowers, despite their differences over many issues, have common interests which are not shared by their allies: they have become "adversary partners". In addition, many of the vastly increased number of independent states in the system are able to exist without having to join the major alliances, or face conquest. Thirdly, ideology has become a major factor in foreign policy. Although its role has been variable, ideological affinities did have an impact during the Cold War which was marked when compared with before 1914. In addition to these changes in the character of contemporary alliances, two more should be added.[21] There has been the rise of a notable degree of peacetime planning, co-ordination, and even integration within some alliances. In earlier times governments did not find it necessary to engage in extensive military preparations in peacetime, but if contemporary alliances are to achieve their primary purposes their members have no alternative. A final characteristic of contemporary alliances has been the reduction of their flexibility: the number of alliances and the frequency of shifts of alliance amongst the major states has decreased.

These changed characteristics of contemporary alliances are not immutable. However, it appears certain that the technological threat will remain so grave that political goals will continue to supersede military goals, and that peacetime co-ordination will remain a prominent feature of operative alliances. But some developments have already proceeded quite far since Dinerstein wrote. Firstly, while the disparity in military power between the superpowers and their allies seems likely to persist, political and economic changes have fragmented diplomatic power in the last ten years, so that the hegemonial authority of the superpowers has been reduced. Secondly, as Dinerstein himself noted, the intense importance of ideology in the Cold War appears to have been transitional; the foreign policies of the United States, the Soviet Union, and the Chinese People's Republic have been characterised by increasing secularisation.

The Roots of Alliances

The literature reveals a wide range of motives behind the alliance policies of different countries. The scheme below is one way of classifying the primary determinant. A variety of motives is usually present in any particular alliance; the categories below are overlapping rather than mutually exclusive.[22]

1. Balance of power considerations

The traditional and still predominant explanation of alliances arises out of "balance of power" considerations. From this viewpoint alliances are means by which states co-operate in order to increase their military power in the hope of preserving international stability. States wishing to attain or maintain equilibrium can do so either by diminishing the weight of the heavier scale or by increasing the weight of the higher scale; their methods have been divide and rule, compensations, armaments and alliances.[23] For most states alliances represent the only option by which they can significantly increase their international power.[24]

Alliances therefore can be regarded as "a necessary function of the balance of power operating within a multiple-state system."[25] Their functions are various: to deter particular countries or alliances which may be threatening to achieve regional or global hegemony; to preserve international order by establishing through the restraint or control of allies a "stable, predictable, and safe pattern"[26] of international politics within an area of common concern; or to join in an existing conflict against a potentially hegemonial power or alliance. In the period of "intensive bipolarity" which characterised the Cold War, alliances served three functions: to add power to that of the protecting superpower; to "draw lines", to leave no doubt in the adversary's mind of the alignment of forces; and to give the superpower a legal reason for intervention to preserve the territorial *status quo.*[27] Where balance of power considerations are primary, therefore, the states forming alliances are either seeking objectives for which their own resources are insufficient, or are seeking to lessen the costs of attaining an objective, or are attempting to attain an objective more quickly than would otherwise be possible[28] or reduce the impact of antagonistic pressure.[29] Clearly, from this perspective "conflicts are the primary determinants of alignments."[30]

The balance of power approach is very useful for understanding some of the motivations underlying alliances. However, it cannot explain everything: there are, for example, deviant cases of "irrational" alliance, which cannot be satisfactorily explained in balance of power terms.[31] Thus the United States has been accused of "pactomania", of "indiscriminately collecting allies whether they were strategically placed or not, strong or weak, developed or underdeveloped."[32] A further proof that alliances are not the mechanistic result of the operation of the balance of power process is that threats, even commonly perceived threats, can result in non-alignment (and neutrality) as well as alliance policy. To understand why alliances are formed, therefore, it is usually necessary to go beyond balance of power considerations, important as they often are.

2. Coalition theories
"Coalition theories" are a very recent explanation of alliance formulation.[33] Their focus is the "size principle", the idea that "participants create coalitions just as large as they believe will ensure winning and no larger."[34] In contrast to alliances in equilibrium theories, in coalition theories "the actors are assumed to be motivated by the single goal of winning, and doing so under conditions that maximise their share of the gain — that is, with as few partners as are necessary to achieve victory."[35] While the "size principle" has merit as an insight — if a rather obvious one — into some alliances, there are very many limitations to this approach as a general explanation. There is, for example, the problem of, defining "winning" in the modern context: how can the spoils of successful deterrence be divided? Furthermore, in deterrent alliances the objective is often to form large alliances rather than the smallest successful coalition. Coalition theories have attracted more attention than influence, even amongst those attracted to quantification.[36]

3. National attributes
Those who explain alliance motivation in terms of "national attributes" emphasise factors other than almost Pavlovian responses to balance of

power considerations. Instead, a variety of other factors has been identified as determinants of the "alliance-proneness" of different nations. These include domestic considerations (especially economic interests), leadership needs, ideological affiliations, and historical experience. The latter appears to be of particular importance. States which have for a long period achieved their objectives by their own efforts, such as Switzerland and Sweden, are less prone to collaborate: on the other hand, states which have been allied tend to remain so.[37] The different attitudes of Norway and Sweden are interesting. Both countries share similar positions, cultures, and attributes, yet the former joined NATO, the latter maintained its vigorous neutrality.

The stark contrast between Sweden and Norway is not typical. In very many cases balance of power considerations can be seen to prevail over national attitudes, however firmly held. Newly independent states do not necessarily shun alliances, and even states which historically, emotionally, and philosophically have shunned alliances have not abjured them in changed circumstances. For a century-and-a-half the United States followed the warnings of Washington against "permanent alliances" and Jefferson against "entangling alliances": within a few years of Cold War, however, the United States was at the heart of multiple alliances and was being criticised for "pactomania".

4. Affiliation theories

"Affiliation theories" do not concentrate on the special attributes of single countries, but instead examine the similarities and differences between one or more countries as an element in their propensity to choose allies.[38] In this respect the significance of the ideological factor has been a subject of considerable discussion and disagreement. Some have argued that a common ideology has been an important factor in alliance formulation, as catalyst and then as cement.[39] Others have argued that ideology has not been a prerequisite for alliances, and usually has been unimportant in what is essentially a marriage of convenience.[40]

The prevailing view is that ideology "may" influence the choice of alliance partners: however, ideology does not rule out marriages of convenience between ideological rivals,[41] or adversary relationships between ideological cousins. While the ideological factor cannot provide a general explanation, therefore, it might sometimes be significant. For example, nations may not be able to align "rationally" because of ideological or historical biases.[42] This possibility was the root of what A.J.P. Taylor has argued was one of Hitler's greatest mistakes, namely his declaration of war against the United States following Japan's attack on Pearl Harbour: his declaration was a fateful act of "gratuitous loyalty."[43] Hitler doubtless felt that Japan was his "natural" ally; however, by declaring war against Japan's enemy, the United States,

Hitler helped to save Britain, and bring about his own defeat.

The ideological factor might be significant on some occasions, but is often not important, for as Liska has put it, "Alliances are against, and only derivatively for, someone or something."[44] Thus the maxim that "politics makes strange bedfellows" remains valid. Churchill's famous 1941 quotation has already been noted. Over thirty years later an equally ideological leader, Mao Tse-tung, expressed a similar recognition of the flexibility of alliance policy: he told the Chinese people that history developed in a spiral, and that the friends of yesterday may be the enemies of tomorrow.[45]

5. Domestic Factors

Several writers have argued that alliance policies are sometimes "closely linked" to domestic needs.[46] In the past, it has been noted that some nations have undertaken programmes of territorial expansion for various domestic reasons, and that they have sometimes combined to form aggressive military alliances to further these ends.[47]

In the post-1945 period, however, domestic considerations have affected alliance policy more through the compulsions of internal security rather than through domestic pressures for self-extension. Political units (as they have throughout history) have offered their military capabilities to other states in order to help maintain friendly governments in power or to perpetuate particular régimes against internal and/or externally supported rebellion or subversion. Certainly, internal factors have played an important part in US alliance policy since the Second World War. While defence against a common threat has been their ostensible justification, an equally important consideration has been the desire to protect weak régimes against internal threats.[48]

It does not require much cynicism to conclude that when weak régimes bang the drum about an external threat, especially if their claim is decorated with ideological demonlogy, they are not engaged in "strategy" in its traditional (outward-oriented) meaning, but they are engaged in furthering their domestic interests. Alliance policy may be a cloak for internal security policy.

Some recent studies have underlined the potential importance of other domestic considerations, including factionalism and intra-governmental bargaining, on the shaping of a country's alliance policy.[49] Nevertheless, however useful in illuminating particular cases, domestic needs cannot *generally* explain the motivation for alliances any more than the other explanations: non-alignment and neutralism are also policies which may be inspired from domestic concerns.[50]

Summary : expediency or principle?

While some nations appear to be more alliance-prone than others, the formation of an alliance is not a matter of principle: alliances are formed for specific contextual reasons. If governments can fulfil their aims without the burden of obligations, then they will, if they are rational. Therefore alliances arise out of communities of interests between states; the interests may be complementary or identical but their achievement requires co-ordination with others. Once the alliance has been formed the actors then can hope to achieve a range of goals. The alliance introduces specific commitments to pursue them; it creates mutual obligations which increase the probability that the partners will act; and it creates a new situation in the external world, which may strengthen the alliance bonds, at least in the short term.[51]

While it may be valid to suggest that policies of non-alignment are the policies which every government would follow in an ideal world,[52] where no power conflicts called for special defence arrangements, in a system where self-interest is the prevailing norm, expediency will inevitably result in alliances.

The Dynamics of Alliances

In their studies of the dynamics of alliances, the so-called traditionalists and the so-called formal theorists[53] have been mainly interested in understanding the factors which affect the cohesion. the size, the efficiency, the decision-making structure, the distribution of benefits, burdens, and influence, and the decay and termination of alliances. The wealth of material is not easily summarised and assessed: all that can be attempted is an indication of the range of ideas about the life of alliances which have been expressed in a multitude of propositions, hypotheses, assertions, and Confucian-like maxims.[54]

The factors making for the solidarity or otherwise of alliances has perhaps been the subject of most general interest. Some empirical support can be found for almost every conceivable theoretical proposition.

The relationship between external threat and alliance cohesiveness is a matter of major significance, for most writers have regarded external threat as the major determinant in the rise and fall of alliances. However, the relationship is not a simple one. Certainly external threat is important in the formation of alliances; given the conventional definition of alliance this proposition is largely tautological. In the course of the life of an alliance external threat can cause allies to draw together, or rally around the alliance leader: on the other hand, a rising external threat can cause allies to defect, or to disagree if they seriously differ about the target, nature, and scope of the threat. A rising threat might produce neutralism as well as alliance cohesion, and some alliances outlive their original enemy. Because of the importance of threats in alliance formation, it is not surprising that most writers consider that perceptions of declining threat are likely to reduce alliance cohesion.

The ideological factor in the life of alliances is one which has attracted much interest, and there is a wide range of opinion about its role in alliance cohesion. Some writers emphasise the stresses and strains caused by ideological homogeneity: others emphasise that it contributes to their smooth operation. Amongst the stresses which have been identified in an ideologically under-pinned alliance are those said to be caused by the difficulty of bargaining and compromise between ideologically sensitive partners, the obscuring of material interests by ideological considerations, and the tendency to splinter amongst purists. Those who argue that ideological affinities cement alliances base their view on the belief that a community of interests in an alliance will be strengthened by the enthusiasm which comes from moral conviction: common ideology strengthens the in-group/out-group dichotomy, and helps partners more easily overcome their differences. There is little agreement about the effects of particular types of ideology. Alliances between authoritarian régimes can be argued to be more unstable, since decisions might depend on the whims of a few individuals, whereas the policies of democratic allies tend to be more broadly based. On the other hand it can be argued that alliances between democratic allies are more unstable, since governments change more frequently than in authoritarian countries. Authoritarian régimes, freer from the constraints of public opinion, can be more flexible, but on the other hand they are not thought to be as predisposed to consult with their allies. Perhaps the most valid assessment of the role of ideology is the view that common values do help to cement an alliance as long as tenets of ideology and doctrinal unity do not become important issues in themselves.

Since "size" is the aspect of alliances most amenable to quantification, it has received much attention from formal theorists. However, their researches have not added much, other than confirmation, to the already widespread and common-sense view that the larger the number of allies, the greater the scope for differences of opinion, and the greater the reduction of efficiency. However, this does not mean that small means streamlined, for even in the smallest alliance particular contextual factors can maximise differences and minimise efficiency.

There are many general propositions concerning the duration and geographical scope of alliances. It can be argued that the longer an alliance endures, the more likely to develop are disruptive stresses and strains, especially if the original threat has subsided. On the other hand, it can be argued that every year added to the life of an alliance increases its legitimacy in the eyes of the partners, and so increases the belief that it is a good thing in itself, almost regardless of occasional strains and the rise and fall of threats. Similarly, geographical factors can have contradictory effects. It can be argued that distance is insignificant, for cohesion is based upon interests: on the other hand, it can be argued that distance between allies is detrimental to unity.

Diametrically opposed positions can be taken on almost all other aspects of the life of alliances. Amongst other factors which have been said to contribute to stresses and strains are: rigidity of organisation, superpower domination, lack of consultation, domestic instability amongst the partners, suspicion of allies, uncertainty of the status of the allies, uncertainties about the exact nature of the commitment, the presence of sub-groups within an alliance, the presence of different strategic priorities, differences in allied capabilities, ignorance about the decision-making structure of other allied governments, differences about issues not concerned with the alliance, and differences about the appropriate share of burdens, influence and rewards. In contrast, amongst the factors which have been said to make for cohesion are: efficient communications between the allies, a degree of economic interdependence, a larger range of common interests than expressed in the alliance, mutual confidence in the competence and military credibility and political dependability of the allies, and a willingness to accept a division of labour on the alliance's military tasks.

Alliance efficacy is closely related to the cohesiveness or otherwise of a particular alliance. While an alliance which is not particularly cohesive can still achieve its goals, clearly its prospects are improved if the partners are in agreement about the approach to be adopted, and are able to co-ordinate their activities. It has been argued that centralized alliances are best suited to imposing cohesion, making rapid decisions, and dealing with changes. On the other hand it has been argued that decentralized alliances are more likely to encourage consultation and adherence, and so establish the foundation for cohesion.

A final set of interests for students of alliances is the difficult question of the distribution of burdens, influence, and rewards. Normally, it might be expected that such distribution will tend towards being one-sided, towards the country or countries which have most "power". However, this does not necessarily follow: several writers have pointed to the advantages possessed by "weaker" allies, in alliances between democratic states, in polarised international situations where a small power possesses important material or strategic assets, or when a large power has committed its prestige to the defence of the small power. While there is never a simple relationship between capability and the ability to influence decisions in alliances, there is often some relationship, and who co-ordinates whom is usually quite clear.

This brief introduction to the complex natural history of alliances should have underlined three points: the wide variety of viewpoints about the dynamics of alliances; the difficulty of advancing propositions of general validity; and the essential impermanence of particular alliances, however many solidifying factors are present.

The Obsolescence of Alliances?

Some strong voices have been heard in the last twenty years arguing that alliances are obsolete, or that they are no longer as important as before. A variety of arguments have been put forward in support of such views, and the factor of nuclear weapons always figures prominently. It is sometimes argued that nuclear weapons have an "equalising" effect: thus, by acquiring independent nuclear power relatively small countries can deter attack by the greatest, thereby depriving alliances of one of their traditional functions. Secondly, it is argued that allies cannot be trusted in the nuclear age, because, whatever commitments have been made in peacetime, no nation would jeopardise its very survival ("would commit suicide") if nuclear was threatened. The risks faced in helping allies in the nuclear age are radically greater than ever before. Thirdly, it is argued that alliances can no longer serve their traditional balance of power functions because of the inflexibility of the modern international situation. In a world of two hostile camps and an uncommitted Third World, movement is very limited. Furthermore, it is also argued that movement would be insiginificant. The two superpowers are so powerful that no alternative grouping could seriously affect them: no state can "hold the balance" as Britain has traditionally done. In addition, the critics of alliances argue that two-bloc systems are inherently unstable and that developing imbalances can only be redressed by arms racing, which results in increased danger and tension. Alliances are therefore said to spread danger rather than buttress stability; they only increase the number of possible nuclear targets. A further argument of the critics is that modern alliances weaken rather than strengthen deterrence, because promises of helping allies in the face of national suicide are incredible; superpower credibility is therefore reduced.

In general terms then it is argued that alliances should be regarded as obsolete because they perpetuate an "old and discredited" system of international politics, namely traditional power politics. They are said to be manifestations of an intellectual time-lag, examples of the way statesmen deal with the problems of tomorrow with the concepts of yesterday — a not unfamiliar phenomenon in politics. Furthermore, it is sometimes argued that if international war continues to decline as an instrument of policy, then the traditional functions of alliances will decline even further.

Such arguments as those above have been advanced from a number of viewpoints. Some French strategic writers, notably General Gallois, have stressed the unreliability of allies in the nuclear age.[55] Some academic observers, notably Morgenthau and Kissinger, have stressed the paradoxes and altered character of alliances in the nuclear age.[56] And some critics of strategic theory, notably Burton, have stressed the misbegotten character of contemporary alliances.[57] From these standpoints, three types of policy prescription follow. Advocates of the first standpoint invariably stress the desirability of independent nuclear forces, either within or outside existing alliances.[58] Advocates of the second standpoint see alliances as "troubled partnerships" not performing all their traditional roles, but still capable of serving some national interests. Advocates of the third viewpoint see non-alignment as the only rational posture in the modern world.

Against the critics of alliances several contrary arguments may be advanced. Firstly, while the flexibility of alliances has been reduced, this does not mean that they are "obsolete": the nuclear age is only thirty years old, and has not provided sufficient case studies.[59] Secondly, while the reliability of allies might have declined, the destructiveness of nuclear weapons enhances deterrence. Even a small possibility of total obliteration should be enough in almost all circumstances to deter most potential aggressors and therefore not put allies to the test. Finally, the presence of a large number of alliances in the world testifies to the confidence of governments that some interests can be furthered by alliance membership, even if not all the traditional ones, in all the traditional ways. Members still find alliances functional for a variety of internal and external security needs. For many states there are circumstances in which they believe that the benefits of alliance membership outweigh the costs. Critical as they were of alliance, France under de Gaulle and China under Mao Tse-tung did not abrogate the treaties to which they had earlier adhered, in the French case the North Atlantic Treaty (1949) and in China's case the Treaty of Friendship, Alliance and Mutal Assistance (1950) with the Soviet Union. Despite Franco-United States differences and Sino-Soviet hostility, the treaties were allowed to remain intact. One day even the leakiest nuclear umbrella might have provided them with some shelter. Or, as a Soviet spokesman put it during the polemics with China, "don't foul the well; you may need the water."

Alliances and the International System

The study of the relationship between alliances and aspects of the international system has fallen into a distinct pattern, reflecting changing concerns about international affairs. This close relationship between theory and its historical context is significant, for it is evident that some of the familiar generalisations about alliances and the international system have been based on a limited range of experience.

The crucial question concerns the stabilizing and destabilizing potential of alliances: basically, do they deter or do they stimulate the propensity of international relations towards tension, crisis, and war?[60] As with all other aspects of alliance studies there have been many viewpoints: alliances have been seen as both the major bastion or order and national survival, and as major catalysts of danger and war. Strong historical experiences have been adduced in support of both sets of arguments.

Those who argue that alliances are fundamentally stabilising largely base their opinion on the nineteenth-century experience, the bipolar stability of the Cold War, and the absence of clearly articulated deterrent alliances when major war broke out in 1914 and 1939. This traditional argument is that alliances have been a major process by which international power has been "balanced", and order maintained. Counteravailing alliances have been formed to deter or to defeat nations or groups of nations which have sought to achieve preponderance. They have sought to maximise stability by aggregating deterrent power, and thereby oppose developing imbalances which might increase the chances of war.[61] Alliances have sustained continuity of policy and have introduced an important element of predictability into a situation by drawing politico-geographical lines and clarifying intent. In addition they have been used to restrain allies,[62] which in the nuclear age has been said to include inhibiting the spread of nuclear proliferation. To the extent therefore that a balance of power policy contributes to international stability — and many practitioners and theorists would claim that there is no feasible alternative — then alliances clearly play a decisive role.

Few balance of power theorists are complacent about the dangers of the approach which they analyse, and sometimes recommend. Few would deny the inherent difficulties, uncertainties, unrealities and inadequacies of balance of power policies.[63] However, while critics of balance of power approaches might quote Martin's comment on 1914-18 with approval,[64] supporters would argue that 1914 has been wrongly assessed: to the latter 1914 illustrated the dangers of failing to pursue alliance policy with due care, and in particular, the danger of failing to make one's intentions sufficiently explicit.[65] Thus those who have argued that alliances are basically stabilising rest their case on the belief that in an imperfect world peacetime deterrent alliances are one of the few instruments by which states can hope to improve the prospect for international stability. A fundamental problem in assessing their stabilising effects, however, is that it is in the nature of things that successful deterrence can rarely be "registered and counted".[66] In contrast, the episodes of unsuccessful deterrence have been obvious and impressive.

The view that alliances are essentially destabilising has been based upon some notable collapses of international order. This criticism has been naturally enmeshed with general critiques of the balance of power concept.

While it might be argued that alliances might contribute to equilibrium in the short term, it is a common view that balance of power systems always contain within them the "seeds of their own destruction", because of a range of subjective and objective difficulties, not the least of which is actually defining "balance". From this perspective alliances have been seen as symptoms rather than fundamental causes of international tension, but certainly symptoms which can exacerbate the unfortunate condition of international relations: they have been seen to have a self-fulfilling nature, which results in them bringing about the tension and confrontation which they were presumably designed to minimise.[67] Not only might the race for alliances intensify conflict, but they might also increase the area and scope of the original conflict. They can stimulate tension in peace, and expand fighting in war. The process by which the struggle in the Balkans became a major European war in 1914 is the classical example used in support of this argument, though the process was not as simple as it sometimes imagined.[68] Other arguments used to support the view that alliances tend to stimulate international tension include the criticism that secret treaties increase unpredictability,[69] that alliances sometimes outlive their usefulness and result in states finding themselves in undesirable situations,[70] that alliances polarize international relations, and that alliances tend to develop their own policy imperatives. The latter may work against tension-reducing policies by the maintenance of a stereotype "threat", or by the development of an activist or interventionist policy from a perceived need to defend every boundary and a determination to take offence at any challenge to one's credibility.[71]

The debate about the relationship between alliances and conflict continues, and still fluctuates with current experience. After a period (roughly 1940-65) in which the stabilizing effects of alliances were often stressed (though not of course by the non-aligned) we have seen from the late 1960s a rehabilitation of the view that alliances are a major source of international tension and violence. The background of this change was the war in Vietnam and the continuing Middle Eastern crisis.[72] While the force of these examples is considerable, their meaning can be upturned. It can be argued that the Vietnam War was a *misapplication* of alliance policy, or power theory, and of Schelling's "art of commitment" (and what human activity is likely to be free of mistakes?). Furthermore, it could be argued that, terrible as it was, the Vietnam War was a lesser evil, and that not to have fought would have been more dangerous to international stability in the longer run; this was certainly the argument of the domino theorists. As far as the Middle East is concerned, it might be argued that formal alliances were irrelevant to the evolution of the situation, and that on the whole superpower involvement has done something to restrain an inherently dangerous situation.

Whatever the arguments, the fact is that many alliances continue to persist. This suggests that many governments believe in their stabilising potential, or at least consider that their destabilising potential is outweighed by more important considerations; and some governments believe that they have no alternative but to join an alliance. This continuing belief in the role of alliances seems substantiated by the rule or norm (Brodie calls it "a kind of etiquette") which, even today, holds that governments must always seek to strengthen rather than weaken alliances, as if such an outcome were self-evidently desirable.[73]

In the light of all the conflicting evidence and viewppoints, a summary of the relationship between alliances and war is not easily achieved.

The safest course is to take refuge in the multi-causality of events, and agree with Liska's masterly fence-sitting verdict that "In themselves, alliances neither limit nor expand conflicts any more than they cause or prevent them."[74]

If states have not been able to secure their interests by "going it alone", then alliances have been their most frequent option. Other alternatives, collective security and neutralism, have not been seen to be satisfactory for those centrally involved.

The basic principle of collective security is that an attack upon one state will be regarded as an attack upon all states. The history of the concept has been a disappointing one for its supporters.[75] It has been a constant illustration of the tremendous gap which can exist between a relatively simple theory and the great complexity of practical reality. Even to the extent that it has been practised, collective security has not been an acceptable alternative to alliances. Indeed, it is very doubtful if the idea of collective security is even feasible with any international situation we are likely to know, because of the objective and subjective requirements of the pure theory.[76]

In contrast to the commitment implied in the ideas of alliance and collective security, many of the new states which were spawned by the decolonisation of the 1950s and which swelled the United Nations, sought refuge elsewhere, in the doctrine and practice of neutralism and non-alignment.[77] The typical new state which emerged during the Cold War was militarily weak, economically underdeveloped, geographically remote from the central conflict, lacking in a foreign policy tradition, and often politically unsettled. For such states a policy of neutralism made tactical sense, militarily and economically, and it also fulfilled national psychological needs. Adopting a neutralist posture in a bi-polar system gave some of these new countries an influence which often exceeded their objective capabilities.[78] Furthermore, as with alliances, if not more so, the neutralist stance was often a function of domestic pressures and considerations. Neutralism flourished for a period as a positive idea, but lost its former significance with the relaxation of Cold War tensions: indeed, the very word "neutralist" already has something of an old-fashioned ring to it.

Alliances have sometimes been considered to be potentially important catalysts towards regional integration. There has been some evidence for this: wartime alliances between German states and between Swiss cantons helped the development of their national communities. On the other hand, alliances are generally thought to break up when common danger disappears, and there is overwhelming evidence for this. In a growing period of peace it is understandable that there might be attempts by the supporters of particular alliances to add more than a military dimension to their relationship, in order to increase the sense of identity amongst the members. This occurred to some extent with NATO at the end of the 1960s, but subsequently there has been little or no enthusiasm for the idea. Generally, the tasks and functions performed by alliances and international integrative institutions are radically different.[79] As Fedder has put it: "While nations may congregate in alliance, they do not merge."[80]

Collective security in its pure theory is a dream. Neutralism and non-alignment seem unlikely to become the "norm" they are sometimes claimed to be, as long as the "ideal" world remains far off. Going it alone will not be a profitable option for some states. Alliances therefore, with all their faults, burdens, dangers, and difficulties seem destined to remain an important feature of the international system, especially for those states most involved in the great issues of world politics. Certain aspects of the character of alliances might continue to change: they will be rigid rather than flexible, they will be declarations of intent rather than vehicles for fighting, there will be fewer rather than more of them, and they may tend to be inward rather than outward orientated. However, they are unlikely to disappear until the propensity of states to utilise military power and force as an instrument of policy becomes obsolete.

Notes

1. This was George Modelski's comment in a review article. The book under discussion was George Liska's *Nations in Alliance. The Limits of Interdependence* (Baltimore: The Johns Hopkins Press, 1962). The comment has a more general application. See Modelski's "The Study of Alliances: A Review", *Journal of Conflict Resolution,* VII, Vol. No. 4, December 1963, pp. 769-76.
2. Ole R. Holsti, P. Terrence Hopmann, and John D. Sullivan, *Unity and Distintegration in International Alliances: Comparative Studies* (New York: John Wiley and Sons, 1973), pp. 249-77.
3. This is an increasingly prevalent view. See, for example, Ole R. Holsti ibid., pp. 226, and Edwin H. Fedder, "The Concept of Alliance", *International Studies Quarterly,* 12, 1968, pp. 65-86.
4. This is the definition used by Ole R. Holsti *et al.,* ibid, p. 4.
5. The phrase is used by Sylvia Kowitt Crosbie, in *A Tacit Alliance: Frnce and Israel from Suez to the Six Day War* (Princeton, N.J.: Princeton University Press, 1974), especially p. 215 ff.
6. William R. Kintner and Robert L. Pfaltzgraff Jr., *SALT: Implications for Arms Control in the 1970s* (Pittsburgh: University of Pittsburgh Press, 1973), p. 309.
7. Raymond F. Hopkins and Richard W. Mansbach, *Structure and Process in International Politics* (New York: Harper and Row, 1973), p. 306.
8. Arnold Wolfers, "Alliances", in *International Encyclopaedia of the Social Sciences,* D.L. Sils, (ed.), (USA: The Macmillan Co, 1968), Vol. 1, p. 260.
9. An interesting but selective introduction to "some international systems in history" may be found in Robert Purnell, *The Society of States. An Introduction to International Politics* (London: Weidenfeld and Nicolson, 1973), pp. 35-65.
10. Liska, op. cit., p. 12
11. The characteristics of this system are revealed through the Editor's Introduction and the useful set of readings in Laurance W. Martin's *Diplomacy in Modern European History* (London: Collier-Macmillan Ltd., 1966).
12. J. David Singer and Melvin Small, "Formal Alliances, 1815-1939. A Quantitative Description", *Journal of Peace Research,* Vol. 3, No. 1 (1966), pp. 1-32. See especially Table 2. Reprinted in J.R. Friedman, C. Bladen and S. Rosen,

Alliance in International Politics (Boston: Allyn and Bacon, 1970), pp. 130-64. Their definition of alliance includes "Defence Pacts", "Neutrality and Non-Aggression Pacts", and *"Ententes"*.

13. See Robert E. Osgood, *Alliances and American Foreign Policy* (Baltimore: The Johns Hopkins Press, 1968), pp. 25-7, and Hans J. Morgenthau, *Politics Among Nations. The Struggle for Power and Peace* (New York: Alfred A. Knopf, 1965, 3rd edition), p. 181 ff.

14. Winston S. Churchill, *The Grand Alliance* (Boston: Houghton Mifflin Co., 1951), p. 370, quoted by Ole R. Holsti, op. cit., p. 223.

15. Martin, op. cit., p. 9

16. Osgood, op. cit., p. 30. Elsewhere, Osgood has judged the quality of statesmen in the past in terms of their understanding of deterrence policy. See *Force, Order, and Justice* (Baltimore: Johns Hopkins Press, 1967).

17. Inis L. Claude Jr., "The Management of Power in the Changing United Nations", *International Organisation*, XV, ii, Spring 1961, pp. 219-35.

18. Inis L. Claude Jr., *The Changing United Nations* (New York: Random House, 1967), pp. 7-13.

19. This conclusion is drawn from Singer and Small, op. cit., Table 2.

20. Herbert Dinerstein, "The Transformation of Alliance Systems", *The American Political Science Review,* Vol. LIX, No. 3, September 1965, pp. 589-601.

21. See, for example, Osgood, op. cit., pp. 25-31.

22. With the exception of the fifth category, "Domestic Factors", the categorisation below is based upon the approaches to alliance formulation analysed by Ole R. Holsti *et al.,* op. cit., pp. 4-14, 219-26.

23. Morgenthau, op. cit., Chapter 12.

24. See, for example, Inis L. Claude Jr., *Power and International Relations* (New York: Random House, 1962), p. 89.

25. Morgenthau, op. cit., p. 181

26. Osgood, op. cit., p. 22

27. John W. Spanier, *Games Nations Play. Analyzing International Politics;* (London Nelson, 1972), pp. 69 ff., 191 ff.

28. Hopkins and Mansbach, op. cit., p. 307-8.

29. Liska, op. cit., p. 26

30. Ibid., p. 12·

31. Ole R. Holsti *et al.,* op. cit., pp. 6, 221.

32. See, for example, Spanier, op. cit., p. 69.

33. This approach has been most closely associated with W.H. Riker, *The Theory of Political Coalitions* (New Haven: Yale Univeristy Press, 1967), especially Chapters 2 and 3. Relevant extracts are reprinted in Friedman *et al.,* op. cit., pp. 263-76.

34. Riker, op. cit., pp. 32-3.

35. Ole R. Holsti's succint summary, op. cit., p. 7.

36. For an idea of the limitations of this approach, see, for example, ibid. pp. 9-10, 69-79, 221-2; Karl W. Deutsch, *The Analysis of International Politics* (Englewood Cliffs, N.J.: Prentice Hall Inc., 1968), pp. 136-40; Steven Rosen, "A Model of War and Alliance" in Friedman, op. cit., pp. 215-37; Bruce M. Russett, "Components of an Operational Theory of International Alliance Formation", *Journal of Conflict Resolution, Vol. XII, No. 3, September 1968* pp. 285-301. Reprinted in Friedman, op. cit., pp. 238-58.

37. e.g. Harold Guetzkow, "Isolation and Collaboration: A Partial Theory of Inter-Nation Relations", *Journal of Conflict Resolution,* 1, 1957, pp. 48-68; and Henry Tuene and Sid Synnestredt, "Measuring International Alignment", *Orbis,* Vol. IX, No. 1, Spring 1965, pp. 171-89. Reprinted in Friedman *et al.,* op. cit., pp. 316-32.

38. Ole R. Holsti *et al.,* op. cit., p. 12.

39. e.g. Osgood, op. cit., p. 20

40. e.g. Wolfers, op. cit., p. 270, see also Morgenthau, op. cit., p. 184.
41. e.g. Tuene and Synnestredt, op. cit., p. 188.
42. Liska, op. cit., p. 27.
43. A.J. P. Taylor, *English History 1914-1945* (Oxford: Oxford University Press, 1965), p. 532.
44. Liska, op. cit., p. 12. Ole R. Holsti and his associates found that between 1815 and 1939 there was only a "moderate tendency" for nations that shared an ideological viewpoint to undertake more binding commitments; there was no support for the view that such alliances would enjoy greater longevity. In fact, they discovered that ideological alliances were less likely than heterogeneous alliances to be renewed or to endure for a long time. op. cit., p. 220.
45. Quoted by John Gittings, *Guardian,* 3 November 1974.
46. e.g. Guetzkow, op. cit. K.J. Holsti, *International Politics. A Framework for Analysis* (Englewood Cliffs, N.J.: Prentice Hall Inc., 1972), second edition, p. 112-13; Liska, op. cit., pp. 34-9.
47. K.J. Holsti, op. cit., pp. 112-13.
48. Ibid., p. 112.
49. e.g. Robin Alison Remington, *The Warsaw Pact. Case Studies in Communist Conflict Resolution* (Cambridge, Mass. : The MIT Press, 1971); and Richard E. Neustadt, *Alliance Politics* (New York: Columbia University Press, 1970).
50. Liska, op. cit., p. 217.
51. See Robert L. Rothstein, *Alliances and Small Powers* (New York: Columbia University Press, 1968), Chapter 2.
52. John W. Burton, *International Relations: A General Theory* (Cambridge, Cambridge University Press, 1965), p. 170.
53. Friedman, op. cit., pp. 127-332, reprints a selection of useful and characteristic "formal theories" on alliance.
54. See note 2 above. This is an invaluable collection of ideas and references for research purposes. The substantive findings of the authors themselves makes this work a most useful starting point for the serious student of alliance.
55. See, e.g., Pierre M. Gallois, "US Strategy and the Defence of Europe", *Orbis,* Vol. VII, No. 2, Summer, 1963. Reprinted in Henry A. Kissinger, *Problems of National Strategy* (New York, Praeger, 1965), pp. 288-312.
56. Hans J. Morgenthau, "The Four Paradoxes of Nuclear Strategy", *American Political Science Review,* Vol. 58, March 1964, pp. 23-35, especially pp. 33-5; and Henry A. Kissinger, *The Troubled Partnership: A Reappraisal of the Atlantic Alliance* (New York: McGraw-Hill, 1965).
57. Burton, op. cit.
58. There has been much debate about the effect of nuclear weapons on alliances. Some argue that they discourage proliferation, by providing a nuclear umbrella, while others argue that they encourage proliferation by underlining the unreliability of allies in the nuclear age. None would deny that nuclear weapons seriously complicate the decision-making structures and processes of alliances. Against what is probably the prevailing view, that nuclear diffusion is likely to produce more stress than stability in any particular alliance, see Liska, op. cit., pp. 269-84, André Beaufre, *Deterrence and Strategy* (London: Faber, 1965).
59. Ole R. Holsti *et al.,* op. cit., p. 26.
60. Clearly, discussion of this problem implicitly refers only to peacetime deterrent alliances. These, however, have become the norm, since aggressive and revisionist alliances have long since been unfashionable, in declaratory policy, if not in practice.
61. One recent writer on the causes of war finds that the evidence of past wars does not support "the respectable theory" that an uneven balance of power tends to promote war. Geoffrey Blainey, *The Causes of War* (London: Macmillan, 1973), p. 248.

62. See, e.g. Liska, op. cit., pp. 138-47, 176-85.
63. See, e.g. Morgenthau, op. cit., Chapter 14.
64. See note 15 above.
65. See Osgood, op. cit., p. 29.
66. Bernard Brodie, *War and Politics* (London: Cassell, 1974), pp. 336-7.
67. Burton, op. cit., pp. 169-85. The one empirical study in this subject tends to support the view of the critics of alliances. Singer and Small found that there was a positive correlation between the formation of alliances and international conflict in the twentieth century, but not for the nineteenth century. J. David Singer and Melvin Small, "Alliance Aggregation and the Onset of War", in Singer (ed.), *Quantitative International Politics: Insights and Evidence* (New York: The Free Press, 1968), pp. 247-86. While their conclusion supported the view that there was a relationship between the level of alliance commitment and the outbreak of war, it left many questions unanswered, and cannot be taken as final proof. Ole R. Holsti *et al.*, op. cit., pp. 35-8.
68. See the explanation of Blainey, op. cit., pp. 235-7.
69. K.J. Holsti, op. cit., p. 117.
70. Brodie, op. cit., pp. 337-8.
71. Morgenthau opposed US policy in Vietnam on the grounds that it was misapplying the balance of power idea. Brodie, op. cit., p. 334. US intervention in Vietnam can also be interpreted as a misapplication through over-eagerness of Schelling's "diplomacy of violence". For the·latter see Thomas C. Schelling, *Arms and Influence* (New Haven: Yale University Press, 1966), *passim.*
72. Ole R. Holsti *et al.*, op. cit., p. 33.
73. Brodie, op. cit., p. 377.
74. Liska, op. cit., p. 138.
75. For excellent analyses of the concept, see Inis L. Claude, *Swords Into Ploughshares. The Problems and Progress of International Organisation* (London: University of London Press, 1964), Ch. 12, and Geoffrey Goodwin, "International Institutions and International Order" in Alan James (ed.), *The Bases and International Order* (London: OUP, 1973) pp. 156-87.
76. Claude, *Swords into Ploughshares*, pp. 227-38.
77. For a discussion of the uncertainty of the idea of "neutralism" see Samir N. Anabtawi, "Neutralists and Neutralism", *The Journal of Politics*, Vol. 27, No. 2, May 1965, pp. 351-61. Reprinted in Friedman *et al.*, pp. 359-67.
78. Spanier, op. cit., pp. 226 ff.: Laurence W. Martin, *Neutralism and Non-alignment* (New York : Praeger, 1962).
79. Christopher Bladen, "Alliance and Integration", in Friedman *et al.*, p. 126.
80. Fedder, op. cit., p. 86.

PART THREE

THE MILITARY POLICIES OF THE POWERS

10 UNITED STATES DEFENCE POLICY

Phil Williams

I The Setting

'Peace, commerce, honest friendship with all nations; entangling alliances with none.' Thomas Jefferson's words of 1801 described the major theme of United States foreign policy for almost the next 150 years. Even today they evoke considerable sympathy from many Americans who regard extensive international commitments as unnecessary and unwise. In the aftermath of the Second World War, however, there was a profound reversal of this traditional policy. The change was gradual at first, but increased momentum in the late 1940s, as America established an unprecedented number of international commitments and obligations. The scale of this involvement was staggering. By 1969 the United States was maintaining 2,270 installations overseas, of which about 340 were major bases. It also had 1,222,000 men stationed abroad in over 30 nations. Not surprisingly budget appropriations for defence were enormous, being somewhere in the region of 70 billion dollars.[1] The departure from the days when security had been only a minor concern could hardly have been more complete.

Yet there was little indication in 1945 that such a departure would occur. The predominant mood at the end of the war was for a return to 'normalcy'. With its enemies completely prostrate it was hoped and expected that the nation would revert to its former preoccupation with domestic affairs and building the 'great society' at home. This was reflected in the speed of demobilization which was restricted only by the availability of 'transportation facilities and by the ability of trained personnel to carry its administrative requirements out.'[2] Indeed, the armed forces had shrunk from twelve million men at the end of World War Two to a million and a half by 1950 when hostilities broke out in Korea.[3] There was no conception of America playing an important military role in the post-war world. In so far as involvement in international affairs was to continue it would be channelled primarily through US participation in the United Nations.[4]

But policy-makers and public alike were soon to discover that the surplus of security they had once enjoyed was over. The war of 1914-18 and the struggle against Hitler had ultimately demonstrated that America could not be indifferent to the balance of power in Europe. The Second World War had completely destroyed that balance. Dramatic and far-reaching changes had occurred with the involuntary abdication of power by the traditionally great states of Western Europe. The resulting imbalance in favour of the Soviet Union could be rectified only if the United States stepped into the breach. Trapped by the 'fatality' of its position as one of the two superpowers in what had already become an essentially bipolar world, the US was increasingly drawn into the affairs of the European continent.[5]

The story of the deteriorating relationship between the superpowers and the deepening American entanglement with Western Europe in the latter part of the 1940s is too well known to be reiterated at great length.[6] The dispute over 'free elections' in Poland and the coup in Czechoslovakia marred relations between America and the Soviet Union; differences over the future of Germany destroyed the remaining vestiges of trust and good faith. As a result, Washington became more and more committed to off-setting Soviet power as well as rehabilitating the states of Western Europe. With the proclamation of the Truman Doctrine, the implementation of the Marshall Plan, and the signing of the North Atlantic Treaty, the foundations of post-war American foreign policy were firmly established.

The objective of the policy was very clearly the containment of the Soviet Union.[7] With the defeat of the Nationalists by Mao Tse-tung's Communist Party in China in 1949 and the outbreak of the Korean War in 1950 the United States also became concerned with containing Communism in Asia. These events had a traumatic impact on United States policy-makers and encouraged a search for allies in the struggle against what appeared to be a global threat. Thus the American attitude towards the conflict in Indo-China was completely transformed. 'The original disapproval of France as an imperial power disappeared altogether in a redefinition of the French as "defenders of the West"' while there was simultaneously a growing antipathy towards the 'Nationalist rebels' led by Ho Chi Minh who 'were steadily amalgamated with the Communist threat'.[8] Indeed it was during the early 1950s that the seeds of American involvement in Vietnam were sown. Material aid was given to the French in Indo-China and attempts were made to establish a bulwark against Communism in Asia with a series of bi-lateral and multilateral alliances. These included defence agreements with Japan, South Korea and Taiwan, as well as the South-East Asia Collective Defence Treaty of 1954. Nor were the United States' commitments extended only to Asia. The Middle East became another area of concern, particularly after the Suez Crisis of 1956. Fear of Communist incursions in this area led to the formulation of what was known as the Eisenhower Doctrine. This was embodied in a Congressional resolution of 1957 stating that the United States was 'prepared to use armed forces to assist' any nation of the area 'requesting assistance against armed aggression from any country controlled by international Communism'.[9]

The role of world policeman dedicated to combatting Communism wherever it appeared culminated in the Vietnam War which, in turn, provoked a reaction among members of the United States public and Congress against what was increasingly being regarded as indiscriminate entanglement in world affairs. The foreign policy of President Nixon was designed to accommodate the pressures for a more limited US role in international affairs. At the same time it was far from the neo-isolationist posture that some critics suggested. The fundamental assumption underlying the Nixon Doctrine was that America could not retreat from the world but could play a less demanding and more discriminating role in it.[10] A more accommodating stance towards the Soviet Union and China was combined with the maintenance of American strength in an attempt to put containment on a more sustainable basis.

American foreign policy since 1945, therefore, has demonstrated a remarkable continuity of purpose.[11] Despite this, the defence planner's task has not been an easy one. Bedevilled by complex issues and faced with a series of difficult choices, policy-makers have had to adjust their decisions and actions to a variety of internal and external pressures throughout the years of Cold War and *détente*. The range of problems was formidable. Not the least of them lay in trying to assess the nature of the threat and the part military power could play in meeting it. Was the Cold War merely an ideological struggle or could Communism be contained through military means? Was the Soviet threat primarily political or military? Should most importance be attached to Soviet intentions or to Soviet capabilities? The answers to such questions would do much to determine the proportion of national resources devoted to defence. There were further problems, however, concerning the delineation of tasks and the allocation of resources within defence. Precisely what functions should each of the Services fulfil? Was it necessary to prepare for small wars as well as large? Should priority be given to nuclear or conventional forces? How much emphasis should be put on deterrence as opposed to war-fighting? Yet other difficulties surrounded America's relationships with its allies. How could the burdens of defence be shared equitably between a nuclear super-power on the one hand and a diverse group of small states on the other? To what extent should allies have to rely on self-help as opposed to American assistance?

The answers to such questions have differed at different times in the light of changing conditions. Indeed, many of the problems have been a source of recurring debate and controversy. By focusing upon them and the way they were handled, therefore, it should be possible to highlight the major features of United States defence policy and the considerations affecting its evolution throughout the post-war era.

II Commitments and Capabilities

One of the major tasks of statesmanship is to establish and maintain a harmonious relationship between commitments or political obligations on the one hand and the means to honour or fulfil them on the other. For Washington, this necessitated careful and continuing assessments of the utility and limitations of military power in supporting its foreign policy undertakings. Not surprisingly consensus on this has sometimes been absent and the enthusiasm with which succeeding administrations have been prepared to allocate resources to military purposes has varied considerably.

Until the outbreak of the Korean War, the Truman Government relied primarily upon economic aid in the hope of restoring the Europeans to a position where their own efforts might suffice in the attainment of their security. This was reflected not only in the programme of Marshall Aid but also in the North Atlantic Treaty which was intended in part to promote a sense of confidence in Western Europe without which social reconstruction and economic progress would have been seriously undermined. As Robert Osgood has argued, the alliance 'was intended to provide political and psychological reinforcement in the continuing political warfare of the Cold War'.[12] Thus the Treaty was the natural concomitant of the Marshall Plan and was designed to reassure the Europeans as much as to deter the Russians. It was felt that the immediate Soviet threat was more political than military with internal unrest, subversion, and diplomatic pressure being greater dangers than armed attack. 'There was no significant fear of a massive Russian invasion.'[13] Although the Europeans were expected to rebuild their military strength, therefore, economic recovery was to have first priority.[14]

With such a view of the Soviet threat, military power could have only a limited role in containment. Until the Korean War, President Truman resisted all pressure for expanding the defence budget and has been criticized for allowing political commitments and military capabilities to become increasingly divergent. One commentator has claimed that 'foreign policy and military policy were moving in opposite directions' with American involvement in the world deepening while the defence budget was declining.[15] The ceiling on the budget was in fact reduced from 15 to 13 billion dollars prior to the Korean War. Yet this reflected the President's conscious priorities. In the light of his commitment to avoid 'deficit spending', an increased allocation of resources to defence would have deprived other government policies, including economic assistance to America's allies, of the funds necessary for their successful implementation.[16] Truman was unwilling to do this on the basis of his assessment of the international situation and how it could best be handled.

Not even a report from some of his senior officials — NSC-68 —

emphasizing the urgent need for conventional rearmament could shake the President's resolve.[17] The Korean War, however, stimulated rearmament on a scale that even the most implacable opponents of the Soviet Union had been reluctant to contemplate. Its imprint on American foreign and defence policy was profound. The departure from isolation had been marked by the Truman Doctrine of 1947, but 'despite its sweeping language, the Truman Administration between 1947 and 1950 had neither the intention nor the capability of policing the rest of the world . . . the real commitment to contain communism everywhere originated in the events surrounding the Korean War, not the crisis in Greece or Turkey.'[18] Not only did containment become firmly entrenched in Asia, but it was given far greater military support in Europe. A reappraisal of Soviet intentions led Truman to declare that 'Communism has passed beyond the use of subversion to conquer independent nations and will now use armed invasion and war.'[19] Parallels between divided Korea and divided Germany caused further anxieties and the threat to Europe was now regarded as a military problem to be countered by military means. The American contingent in Europe was substantially strengthened, German rearmament was set in motion, and what had been a traditional guarantee pact was transformed into a semi-integrated military organization.[20]

The more alarmist feelings, however, gradually disappeared, and a reduction in the scale of the American defence effort occurred as it became obvious that the North Korean attack was not the precursor to an all-out Soviet offensive against the West. This process began under Truman and continued further under his successor General Eisenhower who was elected President in 1952. The new government's estimate of the Soviet threat in fact resembled that prevalent in the White House before the Korean War: the danger was seen as long-term and indirect rather than immediate and blatantly military.

Not surprisingly, therefore, Eisenhower emphasized the need to maintain fiscal and economic integrity for the 'long haul'. He feared that the Communists were trying to provoke the US into spending ever-increasing amounts on armaments. The belief that a 'bankrupt America' was 'more the Soviet goal than an America defeated in war' lay behind the President's 'great equation': security had to be 'reconciled with solvency'.[21] Underlying government policy was the recognition that, in view of the other demands on resources and the commitment to balanced budgets, higher defence expenditure would demand higher taxation which might result in a curtailing of private investment in industry. Eisenhower's faith in the private sector of the economy as the key to the nation's well-being prohibited any such alternative. Furthermore, 'it was widely felt within the incoming administration that, unless the size and rate of defence expenditures were reduced or, at least, stabilized, a vigorous inflation followed by stifling government controls was likely to occur.'[22] This would go a long way to creating a 'garrison state' in which cherished democratic values would be sacrificed on the altar of 'national security'. The immediate result of such concern was a massive reduction in the defence effort going beyond that projected by the Truman Administration. The Korean War had pushed the budget appropriations for defence up to a peak of almost 57 billion dollars for fiscal year 1952. In fiscal year 1955 they were under 30 billion dollars.[23] Although defence appropriations exhibited a gradual trend upward throughout the rest of the 'fifties, it was not until the Kennedy years that relatively rapid increases were initiated once more.

It is apparent then that in the 1940s and 1950s there was no straightforward correspondence between the government's overseas commitments and the development of its military capabilities. Yet this is hardly surprising since neither the Truman nor Eisenhower governments saw the threat as exclusively, or even primarily, military, except during the brief period of acute tension precipitated by the Korean War. Furthermore, Washington neither expected nor intended to meet all the commitments alone. Although Eisenhower's Secretary of State, John Foster Dulles, is often criticized for what is disparagingly termed 'pactomania', the alliances he created benefited the United States to the extent that its allies were to bear an important part of the security burden themselves. In the light of such considerations, the claims of defence and security were not so overwhelming that they could not be moderated against domestic requirements and the needs of the economy as a whole.

The resulting discrepancy between commitments and capabilities was not treated with the same equanimity by Eisenhower's critics as it was by the President himself. When he was succeeded by John Kennedy in 1960, therefore, an attempt to attain a greater degree of correspondence between commitments and capabilities was almost inevitable. Kennedy's talk of 'new frontiers', however, was slightly misleading: containment remained the basic objective of his foreign policy as it had been of his predecessor's. It was not so much that there were new frontiers to defend as existing frontiers being defended more strongly and with a greater sense of urgency by the United States itself. The intentions of the new administration were clearly stated in the President's Inaugural Address which emphasized the willingness of the US to incur heavy sacrifices in meeting the Soviet threat. As he put it, America would be prepared to 'pay any price, bear any burden, meet any hardship, support any friend, oppose any foe' in the cause of freedom. Strong words were to be backed up by strong actions requiring dramatic increases in military capability.[24]

Underlying the new posture was a more pessimistic assessment of the Communist threat and a more optimistic assessment of what the United States could do in meeting it, than had been made by Eisenhower. Indeed, much of Kennedy's defence policy was an attempt to make up what were regarded as shortcomings in the strategic design of the previous administration. The fifties were seen as 'the years the locusts have eaten' in which the leadership of the Western camp had been allowed to languish and American preparedness undermined.[25] Commitments were now to be fulfilled with an eagerness and enthusiasm that would both provide the example for America's allies in framing their own defence efforts and demonstrate to them that Washington could be relied upon to provide substantial military assistance in the struggle against Communism. Thus security was accorded a much higher status in the hierarchy of national priorities than in previous years when, in Kennedy's words, 'we tailored our starategy and military requirements to fit our budget — instead of fitting our budget to our military requirements strategy.'[26] Increases in the defence budget over that of Eisenhower were considerable: defence approprations of just above 39 billion dollars in fiscal year 1960 had climbed to over 47 billion dollars by fiscal year 1964.

They climbed even higher as this activist policy culminated in direct American participation in the Vietnam War. With the increasing unpopularity of the war, however, it became obvious that another reappraisal of American foreign and defence policy was called for. The more radical critics of the war hoped that in its aftermath there would be a significant demilitarization of US policy if not the complete abandonment of containment. The policies of Richard Nixon and Henry Kissinger, while not fulfilling all these demands, recognized them as legitimate grievances. President Johnson's successor acknowledged that Vietnam had become a blatant symbol of United States involvement in the world and accepted the need for a reordering of priorities to give greater attention to urgent domestic problems. The Nixon Administration quickly recognized that the 'American domestic consensus' had been 'strained by 25 years of global responsibilities' and that social and economic difficulties at home demanded retrenchment abroad.[27]

The extent of the consequent readjustment should not be exaggerated, significant though it was. The government did not relinquish its commitments but made clear that less effort was to be directed towards meeting them, particularly in Asia. The point was neatly crystallized in the President's Foreign Policy Report to Congress in May 1973 which stated: 'the United States will keep all of its treaty commitments', but 'we will adjust the manner of our support for our allies to new conditions and we will base our actions on a realistic assessment of our interests.'[28] In essence this meant that although the United States would still be prepared to furnish military and economic assistance to its Asian allies it would 'look to the nation directly threatened to assume the primary responsibility for providing the manpower for its own defence.'[29] There was nothing new about this though, and it did little more than revert to the position held by

Eisenhower and Dulles throughout the 1950s. Once again American involvement in a ground war in Asia was something to be avoided.

The most immediate consequences of this changing attitude were felt in Vietnam itself where indigenous forces began to take over an increasing share of the war from the Americans. As the 'Vietnamization' programme proceeded, American military forces totalling well over half a million men were gradually withdrawn from the area. The American presence elsewhere was also scaled down and included a reduction of 20,000 troops in South Korea and 13,000 in the Philippines.[30] Substantial cuts in the defence budget were thereby made possible. Appropriations that had climbed to 71 billion dollars by fiscal year 1969 were reduced to 66.6 billions by fiscal year 1971. The funds no longer required for defence were directed into civilian welfare programmes, thus giving rise to what was termed the 'peace dividend'. The rising cost of equipment and manpower, especially after the change from conscription to an all-volunteer armed force ensured that this downward trend in defence expenditure was soon reversed. Nevertheless there has been no repetition of the Kennedy-Johnson years when an attempt was made to meet defence commitments almost regardless of the social, political and economic costs to the nation.

It is apparent then that there have been varying degrees of reliance on military means for the implementation of containment. This has had significant implications for the balance between nuclear and conventional weapons in the overall design of American strategic policy. Anxiety about the threat and a willingness to meet commitments in full have generally gone hand in hand with higher defence spending and spectacular increases in conventional armaments, while the more complacent attitudes have been accompanied by restrictions on defence expenditure and greater emphasis on the benefits of nuclear deterrence. Thus the balance between conventional and nuclear weapons has tended to be a somewhat fluid element in security policy.

III Nuclear and Conventional Weapons

Two major alternatives have competed for the attention and favour of defence planners throughout most of the post-war period. One has suggested an almost exclusive reliance on nuclear deterrence, whereas the other has highlighted the limitations rather than the utility of nuclear weapons and advocated 'balanced forces' in order both to deter aggression right across the board and provide an insurance policy should deterrence fail.[31] The differences between them have often centred around the extent to which the United States Government should prepare for limited war.

Before Korea, however, discussion and planning for future hostilities confined itself to the possibility of a total war against the Soviet Union with Western Europe as both the major theatre of conflict and the prize for victory. Little attention was paid to lesser contingencies. The analysis contained in NSC-68, suggesting that strong conventional forces were essential to block the limited challenges likely to occur when the Soviet Union acquired a substantial atomic deterrent of its own, ran against this trend and won little sympathy in the White House. Although the Korean War 'rescued NSC-68 from oblivion', the conventional rearmament it stimulated was merely an interlude between two periods during which major reliance was placed on atomic weapons.[32] The one 'lesson' the Eisenhower Government would not accept from the Korean hostilities was that it should prepare for similar occurrences in the future. It preferred instead to continue the trend towards nuclear deterrence that had begun prior to the war. This was hardly surprising in view of the frustrations, restrictions, and inconclusiveness of limited war. General MacArthur's claim that 'there is no substitute for victory' touched a responsive chord in a nation accustomed to total involvement for total victory.[33] Furthermore, it was felt that the war had occurred because the American commitment to South Korea was not sufficiently explicit. The solution, therefore, appeared to lie in making United States commitments clearer and relating them more closely to the nuclear deterrent.

Thus a vital part of Eisenhower's 'New Look' in defence policy was the 'massive retaliation' strategy publicly articulated by Secretary of State Dulles who suggested that in future conflicts with the Communists, America would not necessarily confine itself to the local arena of hostilities but might carry the war to the Soviet and Chinese homelands.[34] Although Dulles never advocated the absolute reliance on nuclear weapons that he was sometimes accused of, there was still a large gulf between the Secretary's position, which in part saw tactical and strategic nuclear weapons as a cheap substitute for manpower, and that of his critics who resurrected the logic of NSC-68.

The demand for a greater conventional emphasis was adopted with enthusiasm both within and without the Government. It found its most sympathetic audience, and one of its most effective spokesmen, in the United States Army. This was hardly surprising since the Army felt severely handicapped by 'massive retaliation' and its attendant budgetary restraints. The allocation of resources within defence give it only 22 per cent of the funds available compared to the 47 per cent devoted to the Air Force and 29 per cent to the Navy.[35] The embryo of the 'flexible response' strategy developed out of dissatisfaction with this situation. Unable to improve the Army's position within the confines of government, General Maxwell Taylor, Army Chief of Staff, resigned in order to present his case to a wider audience.[36] In a thesis that was simultaneously being elaborated by a number of academic strategists, Taylor argued that a greater limited war capability was essential. It was 'just as necessary to deter or win quickly a limited war as to deter general war.'[37] Eisenhower remained virtually unmoved, however, and in fiscal year 1959 the army was ordered to cut its personnel by about 130,000, although it had already suffered reductions totalling half a million men since Korea.[38]

Far greater success was achieved under the next administration. The consensus that was gradually emerging came to fruition with the change to 'flexible response' engineered by President Kennedy and his Secretary of Defence, Robert McNamara. Control, selectivity and discrimination were all characteristics of a strategic posture designed to provide the choices between 'suicide and surrender' that had been less evident in the era of 'massive retaliation'.[39] The new government wanted the capacity to cope with all kinds of aggression and made immediate improvements in both its conventional and nuclear armouries.

> The most fundamental transformation occurred in non-nuclear fighting forces. Army and marine corps personnel increases leaped 127,000 in two years. During the Berlin Crisis the army temporarily swelled to a force of over one million. By 1965 it had stabilized at a level of almost 970,000 which was about 100,000 more than the Eisenhower-approved total.

The US airlift capacity was also rapidly expanded and tactical air power increased by twenty-five per cent.[40]

The augmentation of conventional forces was designed both to strengthen deterrence and, in the event that it failed, to minimize the likelihood that the United States would have to resort to nuclear weapons — particularly in the context of a European war. Whereas Eisenhower and Dulles had seen escalation primarily as a threat to be wielded, Kennedy and McNamara viewed it far more as a danger to be avoided. Consequently, pressure was put on the Europeans to follow the American example and give priority to conventional armaments in their force structures. Pentagon analysts argued that when allowance was made for the smaller size of Warsaw Pact divisions compared to those of NATO, the defensive task of the alliance was less awesome than had hitherto been thought.[41] The European allies though did not readily subscribe to the new American strategy and it was not until 1967, after the withdrawal of France from the integrated military organization that NATO formally adopted 'flexible response'.[42]

Even then doubts were expressed about the ability of the Western Alliance to withstand a large-scale Soviet invasion without resort to nuclear weapons.[43] Thus it seems unlikely that defence staffs discontinued making contingency plans for the transition from conventional to nuclear hostilities. Whatever the declaratory posture, operational planners could not ignore the possibility that a war in Europe at some stage might cross the nuclear threshold. This raised the question of whether military forces should be organized and deployed primarily for a conventional or a nuclear war. Throughout the 1950s the United States Army in Germany was equipped and trained for both types of hostilities. Even under McNamara the number of tactical nuclear weapons in Western Europe increased enormously, building up to a stockpile of over 7,000 warheads. This dual capacity became more rather than less important as the Soviet Union strengthened its own military establishment and diversified its armoury of tactical nuclear weapons. The tactical nuclear option for NATO, therefore, had to be retained as a deterrent to the Soviet use of these weapons. Whether it could also provide a credible response to conventional aggression was more problematical and involved some difficult issues. At what stage in hostilities should the momentous decision to 'go nuclear' be taken? Would it be delayed until the Western position had so deteriorated that the only alternative to defeat was rapid nuclear escalation? In these circumstances how extensive would the use of nuclear weapons have to be if it were to succeed either in stopping the Red Army or in convincing Moscow that the risks of continuing an advance were not worth taking? It was partly to avoid the possibility that an American President would be faced with such dilemmas that the change to 'flexible response' was made. But although the idea of a strong conventional riposte to conventional attack has remained the basis of US planning ever since, the likelihood of nuclear escalation cannot be dismissed entirely so long as there is a chance that conventional resistance will not suffice to halt a Soviet invasion.

At the same time the strategic balance between the superpowers ensures that an early resort to nuclear weapons cannot be given the prominence it once enjoyed. Massive retaliation provided a credible guarantee of European security so long as the United States was not subject to a reply in kind from the Soviet Union. But American immunity from a Soviet nuclear attack decreased significantly throughout the 1950s and 1960s. Indeed, with the launching of Sputnik in 1957 fears were expressed that in a crucial area of the arms race the US was falling behind the Soviet Union.[44] A very reluctant Eisenhower was persuaded to take steps to improve both the size and the survivability of the deterrent forces. Kennedy and McNamara went much further and much faster, with the result that the United States had regained a position of nuclear superiority by 1962. This made possible the development of a counterforce strategy which promised to minimize damage to the American homeland and thereby enhanced the nuclear guarantee to Europe. The advantage was only temporary, however, and as Soviet missiles increased in number and degree of invulnerability, McNamara admitted that a nuclear war would be 'bilateral' and 'highly destructive to both sides'.[45] The Secretary of Defence gradually moved away from the counterforce and damage limitation options and by the mid-sixties was emphasizing that deterrence depended on the ability to inflict 'assured destruction' upon any opponent even after absorbing a first strike surprise attack.[46] Unwilling to invest further resources in the increasingly difficult task of limiting damage to the United States, McNamara became reconciled to a position of assured vulnerability. Although this undermined the credibility of the nuclear guarantee to Western Europe, the Secretary argued that 'flexible response' made the strategic nuclear umbrella less vital to European security. Thus, United States conventional forces in Germany, which through the 1950s had acted mainly as a potential 'trip-wire' to a nuclear response, were assigned a substantial defensive role in which nuclear weapons were relegated to the background. Significant as this was, it merely added to the range of tasks undertaken by the armed forces of the United States during the Cold War era.

IV   The Role of Military Forces

With the exception of the occupation duties undertaken by the United States Army in Germany and Japan immediately after the end of the Second World War, the major activities of the armed services have been determined largely by the containment policy and the struggle against Communism. As a result they have fulfilled functions going far beyond their role in the prosecution of hostilities. The non-nuclear forces have contributed significantly towards the maintenance of deterrence, they have supported diplomacy during confrontations with the Communist states, and they have been used to intervene in situations which policy-makers regarded as posing either an actual or a potential threat to American security. In the first two of these tasks they have been fairly successful, but in the third the results have been far less favourable with two interventions leading to prolonged and frustrating involvement in intense limited wars.

The role of conventional forces in promoting deterrence has varied considerably according to the nature of the strategic balance. In the 1960s deterrence and defence merged in the strategy of 'flexible response'. United States forces in Western Europe were equipped for a ninety-day conventional war and deterrence was presumed to rest upon the possession and readiness of efficient war-fighting capabilities. A conventional presence has also contributed to deterrence in a more symbolic and less substantial way however. As well as being a visible token of America's commitments to allies, the personnel stationed overseas have acted as hostages to ensure that any attempt to overthrow the *status quo* would involve immediate confrontation or hostilities with the United States. The use of military forces to demonstrate resolve during the process of crisis bargaining is in some respects little more than an extension of this first task. It is no less important for that, however, and has played an integral role in the resolution of international crises on terms satisfactory to the United States. During the confrontation over Berlin in 1961, for example, troop reinforcements were sent to the city in order to demonstrate that Kennedy intended to withstand Soviet pressure and resist Soviet intimidation tactics.[47] Neither the display of military power nor the purposes it was intended to serve were in any way unique. In 1958 the deployment of the American Sixth Fleet which possessed both conventional and nuclear strike capabilities, had an inhibiting effect on the behaviour of Communist China in its dispute with Taiwan over the offshore islands of Quemoy and Matsu.[48]

On a number of occasions the United States has gone beyond demonstrations of military power and adopted a policy of overt military intervention to prevent what it feared could be major communist gains. The first example of this occurred with American entry into the Korean War. Although South Korea was not a close ally of the United States, policy-makers in Washington were anxious to avoid repeating the mistakes of the 1930s and regarded direct intervention as the only alternative to appeasement.[49] Truman in fact saw Korea as 'the Greece of the Far East' and believed that a weak American response to a Communist move in Asia would undermine the confidence of the West European allies.[50] Furthermore, aggression had to be met with a firm stand in its early stages in order to avoid a more widespread conflict when the appetite of the aggressor had grown insatiable on success.

Because they miscalculated the resilience of the South Korean armed forces, United States decision-makers initially thought that American air support would be sufficient to halt the North Korean advance. It quickly became apparent, however that only the active participation of US ground forces could salvage the South Korean position. Within a week of the war beginning, therefore, American land forces were directly involved. At first the results were disappointing, and it was only after General MacArthur's amphibious landing at Inchon caught the North Korean Army by surprise that the war began to go in American's favour.[51] Military success generated its own momentum and the initial objective of restoring the integrity of a non-Communist South Korea was expanded to encompass the reunification of Korea under United Nations auspices. This attempt to go beyond containment and 'liberate' a Communist state was sanctioned by President Truman on the grounds that it would demonstrate to Russia and China that aggression did not pay. With the Communist army in full retreat General MacArthur was allowed to pursue it into the North. He did this with his forces divided into two, a course of action that proved disastrous when Communist China intervened and caught the advancing armies completely off balance. The result was one of the greatest defeats in America's military history as MacArthur's troops were driven back to the thirty-eighth parallel. After this the war became less fluid and settled into a pattern of attrition that persisted until prolonged negotiations finally led to an armistice in 1953.

The pains of adapting to limited war included a profound crisis in civil-military relations. General MacArthur, who believed that Asia should have priority over Europe in American foreign policy, publicly attacked the Truman Administration's conduct of the war and advocated widening hostilities beyond Korea. This was in direct contravention of Truman's orders and, as a result, MacArthur was dismissed from his position as Commander-in-Chief of American forces in the Pacific and UN forces in Korea. The President's action caused considerable opposition within the United States and a government that initially had been praised for its decisive intervention became increasingly unpopular as the war dragged on.[52]

One consequence of all this was a desire to avoid further military entanglements on the mainland of Asia, a consideration that may have been paramount in Eisenhower's decision not to intervene to save the French position at Dien Bien Phu in 1954. The President was less reluctant to act in the Middle East and sanctioned a 'bloodless' intervention in Lebanon in 1958 on the side of a pro-Western government threatened by internal disorder. Fears of a Communist take-over aided and inspired by a left-wing régime in Syria, provoked an intervention which lasted for three months, involved 15,000 men, and succeeded in restoring order. Although US activities were justified in terms of the Eisenhower Doctrine enunciated the previous year, it seems possible that the fears of Communist gains were somewhat exaggerated.[53] This was almost certainly the case with American intervention in the Dominican Republic in 1965, an operation that was implemented by President Johnson with the aim of preventing the emergence of another Communist régime in the Caribbean.[54] Such a contingency was far more remote than the President argued, and the intervention was severely attacked, most notably by Senator Fulbright, Chairman of the Senate Foreign Relations Committee. The resulting controversy, however, was little more than a foretaste of the furor that was ultimately to surround American involvement in Vietnam.

This involvement can only be understood in light of the Kennedy Administration's activism in combatting Communism. The conventional emphasis in the flexible response strategy was accompanied by a novel concern about sub-limited warfare and the United States counter-insurgency role. Kennedy and McNamara were far more anxious than any of their predecessors about the inability of the West to cope with insurgency movements in the developing nations. The vulnerability of containment to these Communist tactics was one of Washington's major preoccupations in the early 1960s, and an integral part of the new defence posture was concerned with filling the gap in Western defences. This task was made particularly urgent by Khrushchev's famous speech of January 1961 in which he promised Soviet support for 'wars of national liberation'. The speech was taken very seriously by the Kennedy Government and seemed to herald a challenge that could not be ignored. McNamara interpreted it as potentially 'one of the most important statements made by a world leader in the decade of the sixties.'[55] Whether Khrushchev's remarks were in fact a serious declaration of intent became irrelevant as the United States acted on the basis that the success of containment depended on demonstrating to both allies and adversaries that Communist-inspired insurgency wars could only end in failure. This helps to explain Kennedy's reaction to the deteriorating situation in Vietnam. Although the United States had been interested in developments in Indo-China through the 1950s, the events there now took on a new significance. Some writers suggest that Kennedy acted on the assumption that if South Vietnam fell to the Communists the rest of Asia would also be lost, but the intervention had a much more positive and dynamic aspect. Vietnam was the test case that would demonstrate unequivocally the futility of Communist insurgencies. It was to be the war to end all wars of national liberation.

Although Kennedy placed his faith in Special Forces trained specifically for a counter-insurgency role, rather than in regular combat units, there were nonetheless 23,000 Americans in Vietnam — about two-thirds of whom were involved in actual hostilities — at the time of his assasination.[56] While this was an insignificant figure when compared with the number of American servicemen to be involved later, it did represent a firm public commitment to South Vietnam. The main changes made by President Johnson were in the manner and intensity with which the war was fought. He changed little in terms of US objectives and continued, probably with greater inflexibility, along the path set by Kennedy.[57] The rest is well-known. The United States discovered that possession of a capability for counter-insurgency was one thing, to fight a successful counter-insurgency war was something very different. American methods in the war went through a series of modifications ranging from 'search and destroy' tactics to the punitive bombing campaign against the North. The results were disappointing at best and not even a massive commitment of ground forces could bring success. As a result the war became even more unpopular than that in Korea. The question of American participation also became bound up with the controversy over the respective roles of President and Congress in the making of foreign and defence policy.

V Institutional Adjustments

Struggle between the executive and legislative branches of government is endemic in American politics. Often described as a government based on the 'separation of powers' the American political system is better understood as a government of 'separate institutions sharing power'.[58] This is particularly important in relation to defence policy and foreign affairs since the constitution provided for the President as Commander-in-Chief while giving Congress the power to declare war and to allocate the funds necessary for the maintenance of armed forces. Although the war powers were never used as widely as was intended, the post-war era saw them fall into almost complete disuse. President Truman established the pattern by failing to request a congressional declaration of war either before or after he committed US troops to the aid of South Korea. There was some concern that Truman had behaved unconstitutionally, but this was lost in the applause as his swift and decisive action won overwhelming support in both houses. The accretion of power to the President continued throughout the Cold War, facilitated by the concentration of information and expertise in the executive branch.[59] It was accepted — although not without occasional rumblings of disquiet — so long as the President acted within the limits of a national consensus on policy. When the consensus broke down in the face of disillusionment and dissent over the Vietnam War, Congress attempted to reassert its own rights and powers and restrict those of the President. The struggle was a long and difficult one, however, and it was not until 1973 that Congress finally overrode President Nixon's veto and set a sixty-day limit to any Presidential commitment of US troops to hostilities abroad.[60]

The war also provoked Congressional hostility to increases in the defence budget. This was an important departure, for Congress had typically acquiesced in the President's budgetary demands. Towards the end of the 1950s it had briefly played a more positive function, and as a result of its initiatives extra funds were set aside for Strategic Air Command's dispersal and alert facilities and for speeding up the Polaris and Minuteman missile programmes. Such activism was the exception rather than the rule, however, and during the 1960s Congress reverted to a more passive review of defence expenditure.[61] It was not until the Tet Offensive of 1968 demonstrated the complete bankruptcy of President Johnson's Vietnam policy that Congress became more assertive in its treatment of the executive's budgetary proposals.

> For fiscal years 1960-69 Congress changed the administration's
> defence budget request by an average of little more than 1 per
> cent. For the fiscal years 1970 to 1973, when dissatisfaction
> became more pronounced and concern about budget priorities
> became more serious, the Congress reduced the administration's
> defence budget request by an average of 4 per cent.[62]

Thus it appears that Congress plays an independent role in defence policy-making only when there is widespread anxiety over the President's actions.[63]

Apart from these formal responsibilities, Congress has acted as a forum and court of appeal for the armed services in their struggles over the allocation of missions and resources. Although there has been general agreement within the defence establishment on the objectives of United States policy, the role and importance of each of the military services in attaining those objectives have been much more uncertain. It has to be remembered, therefore, that 'strategic programs are not the product of expert planners who rationally determine the means necessary to achieve desired goals. They are the result of controversy, negotiation and bargaining among different officials and groups with different interests and perspectives.'[64] Not even the National Security Act of 1947, creating the post of Secretary of Defence and supposedly unifying the military establishment, could alter the situation and succeed in moderating the intensity of inter-service rivalry.

In the 1940s this rivalry took the form of a dispute over the control of atomic weapons. The newly independent Air Force sought to maintain a position of exclusive ownership and attempted to establish its pre-eminence over the older services with the argument that the next war would be won by strategic bombing alone. The fact that from 1947 both the Army and Navy had their appropriations cut in 'each fiscal year until the North Korean attack in 1950' is testimony to the efficacy of its tactics.[65] The two senior services quickly realized, however, that nuclear missions were a means to organizational growth and a greater share of the defence budget, and the Navy established a nuclear niche for itself with the strike carriers, and later the Polaris submarines, while the Army did the same with the development of tactical nuclear weapons. Despite this, they were unable to dislodge the Air Force from its well-entrenched position at the top of the military hierarchy.

Budgetary battles continued throughout the 1950s and were particularly serious because of the limited resources made available for military purposes. The effect on procurement decisions and research and development was particularly important as 'each service launched its own projects independently of the others in the hope of laying claim to some future mission and thereby increasing its share of available funds.'[66] Not surprisingly there was considerable duplication of functions as a result, and at one stage the army developed its own intermediate range ballistic missile, the Thor, while the Air Force was extolling the virtues of a rival IRBM known as the Jupiter. When Robert McNamara became secretary of Defence he saw his task as one of preventing such practices. Regarding decentralized decision-making as an abdication of the authority of the Secretary, as well as a source of waste and inefficiency, McNamara tried to make the allocation of resources within defence a more rational process than it had been under his predecessors. Rigorous techniques of evaluating weapons and force levels were introduced and a Planning-Programming-Budgeting System with its five-year projections of the defence posture was established as an aid to centralized decision-making and long-term planning. One consequence of these innovations was that military judgements about the feasibility and desirability of particular weapons systems, such as the RS-70 strategic bomber, were sometimes overruled by the Secretary on cost-effectiveness considerations.[67] This earned McNamara considerable criticism from Congress, and under his successors the Joint Chiefs of Staff appear to have regained much of their former importance. The implications of a more powerful military voice in defence planning, as well as a more reassertive Congress, remain to be worked out. What does seem apparent, however, is that pressures from both quarters can only make the continued implementation of the Nixon Doctrine extremely difficult, resting as it does on a judicious combination of strength, partnership, and negotiation. Even without such pressures the task of maintaining an equitable balance among these three elements of national policy is formidable.

VI   Current and Future Issues

American defence policy since 1945 has undergone a process of constant evolution and adjustment during which many difficulties have been overcome. One problem that has become more rather than less acute, however, is in deciding 'how much is enough'. What level of military preparedness is necessary to maintain the security of the United States and its allies now that the 'era of confrontation' has given way to the 'era of negotiation'? There is little agreement on the answer to this question. Within the Ford Administration itself there are perhaps irreconcilable differences between those like Secretary of State Kissinger, who emphasize the mellowing of Soviet intentions, and those who follow Secretary of Defence James Schlesinger in highlighting the continued development of Soviet military capabilities. Indeed, the lack of unanimity reflects what may be a growing uneasiness in the United States about *détente*. The Soviet-American relationship has certainly been subjected to considerable strain with the events surrounding the Yom Kippur War of October 1973 and the breakdown of the US-USSR Trade Agreement in January 1975. Whether these setbacks are anything more than temporary irritants along the road to more substantial cooperation remains to be seen. Nevertheless, they have introduced great uncertainties into the superpower relationship.

Such uncertainties make the policy planning task inordinately difficult and have resulted in United States defence policy exhibiting a kind of schizophrenic quality. Nowhere is this more prevalent than at the nuclear level. While Kissinger was working towards agreement with the Soviet Union on limiting strategic armaments, Schlesinger enunciated a targeting doctrine that some critics suggest can result only in another upward spiral of the arms competition.[68] The Secretary of Defence has denied that a further surge in the arms race is an inevitable consequence of the new counterforce strategy but has authorized, nonetheless, an extensive research and development programme to ensure that the United States maintains 'an offensive capacity of such size and composition that all will perceive it as in overall balance with the strategic forces of any potential opponent.' Furthermore, he has argued that 'essential equivalence' between the strategic forces of the US and USSR is vital to American security. The Strategic Arms Limitation Talks have sanctioned asymmetries in the nuclear armouries of the superpowers, but this must not be such that they could be 'exploited for diplomatic advantage' by the Soviet Union.

The principle of 'essential equivalence' also relates to the flexibility of strategic forces and provides a rationale for the move away from an excessive reliance on 'assured destruction'. As Schlesinger commented: 'We do not propose to let an enemy put us in a position where we are left with no more than a capability to hold his cities hostage after the first phase of a nuclear conflict.' There must be alternatives other than a 'massive response' or 'doing nothing' if Washington is not to be coerced in a 'nuclear test of wills'. Thus, a number of 'selective relatively small-scale' nuclear strike options have been added to the larger options already existing. The major assumption underlying these innovations is that the Soviet Union is more likely to be deterred if it knows that the United States can match Soviet actions across the entire spectrum of conflict — including limited nuclear war.

Schlesinger's statements suggest that considerable residual distrust of the Soviet Union exists among US policy-makers. Indeed, a major tenet of the Nixon Doctrine is that despite the relaxation of tension, America must strengthen and revitalize its alliance relationships. Efforts in this direction have had rather mixed results though, partly because they have been bound up with the attempt to redistribute much of the security burden from the United States to its allies. Some limited success has been achieved in Western Europe: in response to pressure from Washington the European members of NATO reluctantly reversed the trend downwards in their defence expenditure that had prevailed from 1964 to 1969. The European Defence Improvement Programme, however, has not succeeded in disarming the Senators who desire a reduction in the American military pressence in Western Europe. Congressional demands for unilateral US troops withdrawal from Europe could well intensify in the future, particularly if the NATO and Warsaw Pact countries are unable to reach agreement on mutual force reductions. In this event the problem of 'defence with fewer men' as part of 'flexible response' would become increasingly acute.[69] But it would not be insoluble. Already there have been suggestions that American forces in Germany be restructured for a short decisive war, while considerable emphasis has been put on the possible use of small discriminate tactical nuclear weapons.[70] Whether or not more substantial moves in these directions occur, it seems probable that the American role in underwriting West European security will continue well beyond the 1970s — unless, of course, Atlantic relations deteriorate even more than they did in 1973 as a result of the Middle East War and the energy crisis.

If real partnership with Western Europe is still a long way off, the prospects in Asia are much more dismal. The 'Vietnamization' programme has proved less an exercise in burden-sharing than a device for disentangling the United States from an unpopular and unprofitable war. Not surprisingly, it has failed to prevent the North Vietnamese from making substantial gains which, in the last analysis, the US has been prepared to tolerate. To conclude from this, however, that defence planners can concentrate solely on the security problems of Western Europe would be a mistake. The American commitment to Japan remains firm. Furthermore, new arenas of conflict may be emerging. The American Navy's use of Diego Garcia as a base for operations in the Indian Ocean could be the precursor to more intense superpower rivalry in the area. The likely effect of this on the *détente* is only one of the many imponderables that will shape the future evolution of United States defence policy throughout the latter half of the 1970s.

Notes

1. These details are taken from *Global Defence: US Military Commitments Abroad* (Washington: Congressional Quarterly Services, September 1969), pp. 37-8.
2. General George C. Marshall, quoted in E.A. Kolodziej, *The Uncommon Defence and Congress, 1945-1963* (Columbus: Ohio State University Press, 1966), p. 35.
3. See ibid. for further details.
4. Ibid., p. 57.
5. See M.H. Armacost, *The Foreign Relations of the United States* (Belmont, California: Dickenson, 1969), p. 6.
6. A superbly balanced account of the origins and development of the Cold War is contained in H. Feis, *From Trust to Terror* (London: Blond, 1970).
7. The rationale underlying the containment policy was outlined in George Kennan's famous 'X' article entitled "The Sources of Soviet Conduct" in *Foreign Affairs,* Vol. 25, No. 4, July 1947. Kennan was later to criticize the manner in which the containment policy was implemented, particularly its militarization. See G.F. Kennan, *Memoirs 1925-1950* (London: Hutchinson, 1968), pp. 354-67 in particular.
8. J.G. Stoessinger, *Nations in Darkness* (New York: London House, 1971), p. 66.
9. The full text of the resolution can be found in *Global Defence,* op. cit., p. 23.
10. See, for example, *US Foreign Policy for the 1970s: Shaping a Durable Peace,* A report to the Congress by Richard Nixon, President of the United States, 3 May 1973, p. 8.
11. This is one of the major themes of J.C. Donovan, *The Cold Warriors: A Policy-Making Elite* (Lexington: D.C. Heath, 1974).
12. R.E. Osgood, *NATO: The Entangling Alliance* (Chicago: Chicago University Press, 1962), p. 30.
13. Ibid.
14. See *The Vandenberg Resolution and the North Atlantic Treaty,* Hearings Held in Executive Session before the Committee on Foreign Relations, United States Senate, Eightieth Congress, Second Session on S. Res. 239 and Eighty-First Congress, First Session on Executive L, The North Atlantic Treaty. *Historical Series.* (Washington: Government Printing Office, 1973), p. 383.
15. S.E. Ambrose, *Rise to Globalism: American Foreign Policy 1938-1970* (London: Penguin Books, 1971). See also S.P. Huntington, *The Common Defense: Strategic Programs in National Politics* (New York: Columbia University Press, 1961), p. 20.

16. See P.Y. Hammond, "NSC-68: Prologue to Rearmament", in W.R. Schilling, P.Y. Hammond and G.H. Snyder, *Strategy, Politics and Defence Budgets* (New York: Columbia Univeristy Press, 1962), p. 278. This volume is an indispensable source of information on the evolution of American defence policy during the later 1940s and early 1950s.
17. See ibid. for a full acount of the Report and its contents.
18. J.L. Gaddis, "Was the Truman Doctrine a Real Turning Point?" in *Foreign Affairs,* Vol. 52, No. 2, January 1974, p. 386.
19. Statement by President Truman, 27 June 1950, the full text of which can be found in H.S. Truman, *Mamoirs Vol. II: Years of Trial and Hope* (New York: Signet Books, 1965), pp. 385-6.
20. Osgood, op. cit., contains an excellent account of these developments.
21. This emerges very clearly in G.H. Snyder's "The New Look of 1953", in Schilling, Hammond & Snyder, op. cit., especially pp. 470-79. See also Huntington, op. cit., Ch. 4.
22. Kolodziej, op. cit., p. 108. Such fears are also discussed throughout Schilling, Hammond & Snyder, op. cit.
23. The figures used throughout this chapter are taken from *Editorial Research Reports on America's Changing World Role* (Washington: Congressional Quarterly, 1974), p.15. They are based on information supplied by the House Appropriation Committee and the Defence Department, and do not include supplementary appropriations for any year.
24. See R. Aron, *The Imperial Republic: The United States and the World 1945-1973* (Englewood Cliffs, New Jersey: Prentice-Hall, 1974), pp. 70-79.
25. J.F. Kennedy, quoted in H. Moulton, *From Superiority to Parity* (London: Greenwood Press, 1973), p. 37.
26. Quoted in ibid., p. 37
27. *US Foreign Policy For the 1970s: Building for Peace,* A Report to The Congress by Richard Nixon, President of the United States, 25 February 1971, p. 7.
28. See *US Foreign Policy For the 1970s: Shaping a Durable Peace,* 3 May 1973, op. cit., p. 40.
29. Ibid.
30. Fuller details can be found in ibid.
31. The argument for 'balanced collective forces' was presented by James Forrestal and is discussed in Kolodziej, op. cit., p. 75.
32. See R.F. Weigley, *The American Way of War: A History of United States Military Strategy and Policy* (New York: Macmillan, 1973), p. 398. An alternative argument is that Truman welcomed the war as an opportunity to increase military spending. See Ambrose, op. cit., p. 192.
33. See J.W. Spanier, *The Truman and MacArthur Controversy* (Cambridge, Mass.: The Belknap Press, 1959) for a comprehensive analysis of the conflict between MacArthur and the Administration.
34. Dulles' original speech was made to the Council of Foreign Relations on 12 January 1954 and published as 'The Evolution of Foreign Policy' in *The Department of State Bulletin,* Vol. 30, 25 January 1954, pp. 107-10. The speech was later clarified and elaborated in Dulles' article, "Policy For Security and Peace", *Foreign Affairs,* Vol. 32, No. 3, April 1954.
35. Huntington, op. cit., p. 413
36. Taylor did this in *The Uncertain Trumpet* (New York: Harper, 1960).
37. Ibid., p. 6.
38. Further details can be found in Kolodziej, op. cit., p. 279.
39. See A.C. Enthoven, Address before the Nuclear War Institute, West Baden College of Loyola University, Indiana, 10 November 1963.
40. See Kolodziej, op. cit., p. 408.
41. See A.C. Enthoven and K.W. Smith, *How Much is Enough?* (New York:

Harper & Row, 1971), especially pp. 117-64.

42. European preferences are detailed in C. Amme, *NATO without France* (Stanford: Hoover Institute, 1967).
43. See B. Brodie, *Escalation and the Nuclear Option* (Princeton: Princeton University Press, 1966) and D. Healey, "Perspectives of Soviet Military Policy", *NATO Letter,* March, 1969.
44. See A. Wohlstetter, "The Delicate Balance of Terror", *Foreign Affairs* Vol. 3, No. 2, January 1959. Wohlstetter's ideas were probably important in the recommendations of the Gaither Committee, a good account of which can be found in M.H. Halperin, "The Gaither Committee and the Policy Process", *World Politics,* Vol. 13, No. 3, April 1961. See also Donovan, op. cit., pp. 130-49.
45. R.S. McNamara, Speech before Economic Club of New York, 18 November 1963.
46. The details of this transition are provided more fully in my "La Stratégie McNamara et La Sécurité Européene", *Revue du Defense Nationale,* June 1973, pp. 97-114.
47. The reinforcements and their effect are dealt with at greater length in W.W. Kaufmann, *The McNamara Strategy* (New York: Praeger, 1964), pp. 257-60.
48. J.T. Howe, *Sea Power and Global Politics in the Missile Age* (Cambridge, Mass.: MIT Press, 1971) provides a fuller account of these developments.
49. See E.R. May, *Lessons of The Past: The Use and Misuse of History in American Foreign Policy* (New York: Oxford University Press, 1973), p. 52
50. An excellent account of the American decision to intervene in Korea is contained in G. Paige, *The Korean Decision* (New York: Free Press, 1968).
51. See D. Rees, *Korea: The Limited War,* for a useful history of the military aspects of the war.
52. Spanier, op. cit., discusses the events surrounding General MacArthur's dismissal while J.W. Spanier and L. Elowitz look at the way the American public reacted to the limited wars in "Korea and Vietnam: Limited War and the American Political System", *Orbis,* Vol. 18, No. 2, Summer 1974.
53. This is suggested in H.K. Tillema, *Appeal to Force: American Military Intervention in the Era of Containment* (New York: Crowell, 1973), pp. 74-83.
54. A good account of the intervention can be found in ibid., pp. 60-65. See also T.H. Halper, *Foreign Policy Crises: Appearance and Reality in Decision Making* (Columbus, Ohio, Merrill, 1971).
55. Quoted in Moulton, op. cit., p. 77.
56. Weigley, op. cit., pp. 456-7, discusses Kennedy's approach to the conflict.
57. An extremely balanced attempt to apportion responsibility for the American involvement is B. Brodie, *War and Politics* (New York: Macmillan, 1973). The assessment differs from that presented here in that it is much more critical of President Johnson and less critical of President Kennedy.
58. See R. Neustadt, *Presidential Power* (New York: Wiley 1960)
59. J.A. Robinson, *Congress and Foreign Policy Making* (Homewood, Ill.: Dorsey Press, 1967) deals at length with this theme.
60. A good account of the struggle is contained in J.W. Spanier and E.M. Uslaner, *How American Foreign Policy is Made* (New York: Praeger, 1974), pp. 68-78 and 132-43.
61. Congressional influence on the defence budget is examined most thoroughly in Kolodziej, op. cit. This is usefully supplemented and updated by A. Kanter, "Congress and the Defence Budget: 1960-1970", *American Political Science Review,* Vol. 66, No. 1, March 1972.
62. E.R. Fried, A.M. Alvin, C.L. Schultze, N.H. Teeters, *Setting National Priorities: The 1974 Budget* (Washington: The Brookings Institution, 1973), p. 407.

63. To see defence policy-making exclusively in terms of a strong executive dominating a weak legislature, however, would be a serious oversimplification. There are often cross-cutting alignments as Congress intervenes in support of particular groups or particular policies and programmes when divisions occur within the executive branch. A well-researched analysis of such divisions exists in relation to the Anti-Ballistic Missile Debate of the late 1960s and is presented in M.H. Halperin, *Foreign Policy and Bureaucratic Politics* (Washington: The Brookings Institution, 1974).

64. S.P. Huntington, op. cit., p. 146.

65. See Kolodziej, op. cit., p. 65. Further details can be found in W.R. Schilling's superb analysis, "The Politics of National Defense: Fiscal 1950", in Schilling, Hammond and Snyder, op. cit.

66. Kaufmann, op. cit., p. 31. Other reasons for inter-service rivalry are described in Halperin, *Foreign Policy and Bureaucratic Politics,* op. cit., pp. 26-62.

67. A useful evaluation of McNamara's achievements as Secretary of Defence is presented in *Congressional Quarterly Almanac 1967*, Vol. 23 (Washington: Congressional Quarterly Services 1968), pp. 971-9.

68. One of the fullest statements of the new strategy was made on 26 February 1974 by Secretary Schlesinger in the *Hearings on the Department of Defence Appropriations for 1975,* held *Before a Subcommittee of the Committee on Appropriations, House of Representatives* (Washington: Government Printing Office, 1974). This paragraph and that following rest heavily on this statement. See pages 69-72 and 95-111 in particular. A critical assessment of Schlesinger's innovations is made by B. Carter, "Flexible Strategic Options: No Need for a New Strategy", *Survival,* Vol. 17, No. 1, Jan/Feb. 1975, reprinted from *Scientific American* May 1974.

69. This problem is analyzed in K. Hunt, 'The Alliance and Europe: Part II: Defence with Fewer Men'. *Adelphi Paper, No. 98* (London: International Institute for Strategic Studies, Summer 1973).

70. See R.D. Lawrence and J. Record, *US Force Structure in NATO: An Alternative* (Washington: Brookings Institution, 1974). The role of tactical nuclear weapons is discussed in L.W. Martin, "Theatre Nuclear Weapons and Europe", *Survival,* Vol. 16, No. 6, Nov./Dec. 1974, and C.S. Gray, "Deterrence and Defence in Europe: Revising NATO's Theatre Nuclear Posture", *Journal of the Royal United Services Institute for Defence Studies,* Vol. 119, No. 4, December 1974.

11 SOVIET DEFENCE POLICY

Ken Booth

From a Western viewpoint, the Soviet armed forces have been the looming ogre in the Cold War drama. The military policy which has directed their powerful muscles has often seemed a mystery. However, a few analysts have shown that it is possible to discover a great deal about some aspects of Soviet military policy.[1] Nearly sixty years of word and deed provide plenty of material upon which to work and speculate.

The above paragraph does not mean that analysing Soviet military policy is straightforward. Indeed, the search for understanding has been obstructed by natural military secretiveness obfuscated and exaggerated by morbid state secrecy. Furthermore, the inevitable problems of analysis have been compounded by a number of attitudes and approaches from Western observers which have distorted the limited knowledge which has been gained. The main difficulties have arisen from a "level-of-analysis" problem, ethnocentricity, and cultural blind spots.

The level-of-analysis problem expresses itself in confused threat assessment. Is the level of concern that of the military contingency planner with the theoretical range of *possibilities* of what an adversary *can* do, or is it the level that of the foreign policy analyst, with estimates of *probabilities* about *likely* adversary behaviour? This distinction between what is possible and what is probable is a crucial one when analysing the difficult concept of "threat", but is often ignored or confused.[2] Ethnocentricity is the tendency to assess the words and deeds of other groups in terms of one's own culture, and invariably with an implicit or explicit belief in the superiority of one's own culture. In military and other fields the standards and assumptions of one's own outlook are often applied to others in a biased way. Thus one hears that "the Soviets do not understand sea power", when it should be quite clear that they completely understand it, but from a different perspective to that of the traditional monopolist maritime nations. Similarly, Soviet behaviour is sometimes characterised as "not making sense" (e.g. the institution of the "military commissars") or of being "mischievous" or "not legitimate" (e.g. their quantitative over-insuring in military terms): in such cases, however, they are simply and rationally acting from different assumptions, or applying different values. Cultural blind spots impinge in other ways. When a lack of imagination makes it impossible even to begin to perceive the world from the standpoint of Soviet decision-makers, it invariably means that Soviet behaviour is assessed by the analyst in terms of his own (Western) vulnerabilities and fears rather than Soviet priorities. Cultural blind spots also result in a tendency to assume that Soviet spokesmen and Western spokesmen mean the same thing when they use what is translated as the same or similar terminology: this is not so, and not to recognise the fact involves a serious risk of misunderstanding Soviet conceptions of such an important idea as deterrence.[3] While understanding Soviet military policy will always be difficult, because of both inherent and Soviet-made obstacles, at least some of the keys are in our own hands.

The Traditional and Revolutionary Heritages

The invaders of Russia in the last 800 years read like a *Who's Who* of military aggression: the Mongols between 1240 and 1380; the Poles 1607-1612; the Swedes 1611-1614, and again in 1709; Napoleon in 1812; Germany and Austria in 1914-1918; Britain, the United States, Japan, France and Italy, 1918-1919; Poland in 1920; and Germany between 1941 and 1944. The Russian people have faced the scourge of war probably more than any other nation, certainly in Europe.[4] Within living memory the Russians lost 45,000 military dead in the Russo-Japanese War, nearly two million military and an uncounted number of civilian casualties in the First World War, 30,000 in the clashes with Japan in the late 1930s, approximately 50,000 in the Soviet-Finnish War, and in the last and worst of the invasions, between fifteen and twenty million in overcoming the gratuitously brutal invasion by Hitler's Germany.[5] Outside Leningrad there are no single graves for individual, if unknown defenders. Each grave in each line contains numerous bodies. The scale of Russian suffering has been heroic: it is almost ungraspable for the traditionally secure and phlegmatic citizen of the British Isles or North America.

Vulnerability to military invasion and pressure has been a characteristic feature of Russian history. In Tsarist times there was a periodic search for secure frontiers, in an effort to stretch as much space as possible between potential enemies and the "huddled defensive community" in the national heartland. Soviet leaders, like their Tsarist predecessors, have never been able to be really confident about their state's security from external threat. This chronic feeling of insecurity can be called "paranoia", but it is no less real for being in the mind.

In such circumstances, the accretion of military power to deter the numerous perceived external enemies, to deal with them from a position of strength, and to fight and defeat them if deterrence failed[6] had been a constant concern and focus of national efforts. It is not surprising that those who have been responsible for that patch of embattled territory have seen their security lying in massive military strength, have defined their security requirements expansively, and have always tended to "overinsure"[7] in quantitative military terms. Objective and subjective requirements have dictated massive military manpower and equipment.

The historic military problem of both Tsarist and Soviet Russia has been to meet the danger to its exposed Western frontier of incursion from countries in Scandinavia and central Europe which were technologically and militarily better developed. With the rise of Japan and then China in the Soviet period a major threat reappeared after a 600-year break on the eastern plains. The experience of vulnerability and disaster has been itensified by some traditional weaknesses in Russian life: on the other hand, calamity was attenuated by some enduring strengths of that system. The chief weaknesses have been: the lack of easily defensible frontiers, without geographical advantages and with immensely long frontiers to defend; an inefficient administrative infrastructure; inadequate transport arrangements, made worse by the vast distances involved; lack of industrial development; technical backwardness; inefficient government; supply problems; and the low educational standards of military personnel. Set against such deficiencies, the country has had some important strengths: the vast space has been an asset in war; there have been abundant natural resources; great manpower reserves; brave and tough soldiers, generally prepared to accept harsh discipline and high casualties in defence of the homeland; and a high prestige attached to military duty. Some of the worst deficiences have been overcome in the Soviet period, but all the strengths remain. Overall, there has been a marked continuity in the Tsarist and Soviet experiences, in terms of geopolitical inheritance, deeply ingrained outlooks, strategic requirements, and military roles.

1917 in fact was less significant in a military sense than some hoped, and others feared. A "revolutionary" element in military policy was prominent in organisation, doctrine, and ambition during the short period of Bolshevik innocence, but gradually many traditional elements necessarily imposed themselves. While the ideological element struggled to survive in aspects of organisation and doctrine, the force of circumstance resulted in increasing weight being given in the modernising Red Army to traditional practices, notably military professionalism. Out of the intermittent struggles between the "professionals" and the "party doctrinaires", there emerged a fusion of the two heritages,[8] the balance of which was symbolically marked in 1946 with the new title *Soviet Army* to replace the existing *Workers' and Peasants' Red Army*.

Strategic Policy

Soviet leaders, like their Tsarist predecessors, have never been confident about their state's security from external threat. The Civil War (1917-20), the foreign interventions (1918-22), the period of "capitalist encirclement" when internally weak, the Nazi threat, Japanese pressure in the Far East in the 1930s, the horrors of the Great Patriotic War, the US atomic monopoly, the formation of NATO, West German rearmament, growing US superiority until the mid-1960s in intercontinental delivery systems, fear of surprise attack, the dangers of polycentrism in Eastern Europe, concern about nuclear proliferation (especially to West Germany), the growing danger from China — all these, in under sixty years, have confirmed and structured deep national and ideological predispositions towards insecurity. The task of a Soviet military planner, who as part of his responsibility has to assume at least "fairly bad" cases when speculating about future military contingencies, can never have been an easy one.

Since 1945 Soviet strategic policy has been dominated by the need to meet the requirements of deterrence and defence against the dominant US enemy,[9] although as the preceding paragraph testified, there have been some other important threats to Soviet security. In addition to reacting to these strictly "defensive" problems Soviet military strength has also been used in a variety of ways to support the advancement of foreign policy.[10]

The great victories of the Red Armies in 1945 promised to solve the old problem of having to deal with incursions from the West: not only had Germany been crushed, but the Soviet Union had been able to occupy a belt of states in Eastern Europe which would serve as a forward defence zone. The full promise of this achievement was short-lived. The new Soviet defensive position was soon outflanked, and was faced by what must have been seen as a potentially greater threat than ever before, that of the United States with its massive air and naval power, including a monopoly of atomic weapons. However mighty the Soviet Army was, and however impenetrable its forward perimiter might become, the Soviet heartland was henceforth exposed to the possibility of the most terrible destruction. As the Cold War intensified, Soviet problems grew with the formation of NATO and the rearmament of West Germany.

Stalin, from his own paranoid perspective, must have thought by the early 1950s that he had done a satisfactory job in deterring US atomic-backed power, and in strengthening the general defensive position of the USSR. Soviet-manipulated regimes in Eastern Europe consolidated the forward defence zone: Soviet forces were deployed there to control internal developments and to extend Soviet deterrent and defensive capabilities. In particular, Soviet forces were deployed with such offensive potential that Western Europe became an explicit hostage to the USSR in the event of war. In manpower and hardware Soviet military resources were developed to defend the homeland against attack from land, sea or air. In the background Soviet research and development in modern weapons were pushed along at a pace which surprised many in the West, and soon produced an A-bomb, long-range aircraft and a range of tactical and strategic missiles. As a result of these developments the US homeland for the first time became vulnerable to massive destruction. While Soviet military doctrines appeared to be frozen by Stalinist orthodoxy ("the permanently operating factors"), in the most important respects the assimilation of the military-technical revolution was proceeding rapidly.

Soviet strategic policy in the immediate post-war years was dominated by the possibility of war with the United States. Nevertheless, it was also associated with a foreign policy which sometimes exhibited signs of bellicosity and which gave the weakened and war-weary countries of Western Europe plenty of reason to fear a "march to the Channel". This fear, which stimulated the Western alliance and increased Western military efforts, is now generally believed to have been much exaggerated: it is arguable that, whatever Stalin's dearest ambitions about extending the camp of socialism, his Cold War bellicosity was a manifestation of weakness rather than a portent of aggression. When Stalin did use the military instrument to advance foreign policy it was done in a cautious manner. The consolidation of the Soviet bloc in Eastern Europe involved few military risks. In fluid situations elsewhere Stalin was tempted to probe to see where the boundaries of the post-war world might settle. With varying degrees of involvement, the military instrument was used to support policy over Iran, Greece, Turkey, Sinkiang, Berlin and (by proxy) Korea. Soviet policy in each case was cautious: in each case Stalin was also ready to accept failure.

Stalin's death had many repercussions, not the least in military policy. The most novel development was a defence debate involving the party and military hierarchy about the character of modern war and about the strategic policy which the Soviet Union should adopt.[11] The eventual strategic outcome, however, was the result of the interplay between factional disputes, perceptions of US policy, technological dynamism, developing doctrine, and bureaucratic politics among the services.

Although the US atomic monopoly had been broken, Soviet military planners in the middle and late 1950s still faced the problem of a possible preventive or pre-emptive attack. Consequently, great efforts were made to improve air defence and defence against a strike from the sea. Long-range bombers and ICBMs were developed to deter war, and to strike back if war broke out. Soviet ground forces in Eastern Europe and Western Russia remained deployed to keep Europe a hostage. Their training and equipment was improved as they prepared to fight a nuclear World War III in central Europe. The Warsaw Pact was established in 1955 for a mixture of political and military reasons, including rationalising the military preparations for coalition warfare in modern conditions. Extrapolating into the nuclear age the old military maxim that "attack is the best form of defence" Soviet forces were deployed to take the initiative at the outbreak of war, and to conduct a mobile and hard-hitting campaign aimed at occupying Western Europe.

In 1960, partly because of economic strains and partly because of his growing confidence in the stability of the balance of terror,[12] Khrushchev amended the traditional emphasis on the ground forces, and instead moved towards a more ostensibly nuclear defence posture. This has been characterised as "minimum deterrence": his domestic critics later called it "nuclearmania". Khrushchev argued that if nuclear war broke out it would be settled within a few days: priority resources had therefore to be diverted to the forces which would play a dominating role in that exchange (that is, strategic offensive forces and the air defence). Other forces could be reduced, because of their secondary military role and because manpower and other shortages in the economy placed a premium on cutting labour-intensive services and "metal-eaters". Parts of the armed forces faced a swingeing one-third cut. Not surprisingly, Khrushchev's axe was very unpopular amongst the military establishment and their supporters. Financial cuts, large-scale dismissals ("the cold purge") and changed mission structures threatened important vested interests within the military profession, while the "one variant" doctrinal emphasis was considered to involve a dangerous inflexibility. In October 1964 the military establishment was not sorry to see Khrushchev ousted.

The military establishment had other reasons for dissatisfaction with Khruschev's strategic policy. In addition to what they regarded as his unsatisfactory doctrinal shift, and its accompanying cuts, they were anxious about his foreign policy, which his detractors were later free to describe, with some accuracy, as "adventurist". Khrushchev's impulsive character, his susceptibility to the temptation of "quick-fix" solutions, and his ambition, resulted in his using Soviet military power – the image of it, if not the reality – in a highly prominent fashion to support his foreign policy objectives. The alarms of the "missile gap" period were the outcome.[13] Between 1957 and 1962 Khrushchev practised what has been variously called "missile diplomacy", "psycho-strategic warfare", or less grandly, "rocket-rattling". Over crises in the Middle East, the Chinese offshore islands, Berlin and Cuba, Khrushchev engaged in threatening behaviour, although not to the extent (he hoped, and presumably expected) of provoking war. Western resolve held. Despite the advantages which the Soviet Union seemed to possess at the time, Khrushchev failed to make his country the "wave of the future" which it threatened to be. The problem for the Soviet military establishment was that Khrushchev was carrying out his crisis-prone foreign policy without full control of events (he could not be sure of US reactions) and without the actual military capability which his declaratory policy suggested he had. Their sense of vulnerability was increased by the massive strategic efforts instituted under President Kennedy. The Cuban missile crisis of October 1962 was the *dénouement* of Khrushchev's activist strategic policy: it ended his "hare-brained" schemes, it exposed the strategic inferiority of the Soviet Union, and it underlined important aspects of the efficacy of US conventional military power.

Khrushchev worked hard to relax international tension after Cuba. Arms control played a part in this, as symbolised in the Partial Test Ban

Treaty of 1963. In most respects up to this point (including his ostensible commitment to national liberation struggles) Khrushchev's strategy had provoked the United States to take actions which he would not have wished. In particular the build-up of strategic offensive forces by the United States meant that the Soviet Union, which had taken the lead in strategic missilery in 1957, had itself to undertake a major effort throughout the rest of the 1960s to regain some sort of recognised "parity". That this was achievable was largely the result of the halt in the numerical production of ICBMs by the United States.

In some respects, however, Khrushchev's contribution to strategic policy did not have merit from the Soviet viewpoint. He used military aid to support foreign policy in a generally effective way. Since the first days of the Revolution Soviet leaders had offered military assistance to support the enemies of its enemies. Khrushchev continued this, and military aid played a part in his breaking of Stalinist isolation and the two-camp image. Soviet military as well as foreign policy took on a more global character. In addition to military aid, there were also important developments in military procurement. However, because of the long lead-times of modern weaponry, these efforts did not become visible until the middle and late 1960s. New missile programmes were begun which aimed to try at least to match US strategic offensive power. Furthermore there was priority given to air defence, including the challenging idea of BMD. The apparent success of the post-Khrushchev leadership, especially in terms of improving the "strategic balance", owes more to the foundations set in Khrushchev's later years than the present leaders would be willing to admit.

The dominating feature of the strategic policy of the Brezhnev and Kosygin regime in the second half of the 1960s was the progress towards what is generally regarded as more or less "parity" in strategic offensive power. Between the early 1960s and the early 1970s, the Soviet Union caught up with the United States in numbers of land-based ICBMs, from a three-to-one inferiority to a slight lead. The Soviet lead was even greater in deliverable megatonage and missile "throw weight", but the United States retained an impressive lead in deliverable warheads and in the main branches of the relevant technological expertise. The US lead also included ABM technology, which had been originally dominated by the Soviet Union. Given its inferior industrial base, the Soviet effort was nevertheless notable, even though its achievement did depend on the US decision to replace the doctrine of nuclear "superiority" with that of "sufficiency" and "parity". The first SALT agreements of May 1972 were the mark of Soviet strategic progress: they had moved from the inferiority of 1962 to one of real strength, new confidence, and recognised formal parity in offensive and defensive systems.

The next most interesting trend since the mid-1960s has been the development of greater airlift and naval capabilities. Continuous attention to Soviet air power in the 1960s has resulted in a much improved capability. The growth of airlift potential has been particularly notable, and this was demonstrated operationally in the reinforcement lifts to the Middle East after 1967 and the combat landing in Czechoslovakia in 1968; in addition, it has shown its scope in large-scale exercises.[14] However, it has been the developing strength of the Soviet Navy which became the focus of particular interest amongst the traditional mono-poly naval powers at the turn of the 1960s/1970s.[15] The improved quality and the forward deployment of units of the Soviet Navy was primarily motivated by the general war requirements of strategic deter-rence and defence, in particular meeting the nuclear threat represented by strike-carriers and *Polaris/Poseidon*. Until recently the theme of this effort was of Soviet progress being outflanked by the improving techno-logy of the US Navy. As far as SLBMs are concerned this is still the case, with *Trident* promising to add complexity to an already immense prob-lem; however, it has not been as easy for the strike-carriers of the US Navy to outflank their shadowers. In addition to their general war tasks, the Soviet naval units which have been drawn forward have been used on a number of occasions, and in a number of ways, to support Soviet foreign policy in low-level, non-risk activities off West and East Africa, the Persian Gulf, and during crises in the Middle East and the Indian sub-continent.[16] The new strength and activities of the Soviet Navy have markedly complicated Western naval planning, and to a lesser extent, foreign policy. However, serious weaknesses remain in the Soviet Navy's capability: for the immediate future at least it lacks the capability to launch and sustain a large intervention.

While the Soviet Navy has achieved a new significance since the mid-1960s, the Ground Forces have re-established some of the importance which they lost under Khrushchev. There has been a pronounced mili-tary build-up on the ground in both Eastern Europe and the Soviet Far East, where the confrontation with China became increasingly serious at the turn of the 1960s/1970s: the Soviet forces developed more striking power and a greater flexibility in doctrine. The forces in Eastern Europe continued to provide a range of defensive and offensive capabi-lities in the anti-NATO context, and also contributed through their looming military might to the support of Soviet diplomatic positions, especially in the conferences on European security and mutual force reductions. In addition, the Soviet forces in Eastern Europe remained a major factor in the prosecution of Soviet objectives in the region, by latent or actual threat. The invasion of Czechoslovakia in 1968 under-lined their importance, as has the technique of "mobilisation by manoeuvre".[17] Soviet military might, and the demonstrated will to use it, sets the limit to the independent aspirations of Eastern European countries.

Overall, the results of the first decade of strategic policy under the Brezhnev leadership have been satisfactory to the military establishment. At the level of general-purpose forces Soviet capabilities and doctrine are more well-rounded. At the strategic level the inferiority of the Khrushchev period has been replaced with large and effective capabilities and formal parity. In addition, this strategic policy has been allied to a policy of "peaceful co-existence" which has been much less risk-prone than under Khrushchev. One consequence of these developments is that relations between the Party and the military establishment have improved markedly from the final stages of the Khrushchev period.[18]

Military Policy in the Domestic Environment

Outside observers invariably and not surprisingly perceive the Soviet military juggernaut in foreign policy terms. However, its role and impact in Soviet domestic affairs is by no means uninteresting or lacking in importance.

The Soviet armed forces have performed a number of important internal roles. Border patrol has been a traditional one; its orientation has always been inwards, to check defection, as well as outwards, to prevent intrusion. In addition the armed forces have contributed directly on a number of occasions to internal security in times of crisis, notably in the suppression of several insurrections. The armed forces also undertake a variety of socialising functions; the institution of conscription has been used as an instrument of political indoctrination, nation-building, youth control, and social conformity. For a mixture of historical and practical reasons, however, relations between the civilian and military sections of the Soviet community have continued to be reasonably close, with none of the outright anti-military hostility which has been manifest in many Western industrialised countries. While the military profession might not have all the prestige and attractiveness of former generations, it is still seen as an accepted and useful part of national life. Together, the range of domestic functions performed by the armed forces contribute in important ways to the effectiveness of the Soviet political system. One is tempted to conclude that if Soviet leaders did not feel that they needed an army for external reasons, they would have to invent one for internal reasons.

Military policy is also important in the domestic environment because of its economic aspects. The problem of estimating actual Soviet defence expenditure, and the consequential burden is difficult and familiar.[19] The range of estimates put forward has been very wide, but a common view is that despite the different GNPs (the Soviet GNP is variously estimated at between 50-70 per cent of that of the United States) their spending on defence is roughly comparable, though in some respects the Soviet Union is able to buy more for the same money, because Soviet military manpower is relatively cheap. Recent levels of military spending have been something of a burden: some parts of the Soviet economy (especially investment in the civilian sector) have been sacrificed in order to maintain and develop modern armed forces, with all their special and expensive equipment. However, there seems little reason to suppose that Soviet leaders will cease to press for, and receive, the military equipment which they consider necessary for the country's security. The "resource allocation" problem has always been a major one for the Soviet leaders in recent years, and is even more so since civilian commitments have become more of a constraint than previously. This development has added an additional but bearable strain to the mysterious processes of defence decision-making in the Soviet Union.

Defence Decision-Making

Knowledge about the processes by which defence policy has been formulated in the Soviet Union has always been limited.[20] However, over a twenty-year perspective two trends have been perceptible: decision-making today is more bureaucratic than in Stalin's time, and in some senses military "influence" has increased.

Defence decision-making in all countries is characterised by informal as well as formal processes. This generalisation is certainly true of the Soviet Union. Indeed, some major committees concerned with defence are not statutory, although they have been constant and important features of the process. In general, those who have concentrated their attentions upon the formal processes tend to under-estimate the influence which the military establishment can exert on policy: on the other hand, it is easy to exaggerate the character and extent of military influence.

The Soviet tradition has been one of firm civilian (Party) control; indeed, there has been a recurring fear of undue military influence. As a mark of this the military establishment has been formally excluded from decision-making power (though not close consultation). At the top of the Soviet hierarchy is the Politburo, which in its long history has not normally included the Minister of Defence.[21] The Party leaders in the Politburo have reserved for themselves the right to make decisions on the employment of forces and on peace and war.[22] On military questions below this level the formal position is that military policies are passed by the political leadership to the Ministry of Defence, where they are then put into operation by the relevant body, be it the General Staff, the Military Academies, or the Chief Political Directorate of the Armed Forces. Military doctrine (such questions as future types of war or weapon employment) is evolved in these bodies.

Linking the political and military hierarchies are several joint committees, where details of policy are probably worked out. By far the most important of these bodies — if it actually exists — is the so-called "Defence Council". This is a mixed Party-military body at the highest level of representation. Doubts about the Defence Council include its exact character, as well as its existence, although the balance of scanty evidence supports the latter. The Defence Council has been described as a sub-committee of the Politburo which actually formulates defence policy and submits it for ratification to the Politburo: alternatively, it has been seen as essentially a military-political linking body, a channel for advice and co-ordination. One of the few pictures of typical political-military consultation at the top level describes procedure as being highly regular, business as being cyclical, mainly concerned with incremental decisions and probably strictly confined to the military field. Mixed politico-military questions (e.g. SALT) would probably be decided by the political leaders themselves, with military specialists invited as advisers only.[23]

The formal position, therefore, is one of firm civilian control, constitutionally and in practice. However, this should not be taken to mean that the military establishment is not able to affect the thinking of the Party leadership. Indeed, in some respects their influence has grown in recent years: certainly their opportunities have increased. However, this is not the result of a drop in traditional Party vigilance, or of exceptional military pressure, though the trend has been encouraged by a more collective Party leadership and a military establishment with some assertive characters. The main factor behind the growth of influence has been the thrust of events. With frequent regularity in recent years the mere logic of certain situations has caused the Soviet leaders to seek the advice of their military specialists. The invasion of Czechoslovakia, the confrontation with China, SALT, the continuing Middle East crisis, military aid diplomacy, forward naval deployment, MFR — all these have required specialist military advice. Events have pulled the military establishment into the decision-making process, and this has been encouraged by leaders with the bureaucrat's tendency to seek advice and spread responsibility. The military establishment, with its recent memory of the Khrushchev years, has not hesitated to accept the increased advisory role.

The informal aspects of the political-military relationship tend to become important when the military establishment fails to achieve its objectives through the formal channels, or when it wishes to protest against decisions which it regards as threatening to its interests.[24] Various opportunities can be exploited. For example, it may cultivate personal relations with individual political leaders, who for obvious reasons have usually been interested in developing harmonious relations with military leaders; alternatively, the military establishment might take its case to wider party and government opinion, in the hope of affecting decisions from below. The more notable manifestations of military criticism include opposition to Khrushchev's proposed force cuts in the early 1960s, the attempts to influence budgetary decisions in 1966 and 1967, scepticism about arms control (including initial opposition to SALT, and continuing scepticism about the exercise for all but tactical utility) and some agitation against the idea of *détente*.[25] Although there have been important differences of opinion between the political and military hierarchies — indeed there is always likely to be a degree of tension in the relationship between a professional officer corps and a totalitarian party[26] — there remains a vital area of interdependence. Because of the Party's traditional preoccupation with security, the need to have military backing for policies, and the increased military content of important areas of foreign policy, the Party is both reliant on and susceptible to military advice and/or influence. As a result of the favourable combination of factors in recent years it is not surprising that the Soviet military establishment, in the view of one close observer, "is consulted at an earlier stage and in greater depth on foreign and defence policy than ever before."[27] Despite this, however, there seems little doubt that on all major matters of military policy the Party has, and intends to keep, the final word.[28]

One interesting feature of the making of Soviet military policy is that there has not grown up, as in many Western countries, a habit of public defence debating, in press, parliament, or academic circles. The Soviet Union lacks the phenomenon of academic strategists in universities, or civilian specialists in ostensibly independent research institutes, or unofficial newspaper defence correspondents. Defence is never a ball in the parliamentary arena. This does not mean, however, that the phenomenon of "defence debates" is entirely absent: as earlier discussion has indicated, there have been both differences of opinion and outlets for its expression. In fact, in the post-war years there have been three periods of marked discussion about military matters: the mid-1950s, the mid-1960s, and from 1972 to the present. As the debating occurs in a distinctive political and cultural *milieu,* it is hardly surprising that the activity is rather different from the Washington model. The debates are more cautious, they are technically rather than politically-inclined, and "outsiders" have no role. Military affairs are dealt with by a smaller, more inbred and more professionally-involved group than in the West.

It is hoped that the brief sketch which has been given shows that while ultimate authority on defence matters resides in the Politburo, the formulation of military policy in the Soviet Union, especially below the level of very basic issues, is always likely to be very much more messy than administrative wire-diagrams or simple decision-making models might suggest. The policy process, which is always complex enough, has become much more so than in Stalin's time, when the system was relatively dominated by one man, and when clearer military imperatives resulted in requirements-led-innovation. Since the mid-1950s, and especially since Khrushchev's fall, various aspects of bureaucratic politics have come to the fore. There has been more formalism, greater bureaucratic activism, increased professional expertise, newer techniques in decision-making, and a diffusion of responsibility on non-vital matters. Furthermore, interest group involvement has been at a higher level than was conceivable under the Stalinist model. In weapons procurement the relevant ministries, scientific research institutes, and design bureaus bring influence to bear, and there is no lack of inter-service rivalry and competition within the traditionally army-dominated system. "Weapons dynamics" and economic factors also have their pull on the procurement process.[29] The increasing complexity of the factors involved adds considerably to the problems of policy-making in this difficult area.

Looking to the future, it might be expected that the increased bureaucratisation of the military decision-making process will make policy more expert, more incremental, and less susceptible to one man's proclivity to "hare-brained schemes". At the same time it could mean that mistakes will be carried through with ever-more efficiency.

Alliances and Soviet Strategy

Soviet troops have had far less operational experience since 1945 than their counterparts in the armed forces of the major Western military powers. It is a marked irony, therefore, that what operational experience has been gained by Soviet troops has been at the expense of some of its ostensible allies, notably Hungary, Czechoslovakia, and China. When contemplating the relations between the socialist allies one is reminded of the comment: "With friends like these, who needs enemies?"

In February 1950 the Soviet Union and the People's Republic of China signed a Treaty of Friendship Alliance and Mutual Assistance.[30] This Soviet-dominated alliance confronted the Western powers with two apparently united Communist giants, and in so doing increased their individual deterrent power and general political strength, for example during the Korean War.[31] From the late 1950s onwards, however, the strains in the Sino-Soviet military relationship grew, and both the political and military relationship deteriorated rapidly after 1960. While military relations with the United States became more manageable through the 1960s from a Soviet viewpoint, those with China appeared increasingly dangerous, judging by both word and deed. In 1969 there were clashes, and much talk of war in many quarters. Although there have been periodic alarms the situation appears to have stabilised since that time, and most observers believe that the possibility of major war has receded. As time passed the military attractions of a "surgical strike" by the Soviet Union against China's growing strategic potential have diminished. Nevertheless, the impressive Soviet military build-up in the Far East[32] indicates its determination that any negotiations will take place against a background of Soviet military superiority, and that any clashes which do break out will be won.

The growing military problem of China in recent years has to some extent diverted the Soviet preoccupation with Europe. Nevertheless, the traditional significance of Europe remains, and one reflection of this has been the growing importance of the Warsaw Pact in the conduct of Soviet foreign and military policy.

The Warsaw Treaty of Friendship Co-operation and Mutual Assistance was signed between the Soviet Union and seven Eastern European states in May 1955.[33] It is generally agreed that is origins were primarily political rather than military. In part it was a Soviet attempt to deal with a number of immediate problems: these included the desire to offset the entry of West Germany into the Western European Union and NATO, the desire for a propaganda counter to NATO, and the need to provide a rationale for military movements in Eastern Europe after the Austrian State Treaty. Important as these were, however, the Pact was basically to be understood as a means of rationalizing and institutionalising Soviet political and military authority in Eastern Europe on a more acceptable basis.[34] In addition to Soviet purposes, the Pact was also to serve – and continues to serve – some internal and external interests of some of the socialist regimes in Eastern Europe. While the latter's input into the alliance is not to be overlooked, the evolution of the Pact has been related in the main to Soviet attempts to deal with the problems of an evolving Eastern Europe in a world of change.

For its first five years, until 1960-61, the political and military activity of the Warsaw Pact was very limited. Since that time a combination of factors have worked to increase its significance for its members. The first notable development was the start of a series of major joint military exercises at the start of the 1960s. While the military side of the Pact progressed through the mid-1960s, however, political tensions within Eastern Europe troubled the Soviet Union. The swing from Soviet-defined rectitude of Albania, Romania, and then Czechoslovakia each demanded attention, and the Pact was used in attempts to deal with the various problems by exclusion, pressure, threat, or directive. By 1967 the Pact was playing a novel role in Soviet-Romanian relations in particular; it had become an important channel for communication and conflict resolution.[35] Unfortunately for all concerned, this embryonic development was not able to contain what the Soviet leaders and their Eastern Europe supporters regarded as the dangerous side of Czechoslovakian "socialism with a human face". In late August 1968 an invasion was carried out after the failure of multilateral diplomacy backed by military demonstration. The Warsaw Pact had been prominent in the build-up of military pressure in the summer of 1968, but command of the actual invasion was handed to General Pavlovski, the Commander-in-Chief of the Soviet Ground Forces. This episode appears to confirm Mackintosh's thesis that in its military sphere the Pact is not intended to be an operational command-and-control headquarters, but rather an administrative authority, designed to organise and co-ordinate the activities of the members. It is a War Office rather than a Supreme Headquarters.[36]

The Warsaw Pact has grown in both military and political importance since 1968. The Soviet leaders recognised that the mechanism needed changing, and this was done in the Budapest reforms of March 1969. The reforms involved some reorganisation of the military side of the alliance, including the granting of a larger formal role to the non-Soviet members. One result of the increased attention given to the Pact since 1969 is that its military aspects have improved in almost all respects. While manpower levels have remained roughly stable, defence spending has increased, and the quality and quantity of modern weapons and logistic back-up have improved notably. This improvement in combat power seems to be consistent with the increased force requirements of a readjusted military doctrine for the European theatre, which involves the possibility of prolonged conventional operations in the opening stages of hostilities.[37]

Alongside the "perfecting" of the military organisation of the Pact there has been an upgrading of its political role. Especially in the immediate aftermath of the invasion of Czechoslovakia this involved the stressing of the socialist nature of the alliance, one manifestation of which was the Brezhnev doctrine. Parallel with Soviet attempts to use the Pact to improve Eastern European integration have been efforts to use the Council for Mutual Economic Aid (COMECON). Since 1968 the Pact has continued to be used in a conflict containment role; this has involved the independently minded Romanians, but less predictably it also included East Germany, which for a time exhibited its disapproval of the Soviet and other Eastern European responses to West Germany's *Ostpolitik*. The crisis in Czechoslovakia was an important experience for the non-Soviet allies: it gave them a dramatic lesson of the limits of diversity which Soviet leaders were willing to accept. On the other hand, they have probably also learned from the Romanian experience that there is room for manouevre within the Pact, if haste is avoided and certain ground-rules are obeyed. While the Soviet Union continues to have the last word, the opportunities for the non-Soviet allies to have some voice widened at the start of the 1970s, when discussions began on various aspects of European security.[38]

Current Issues and Future Problems

While military security probably remains more of a preoccupation for Soviet leaders than the leaders of the other major powers, the Soviet Union is more secure than ever before. Objectively, no state dare now attack it, without receiving almost certain and unacceptable punishment: subjectively, few men in Soviet decision-making circles believe that major war is likely in the foreseeable future. This does not mean that the effort devoted to military policy can be relaxed. An ingrained sense of danger rules against complacency, while to the extent Soviet leaders feel secure, it is seen as being the result of military might and preparedness. For both internal and external reasons military policy will remain a major commitment for Soviet society, in time, energy, and resources.

The Soviet leaders have reason for satisfaction with most aspects of military policy in the domestic environment, certainly when comparing their lot with their counterparts in some Western countries. At the highest level, relations between the military and political hierarchies has greatly improved since Khrushchev's time, with a "rejuvenated" High Command and a more like-minded political leadership.[39] While there has been compromise on both sides, the improved relations have largely involved a sympathetic party hierarchy meeting military preferences on matters such as doctrine, character of effort, and the general relationship between defence posture and foreign policy. The improved relationship has not ruled out disagreements on such matters as missions and budget, but something of a "compact" has come into existence between the Party of Brezhnev and the military establishment of Marshal Grechko.[40] At a lower and more general level of civil-military relations it appears that if military life does not always have the same high prestige it had formerly, this is in part a reflection of its earlier inflated position, in part a reflection of the absence of immediate danger, and in part a reflection of other desirable job opportunities. There has been no significant manifestation of the anti-military attitude which has characterised civil-military relations in the West, and such a development in the foreseeable future appears unlikely. On resource allocation questions it is clear that the Soviet leadership has been conscious of the defence burden, and the opportunity costs involved. Although for historical and political reasons the Soviet leaders will always be vulnerable to demands bearing upon security issues, military requirements are not likely to be met as expansively in future as they have been in the past; the military establishment will have to work hard to establish its claims, though "vital" claims will always be met. In recent years the demands have included a notable inter-service debate on missions, with the Commander-in-Chief of the Navy, Admiral Gorshkov, playing a dominant but not exclusive role.[41] To an increasing extent the problem of meeting multiple demands for money is being met by efforts to achieve greater efficiency in military procurement and improved organisation and decision-making.[42] While economic factors may shape military policy to a larger extent than hitherto, there is no reason to suppose that the Soviet armed forces will fail to receive what is considered to be essential for the maintenance of their strength.

As far as the external aspects of military policy are concerned, the strategic priorities of the post-war period have remained consistent: creating the capability and doctrine to deter war, to fight a war successfully if one should break out, and to have the military bargaining chips to be able to deal with the world from a position of strength. Behind the Soviet efforts there has been a "damage limitation" philosophy which Wolfe and other writers have talked about. Expressed more positively but less practically by Erickson the influential principle might be called "assured survivability".[43] Translated into current doctrine this means a counterforce strategy coupled with both active and passive defence measures.

All the branches of the armed forces have a general war orientation. The primary missions of the Strategic Rocket Forces and the Air Defence Command are strategic deterrence and the defence of the homeland (damage limitation) by counterforce and active air defence. While the SALT agreements have restricted the expansion of BMD coverage, much attention has been drawn to the recent new weaponry of the strategic offensive forces which, added to their concern with pre-emption and counterforce suggest that "superiority" is a desirable military preference, even if it is not politically or economically achievable — or even military meaningful.[44] While the massive spurt in Soviet strategic forces from the mid-1960s was dramatic and has given them a lead in launchers and "throw weight", they remain significantly behind the United States in the deployment of advanced technology (such as MIRVs, ABMs, and MARVs).[45] In its achievement of rough parity the SALT exercise has been a useful vehicle for Soviet strategy, although the political rationale has perhaps been a major one throughout.[46]

If not as dramatic as the strategic offensive forces, the build-up of Soviet general purpose forces has been an equally interesting development. In this respect there has been a "revival" of the Ground Forces, whose traditional position slipped under Khrushchev. The current numbers and capabilities of the Ground Forces are impressive, but so are their commitments: in a sense theirs is a three-front commitment, involving Eastern Europe, NATO, and China. In addition to policing Eastern Europe the primary roles of the Ground Forces remain the provision of defensive and offensive capabilities in Europe and the Far East. They are deployed to be in a position to break out and win should war occur: this means that their concept of operations is based on the *blitzkrieg* principles of speed, hitting power, and mobility. For a long time their doctrine had a nuclear emphasis, on the assumption that any war in central Europe would be certain to escalate: this idea has recently been amended, in favour of a doctrine which envisages the possible conduct of prolonged conventional operations by Warsaw Pact forces in the opening stage of hostilities, and this major shift explains the build-up of combat power in Eastern Europe, which has so exercised Western planners. Alongside the strengthening of the ground forces there has been an improvement in air power, with considerable attention being given to the capabilities designed for strike, reconnaissance, interception, and tactical air support.[47] In addition, strategic air lift potential has been a notable development. As with the strategic forces, the missions of the ground and air forces remain basically unchanged: the current improvements simply represent the continuing Soviet efforts to perfect the capabilities and doctrine of the services for the successful prosecution of their missions. This generalisation has also been true for the Soviet Navy, whose growth from the early 1960s provoked an excited thrill for many in the traditional naval powers.

The Soviet Navy in the last ten years has significantly improved its combat capability, has considerably expanded its area of operations, and has developed a different concept of operations. However, there has been a marked stability in its primary mission structure.[48] The priority general war missions remain: to counter the *Polaris/Poseidon* threat, to neutralise the strike carriers, to contribute to Soviet strategic strike, to maintain command of the sea in the four fleet areas, and to provide flank support for land operations.[49] The general war missions of the Soviet Navy have remained stable since the early 1950s (except for the addition of the SLBM problem). At the turn of the 1960s/1970s, however, the Soviet Navy in forward deployment demonstrated on several occasions a novel activism in support of foreign policy. This has led a number of analysts (and certainly Western naval establishments) to argue that this represents a significant shift in the emphasis of mission structures towards such peacetime employment.[50] The emphasis in the "Gorshkov series" on naval support of state interests has been said to support this argument, although it is most likely that Gorshkov was engaged in the business of advocacy in an inter-service debate, rather than announcing policies which had been accepted.

While the recent naval developments demand attention from adversaries and potential adversaries, it is not yet clear whether the activism represents a temporary phase, resulting from the thrust of events, or whether it represents a major shift in policy towards the naval support of state interests short of war. It remains to be seen whether the phase of activism is an aberration or a precedent.[51] While the disparity between Soviet and Western naval capabilities has narrowed in recent years, and thus the tactical threat posed to Western shipping in the event of war has grown dramatically, important gaps remain in the discharging of some priority missions. "Sea control" is a feasible objective in the fleet areas, but the priority damage — limitation mission against *Polaris/Poseidon* — and soon *Trident* — is likely to remain unachievable. This certainly does not mean that US SLBM platforms will be allowed a free ride by the Soviet Navy. Making the maximum use of whatever is available is a well-developed faculty in the Soviet military outlook.

Overall, the individual branches of the Soviet forces have reason to be satisfied with their current position, particularly when compared with the early 1960s: doctrine is better developed and more flexible, capabilities and missions are better matched, and the defence posture fits more comfortably into the régime's foreign policy. But military policy does not stand still: the dynamics of politics and technology force reconsiderations. As the mid-1970s have approached the Soviet Union has been at one of its periodic cross-roads, in which important aspects of military policy have been discussed and argued over. The questions have been the perennial ones: resource allocation, allocation and structure of missions, the level and character of military effort, doctrine, and future requirements.[52] While the detailed outcome of the debate remains to be seen, the objectives of the Soviet leaders, and the constraints within which they work, do not allow great scope for change in the main outlines.

Relations with the United States will remain the most important strategic problem for the Soviet leaders. While their strategic relationship has been largely stabilised, the difficulties encountered in SALT, including the momentum of the background arms racing, ensures that this relationship will remain a major preoccupation for both sides. Although the Soviet position on the strategic balance has improved significantly since the early 1960s there are still reasons to cause them anxiety and continuing vigilance: the quality and quantity of US procurement, the diversification of its building programmes, and the Schlesinger targeting doctrine are the most important. These relative weaknesses also explain why simple "parity" as such is not likely to be a satisfactory concept for the Soviet military leadership: from a military viewpoint, their desirable aim is likely to be "parity plus", "superiority in the guise of parity" or even "superiority" — in each case without provoking the United States to a further round of the arms race. The existing SALT agreements have symbolised the progress achieved, and have given the basis for some hope for further relative gains in future. As far as strategic procurement is concerned, therefore, competition with the United States is likely to continue more or less vigorously, although the competition is in a sense ritualised, because the policies of both sides are constricted by a determination to avoid nuclear war. Ritualised competition is not necessarily safe: it does not rule out mistakes, misunderstandings, irrational behaviour, or deliberately risky behaviour to test the rules.

Europe remains the major area of commitment for Soviet military manpower. Controlling change in Eastern Europe will continue to have an important military element, and will involve many problems as the region evolves through a complex inter-relationship between internal developments and foreign policy. The Warsaw Pact now involves a greater non-Soviet contribution than the Soviet rulers originally intended, though militarily and politically it remains dominated by the Soviet Union, and will remain so as long as Soviet leaders feel that their own armed forces are their only guarantor of security, and that control of Eastern Europe is essential to that security. As far as the NATO-oriented functions of the Soviet forces are concerned the balance of military power seems likely to remain heavily in their favour, without any unacceptable sacrifices. However, some technological developments revealed by the 1973 Middle Eastern War (notably in anti-tank and anti-aircraft weaponry) promise to increase the strength of defensive formations, and so will help NATO maintain its threat of posing enormous costs should an offensive incursion take place. Short of a radical political or technological change in Europe therefore, it remains difficult to foresee circumstances in which Soviet leaders will see it in their interests to carry war across the now crystallised 1945 truce lines.

If European war remains improbable, this does not decrease the usefulness of the Soviet forces which are deployed towards the West. These forces aggregate into an impressive array of military power, which plays an important if sometimes indefinable role in supporting the Soviet Union's European diplomacy. The ability of Soviet leaders to talk against a backdrop of great military strength not only affects their own predispositions, but also the perceptions of those with whom they are dealing. While the negotiations at the European security conference in 1973-74 showed that Soviet military power could not easily be translated into political influence, their military strength has given them more leverage in the talks on mutual force reductions. It gives them the confidence to play for time, and the opportunity to press their favoured proposals in the knowledge that any agreement is likely to be an improvement, while the no-agreement fall-back position will only mean the continuation of a satisfactory *status quo*. Because of the Soviet ability to talk from strength and its relative freedom from domestic pressures, it is hardly surprising that MBFR was sometimes dubbed "Much Benefit For Russia".

In terms of active military engagement it is the Sino-Soviet frontier rather than the old Iron Curtain which will be the most likely scene for fighting. The possibility of hostilities cannot be ruled out, but as the costs of any conflict increase with time, the likelihood that war will be a chosen instrument of policy is likely to recede. However, the military instrument will remain an important factor in the confrontation with China. The threat of swift and massive military action, for deterrence and coercive bargaining, will remain a thought-provoking feature of the Soviet posture. The most likely prognosis for the old allies is a prolonged relationship of "neither war nor peace".

As far as the rest of the world is concerned, the Middle East is an area of major military anxiety. Direct Soviet military commitment has always been limited, but the very large quantities of military assistance which it has despatched into the area have been a major tool in its efforts to penetrate and maintain an influential role. The Soviet record in this unstable and dangerous area has been variable, like that of earlier external powers: the record also suggests that Soviet policy will tend to be cautious as far as direct military involvement is concerned, that the Arab-Israeli conflict will always provide opportunities for leverage for a benevolent arms supplier, and that local nationalisms will always be a severe constraint on Soviet or any external influence. In any relationship between a Middle Eastern and an external country, *who* is using *whom* is not always as it seems.

In the Middle East as elsewhere, the possible significance of the extending capability of Soviet military potential has received much attention. The Soviet leaders have options which were not there previously. At the least, these developments facilitate the provision of military assistance, and this together with visible presence helps to complicate Western planning, and gives support to Soviet foreign policy, albeit at a low level, in areas such as the Eastern Mediterranean, the Persian Gulf, West Africa and the Indian Ocean. If there has been some alarmism about the threat to Western interests represented by the forward deployment of units of the Soviet Navy, these instruments certainly can support an incremental foreign policy in relation to specific regions and countries. However, the intervention potential of the existing forces should not be exaggerated; the optimum level of Soviet building in this respect may have already been reached. Furthermore, it should not be forgotten that forward deployment might bring undesirable complications to Soviet foreign policy, as well as to the foreign policies of its adversaries. The Soviet Navy has major weaknesses in terms of its development into a world-wide intervention capability: the gap between an ability to project a presence and the ability to sustain large-scale operations in a hostile environment is considerable, and it is far from apparent that the Soviet leaders intend to develop the latter capability. An embryo exists, in the form of naval infantry, experience in forward deployment, and a medium-sized carrier, and these developments are sometimes aggregated and extrapolated into an intervention capability: however, there are persuasive reasons for thinking that the motives behind each of the developments was largely self-contained.

In assessing the continued build-up of Soviet strategic and general purpose forces, Western observers are faced with the perennial problem of relating intentions and capabilities. In particular, they have to ask themselves the question: is *détente* compatible with a continued expansion of Soviet military potential? From the Soviet viewpoint there is certainly no contradiction between the two: the conditions for peaceful coexistence are only made possible by the impressive military strength of the Soviet Union. This traditional view that military strength is at the basis of security is more prevalent in the West than some commentators would allow: the Harmel Report established in 1967 that defence and *détente* were to be the twin pillars of NATO, while the quantity and quality of US military procurement is often overlooked as we project our anxieties eastwards, towards the only country which has us targeted.

Notes

1. The following works by the figures who have dominated the study of Soviet military policy in the last decade will provide a sound and detailed introduction to the subject: John Erickson, *The Soviet High Command 1918-1941: A Military-Political History* (London: Macmillan & Co. Ltd., 1962), and *Soviet Military Power* (London: Royal United Service Institute, 1971); R.L.

Garthoff, *How Russia Makes War* (London: Allen and Unwin, 1954), and *Soviet Military Policy: A Historical Analysis* (London: Faber and Faber, 1966); J.M. Macintosh, *Juggernaut: A History of the Soviet Armed Forces* (London: Secker and Warburg, 1967); Thomas, W. Wolfe, *Soviet Strategy at the Crossroads* (Cambridge, Mass.: Harvard University Press, 1964), and *Soviet Power And Europe* (Baltimore: The Johns Hopkins Press, 1970). In addition, each has written numerous articles in professional jsournals.

2. This problem is discussed more fully in Michael MccGwire, *Soviet Naval Developments: Capability and Context* (New York: Praeger, 1973), pp. 1-5, 31-33.

3. For two excellent analyses of this concept see Peter H. Vigor, "The Semantics of Deterrence And Defence", and Geoffrey Jukes, "The Military Approach To Deterrence And Defence", Chapters 25 and 26 respectively in Michael MccGwire, Ken Booth, and John McDonnell, *Soviet Naval Policy: Objectives and Constraints* (New York: Praeger, 1974). See note 9.

4. Self-inflicted terror, of course, has also been on a staggering level.

5. Estimates put military casualties between 7.5 and 13.6 million, and civilian casualties at 7,500,000. The British figures were 264,443 and 92,673 respectively. The United States had slightly more military casualties, and many fewer civilian casualties than Britain. It is not insignificant that in this and other examples Russian war dead are counted to the nearest thousand, while Britain and the United States are able (and willing) to do it to the last individual.

6. This is J. Malcom Mackintosh's definition of "strategic policy" from the Soviet viewpoint, in his "Soviet Strategic Policy", *The World Today*, Vol. 26, No. 7, July 1970, p. 272.

7. Many observers have noted this tendency. See, for example, ibid., p. 270.

8. This is the thesis of M. Garder, *A History of the Soviet Army* (London: Pall Mall Press, 1966).

9. Soviet strategic thinking does not make the same doctrinal distinction between *deterrence* and *defence* which is made by Western strategists. In Soviet thinking the one is an extension of the other, or even synonymous. The Soviet conception is the traditional military view which comprehends deterrence in terms of a threat by an impressive war-fighting capability. The Anglo-American conception, on the other hand, has crystallised into the idea of *mutual* deterrence, in which the capabilities and doctrines developed might be significantly different from those desirable for an effective war-fighting capability; furthermore, the idea of mutual deterrence also includes the idea of being solicitous about mutual vulnerability and about the survivability of the adversary's retaliatory forces. None of these conditions are important from the traditional viewpoint. Furthermore, the synonymity of deterrence and defence from the Soviet viewpoint means that their military thinkers have given much more explicit attention to fighting and winning a nuclear war than Western (especially civilian) strategists: there is no mental blockage caused by the thought that deterrence might "fail".

10. In addition to the books cited in note 1, two mongraphs which provide overviews of the period are Geoffrey Jukes, *The Development of Soviet Strategic Thinking Since 1945* (Canberra Papers on Strategy and Defence, No. 14, 1972) and Ken Booth. *The Military Instrument in Soviet Foreign Policy, 1917-1972* (London: Royal United Service Institute, 1974).

11. Herbert S. Dinerstein, *War and the Soviet Union* (New York: Praeger, 1962), *passim*.

12. This had already been manifest in 1956 when Khrushchev revised Lenin's doctrine about the fatalistic inevitability of war between the two systems. Khrushchev declared that "war is not fatalistically inevitable. Today there are mighty social and political forces possessing formidable means to prevent the

imperialists from unleashing war."

13. Although they focus too narrowly on the "strategic" motivation behind Khrushchev's policy in these years, a most interesting account is provided by A.L. Horelick and M.R. Rush, *Strategic Power and Soviet Foreign Policy* (Chicago: Chicago University Press, 1966).

14. While the attention of commentators has been drawn to the great Soviet naval debate, Erickson has been one of the few analysts stressing the developing potential of Soviet air forces. See his *Soviet Military Power*, pp. 61-5.

15. The two volumes edited by Michael MccGwire (notes 2 and 3 above) contain a large number of papers providing factual material on this contentious issue, and also reflect the wide range of serious opinion on the subject.

16. For a summary of these activities see Robert G. Weinland, *Soviet Naval Operations – Ten Years of Change* (Center for Naval Analyses, Professional Paper 125, August 1974).

17. See Erickson, *Soviet Military Power*, pp. 93-5.

18. A summary of recent trends is given by John Erickson, "Soviet Military Policy. Priorities and Perspectives", *The Round Table*, No. 256, October 1974, pp. 369-79.

19. Studies of Soviet military policy have concentrated overwhelmingly on the more exciting and dangerous aspects of the subject, such as doctrine and equipment: the economic factor has invariably been taken as a given. Introductions to the problems involved in analysing this topic are given by Philip Hanson, "The Analysis of Soviet Defence Expenditures", in MccGwire, Booth, McDonnell, Chapter 7; Raymond Hutchings, "Soviet Defence Spending And Soviet External Relations", *International Affairs*, Vol XLVII, No. 3, July 1971, pp. 518-31; *The Military Balance 1970-71* (IISS), pp. 10-12.

20. We should also be conscious of how little we know of the *how* and *why* of defence policy "making" in the West also.

21. There have been two exceptions: Marshal Zhukov between February 1956 and October 1957, and Marshal Grechko from April 1973 to the present (January 1975).

22. The comments in this and the next paragraph are based on Malcom Mackintosh, "The Soviet Military's Influence on Foreign Policy", *Problems of Communism*, September–October 1973, and in MccGwire, Booth, McDonnell, op. cit., Chapter 2.

23. See Matthew P. Gallagher, "The Military Role in Soviet Decision-Making", Chapter 3 in MccGwire, Booth, McDonnell, op. cit. Also his *Soviet Decision-Making for Defence: a critique of US Perspectives on the Arms Race* (New York: Praeger, 1972), with Karl F. Spielmann.

24. Ibid.

25. Ibid.

26. This is one of the central theses of R. Kolkowicz, *The Soviet Military and the Communist Party* (Princeton: Princeton University Press, 1967).

27. Mackintosh, "The Soviet Military's Influence On Foreign Policy", op. cit.

28. This view is supported by all the available Soviet press material on Army-Party relations, ibid. The concern with the issue is on implicit recognition of its sensitivity.

29. On a range of the more complex factors involved, see Edward L. Warner III, "The Bureaucratic Politics of Weapons Procurement", and John McDonnell, "The Soviet Defence Industry As A Pressure Group", Chapters 5 and 6 in MccGwire, Booth, and McDonnell, op. cit.; David Holloway, "Technology and Political Decision in Soviet Armaments Policy", *Journal of Peace Research*, No. 4, December 1974.

30. Useful background is provided by Raymond L. Garthoff (ed.), *Sino-Soviet Military Relations* (London: Praeger, 1966).

31. See, for example, the essay by Malcom Mackintosh, "The Soviet Attitude" in

M.H. Halperin (ed.), *Sino-Soviet Relations and Arms Control*)(Cambridge, Mass.: MIT Press, 1967) pp. 193-226.

32. Soviet manpower deployed on the border with China rose from 15 divisions in 1968 to 45 divisions in 1974.

33. For the evolution of the Pact see Malcom Mackintosh, 'The Evolution of the Warsaw Pact', *Adelphi Paper,* No. 58, June 1969, and "The Warsaw Pact Today", *Survival,* Vol. XVI, No. 3, May/June 1974, pp. 122-6; R.A. Remington, *The Warsaw Pact. Case Studies in Communist Conflict Resolution* (Cambridge, Mass.: The MIT Press, 1971); T.W. Wolfe, *Soviet Power and Europe, op. cit., passim.*

34. The formal Soviet military position in Eastern Europe does not depend exclusively on the Warsaw Pact. It also has a series of bilateral treaties with the countries of the area.

35. Remington, op. cit., pp. 8, 56-93.

36. Mackintosh, "The Warsaw Pact Today", p. 122-3.

37. John Erickson, "Soviet Combat Force on Continent Grows", *NATO Review,* No. 3, June 1974, pp. 18-21. First published in *The Times,* 19 February 1974.

38. For post-1968 trends see note 33, plus Daviid Holloway, "The Warsaw Pact in the Era of Negotiation", *Survival,* XIV, No. 6, November/December 1972, pp. 275-9; and Robin Alison Remington, "The Warsaw Pact: Communist Coalition Politics In Action", *The Yearbook of World Affairs* (London: Stevens and Sons, 1973), pp. 153-72.

39. Erickson, *Soviet Military Power,* pp. 13-40, and "Soviet Military Policy: Priorities and Perceptions", pp. 377-8.

40. Ibid.

41. See, for example, John Erickson, "Soviet Defence Policies and Naval Interests," and Robert G. Weinland, "Analysis of Admiral Gorshkov's Navies In War and Peace", Chapters 4 and 29 respectively in MccGwire, Booth, McDonnell, op. cit.

42. See, for example, David Holloway, "Technology, Management and the Soviet Military Establishment', *Adelphi Paper,* No. 76, April 1971, and his "Technology and Political Decision in Soviet Armaments Policy", op. cit.

43. John Erickson, "Soviet Military Policy: Priorities and Perceptions," p. 374.

44. On 3 July 1974 Dr. Kissinger declared: "And one of the questions we have to ask ourselves as a country is what in the name of God is strategic superiority? What is the significance of it politically, militarily, operationally at these levels of numbers? What do you do with it?" According to Erickson, the Soviet command would simply answer: "Use it". Ibid., p. 370.

45. And as Kissinger has pointed out to some SALT critics, it is warheads not launchers which destroy targets.

46. Booth, op. cit., pp. 20-23.

47. See note 37 above.

48. MccGwire, Booth, McDonnell, op. cit., Editors' Introduction.

49. MccGwire, op. cit., especially Chapters 16 and 25.

50. For a well-reasoned example of this approach see Robert G. Weinland, "The Changing Mission Structure of the Soviet Navy", *Survival,* Vol. XIV, No. 3, May/June 1972, pp. 129-33.

51. See note 48.

52. The present debate is assessed by John Erickson in "Soviet Military Policy: Priorities and Perceptions", op. cit.

12 CHINESE DEFENCE POLICY

John Baylis

The task of studying the defence policy of any state is inevitably a difficult one, given the universal preoccupation with secrecy which is so characteristic of the security field. For the Western student of Chinese defence policy the problems are particularly complex. Not only does he have to face the linguistic and semantic difficulties, but also those of a heritage, culture and ideology so alien to his own. These problems are further compounded by the scarcity of reliable information available due to the lack of documentary sources, memoir material and scholarly Chinese writings on the subject. The evidence available to the analyst therefore is, of necessity, fragmentary and often ambiguous. As Coral Bell quite rightly points out, "the observer is in no position to offer certainties, only a tentative assessment subject to modification as further evidence comes in."[1] Despite these difficulties, the attempt to interpret the defence policy of a country as important as China, especially as it emerges from its isolation to play a greater role in international affairs, is one which must be undertaken.

The Historical Legacy

Throughout its long and impressive history China has always regarded itself as the centre of world civilization. Even the term China (Chung-Kuo) meaning the "Middle or Central Kingdom" conveys the idea of a "large universe revolving around a primary directing force" represented by China.[2] For much of its long history, Chinese military, cultural and economic prosperity over its Asian neighbours enabled successive Chinese dynasties to establish China at the centre of a system of tributary states which were expected to be submissive and pay tribute to "the Middle Kingdom".

This feeling of China's universal superiority, however, received a severe setback in the nineteenth century when Chinese weakness and the advanced technology of many Western states enabled them to force the Chinese to open up their ports to foreign trade and cede their territory in a series of "unequal treaties". To a people as proud of their past glory and civilization as the Chinese, such domination by foreigners, and therefore by definition barbarians, was a humiliation which has provided a stimulus to all Chinese leaders since. This feeling of humilitation was summed up by the founding father of Republican China, Sun Yat-sen, when he said, "We are the poorest and weakest country in the world, occupying the lowest position in world affairs; people of other countries are the carving knife and we are the fish and meat."[3]

The obsessive concern with their humiliations at the hands of Western states in the nineteenth century led to a debate which continued for much of the late nineteenth and early twentieth century about how China could recover her position in the world. Of the two main schools of thought which emerged in this debate, there was one school which argued that only minor changes were necessary to re-establish China's position in the world. Western technical skills would have to be adopted, particularly in the military field, which would be used to eliminate foreign interference in Chinese affairs. China would then be able to continue on the basis of her unchanging Confucian principles. There was, however, another school of thought, whose members argued for a more revolutionary change which would sweep the discredited old order away. What was needed, so the argument went, was a new system of belief, a new philosophy which would replace the outworn Confuciansim. To some of the revolutionary school, the new Marxist-Leninist doctrine after 1917 was especially appealing. The explanation of imperialism in particular provided a convincing inter-pretation of the misfortunes which had befallen China and at the same time a "doctrine of certain hope".[4] Capitalism was responsible for China's problems but capitalism was in decay and about to be replaced by the superior Communist system.

The Communist Party, however, was neither the only, nor the most powerful revolutionary movement in China during the first half of the twentieth century. Following the fall of the Manchu dynasty and the foundation of the Republic in 1912, Sun Yat-sen's Nationalist party grew in strength until it achieved power in 1928. The clash between the two movements led to a struggle for power which characterized the Chinese political scene for much of the period between the 1920s and 1940s. Despite their major ideological differences, however, both Nationalists and Communists desired the restoration of Chinese pre-eminence in world politics. Both movements strove, often in uneasy alliance, to free their country from the Japanese invaders and both envisaged the restoration of Chinese control over various territories which had traditionally belonged to China. Both Nationalist and Communist leaders have also on numerous occasions expressed similar views on China's past and future in terms of its traditional superiority and its future importance in world politics.[5]

One of the central objectives therefore of whichever power emerged triumphant from the Civil War was likely to be the restoration of China to a position of some significance in the international system. As China also had not been slow traditionally to use force[6] to achieve its objectives many predicted that a strong Nationalist or Communist government would, if necessary, use military means to recover those lands deemed to be part of China and to re-establish her position in world affairs. The victory of the Communist forces in 1949 seemed to further reinforce this view. Marxism-Leninism taught that there could be no peace between socialist and capitalist camps. It emphasized the duty of all true Communists to transform non-socialist countries into socialist ones and the only way to achieve this was through revolution. According to Mao: "Revolutions and revolutionary wars are inevitable in class society . . . without them it is impossible to accomplish any leap in social development and to overthrow the reactionary ruling classes, and therefore impossible for the people to win political power."[7] China's new ideology also stressed the utility of armed force to achieve political objectives. To Mao not only did "political power grow out of the barrel of a gun" but also "with guns the whole world can be transformed".

To some observers of contemporary China in October 1949, therefore, the combination of its irredentist claims, Great Power pretentions and its Communist ideology was a portent of aggressive Chinese policies in international relations in future. China could be expected to use force to recover its territories in Asia and thereby enhance its own power and extend Communist influence.

China's Use of Force in International Relations

Since 1949 the debate about how far these fears have been justified has characterized much of the literature written about Chinese foreign and defence policy. Viewing exactly the same evidence different observers have come to widely conflicting conclusions. Some argue that Chinese actions in the military field demonstrate an inherently aggressive and expansionist policy. Others contend, quite the reverse, that China has been extremely cautious and indeed defensive in its utilization of armed force as an instrument of foreign policy.

To those who hold the former view, Chinese operations, such as those in Tibet, Korea and on the Indian border, as well as the continuing vocal and material support for wars of national liberation, all illustrate China's aggressive intentions against her neighbours. Such actions, it is often contended, demonstrate the determination of Chinese leaders to recover all those lands regarded as being part of the old Chinese empire.

There are others who interpret the evidence available more in terms of the influence of ideology on policy-making than of traditional territorial claims. Franz Michael, for example, writing in 1971, argued that China was interested in the "far more important form of "expansionism" . . . the spread of Communist revolution".[8] For Professor Michael, the pursuit of international Communism and the mission to spread Marxism-Leninism throughout the world are the decisive factors in China's policies abroad. According to this view also, the acquisition of nuclear weapons by the Chinese has facilitated a much more militant policy towards Asia and a more vigorous support of "wars of liberation", such that "the clear intent of current Chinese policy is to promote, foster and support Communist revolutions."[9]

Those who hold a different view of Chinese military policies since 1949 do not deny that China has constantly issued bellicose statements, made verbal assaults on the *status quo* and called for the overthrow of foreign governments. They accept that China has given material and moral support to revolutionary movements throughout the world. They also recognize that the Chinese leaders undoubtedly seek greater power and influence in world affairs. What they do reject, however, is that all this adds up to "expansionism" by the People's Republic of China.

In terms of assessing the validity of these two arguments, much, of course, depends on how the word "expansionism" is defined. If it is taken to mean simply an attempt to extend a nation's sphere of influence and interest, then undoubtedly China is an "expansionist" power. But then most states, particularly the larger states, fit into this category. Such a definition as this hardly corresponds to the usual interpretation given to the word in international relations. If, on the other hand, it is interpreted as it more commonly is, to involve "a sustained effort to exercise direct control over people and territory beyond a nation's borders',[10] then on the evidence available it would be difficult to conclude justifiably that China is an "expansionist" power. As Professor Peter Van Ness points out in a recent study of Chinese military policy:

> ... despite Peking's inflammatory rhetoric and its formidable military power, Chinese behaviour in foreign affairs has been surprisingly circumspect. In the 21 years since the establishment of the People's Republic, Chinese military units, with the exception of the Korean War, have rarely, and then only briefly, engaged in combat operations beyond or adjacent to China's borders.[11]

The validity of this view can be illustrated from an examination of Chinese military activity abroad during the period since 1949 which can be classified in three main categories: conflict over boundaries; military action in support of neighbouring Communist states; and support for wars of national liberation.

1. Conflict over boundaries
China's most significant border clash occurred with India in the short war of 1962 and would seem at first glance to provide *prima facie* evidence for the conventional image of an aggressive China. Chinese forces initiated the first large-scale attacks of the war between 20

September and 20 November 1962 with simultaneous advances in the North East Frontier agency and Ladakh and swept Indian forces from all disputed territory. According to most informed commentators of the war, however, the Chinese initiative resulted from India's persistence in its "forward policy".[12] After years of passivity in the long-standing border dispute between the two countries the Indian Government appears to have sown the seeds of war by sending small patrols into the unpopulated Himalayan valleys and plateaux. Although the Indian initiative posed no threat to China, it coincided with a number of other events which came to common focus for Chinese leaders in 1962. An unprecedented resurgence of Chinese Nationalist attention in "reconquering the mainland", Nationalist and American support for Tibetan insurgents; the vulnerability of the only military road linking Sinkiang with Tibet which traversed the Aksai Chin plateau at the Western end of the Sino-Indian border; and problems in Sinkiang on the Sino-Soviet border, all added up in Chinese eyes to the possibility of Soviet-American collusion with the Indian advances.[13]

Seen in these terms the PLA attack on Indian forces, followed by a unilateral ceasefire and withdrawal from the North East Frontier agency, suggests a limited action on the part of the Chinese leaders faced with what they perceived to be a growing threat to their security.

The other major boundary dispute in which China has used military force is that with the Soviet Union. With the deterioration in the relationship between the two states in the late 1950s and early 1960s, the disputed border territories in Sinkiang and along the Amur and Ussuri rivers flared into open conflict culminating in the major clashes of 1969. The legal position over the disputed territories and over what the Chinese describe as the "unequal treaties" imposed on China by the Russian Tsars is a highly debatable one. On the evidence available, however, the Chinese appear to have been no more aggressive in pressing their demands than the Russians[14]. Certainly the actions of the PLA cannot be construed as evidence of the aggressive and expansionist policies of the Peking Government as the Russians would have everyone believe. Indeed from a Chinese perspective quite the reverse would appear to be true. The actions of Soviet forces and the massing of between 45 and 47 Soviet divisions and rocket forces along the border probably suggests to the Chinese the possibility, or indeed the likelihood, of a Soviet attack on China.

In the case of both the Indian and Soviet borders, therefore, it would appear that the Chinese use of force was not "expansionist" in the sense in which it has been defined. In both cases, as one commentator has pointed out, "the location of the border line became an issue after other differences had arisen between China and the two countries, both of which had been friendly with China."[15] The implication would seem to be that the territory itself may not have been as important as other questions in the wider dispute which had arisen in both cases. In the same period as China was in conflict with these two states, she signed border treaties with five neighbours, Burma, Nepal, Mongolia, Pakistan and Afghanistan, delineating common borders between herself and them. In these negotiations Chinese leaders also often made generous concessions to the individual states.

2. Military Action in Support of Neighbouring Communist States

Chinese operations in Korea between 1950 and 1953 and North Vietnam between 1965 and 1968 provide the main illustrations of the use of Chinese military forces in combat operations in territory clearly outside Chinese borders.

Chinese intervention in Korea in the Autumn of 1950 and the commitment of a force of around 300,000 over a three-year period is often cited as a clear illustration of Chinese aggressive intention. Once again, however, the evidence does not seem to lead to the conclusion that China was behaving aggressively. As Allen S. Whiting has pointed out, China was probably not involved in the planning of the initial attack by the North on the South and only intervened when the existence of a Communist government in the North and its own security appeared to be at stake.[16] Chinese troops were only used in support of the government of North Korea after UN forces had crossed the 38th parallel, ignoring warnings from Peking, in an attempt to unify the country by force. From a Chinese point of view the use of force was designed to keep a neighbouring Communist government in power but perhaps more importantly, Chinese forces were committed to counter, what was perceived to be, a major threat to the security of China itself by preserving a vital buffer zone which protected areas of critical industrial importance to the new Communist régime in Peking.

In the case of North Vietnam, Chinese troops were not in direct combat operations as they were in Korea but their intervention does appear to have served a similar function. Chinese forces were sent to North Vietnam in 1965 presumably on the request of the Hanoi Government after the beginning of the American bombing campaign against the North and the large-scale intervention of American combat forces. At no time between 1965 and 1968 were there more than 50,000 Chinese troops in North Vietnam and the tasks they performed were mainly engineering and construction functions, maintaining and rebuilding bridges, roads and railway lines destroyed by American bombing. In so doing they helped relieve North Vietnamese forces for operations against the South and also to deter an American invasion of the North which would have directly threatened the security of China itself. In March 1968 after President Johnson's decision to end the major bombing campaign, the expeditionary force returned to China. As in the case of Korea, Chinese forces withdrew as soon as they were no longer needed. It also appears that little or no attempt was made to utilize their presence on foreign soil to achieve the kind of political

247

control which the presence of the Soviet Army has made possible in Eastern Europe.

An appraisal therefore of all of the cases of direct Chinese military activity in border disputes and assistance to neighbouring governments reveals a pattern of military involvement for limited objectives. In all of the operations cited after hostilities had ended, Chinese forces were withdrawn once the limited objectives were secured and there was "virtually no gain for China in terms of expanded territory or political control as a result of its military actions".[17]

3. Support for Wars of National Liberation

This view of China as cautious and defensive in its use of armed forces outside its own boundaries is challenged by some who argue that "Peking's disinterest in old-style empire-building has deflected Western attention"[18] from the indirect form of Chinese expansion which takes the form of the support for foreign revolutions. According to this argument, Chinese leaders are engaged in fostering world revolution by providing moral and often material support for individuals and organizations engaged in making revolution against their governments. The validity of this view would seem to be strengthened by the wealth of evidence available on Chinese assistance to insurgent movements all over the world. It is often pointed out that Chinese leaders support many revolutionary groups by offering them training facilities and instruction in China, weapons and financial assistance.

The Chinese have made it plain, however, and past experience would seem to reinforce their public statements, that revolutionary movements must rely essentially on their own efforts and resources to gain power. This concept of "self-reliance" is, from a Chinese viewpoint, one of the most important tenets of Maoist revolutionary doctrine. In his famous, but often misunderstood, article entitled "Long Live the Victory of People's War" written in 1965, Lin Piao spells out the Chinese view that revolution cannot be exported and that insurgent forces must be almost entirely self-sufficient if they are to succeed.[19] This contention would seem to be confirmed by an empirical study of Chinese policies towards insurgent movements in Thailand undertaken by Daniel Lovelace. According to this study the Chinese, in this particular case, lived up in practice to the principle of self-reliance. On the basis of his research Lovelace concludes that Chinese support "is certainly not a recipe for direct CPR involvement or control of revolutionary movements."[20]

Once again therefore it would seem that the customary picture of an aggressive China supporting and controlling revolutionary movements throughout the world as part of Peking's grand design for world revolution does not seem to conform strictly to reality. China does attempt to influence the internal politics of other states from time to time by providing support for those domestic forces whose policies it favours. In this, however, it is perhaps not too unlike virtually all the other major powers. As with the other examples of the more direct use of force by the People's Republic, the limitation on Chinese support of wars of national liberation, stemming from the concept of self-reliance, would seem to further confirm the contention that while China may be a revolutionary power, it would be difficult on the basis of the evidence available to describe her as an "expansionist" power.

The Use of Chinese Forces in the Domestic Context

Besides the limited use of force as an instrument of foreign policy, the Chinese leaders have also used their armed forces for a variety of specific domestic purposes. In fact a strong case can be made that the PLA is seen by the leaders in Peking as being just as important in the domestic as in the international context. At times it has probably appeared even more important. The domestic purposes which the armed forces have served range right across the spectrum, from the direct and physical use of force to reincorporate traditional Chinese territories into the new Communist state, to the peaceful ideas of the PLA in a whole host of roles in support of the Chinese economy and the political leadership.

The Physical Use of Force in the Domestic Environment

Following the Communist victory over the Nationalist forces in 1949, the PLA had a number of limited, but nevertheless pressing functions to perform internally. These, according to Liu Shao-chi, speaking in May 1950, included the occupation of various territories considered to be an integral part of China.

Amongst the first tasks of Chinese forces was the occupation of Tibet and the invasion of Taiwan. On 2 September 1949 the New China News Agency (NCNA), circulated an article entitled "Foreign Aggressors must not be allowed to annex Chinese territory", in which the determination of the new régime to "liberate all Chinese territory including Tibet, Sinkiang, Hainan and Formosa" was made absolutely clear.[21] By April 1950 Sinkiang and Hainan had been seized, leaving Tibet and Formosa on the list of unfinished business. Preparations for the occupation of Tibet began in January 1950 as soon as the South-West of China had been liberated. In October a force of 40,000 men crossed into Tibet and captured the town of Chamdo in the east in what was to be the first and the last major engagement of the invasion. By 23 May 1951 an agreement had been reached with the Tibetan authorities for "the peaceful liberation of Tibet" and by February 1952 the Military Region of Tibet had been established. For the Communist Chinese, Tibet, which had never been generally recognized as an independent state, was within what was recognised, even by the Nationalists, as the proper limits of the Chinese domain. They felt therefore not only justified in taking such action but also confident that outside powers would not intervene on behalf of the Dalai Lama.

The new Chinese leaders held the same expectations about the invasion of Taiwan. The determination to undertake the invasion, which was to be "the principal task" of 1950, was further reinforced by President Truman's announcement on 5 January 1950 that the United States recognized China's legal claim to Formosa. He also promised that the American Government had "no intention of utilizing its armed forces to interfere in the present situation."[22] Preparations for the invasion, however, by General Ch'en Yi's force of about 300,000 were frustrated by the outbreak of the Korean War and the radical change in US attitudes. Following the invasion by North Korea, President Truman announced on 27 June that the Seventh Fleet had been ordered to the Taiwan straits to prevent any attack on Formosa. It was at this point, according to Whiting, that Peking tacitly admitted the 'futility of attacking Taiwan as long as the threat of American intervention remained."[23] Since then no really determined efforts have been made to take Taiwan through the use of armed force. Even the two Taiwan Straits Crises of 1954-55 and 1958 must be viewed more in terms of China's wider political objectives[24] than as a serious attempt to overthrow Chiang Kai-shek's Nationalist Government on the island.[25]

The Peaceful uses of the PLA

Apart from the more traditional use of armed forces in support of both foreign and domestic policy, the PLA also holds a unique place amongst the world's armies in terms of the extent of the role it has played in the economy and more generally in the political system.

The role of the PLA during the Civil War in supporting the peasantry in various forms of production was carried on after the Communist victory, becoming at times even more important than the more military functions of the army. The army's work in this field ranged from agricultural production, water conservation and flood control to industrial production and management. Such activity reached a peak during the Great Leap Forward period when, according to Chinese sources, the army contributed respectively 59, 44 and 46 million man-days of labour to the economy in the years 1958-60.[26]

As well as this important economic function, the PLA has also at various times played a critical political role. In particular, the army and militia have played a role, especially in the late 1950s and 1960s, in the politicization of Chinese society. The "Everyone a Soldier Movement" launched in the autumn of 1958 during the first months of the Great Leap Forward and the "Learn from the PLA" movement in 1964 were both attempts to use the army and militia as vehicles of political education. In the case of the latter campaign, the PLA was held up as a revolutionary model for Chinese society. According to the slogans of the campaign the army was worthy of emulation by the rest of society because its working style had enabled it to achieve the Maoist goal of being both ideologically correct and professionally competent.[27]

In practice, however, despite this stress on the army's success in achieving the Maoist goal, the task of combining the two elements of ideological rectitude and professional skill has been far from easy. For much of the period since 1949, in fact, the contradiction between the political and professional roles of the army has been a continuing characteristic feature of civil-military relations in China. The problem for both military and political leaders has been how to reconcile the need to create a modernized army capable of operating effectively in a highly complex technological environment, with the need to ensure that such an army retains its revolutionary character and remains amenable to political direction.

"Revolutionization" versus "Professionalization"

The "revolutionization" versus "Professionalization", or "red" versus "expert", debate had its origins in the change in the role and primary function of the PLA after victory in 1949. In the Civil War, the PLA was the nucleus of the revolution. Its tasks were difficult and demanding but in many ways were relatively uncomplicated. The army played its part in the political struggle of winning popular support and performed its military function of wearing down and defeating an identifiable opponent. Once victory has been achieved however the roles and functions of the PLA changed dramatically. Now, instead of being a force designed solely to overthrow the established authorities it became itself an instrument of government policy with a wide spectrum of international as well as domestic objectives to fulfil. As John Gittings aptly puts it, "By the very act of victory, the PLA had transformed itself from a free-wheeling revolutionary army to a predominantly garrison army of national defence."[28]

Although the initial steps of military reform were laid down in the Common Programme of the People's Political Consultative Conference in September 1949, [29] the real impetus to undertake a programme of modernization first became apparent during the Korean War. Despite the initial Chinese successes, later setbacks soon demonstrated the inherent weakness of the army engaged in action against a sophisticated opponent using the advantages of modern technology. Without the benefit of indigenous armaments industries, the obvious source of modernized equipment and techniques was China's new ally, the Soviet Union, with whom she had signed a treaty of "Friendship, Alliance and Mutual Assistance" in 1950. The gradual reliance on the Soviet Union for weapons systems led also to the attempt to emulate the Soviet model in terms of military organization as well as strategic doctrine. A system of formal ranks was introduced and specialized service branches were created in the PLA similar to those in the Soviet Army. Conscription was also adopted on Soviet advice as a means of securing the necessary quality of recruits which would be capable of learning the technical skills associated with a modern military force. According to the editorial of the *People's Daily* in July 1954, "The Soviet Army provided the PLA with a great example, the future PLA would resemble the Soviet Army of today."[30]

The transformation of the PLA from a revolutionary guerrilla force of volunteers to a mixed conscript/professional army, soon brought some sections of the new officer corps into conflict with the party leadership. Growing impatience with political control and pressure for an accelerated programme to improve the Chinese military posture led to conflict in the mid-1950s. The military "modernizers", however, were faced with a hostile coalition of other military and civilian interests who desired an acceleration of economic development through the reduction of the military budget. The "anti-modernization" lobby seems to have been strengthened at this time also by a growing disenchantment with the Soviet model in both economic and military spheres which was emerging in some sections of the party. Increasing questioning of Soviet practices and growing economic difficulties requiring concentration on the problems of reconstruction led in April 1956 to a partial reaction against the programme of military modernization in the "Ten Great Relationships". Mao agreed that modern armed forces were necessary but declared that military expenditure must be reduced rather than increased to facilitate an acceleration of economic development.[31] The pursuit of a modernized army remained an important objective but equal priority was given to the army's non-military functions in the spheres of production work and politicization as well as the importance of political control over the army.

The consensus which the 1956 compromises attempted to achieve between "professionalization" and "revolutionization" gradually broke down however, in the following two years. Many professional combat officers became more and more critical of government policy as less stress was placed on modernization and more on production work, politicization and political control. The increasing emphasis on domestic functions also came at a time when serious strains were appearing in the Sino-Soviet alliance. Soviet support for Chinese actions in the Quemoy Crisis of 1958 came only after China had borne the greatest risks. Further questioning of the Soviet military model which this caused seems, in large part, to have been an important contributary factor in the readoption by the CCP of the traditional Chinese revolutionary model which had been so successful before 1949. The concept of People's War was given renewed emphasis and the militia was strengthened in an attempt to improve China's defence posture without reducing the army's participation in domestic political and economic projects and without reducing the funds set aside for the civilian economy.

From the professional military point of view, however, the militia was no substitute for highly trained and well-equipped armed forces. To many senior officers the renewed stress on People's War and the concern with non-military roles was seriously detrimental to the fighting capability of the Chinese Army. The articulation of their objections to the changing emphasis in military policy dictated by the party led, however, to the purging of the Minister of Defence, P'eng Teh-huai and some of his colleagues in 1959.[32] Once again the supporters of modernization and professionalization seemed to have been defeated by those who wished to preserve the revolutionary character of the Army. Although this was true, to a certain extent, as in 1956, the solution to the crisis in civil-military relations was more of a compromise than it seemed. While stressing the continuing priority given to the domestic role of the PLA, P'eng's successor as Minister of Defence, Lin Piao, also continued the task of modernizing the armed forces. He intensified political training in the PLA and rejuvenated party branches throughout the military hierarchy but he also devoted considerable effort to the development of nuclear weapons as well as the creation of new machine-building ministries charged with the production of sophisticated military weapons.

A similar set of grievances followed by a compromise solution which nevertheless largely reasserted revolutionary principles occurred in 1964-65. The decision to use the PLA to a much greater extent as the focal point of the Great Proletarian Cultural Revolution and the intensification of the Vietnam War led military leaders, like Lo Jui-ching, the Chief of Staff, once again to emphasize the professional qualities of the army. Lo Jui-ching urged that less emphasis should be given to the PLA's domestic roles and improvements should be made in China's military preparedness.[33] To the Chinese Chief of Staff, the threat of an American attack on China following its direct involvement in Vietnam meant that there were "a thousand and one things to be done".[34] Amongst the most important of these was the task of improving the size and effectiveness of the conventional standing forces. In the new circumstances, what was needed, according to Lo, was a new strategic posture in which the emphasis should be placed less on the People's War concept and more on the professional option of a nationally coordinated, technologically sophisticated defence.

The public criticisms of Lo's suggestions concentrated on the question of enemy intentions and the efficacy of the reliance on the People's War concept. In opposition to Lo, Lin Piao questioned his estimate of the likelihood of an American attack on China and called for an increased rather than a decreased reliance on People's War. In private Lo's campaign for greater modernization became inextricably linked with the struggle for political power, such that his proposals were deliberately exaggerated by the coalition of bureaucratic interests who opposed him. According to W.W. Whitson, "Lo was accused of concocting an elaborate rationalization for proposals whose real purpose was to force the disengagement of the PLA from political activity, reduce its political reliability and thus encourage the spread of revisionism in China."[35]

Although Lo Jui-ching like Peng Teh-huai was purged, the solution which followed his dismissal, as on previous occasions, was again something of a compromise. Predictably increased emphasis was placed on the political roles of the PLA. At the same time, however, while many of Lo's proposals were rejected there were some which were nevertheless accepted. His suggestions, for example, that defences in the south should be reinforced and that aircraft production should be expanded, were both put into effect. Despite the stress on the revolutionary characteristics of the PLA also during the Cultural Revolution and the increasing role of the army in political affairs, the modernization of the navy and the priority given to nuclear testing were also continued with little interference.

A similar pattern of gradually continuing the process of modernization of the PLA with the parallel stress on revolutionary principles has characterized Chinese defence policy since the fall of Lin Piao in September 1971. Although the issues at stake in the purging of Lin Piao were far more complex than simply "professionalism" or "revolutionization" in the PLA, amongst the chief concerns of the anti-Lin coalition, led by Chou En-lai, was the determination to reimpose party control over the Army. In some ways Chou En-lai's "New Course" which emerged after Lin Piao's fall from power represented an attempt to get away from the more extreme revolutionary manifestations of the Cultural Revolution. It did nevertheless signal an attempt to ensure that "the party controls the gun". Following Lin's demise a concerted nation-wide campaign was undertaken to down-grade the role of the military and to reassert party control. Evidence exists that altogether 56 leading military figures disappeared in the purges which followed Lin's fall, five of whom were Politburo members.[36]

Differences also apparently existed, as on previous occasions, over attitudes towards the Soviet Union. Some evidence exists that Lin Piao and some sections of the professional military machine were opposed to the designation of the Soviet Union as the primary threat and the proposed limited *rapprochement* with the United States.[37] From the military viewpoint closer American relations meant the possibility of antagonising Moscow and therefore increased the danger of an unwelcome Sino-Soviet war. It also further reduced the opportunity for patching up the differences with the Soviet leaders which would have enabled the PLA to return to the kind of military co-operation which had been characteristic of the 1950s.

At the same time, however, as the attempt was made to reimpose political controls and the possibility of improving relations with the

Russians was firmly rejected, the task of modernizing China's armed forces was pushed ahead. In the period since 1971, China has been seen building up a stock-pile of between two and three hundred nuclear devices and has continued to develop an IRBM, MRBM and a limited ICBM capability. At the same time as China's strategic nuclear forces have been steadily improved there is some evidence that an increasing effort is being made to arm a proportion of PLA formations with modern weapons which are now becoming available from the growing Chinese armament industry. Emphasis is still placed on the People's War concept but it would appear that attention is increasingly being given by Chinese leaders to the conventional inadequacies which have been a feature of Chinese defence policy since 1949.[38] The professional fighting capability of the PLA has also probably been improved by the relative reduction which seems to have taken place in the utilization of the PLA in domestic economic and political functions.[39] Such functions are undoubtedly still an important part of PLA activity but not on anything like the scale of the Cultural Revolution and its aftermath.

Alliances and National Self-sufficiency

The domestic debate both within the PLA and the Party and between sections of both over the question of "professionalism" and "modernization" are linked very closely, as has been suggested, with differing ideas on the value of alliances, particularly the alliance with the Soviet Union.

In 1949 the creation of a new Communist state in a hostile world at the height of the Cold War seemed to make sound political, military, economic and indeed ideological sense to the new leaders in Peking. For some time following the signing of the treaty with Russia in 1950, China's strategic policy was based on the assumption that the United States was the major threat and that the Soviet Union would remain a reliable ally. Reliance on the Soviet Union was particularly important in terms of the supply of the much-needed military hardware and the nuclear guarantee which Russia was also able to offer. The benefits of the alliance became particularly clear in October 1957 with the agreement signed by the two governments on "New Technology for national defence". According to subsequent Chinese sources, the agreement included a Soviet promise to "provide China with a sample of an atomic bomb and technical data concerning its manufacture."[40] The Russian leaders also supplied China with an experimental reactor and undertook to train Chinese atomic scientists at the Joint Institute for Nuclear Research at Dubna in the Soviet Union. With the help of Soviet military aid therefore, China began to develop not only her own conventional defence forces, but also took the first tentative steps towards the production of a nuclear force.

Despite the military advantages to China of the Soviet alliance, the seeds of future discord appear to have existed from the beginning. Even during the two and a half months of negotiations which resulted in the Sino-Soviet Treaty of 1950, Mao did not obtain the kind of satisfaction he expected. To be sure, according to the Treaty, Soviet rights in Manchuria were to be surrended but not for three years. Soviet credits to the new state of 300 million US dollars, were hardly over-generous to a country the size of China with all the difficulties of reconstruction she faced. Soviet interests were also to be perpetuated in Sinkiang by means of the far-from-equal joint-stock companies.

Difficulties in the alliance also seem to have occurred in the first year of the Korean War. Although China's intervention in the war was eventually to open "the flood-gates of Soviet aid" it would appear that the assistance was not at first forthcoming on anything like the kind of scale the Chinese expected. In his analysis of the Sino-Soviet relationship at this time, John Gittings detects "a degree of coolness towards the Soviet Union which only diminished as Soviet aid became available on a more generous scale."[41] Despite more substantial aid later in the war, the Korean experience seems to have had a significant impact on the Chinese attitudes towards her ally, particularly in retrospect. In later Chinese polemics with the Soviet Union, the leaders in Peking have clearly demonstrated their dissatisfaction with the way they were treated by the Kremlin during the war. In a letter from the Central Committee of the CCP to the Central Committee of the CPSU in May 1964, the Chinese claimed to have shouldered heavy sacrifices and stood in the first line of defence in Korea "so that the Soviet Union might stay in the second-line".[42]

Chinese uneasiness over too great a reliance on the Soviet Union which was a product of the gradually deteriorating relations during the 1950s came to a head following the second Taiwan Straits Crisis in 1958-59. It would appear from the limited evidence available that the Soviet Union attempted to get the leaders in Peking to accept proposals for increased integration of the Chinese defence effort with other Communist bloc countries. At the same time as Marshall Peng Teh-huai negotiated with Soviet officials on questions such as these, however, the general trend in Chinese foreign policy was in the opposite direction towards greater "self-reliance" symbolized by the Great Leap Forward movement.[43] Despite the opposition of those like Peng Teh-huai, greater emphasis was increasingly being placed on Chinese solutions to Chinese problems and the inadequacy of reliance on other countries in in the economic, political and military fields.

The questioning of the value of the alliance with the Soviet Union and the growing stress on national control in the defence field was felt particularly in the field of nuclear technology. During the 1958 negotiations, the Russians appear to have back-tracked slightly in their 1957 commitment and refused to supply the Chinese with nuclear weapons or technology unless they retained effective control over these weapons.

To many Chinese leaders such Soviet control over China's nuclear weapons, together with the proposals for increased defence integration, would have made the Chinese almost totally dependent on the Soviet Union for their security. There was growing evidence of the unreliability of the Soviet leaders to pursue policies in line with Chinese interests, and to a nation as proud as China this was something that the leaders in Peking were not prepared to accept. Soviet attempts at accommodation with the West at a time when "the east wind prevailed over the west wind" convinced many Chinese leaders that the Russian guarantee was of little value. Even before the Soviet Government therefore had unilaterally torn up the 1957 agreement in June 1959, the Peking leadership had already decided to develop an independent deterrent of their own.[44] The pressing need for such a force under their own control was clearly spelt out by Chen Yi in an interview with an Australian film director, John Dixon, in September 1963. In answer to the question of why China needed to construct her own nuclear force when the Soviet Union had given assurances about the defence of China against foreign aggressors, Chen Yi replied: "In the first place, what is this Soviet assurance worth? . . . How can one nation say that they will defend another — these sorts of promises are easy to make, but they are worth nothing. Soviet protection is worth nothing to us."[45]

The Chinese view of the utility of nuclear weapons is thus in many ways similar to that of the French. For the Chinese in their search for equality with the United States and the Soviet Union to re-establish her place in the world, nuclear weapons are the supreme symbol of national self-reliance. In a comparative study of the Chinese and French nuclear programmes, B.W. Augenstein has shown that statements by the leaders of both states reveal a high degree of similarity in the Chinese and French positions. Both see the development of national nuclear forces as the "marks of national greatness, and political power and importance".[46] In both cases also the possession of nuclear weapons has been an important symbol of sovereignty and of the reluctance of either government to rely on alliances for their national security.

China's National Defence Doctrine: The People's War Concept

The perception of a very real threat from the United States together with the refusal to compromise with the Soviet Union meant that Chinese leaders in the late 'fifties and early 'sixties deliberately accepted that they would render themselves temporarily more vulnerable to the danger of enemy attack. Without Soviet assistance and without any form of nuclear deterrence in the short term, the Chinese leaders had the task of developing an effective national security doctrine initially against the perceived American threat and subsequently against what became the dual threat from both the "imperialists" and the new "social imperialists" in the form of the Soviet Union. Given the perception of the threat, and the historical and ideological perspectives of Chinese leaders, China's vulnerability and weakness dictated a defensive and deterrent strategy based on the People's War concept.

Mao recognized that if the "imperialists" attacked they might use nuclear weapons as well as bacteriological and chemical agents. In order to defeat China, however, such an attack, according to Mao, would have to be followed up by an invasion of ground forces. It was here that the supremacy of the Chinese People's War concept would be felt. Such attacks, Mao maintained, would be countered by "a protracted broken-backed war supported by the "aroused masses" of people and fought by the large regular forces, local forces and massive militia developed under the concept of "everyone a soldier". These forces would combine mobile conventional war with widespread independent guerrilla warfare."[47]

The idea behind Maoist strategy was to trade "space for time" and to achieve "active defence in depth". The task of the PLA forces was to lure the enemy deep into Chinese territory. In so doing hostile forces would be "bogged down in endless battles and drowned in a hostile human sea".[48] The defeat of the invading forces would thus be achieved by "wearing them down, defeating them piecemeal and finally driving them from the country"[49] in the same kind of operations which had proved so successful against Chiang Kai-shek's forces. It is perhaps possible to speculate that it was the prospect of fighting such a protracted indecisive campaign that discouraged the Soviet leaders from attacking China in the periods of more extreme hostility since 1969.

As well as being a defensive strategy, therefore, Mao's concept of People's War is also, and perhaps more importantly, part of China's deterrent strategy. In the period of conventional and nuclear weakness, the Chinese leaders appear to hope that the declaration of their determination to fight a long-drawn out guerrilla campaign will deter potential enemies by convincing them that the attempt to conquer China would be too costly.

It would, however, perhaps be wrong to view such a strategy simply as a "doctrine of necessity" as some have done.[50] Despite the inadequacies of the Chinese military machine, the vastness of China and the size, experience and morale of the PLA could well prove as decisive as Mao claims in a conventional or even a limited nuclear battle on Chinese territory. Certainly an opponent, even one with a greatly superior military establishment like the Soviet Union, would have to think very seriously about the possibility of having large numbers of troops tied down in an indecisive campaign over a long period, before initiating an attack on China. Such an opponent would also have to consider the effect of such a campaign on its military forces in relation to its other major adversaries. In this sense, the deterrent value of the threat to engage in a conflict using People's War tactics is likely to be high.

The doctrine does nevertheless have at least one fundamental weakness, as a number of commentators have pointed out. It is based on, the very doubtful assumption that after an initial nuclear strike by either the United States or the Soviet Union, China's enemies would necessarily feel the need to invade Chinese territory using ground forces.[51] Many observers have speculated on the possibility, for example, that the leaders in the Kremlin might undertake a "surgical" strike against Chinese nuclear facilities before she became a significant nuclear power. It is arguable that such an attack could have achieved the desired objective successfully without recourse to a follow-up operation by Soviet ground forces.

Chinese Attitudes Towards Nuclear Weapons and Deterrence

It's often argued that this weakness in Chinese strategic thinking is due to a misunderstanding of the significance of nuclear technology. Those who take this view point to Mao's celebrated image of the atomic bomb as a "paper tiger" and his emphasis on the superiority of "men over weapons". Mao is said to argue that "weapons are an important factor in war, but not the decisive factor; it is people, not things, that are decisive." Some commentators argue that this tendency to underestimate nuclear power has resulted in a rather irresponsible and cavalier attitude on the part of Chinese leaders to nuclear war. This theme, perhaps not surprisingly, is one that the Russians often develop. Soviet sources quote Mao as saying that even if half the population of the earth is destroyed in a nuclear war, this would not be so bad because such a war would destroy capitalism and leave socialism victorious. Chinese attitudes towards disarmament and arms control, particularly the refusal to sign the Test Ban Treaty and the Non-Proliferation Treaty, are also frequently cited as evidence of Chinese irresponsibility.

This interpretation of the Chinese view of nuclear weapons is, however, misleading and largely incorrect. Careful analysis of what the Chinese say and what they have done in various crisis situations reveals that they have been very keenly aware of the disastrous implications of a thermonuclear war for China and for the world.[52] To say that atomic weapons are "paper tigers" does not mean, from the Chinese viewpoint, that they are powerless. It means that the Chinese believe that they are not as powerful as they appear to be. Contrary to the Soviet view in the late 1950s, the Chinese believed that it was possible to support wars of national liberation without such wars escalating into nuclear conflict. In this they would seem to have had a more realistic appreciation of the political limitations of nuclear weapons than the Russians.

One of the reasons for the misunderstanding of Chinese attitudes towards nuclear weapons is that China herself has been reluctant to develop her ideas publicly on the subject. The vagueness, however, of Chinese theories on nuclear deterrence obviously does not necessarily mean that the Chinese are unaware of the realities of nuclear power. It would seem the reverse, that the Chinese are pursuing a policy of "calculated ambiguity"[53] in terms of her strategic doctrines designed to maximize the uncertainties of opponents about Chinese intentions as well as her capabilities. The value of such an approach is particularly evident for a power like China engaged in the laborious process of trying to develop an effective deterrent against vastly superior opponents. Although attempts have been made to disperse and harden part of the small Chinese nuclear force, there is little prospect in the near future, given China's technological and economic weakness and the superiority of her potential enemies, that she will be able to produce and deploy an invulnerable retaliatory capability. Without such an effective second-strike force, the credibility of her deterrent is likely to remain in grave doubt. The belief by other powers, however, that China's leaders are irresponsible and the tacit encouragement of that belief by China may serve to obfuscate this weakness. The development of quick reaction techniques and early warning capabilities by the Chinese helps in a way to enhance this uncertainty about China's likely reaction in a crisis. Such capabilities probably appear to China's opponents, rightly or wrongly, as the basis of fire-on-warning tactics. As Harry Gelber has pointed out, such "tactics may involve grave dangers and instabilities, but China's opponents cannot assume, especially in the absence of clear declaratory policies or of a strategic dialogue between Peking and the outside world, that she might not adopt them."[54] A nuclear strike by China's limited nuclear force against a superior enemy's cities or those of his allies might not be a credible policy for a rational power, but there can perhaps be no assurance, particularly for the Russians, that an "irresponsible" Chinese government might not adopt such a policy under certain circumstances. In this sense it is possible to speculate that the Chinese reluctance to develop their ideas about deterrence is in itself "an important component of its deterrent doctrine."[55]

Despite the advantages, however, of this vagueness and "calculated ambiguity" in Chinese strategic doctrine there are also dangers. The view that a power is irresponsible and perhaps irrational may encourage the formation of an alliance against it and the attempt to isolate that state in the world community. A similar impression may also lead to a pre-emptive strike against the state's nuclear facilities to prevent the emergence of a nuclear power which seems to endanger world peace. It was perhaps the fear of both of these possibilities which was largely responsible for the major shift in Chinese foreign policy in 1971. The threat of a Soviet attack and of Soviet-American collusion seems to have caused a reassessment of Chinese policy to alleviate the dangers of both. It was perhaps hoped, by those who supported the new policy in Peking, that a partial *rapprochement* with the United States would enhance China's national security by discouraging a Russian attack and break the alliance which was developing between the two superpowers. In this it seems to have had some limited success.

China's emergence from isolation to play a greater role in the international community and her concern to improve her strategic vulnerability may, as time goes on, force her to define her views on deterrence more clearly than she has done in the past. As Chinese nuclear forces develop further the thinking behind that development is likely to become more obvious to the outside world. The strengthening of the Chinese force may also perhaps lead to an increased confidence in Peking which will encourage Chinese leaders to enter into the strategic debate with the other two superpowers as a means of achieving their security. In the past the doctrine of "strategic ambiguity" was largely a product of China's weakness. Increased technological sophistication as well as greater contacts with other states may in time not only lead to a more public debate in China but also Chinese participation in the strategic dialogue with other nuclear powers.[56]

Conclusion

Whether or not this does occur, Chinese defence policy for some time to come is likely to be based as it is today on the twin pillars of deterrence provided by the People's War doctrine and nuclear armaments.[57] People's War attempts, through the mass mobilization of the nation's population and the adoption of Mao's revolutionary strategy to deter or repel any conventional invasion by a foreign power. Nuclear deterrence, on the other hand is designed to deter a strategic attack on China through a threat to use the most sophisticated weapons of modern technology. There is a sense in which these two extremes represent the product of the continuing struggle between revolutionary principles and modernization or professionalism which, it has been argued, has pervaded Chinese defence policy since 1949. Although one or other of these influences has at times tilted the balance of defence policy in certain directions, in general Chinese policy has reflected a compromise between both.

Whether this compromise will continue in the future will depend very largely on what happens in China after Mao. A much more radical régime may encourage the even greater military involvement in production work characteristic of the more "heady" days of the Cultural Revolution. Such a régime may also use its growing military strength to encourage more directly revolutionary activity in other countries and attempt to expand its control over neighbouring states and territories. On the other hand, the control of the Chinese Government by certain sections of the military could also be expected to produce a radical change in policy. Relations with the Russians might then be patched up as many military leaders have wanted in the past. This could lead to the rapid modernization of Chinese conventional strength and the readoption of Soviet military techniques and organization.

Although these or similar permutations may in fact occur, the most likely event perhaps, in the short term at least, is the continuation of Chinese policies along much the same lines as at present. Similar policies to those adopted by the past and present leadership would be likely to bring familiar swings between more, or less, emphasis on the revolutionary or professional roles of the PLA. The general direction and balance of policy would be likely, however, to continue the parallel development of both. There would continue to be an emphasis on the importance of People's War and the domestic function of the Army. At the same time, the equipment and training of the PLA would continue to be improved. This would mean the further modernization of the Chinese conventional capability, and the development of a second-strike capability in the nuclear field, either through the development of effective mobile-launchers, a submarine-launched ballistic missile capability, or both.[58] If China continues to go it alone, however, the emphasis of such a régime on simultaneous economic development would be likely to result in relatively slow military improvement, particularly when compared with the Russians or Americans. For this reason it is probable that, in the short term at least, "strategic defence, rather than offensive capability, is likely to retain first priority" in Chinese defence policy.[59]

Once China has built up her economic and military strength however, in the longer term, the great imponderable is how she will be likely to use it. Milovan Djilas in his study of *The New Class*[60] in the Soviet Union, identifies two distinct periods in the history of Soviet foreign policy. The first period is what he describes as "a revolutionary phase" which was essentially defensive and cautious due to Soviet weakness. As the Soviet Union built up her economic and military resources, however, Djilas argues that the first phase gave way to a new more aggressive "imperialist"phase in Soviet policy. If China can be said to be in the "revolutionary" phase at present, it remains to be seen whether she will eventually utilize her enormous potential strength in a more expansionist way than has characterized her defence policy in the past.

Notes

1. Coral Bell, "China: The Communists and the World", in F.S. Northedge (ed.), *The Foreign Policy of the Powers* (London: Faber and Faber, 1974), p. 120.
2. Robert A. Scalapino, "The Cultural Revolution and Chinese Foreign Policy", *Current Scene: Developments in Mainland China,* VI, No. 13, 1 August 1968.
3. Sun Yat-sen, San Miu Chu I (Three People's Principles) (Taipei, Taiwan: Cheng Chung, 1954), p. 6, Quoted in Liu, *China as a Nuclear Power in World Politics* (London: Macmillan, 1972) p. 14.
4. Arthur Huck, *The Security of China* (London: Chatto and Windus, 1970), p. 20.

5. For a discussion of similar statements by Chiang Kai-shek and Mao Tse-tung, see Huck, ibid., p. 21-2.
6. See Liu, op. cit., p.11.
7. *People's Daily*, 31 March 1964.
8. Franz Michael, "A Design for Aggression", *Problems of Communism*, January – April 1971, p. 63.
9. Ibid.
10. Peter Van Ness, "Mao Tse-tung and Revolutionary "Self-Reliance"," *Problems of Communism*, January – April 1971, p. 69. Much of the argument which follows in this section owes a great debt to this article by Professor Van Ness.
11. Ibid.
12. See, for example, Neville Maxwell, *India's China War* (New York: Pantheon, 1970) and Allen S. Whiting, "The Use of Forces in Foreign Policy by the People's Republic of China", *The Annals of the American Academy of Political and Social Sciences*, Vol. 402.
13. For a development of this argument see Allen S. Whiting, ibid., pp. 58-9.
14. See Harold C. Hinton, "Conflict on the Ussuri: A Clash of Nationalisms", *Problems of Communism*, January – April 1971, and Peter Van Ness, op. cit.
15. Van Ness, op. cit., p. 70.
16. Allen S. Whiting, *China Crosses the Yalu* (Stanford, Calif.: Stanford University Press, 1968).
17. Van Ness, op. cit., p. 70.
18. Michael, op. cit., p. 63.
19. Some have wrongly interpreted this article as a blueprint for world-wide revolution.
20. Daniel Lovelace, *"People's War" and Chinese Foreign Policy: Thailand as a Case Study of Overt Insurgent Support*, unpublished Ph.D. dissertation, Claremont Graduate School, 1970, see pp. 215-18, quoted by Van Ness, op. cit., p. 71; see also Daniel Lovelace, *China and "People's War" in Tailand, 1964-69*, China Research monograph No. 8 (Berkeley, Calif.:University of California, 1971).
21. Quoted in John Gittings, *The Role of the Chinese Army* (London: Oxford University Press, 1967), p. 32.
22. See ibid., p. 40.
23. Allen S. Whiting, op. cit., pp. 63-4.
24. China, in part at least, initiated the crises particularly in 1954 to test the alliance with the Soviet Union.
25. Besides the invasion of Tibet and the preparations to invade Taiwan, the PLA were also involved in this period in "bandit suppression". See Gittings, op. cit., pp. 32-7.
26. Gittings, op. cit., p. 182. See also Stephen A. Sims, "The New Role of the Military?", *Problems of Communism*, November–December, 1969, p. 28.
27. As Gittings points out, the campaign was designed to "publicize throughout the country the techniques and activities of political education and control which had been practical in the PLA since 1960 – the army's proper handling of the "four first" relationships, its "revolutionary work-style", the emulation campaigns and the five good soldier and four good movements." See Gittings op. cit., p. 256. The PLA was also used in important administrative and peace-keeping roles during the GPCR.
28. Gittings, op. cit., p. 25.
29. The Conference specified that China should have a "unified army" which should be modernized and an air force and navy should be established. See Gittings, op. cit., p. 119.
30. *People's Daily*, 1 January 1952. Quoted in Gittings, op. cit., p. 125.
31. See Harry Harding, Jr., "The Making of Chinese Military Policy", in W.W. Whitson (ed.), *The Military and Political Power in China in the 1970s*, p. 375.

32. See David A. Charles, "The Dismissal of Marshall P'eng Teh-huai", *China Quarterly,* October–December 1961.
33. See Maury Lisann, "Moscow and the Chinese Power Struggle", *Problems of Communism,* November–December 1969, p. 34.
34. See Harding, op. cit., p. 377.
35. Harding, op. cit., p. 379.
36. See Jurgen Domes, "New Course in Chinese Domestic Politics: The Anatomy of Readjustment", *Asian Survey,* Vol. XIII, No. 7, July 1973, and Parris H. Chang, "Regional Military Power: The Aftermath of the Cultural Revolution", *Asian Survey,* Vol. XII, No. 12, December 1972.
37. See Henry S. Bradsher, "China: The Radical Offensive", *Asian Survey.* Vol. XIII, No. 11, November 1973, p. 1004.
38. See *The Military Balance 1974-75* (London: International Insitute for Strategic Studies).
39. Many leading military figures purged during the Cultural Revolution have also been brought back to key positions. See Bradsher, op. cit.
40. "Statement by the Spokesman of the Chinese Government – A Comment on the Soviet Government's statement of 21 August", *People of the World, Unite, for the Complete, Thorough, Total and Resolute Prohibition and Destruction of Nuclear Weapons* (Peking: Foreign Languages Press, 1963) p. 30. Quoted in Lui, op. cit., p. 34.
41. Gittings, op. cit., pp. 119-20.
42. *Peking Review,* 8 May 1964.
43. See Gittings, op. cit., p. 232.
44. See Liu, op. cit., p. 34.
45. See Huck, op. cit., p. 65.
46. B.W. Augenstein, "The Chinese and French Programme for the Development of National Nuclear Forces", *Orbis,* Vol. XI, No. 3, 1967.
47. Ralph L. Powell, "Maoist Military Doctrine", *Asian Survey*, April 1968.
48. Ibid., p. 243.
49. Huck, op. cit., p. 61.
50. Ibid.
51. See Powell, op. cit.
52. See M. Halperin, "China's Strategic Outlook", in Alastair Buchan (ed.), *China and the Peace of Asia* (London: Chatto and Windus, 1965), p. 101.
53. This is the term used by Harry Gelber in "Nuclear Weapons and Chinese Policy", *Adelphi Paper*, No. 99 (London: IISS, 1973), p. 21.
54. Ibid.
55. Ibid. p. 22.
56. See ibid., p. 22.
57. See *The Military Balance, 1974-75* (London: IISS, 1974), p. 48.
58. With the continuing priority concern with internal problems it may well be that conventional weapons modernization may have priority over strategic weapons. For such an argument see W.W. Whitson, "Domestic Constraints on Alternative Chinese Military Policies and Strategies in the 1970s", *The Annals of the American Academy of Political and Social Sciences*, Vol. 42, July 1972, p. 50.
59. Ibid., p. 40.
60. Milovan Djilas, *The New Class* (New York: Praeger, 1957), pp. 178-9.

13 BRITISH DEFENCE POLICY

John Baylis

The nature of British defence policy since 1945 has been characterized
largely by the process of continual adaptation to the changing circumstances and problems caused by the devolution of Empire. Fundamental
changes in Britain's foreign policy throughout the post-war period have
led inevitably to important changes in the defence sector. The military
instrument which for so long had been predicated on sustaining the
global responsibilities inherent in Great Power status have increasingly
had to be modified and adjusted to suit Britain's declining diplomatic
role in the world.

A superficial examination of the relationship between foreign and
defence policy reveals that in general the two related areas of policy
have to a large extent been in line. Britain's diplomatic posture for
much of the post-war period, despite the gradual process of decolonization, was grounded on the traditional world role and defence policy
was directed towards providing the world-wide capability to perform
the tasks inherent in such a role. To a large extent also the diplomatic
withdrawal from Empire has been paralleled, and in most cases
symbolized, by the gradual contraction of the military effort towards
a concentration on Europe.

A much closer examination of the relationship, however, reveals
that in many other respects foreign and defence policy have never in
fact been very closely related.[1] A more detailed analysis of the process
of decolonization in particular suggests that defence arrangements were
not always adequately related to the time-table and consequences of
withdrawal. It would seem that very often decisions about defence
requirements were taken by the Ministry of Defence in apparent dis-
regard of the policies of withdrawal which were being taken by the
Foreign and Colonial Offices.[2] The failure of the departments concerned
to co-ordinate foreign and defence policies in this important field meant
that instead of an overall, integrated course of action, several independent and often contradictory lines of policy were often pursued.

The result of this lack of overall political direction and co-ordination
of defence and foreign policy has been that defence policy throughout
the period has been in a state of flux as attempts have been made to
meet changing international as well as domestic circumstances.[3] In one
sense the problem has been partly psychological. Decision-makers
responsible for the formulation of policy in both the foreign and
defence fields have been constantly faced with the problem of

reconciling past images with the harsh realities of the moment. The clash between the traditional image of Britain as a Great World Power and the increasing reminders of her reduced diplomatic, military and economic capabilities produced a psychological environment during the period after 1945 which made it difficult for those responsible for making important foreign and defence policy decisions to constantly modify and readjust policy.[4]

This process of constant adaptation and readjustment has taken place in most of the more important areas of policy. Continuous adjustments in emphasis, for example, have taken place between the three overlapping circles of British external relations: the Commonwealth, the United States and Europe. In consequence, there has been constant adaptation by the military to adjust to the changing emphasis on these different areas with the disparate variety of operations which this has necessitated. Adjustment in emphasis has also been made between commitments and capabilities; between conventional and nuclear forces; between ideas concerning total war and limited war; and even between service autonomy and centralization within the machinery responsible for defence policy formulation. Because these issues and the process of adjustment which they reflect characterize much of the nature of British defence policy since 1945 it may be useful to focus attention on each of the questions in turn. In so doing it is hoped to provide a coherent picture of the essential features of the evolution and determinants of policy in the post-war period.

Readjustment of Roles

The immediate post-war period was essentially one of transition and uncertainty in defence policy as planners attempted to take stock of the changed external and domestic circumstances in the post-war world. Attlee saw the 1946 Defence White Paper as a 'stop-gap' and Anthony Eden claimed that it was not so much a 'statement relating to defence but a progress report on demobilization'.[5] This cautious and tentative approach of the government towards defence in these years was reflected in the adoption of a Ten-Year Rule in 1946 which like the ten-year rule of 1919 was a directive to the military to plan on the official assumption that there would be no major war for a decade.[6] In this uncertain environment, with no identifiable enemy as yet to plan against, defence planners searched for a viable security system for the future. With the mood of disengagement in the United States, some form of Commonwealth defence arrangement seemed to many to be the most fruitful.[7] On the basis of the decision of the Imperial Conference of 1926, the general defence of the Empire, in the form of the defence of the Empire's lines of communication, was the responsibility of the United Kingdom, assisted by such forces as the dominions could provide. Although by 1945 it was recognised that this scheme was obsolete, it was hoped that the system of informal co-operation would continue with greater sharing of the burdens of Commonwealth defence. In 1946 and 1947 this idea was accepted when the principle of allocating zones of responsibility within the Commonwealth was adopted by a number of Commonwealth members. A system of regional association was established and over-all co-operation obtained by the creation of a system of Commonwealth Liaison Officers.

Although this loose arrangement was subsequently formalized to a certain extent with the ANZAM agreement of 1949 when the government of the United Kingdom, Australia and New Zealand agreed to co-ordinate defence planning, the Commonwealth defence idea was not to prove the long-term solution to British security problems which many had hoped that it would. The hopes of the Chiefs of Staff in 1945-6 that India would become the centre of the regional Commonwealth grouping had to be abandoned with the loosening of ties between the two countries after Indian independence in 1947. The movement of Australia and New Zealand towards increasing dependence on the United States for their security following the ANZUS treaty of 1951 also helped to create a feeling of disillusionment in Whitehall with Commonwealth defence arrangements.

One of the most important influences directing the attention of defence planners away from ideas of Commonwealth defence was events in Europe. The coup in Czechoslovakia and the Berlin crisis in 1948 finally convinced the Labour Government that the Soviet Union was the potential enemy and that the greatest danger to British security lay in Europe. The realization of this fact led Bevin to try and "entangle" the United States in the defence of Europe and re-establish the 'special relationship' between Britain and America which had been built up during the Second World War.[8]

Relations with the United States following the end of the war had deteriorated with the end of Lend-lease, the passing of the McMahon Act and disagreements over Palestine. The growing American perception of Soviet intransigence and the gradual emergence of the Cold War, however, led to a reversal of the process of demobilization and retreat to isolationsim in the United States.

The movement away from the Commonwealth defence idea therefore led increasingly throughout the late 1940s towards alliance defence arrangements predicated largely on American assistance. The renewal of the bilateral Anglo-American 'special relationship' in the defence field after the relapse of 1945-6 had begun (tentatively) in the latter part of 1946 when there was a continuation of staff contacts and exchange of officers. The exchange of air force officers in particular helped facilitate the despatch of two groups of American B29's to Britain in July 1948 as part of the Western response to the Berlin crisis.

In February 1947, after Britain's famous warning that the state of the economy made it impossible to continue to assist the Greek Government in the Civil War against its Communist opponents, the United States stepped into the breach under the banner of the Truman Doctrine. Britain was also largely responsible for tying the United States much closer to Europe in this period, firstly through economic aid under the Marshall Plan and secondly, following the European Brussels Pact of 1948, through the North Atlantic Treaty Organization established on 4 April 1949, which represented a major triumph in post-war British diplomacy.

The most productive part of the evolving relationship with the United States in defence matters was, however, in the nuclear field. After Anglo-American nuclear co-operation ceased following the McMahon Act of 1946, Britain continually pressed the United States to resume collaboration and amend the Act. Up until the testing of her first atomic bomb, Britain was largely unsuccessful in restoring wartime co-operation. With the Monte Bello test on 3 October 1952, however, when it was evident that Britain had joined the nuclear club, "the hallowed doors of nuclear co-operation gradually opened up." The gradual easing of restrictions began with the *modus vivendi* of 8 January 1948 and was followed by the Atomic Energy Act of 1954 which permitted the sharing of data on the external characteristics of nuclear weapons in terms of size, weight, shape, yield and effect.

The climax to Britain's post-war attempts to share nuclear information with the United States came in 1958 with the amendments to the Atomic Energy Act of 1954. Following the serious break in Anglo-American relations over Suez in 1956, Macmillan, on returning to office in January 1957, moved swiftly to restore the harmony of the 'special relationship' which had been ruptured in the Anglo-French invasion of Egypt. The most important outcome of this British diplomatic offensive was the amendments to the 1954 Act whereby Britain was given even more preferential treatment in the nuclear field than she had achieved hitherto. The new amendment permitted the exchange of information about the design and production of nuclear warheads and the transfer of fissile materials to countries which had made "substantial progress in the development of atomic weapons". As Britain was the only ally to qualify under this stipulation she was the only beneficiary from the amendment.

Suez was also ironically a milestone in the return to collaboration in the field of delivery systems. Macmillan's Bermuda meeting with President Eisenhower in March 1957 resulted in the installation in Britain of sixty Thor liquid fuelled Intermediate Range Ballistic Missiles under a two-key system. At the time Britain's delivery system was based on the V Bomber force and the projected Blue Streak missile was largely independent of the United States. Following the launching of Sputnik by the Soviet Union on 4 October 1957 and the subsequent advances in the accuracy of Soviet and American ballistic missiles, however, the British delivery system became increasingly vulnerable. In an attempt to overcome this and also because of its escalating costs, Blue Streak was cancelled in April 1960 and the decision was taken to rely more heavily on the Americans by buying Skybolt from them to augment the V Bomber force.

The Anglo-American 'special relationship' was temporarily jeopardized once again in the autumn of 1962 when the Americans decided to end research and development on the Skybolt missile allegedly because of the increasing vulnerabilty of aircraft on the ground to a surprise first strike by Soviet missiles. The offer by President Kennedy of Polaris missiles to Britain at the Nassau meeting in December 1962, however, did a great deal to improve and consolidate Anglo-American relations and help preserve in greatly modified form Britain's independent deterrent.

Despite improved Anglo-American relations in the diplomatic as well as in the defence fields after Suez, the rupture in relations caused by the Suez incident led, although belatedly and reluctantly, to a reappraisal of Britain's role in the world and the gradual movement towards concentrating her political, economic and military effort on Europe.

Throughout much of the post-war period, although defence planners had been reluctant to concentrate the defence effort in Europe, the Continent had nevertheless been a high priority in terms of Britain's commitments. In 1947 Britain had signed the Dunkirk Treaty with France against the possibility of a resurgent Germany and in 1948, with the clear identification of the Soviet threat, the Brussels Pact was formed to establish a larger defence structure to facilitate Western European security.[9] This was followed by the North Atlantic Treaty of 1949 whereby Britain managed to achieve not only further European collaboration but also the long-sought-after American guarantee to defend Europe against Soviet invasion.

Symptomatic of Britain's ambivalent attitude towards Europe was the debate which continued throughout the late 1940s and early 1950s over whether Britain should adopt a Continental or a "limited liability" strategy.[10] The traditional penchant for a limited contribution to European defence was reinforced after the Korean War when the fear of an imminent Soviet attack on Western Europe had died down. In 1952 almost immediately after the Lisbon Conference, Britain took steps to water down the over-optimistic force levels accepted at that NATO meeting.[11] The 1952 Global Strategy Paper in particular argued that manpower targets could be considerably reduced because of the advent of tactical nuclear weapons.[12] European defence remained important but the Government was unwilling with its world-wide commitments to concentrate effort and resources in Europe.

The government was forced, however, to compromise its position over the European commitment a little in 1954 when the question of

German rearmament and the European Defence Community threatened to split the Western alliance. On the one hand German rearmament was needed to meet the growing conventional deficiency between East and West but on the other hand lingering French fears of a revisionist Germany had to be allayed. Through its proposals at Paris in 1954, Britain was able to secure German rearmament inside NATO and at the same time safeguard French sensitivity over the German issue by guaranteeing to keep a force of 55,000 men permanently stationed in Europe until 1994.

Despite the significance of this commitment in the sense that it represented a reversal of traditional British policy towards Europe, throughout the 1950s and early 1960s the relative stability created in Europe through the creation of NATO and the Warsaw Pact led to a decreasing emphasis in British defence policy on European affairs. There was a concentration instead on performing the continuing tasks and commitments overseas in the Far East and Middle East. The neglect of Europe to a certain extent, which was symbolized by the borrowing of troops from NATO at times to alleviate the ever-growing strains, caused by the over-stretch of forces East of Suez, continued until the 1960s. It was only then that financial issues and the dangerous imbalance between commitments and capabilities were to lead to a fundamental reassessment of defence priorities and the concentration on Europe. The new European orientation initiated by the first application to join the Common Market in 1961 was taken further in the defence field with the limited retrenchment announced following the 1966 Defence Review and came to fruition finally with the January 1968 White Paper which speeded up the withdrawal of forces from the Far East and Persian Gulf to take place by 1971.[13]

Military Operations

This gradual and uncertain process of retreat from Empire and the constant search throughout the post-war period for a new role has had a significant impact on the kind of miltiary operations that the armed forces were called upon to perform.

At the end of the Second World War, the armed forces were immediately involved in numerous military commitments throughout the world. Quite apart from the inescapable need for armies of occupation in Europe – in Germany, Austria and Venezia Giulia – there was also a need to occupy and control various colonies, both her own and those of other powers. Occupation armies were needed in particular in ex-Italian colonies in Africa and also in many parts of the Far East which had until recently been occupied by the Japanese. Also quite apart from British territories such as Malaya, Singapore, Burma and Hong Kong, both British and Indian forces assisted in the reoccupation of the former Dutch and French colonies in the East Indies and Indo-China.

These latter duties soon brought them into direct conflict with nation-alist forces until the old colonial powers were able to return.

Although the liquidation of occupation responsibilities were not finally completed until the mid-1950s, the focus of attention of military planners from 1947-48 onwards increasingly centred on the two main, and often competing, strands of British foreign policy; the European and the overseas roles. In Europe after the successful show of force against the Yugoslavs over Trieste in 1945 and the campaign against the Communist forces in Greece in 1946-47, the armed forces settled down to a peacetime role of operating within an alliance; firstly the Western European Union (WEU) and later NATO, to deter Soviet aggression in Western Europe.

The kinds of skills and equipment required for a role of this sort were totally different to those needed for operations in overseas territories. As BAOR trained for large-scale conventional and later nuclear, chemical and biological operations in Europe, the gradual and often reluctant withdrawal from Empire increasingly necessitated policing, anti-terrorist and anti-insurgent operations in many different environments and terrains as the tide of nationalist sentiment demanding independence grew. As one writer rather elaborately puts it: ". . . just as the marches of neglected, underpaid red-coats and their thundering volleys had once marked the surge of British expansion, so the soldier in Khaki drill or battledress guarded the hesitant retreat from Empire. While the politicians havered, while authority crumbled, the soldier tried to keep order."[14] Although this view rather under-estimates the difficult tasks that statesmen faced and the often intract-able problems with which they grappled, the fact remains that the armed forces were often left to "hold the ring" against indigenous rioting and terrorist activity as politicians reluctantly worked out their timetables of withdrawal. This pattern of events was repeated in the Middle East, in Africa, in the Carribean and in Asia and the Far East.

In the Middle East, the armed forces conducted operations against terrorist groups in Palestine, in Egypt and in Cyprus in the late forties and early fifties as the British governments, despite the declining importance of the bases in these areas, attempted to find political solutions which would guarantee a continuing presence; only to find that at the end of the day they were compelled to withdraw. The same was true of British possessions in Africa, Asia and the Carribean, where between 1947 and 1967 the military were involved in maintaining order at one one time or another in British Guiana, British Honduras, Kenya, Aden, the Gold Coast, in Hong Kong, Jamaica, the Cameroons, Zanzi-bar, Borneo, Tanganyika, Uganda and Mauritius. In the Far East also British troops successfully fought a protracted counter-insurgency campaign in Malaya against Communist guerrillas between 1948 and 1960 which enabled the colony to progress smoothly to independence with a relatively stable democratic régime.[15] A similar operation with equal success was fought in Borneo between 1963 and 1966 when Indonesia's President Soekarno attempted to prevent the integration of Sarawak and Sabah into the newly formed Malaysian Federation through his policy of confrontation.[16]

More recently British troops have also become involved in counter-terrorist activities much nearer home against the IRA in the domestic context of Northern Ireland. Despite some similarities with counter-insurgent campaigns in other countries, operations in the British Isles, in a predominantly urban environment, have required new techniques and created new problems which the Army has had to solve. Once again the armed forces have been asked to deal with the bombings, snipings and assassinations of the terrorist campaign while the politicians grapple with the complex and confusing political issues in an attempt to find a satisfactory solution to Ulster's problems.

In contrast to these irregular campaigns the armed forces have also been engaged in campaigns requiring vastly different expertise and training. In June 1950, for example, British forces became involved in fighting a conventional war against Communist forces following the invasion of South Korea by forces from the North. For defence planners in Britain the campaign against North Korea in support of the South was important from two points of view. On the one hand, and most obviously, the Commonwealth Brigade was important in helping the United States and the United Nations to prevent Communist aggression and expansion in Korea and thus indirectly in the Far East as a whole: aggression which if allowed to spread would, it was thought, threaten British interests in the area.[17] It was also important, however, from another and perhaps from the British perspective, more important point of view. To many in Western Europe the invasion of South Korea was seen merely as a feint, an act of deception by Stalin, to distract the attention of the Western world away from Europe prior to a concerted Soviet invasion. In these early days of NATO and American involvement in Europe which Ernest Bevin had worked so hard to achieve, the Attlee Government considered that it was vital for political reasons to demonstrate British, and therefore Western European support for the United States in the Far East to ensure continued American military support in Europe against the perceived Soviet threat.

In the majority of cases, British military operations, whether of a policing, anti-terrorist, counter-insurgent or conventional variety were largely successful in achieving the main political objectives laid down. The relative utility of military power as an instrument of state policy in the post-war period has, however, derived not only from the successful use of military force in various circumstances but also often from the threat of the perceived potential which British forces symbolised. This was particularly the case in the Kuwait operation in 1961, when the landing of British forces in Kuwait forestalled a threatened annexation by the neighbouring Iraq. One recent study of the operation points out that with all of the inadequacies of the operation from the British side and the Iraqi superiority in numerical terms and in terms of much of their equipment, even taking into account the more nebulous questions of morale, training and leadership, the British would have been very hard-pressed to have met a concerted invasion by Iraq had it taken place.[18] As it was, despite the deficiencies of the military operation, Kassem did not invade largely perhaps because of the commitment which the British government had made and the potential which the forces on the ground represented.

Despite the relative inadequacies, particularly of equipment, which were highlighted by the Kuwait operation, the forces which existed did enable the government to respond, even if partly fortuitously, to a perceived problem in a relatively short period of time. This was not the case, however, during the Suez crisis in 1956. Despite the lip-service which had been paid to the concept of a highly mobile strategic reserve in the White Papers from 1954 onwards, the over-riding importance of the deterrent and the limited resources available pre-cluded any major improvement in conventional capability. Conse-quently when the government was faced with a situation over the nationalization of the Suez Canal in 1956, because of the deficiencies which existed it was unable to respond with the kind of swift and mobile operation which would have been necessary to have achieved the desired results.[19] Although the crisis broke on 26 July, the military preparations were not complete until mid-September and even then after the initial bombardment of Egyptian airfields on 31 October, the Anglo-French assault on Port Said did not begin until 5 November because of the long sea voyage from Malta.

Suez, in many ways, symbolises the kinds of problems which military planners have faced in the post-war years. Successive govern-ments throughout the period, largely because of their assumptions of Great Power status, have continually called upon the military to per-form a whole variety of disparate and different tasks all over the world, necessitating different skills and equipment while at the same time reducing the manpower of the armed forces and drastically cutting the expenditure available for the variety of weapons necessary for such operations. Under these circumstances the military forces have been forced to continually adjust to the new circumstances and improvise as best they can. This was true in the Suez crisis and such a pattern characterises many of the other campaigns undertaken since 1945. The failures when they have occurred have usually been due to the lack of coherent and clear political direction rather than ones of operational skills and military performance.[20]

Commitments and Capabilities

The constant adjustment and search for a new role and the pressures on the services performing many different operations have to a large extent been a consequence of the imbalance which has existed for much of the post-war period between commitments and capabilities. In 1947 the decision was taken to give India independence, thus in part relieving Britain of one of her biggest commitments. The problem for British defence planners, which does not seem to have been immediately recognised, was that it also deprived her of Indian military manpower which had been traditionally used to garrison the Empire. Despite the loss of the cornerstone of the Empire, the remaining areas of British sovereignty, various residual obligations and perhaps most importantly 'the habit of influence', all helped to sustain the impression that Britain remained a Great Power in Asia. At the same time conditions in Europe required active participation in an alliance with the maintenance of substantial conventional forces permanently on the ground.

The attempts to fulfil this dual defence policy between 1947 and 1967 put increasing strain on the defence establishment as attempts were made to perform numerous commitments with decreasing manpower and financial resources. Following the loss of Indian manpower, various decisions were made in 1956 and 1957 to cut service manpower, largely for economic reasons.[21] Eden announced the reduction of forces from 800,000 to 700,000 men in 1956 and planned for a reduction to about 450,000 by 1960 or 1961.[22] His plans were cut short by Suez; but in the reappraisal of military policy which followed Duncan Sandys, the new Defence Minister, planned for an abolition of conscription by 1962 and the reduction of service manpower from 690,000 to 375,000 by that year.[23] The services were therefore being asked to continue performing traditional commitments during the early 1960s with half of the manpower available in 1956.

There were also the problems caused by rising prices and technological advances which were made considerably more difficult by the gradual reduction in defence spending. Following the massive rearmament programme initiated by the Labour Government in 1950, the plan to spend 10 per cent of GNP on defence was gradually 'stretched out' by the Conservative Government such that it was finally reduced to 6.6 per cent when the Conservatives left office in 1964. At the same time the cost and complexity of weapons systems, particularly those required to retain a global military capability and nuclear delivery system, began to escalate rapidly. The aircraft carriers which in the 1930s had cost £3 million were costing £60 million by the mid-1960s and the cost of army equipment increased four-fold in the twenty years after the war. As Michael Howard rightly points out, "in order to continue to carry out their traditional tasks, the services were compelled year by year to demand bigger appropriations from a Ministry of

Defence which year by year had a smaller proportion of the national income from which to meet their requirements."[24]

In the years after the Kuwait operation in 1961 as East of Suez commitments were increasingly tested in South-East Asia, South Arabia and East Africa, the material and manpower difficulties created more and more difficulties.[25] The 1966 Defence Review made the point of emphasising the over-stretch of British forces but did little either to reduce the commitments or increase the capabilities of British military forces by providing the manpower, mobility and resources which were necessary. The difficult political decisions required to improve the balance were eventually brought about largely by financial crisis rather than rational strategic planning. It was felt that the continuing economic problems required major cuts in government spending. In order to make cuts in social expenditure more palatable to various sections of the Labour Party, the Government felt it necessary to introduce retrenchments in the defence field as well.[26] In 1967 and 1968 therefore, faced with a rapidly deteriorating economic position, the Wilson Government finally decided to withdraw forces from East of Suez, thereby cutting commitments and bringing them more into line with the resources available. As one commentator put it, the right decision had been made but largely for the wrong reasons.[27]

Nuclear and Conventional Forces

The asymmetry between commitments and capabilities has been, to a large extent, due to the reluctance of succeeding governments to provide the necessary conventional forces.[28] Here again, there has been a constant process of adjustment in emphasis between nuclear weapons systems and conventional forces.[29] With the watering down and stretching out of the Labour Government's rearmament programme by Prime Minister Churchill in 1951, emphasis in British defence policy increasingly became focused upon nuclear weapons. For most of the period from the Global Strategy Paper of 1952 to the Chiefs of Staff Paper of 1962 the policy of nuclear deterrence was stressed in the Defence White Papers. The most explicit statement of the nuclear deterrent doctrine came in 1957 with the Sandys White Paper.[30] Following the humiliation of Suez, when even the United States had actively opposed British policies, it was felt that both for political and military reasons emphasis should be placed on building up an independent nuclear deterrent. The White Paper announced that for the next five years Britain was to upgrade the priority accorded to the nuclear deterrent. Thermo-nuclear weapons would be added to the existing atomic armoury and the V-bombers would be supplemented by ballistic rockets as they became available.

The significance of this was particularly important in relation to the provision of conventional forces. As one writer has put it, "nuclear deterrence not only held the centre of the strategic stage but its shadows extended into the wings."[31] Despite the announcement in White Paper after White Paper that the Government intended to improve conventional equipment, declaratory policy never really became actual policy and resources were concentrated mainly on the nuclear field. Even after the increasing emphasis on providing limited war forces for likely threats East of Suez contained in the 1962 Chiefs of Staff Paper, limited improvements in mobility were stifled by the decision of the Labour Government to impose a defence spending ceiling in 1964 of £2,000 million. At the same time no attempts were made to cut commitments. The Services, therefore, it would seem, were being asked to perform the same roles as before at less cost on the assumption that the Labour Government could meet foreign and defence policy issues more skilfully than their predecessors.

The attempt by the Labour Government between 1964 and 1968 to bring the nation's military capabilities into balance with its economic resources and foreign policy objectives, had its effects on the place and priority of nuclear weapons within over-all defence policy, however. While in opposition the Labour Party had by 1964 become rather belatedly critical of the emphasis which the Conservative Government was placing on nuclear weapons.[32] Once in power, however, their policies were not as drastic as many had feared. The independent nature of the deterrent was played down but the decision was taken to continue with the nuclear force despite the feeling of many in the party that the force should be abandoned.

The most immediate problem facing the Labour Government when it came to power was the question of the MLF proposed by the US to solve the issue of nuclear sharing in NATO. Prime Minister Harold Wilson's response, seemingly an attempt to sink the MLF proposal, was to put forward his own idea of an Atlantic Nuclear Force (ANF), whereby Britain's nuclear forces would be integrated into an alliance framework.[33] Although the proposal was of more political than military importance it did set the tone of the Labour Government's desire to play down national control of nuclear forces and emphasize alliance requirements. The difference between Labour and Conservative Government policies towards nuclear weapons, however, was more verbal than substantive. In general the Labour Government did not reverse the nuclear conventional balance of British forces, rather it attempted to integrate the two components more effectively in its over-all strategic and foreign policy.

Healey's answer to the growing disparity between the conventional forces of NATO and those of the Warsaw Pact was the adoption of a strategy of "flexible escalation". This was an attempt in integrate and balance the deterrent and defensive elements of NATO strategy within a framework which would be politically and economically acceptable to member governments. The essence of the doctrine being that NATO should have sufficient conventional forces to deal with small-scale incursions or to hold a large-scale invasion for a few days while negotiations took place, after which time tactical nuclear weapons would have to be used. Healey's argument was that the enemy would be deterred because it would realise that NATO would have no alternative but to use tactical nuclear weapons at an early stage in an all-out conventional war. The initiation therefore of a large-scale attack in Europe posed the risk for the Soviet Union of escalation to strategic nuclear conflagration; a risk they would be unlikely to take.

Ideas about Total and Limited War

Denis Healey's attempt to balance nuclear and conventional forces has been part of the attempt to integrate the general total war and limited war notions into an overall coherent strategic framework.[34] Up until the early 1960s strategic theory in Britain hinged on the assumption that the nations involved in war would devote their whole national effort to the object of winning the war on a global scale. British strategic thinking in this early post-war period was symbolized by the Global Strategy Paper of 1952. The paper, which was prepared by the Chiefs of Staff at the prompting of Winston Churchill, contained three sections: one on deterrence, one on NATO, and the other on overseas responsibilities. Although the full rigour of the paper was never translated into policy, the primary point of the document relating to the importance of nuclear deterrence was immediately accepted and remained the basis of British defence policy for the remainder of the fifties. The general assumption behind strategic thinking was that the deterrent would be effective against threats both of a Cold War as well as a Hot War variety. As the 1954 White Paper pointed out, 'As the deterrent continues to grow, it should have an increasing effect upon the Cold War by making less likely such adventures on the part of the Communist world as their aggression in Korea.'[35]

Despite the continuation of the Total War theme throughout the 1950s, certain lines of policies emerged during the period which were to harden into central prongs of British defence policy in the years after 1957 when the launching of the Soviet Sputnik made the strategy of Massive Retaliation less credible. The most important of the new developments initially was the plan for a central strategic reserve which could be air-lifted to overseas theatres when trouble broke out. Although this need for more mobile conventional forces remained a declared aim of the government from 1954 it was more important as a concept than as a policy until priority was given to building up transport command in the late fifties. The only Service to take up the limited war theme with any enthusiasm in the mid-fifties, however, was the Navy.[36] The Navy's search for a new role after the broken-backed warfare concept had been discredited, caused it to settle by

1957 for a limited war role.[37] Although the Admiralty insisted that the Navy still had an anti-submarine role in the event of general war, the limited war priority became henceforward the basis of naval planning and emphasis was placed on naval task forces.

The relative success of the Kuwait operation in 1961 crystallised ideas which had been prevalent for some time. A new Chiefs of Staff Paper was produced in January 1962 which laid the emphasis much less on the total warfare idea and more on the need to maintain the capability to counter limited threats which might emerge East of Suez. From 1962 onwards therefore, resources were increasingly channelled into providing greater mobility for the forces to perform small brush-fire operations overseas. Transport aircraft became a higher priority in an attempt to make the air-lifted strategic reserve concept a reality. More resources were allocated to the Navy to develop its carriers as the central element in the seaborne task forces. This move toward up-grading the limited war component of British strategy was confirmed by the events of the following two years when, against a background of almost continuous international tension East of Suez, one emergency after another dominated Whitehall's attention.

The overstretch, however, of British forces caused by the attempt to retain an independent global and limited war capability, while at the same time not increasing the financial resources required for such a capability, led to the readjustment of strategic thinking between 1966 and 1968. Henceforth although Britain was to retain a small capability for limited extra-European operations, the main focus of attention was to be Europe where it was recognised that both Britain's conventional and nuclear forces must be integrated more effectively into an alliance framework. The key word in British strategy was to be 'inter-dependence' rather than 'independence'. Increasingly the total war theme was played down and the emphasis placed on deterring Soviet aggression in Europe by co-ordinating nuclear and conventional components into an effective general and limited war alliance strategy.

Institutional Readjustment

Parallel to, and partly responsible for, this constant process of adjust-ment and readjustment which has characterized British defence policy has been a continuing process of adaptation within the institutional structure for policy formulation. In 1946 the wartime expedient was put on a permanent footing when a Minister of Defence was appointed with responsibility for co-ordinating the Services. Beneath the Minister came a series of committees, the most important of which were the Defence Committee of the Cabinet and the Chiefs of Staff Committee. This process of "defence by committee" was, however, sharply criti-cised in the post-war period for arriving at decisions based on com-promise. Montgomery in his memoirs draws a picture of intense inter-

Service rivalry for the scarce funds available. There was, he maintained, little overall coherent strategic planning, and no unified defence policy.[38] This was largely due to institutional weaknesses. In particular, the Minister's powers remained inadequate to secure a unified policy and the Defence Committee failed to perform its statutory function of integrating domestic, foreign and military policies.

The first real attempt to modify the system in order to overcome the continuing problems of resource allocation came in 1955 when Sir Anthony Eden announced an expanded interpretation of the Minister of Defence's role, to include ensuring that the "composition and balance" of each Service conformed to the government's policy.[39] Almost immediately the Suez débâcle occurred, after which a new review of defence policy was initiated by Eden's successor, Harold Macmillan. Once again the powers of the Minister of Defence were extended. Duncan Sandys, the new incumbent, was authorized on 24 January 1957, to decide matters of general defence policy affecting the "size, shape, organization and disposal of the armed forces and their equipment and supply including defence research and development." These new powers of the Minister of Defence were confirmed in July 1958 in a White Paper on the *Central Organization for Defence*.[40]

This movement towards further centralization and utilization of his new powers by the Minister caused resentment amongst the Service Chiefs who saw their traditional autonomy and traditional influence in the decision-making process gradually being eroded. As a result of their pressure the July 1958 White Paper represented a compromise between the Minister's inclination to carry the centralization of authority further and the Service Minister's to maintain their independence. Although the overall authority of the Minister was asserted, the Chiefs of Staff Committee retained their collective responsibility to the government for collective advice and their right of direct access to the Prime Minister. Sandys' attempt to confine the Service Ministers to the new Defence Board which was to deal with purely military matters was also overruled by the Cabinet and their attendance at the Defence Committee was left to the discretion of the Committee.

The failings of this compromise solution became increasingly evident with the replacement of Duncan Sandys by Harold Watkinson in October 1959. The different personalities of the two men led to the realization of how little the changes which had been carried out under Sandys' direction had affected central control of defence policy formulation. The Minister had been given explicit responsibility for the 'formulation and general application of a unified policy' but he had not been given the necessary machinery to carry it out. The internecine struggles between the three Services for appropriations as well as their power of initiative in policy formulation and in procurement remained as great as ever.[41]

Further attempts to readjust the machinery came in 1963 with the

Thorneycroft-Mountbatten reforms.[42] On the prompting of the Chief of Defence Staff, Lord Mountbatten, and Mr. Peter Thorneycroft, the incumbent Minister of Defence, the Prime Minister initiated an independent inquiry under General Ismay and Lieutenant-General Sir Ian Jacob into the organization of the defence machinery. The recommendations in their report (which was ready with astonishing speed in two months) became the basis of the White Paper which was presented to Parliament in July 1963. A single Ministry of Defence was established under a Secretary of State, absorbing the existing Service Ministries. In their place, signalling their reduced status, Navy, Army and Air Force Departments were established. Broad issues of defence policy would still be settled at Cabinet level but the Defence Committee would be replaced by a Committee on Defence and Overseas Policy. The service Boards were to remain in being but only as subsidiary managerial instruments of a central Defence Council where the Ministers, the Chiefs of Staff and the Chief Scientific Adviser would deal with major policy questions. In general the reforms amounted to an "administrative revolution" in the field of defence policy formulation and a great leap forward towards greater centralization. The powers of the Secretary of State were greatly enhanced and the status of Service Ministers was drastically reduced, thus downgrading the independence and autonomy of the Service Ministries.

Further modifications and refinements occurred in 1967 when the Service Ministers were removed and replaced by two Ministers, one for personnel and logistics and the other for research, procurement and sales.[43] Again in 1970 these two ministerial posts were merged to form a single post for personnel, equipment, research and logistics.[44] Finally, following the Rayner Report in 1971, a central procurement excutive was established and a Minister of State for procurement was set up.[45]

Since 1945 therefore, there has been a continual process of adjustment within the central organization of defence. This has meant that the Ministry of Defence and the higher echelons of the Services have been in a state of continuous flux at a time when they have had to carry out continuous reappraisals and make constant adjustments to British defence policy. Plans have had to be revised to conform to new decisions at a time when the defence structure and the chain of command was constantly melting and re-forming. The end result of this constant process of adaptation has been that British defence policy in the post-war period has not been distinguished by clarity or consistency of purpose.[46]

This conclusion, however, in no way detracts from the value of the defence establishment which was maintained during the period. The successful completion of numerous military operations testifies to this fact. Notwithstanding the problems caused by inter-Service rivalries and the failure of the overseas base policy, the military achievement was considerable. Despite the lack of clear political direction and the limited resources available the Services adapted to the changing environment with great alacrity. The preoccupation with the nuclear deterrent in Whitehall did not prevent the Services from developing new approaches to the problems of overseas security. The operational record of the Services attests to their success in developing an effective system for the provision of military support for British foreign policy in the post-colonial era.

Current and Future Issues

In some important respects the process of adjustment for the Services, and for defence policy in general, which has characterized much of the post-war period is likely to continue into the future. While changes in the domestic and international environments which might significantly change the nature of British defence policy in the future cannot be foreseen, it seems likely that for the rest of the 1970s and longer, Britain's security interests will be concentrated in Europe. Although the main direction of policy may have been decided upon, however, many other significant choices nevertheless remain to be made within the confines of the general parameters of the European defence orientation.[47]

One of the major questions for the future is whether Britain's security interests will be concentrated in a solely European defence organization or whether they will continue within an Atlantic Alliance. In recent years as Britain has built up closer political and economic ties with other European countries, she has also, for obvious political reasons, been moving increasingly towards greater identification with the European caucus within the alliance. This was demonstrated when Denis Healey took the initiative in forming the Eurogroup within NATO. This informal grouping of Defence Ministers and NATO Permanent Representatives of ten European countries meets on a regular basis to explore and promote measures designed to improve the European contribution to collective defence and to achieve a more effective result from the available resources.[48]

Besides the political pressures for increased defence integration with other European states stemming from the British applications to join, and subsequent membership of the EEC, there are also strong and increasing economic pressures pushing in this direction. The major determinant of British defence policy in the post-war period has been, and still is, one of finance.[49] With the declining percentage of GNP spent on defence and the escalation of weapons costs, it was perhaps only natural that Britain should seek closer collaboration in the weapons procurement field with other European states. The most important of these projects has been the Jaguar close support and attack aircraft produced by Anglo-French companies and the Multiple Role Combat Aircraft (MRCA) produced by three nations Britain, Italy and West Germany. This tentative move towards joint procurement has led many to push for the establishment of some form of European procurement agency to integrate weapons development for the European members of NATO as a whole.[50] Some commentators have gone even further and argued that because of the need to harmonize European defence and foreign policies at a time of increasing uncertainty over the scale of the long-term American presence in Europe, Western European states should form a European defence community to co-ordinate European defence efforts and supplement their own security.[51]

Such a project, however, poses a number of fundamental difficulties. Firstly, and perhaps most important, there is the problem of establishing a European defence community which would be able to give the kind of political direction to co-ordinate the national defence policies of West European states, before political union is in fact achieved. The question is whether such a European defence organization would be a spur to further political cohesion or whether, as perhaps is more likely, political union is a prerequisite for an effective European defence community in the first place.[52] On top of this obvious political problem there is also the difficulty of the form and composition of such an organization. Should it be based on the old Western European Union, outside NATO and including France, or should it build on the foundations of the Eurogroup within NATO and exclude France? Both organizations or any other European defence arrangement which could be envisaged would face the same problem of its relations both with NATO and with the EEC.

For Britain the dilemma which this creates is particularly acute. Largely for political reasons there is an incentive to forgo stronger ties in the defence field with other EEC members, particularly the French. On the other hand traditional friendship and ties with the US as well as the recognition of the necessity of the American guarantee for Europe would seem to suggest a continuing emphasis on the Atlantic Alliance. The problem for the government therefore is how far to move towards increased European defence integration which might be detrimental to the defence relationship with the United States. This difficulty can be clearly seen in the debate over the future of Britain's deterrent. If the government decides to remain a nuclear power, there is the choice between producing, and paying for, the next generation of missiles and warheads unilaterally; buying from the United States; or collaborating with other European states. Mainly because of the very high costs of "going it alone", apart from the policy of producing her own MRV or MIRV warheads, it would appear that an independent British effort to produce a 'follow-up' to Polaris is out of the question.[53] If the government therefore decides to produce a credible deterrent, the real choice is between buying the American Poseidon or Trident systems or European collaboration in the nuclear field, perhaps with the French in particular.[54] Both options, however, create problems for

British defence planners.

As far as an Anglo-French force is concerned, despite the obvious gains to be made in technical and economic collaboration, the political issues involved would seem to preclude, at least at present, any concrete co-operation. France's desire to retain her independence from the USA and Britain's interest in retaining the advantages of co-operation with the Americans in nuclear terms, together with the desire of both governments to retain independent operational control of their forces, suggests that there will have to be a radical change in political thinking in both capitals if an Anglo-French nuclear force is ever to become a reality.[55]

On the other hand, although a continuation of the 'special relationship' with the US in the defence field on the lines of the Nassau agreement would perhaps be the answer for Britain, present political and economic issues would make this much more difficult than in 1962. Britain's identification with Europe and French criticism of Britain's close ties with the United States would make another simple bilateral agreement between the two countries perhaps less likely, at least on the favourable terms of the Polaris agreement. The stipulation that Britain would on this occasion have to pay a share in the Research and Development costs of Poseidon or Trident would also make it an extremely expensive proposition.

This dilemma in the nuclear field highlights the central problem within the alliance for Britain. Although further collaboration with other European states in the defence field is necessary and possible, the solution of the most important aspects of European security seem unlikely to be achieved until some form of closer political integration takes place. This, however, is an increasingly more distant prospect with the continuing difficulties and uncertainties in Europe, especially after the energy crisis following the Yom Kippur War of October 1973. At the same time, Britain's decision to identify formally with the EEC and the movement, however slow, towards the ideal of political union, has involved at least a psychological loosening of ties with the USA. As such, the prospects of increased collaboration with the Americans become politically and economically more difficult.

Despite this uncertainty in Britain's relations with the United States and other members of the EEC, however, the incentive for collaboration of some form with other states continues to grow. The main pressure, as usual, is financial, emanating from the continuing decline in the percentage of GNP which the government is prepared to spend on defence. As British defence expenditure is reduced to the level of other European members of NATO,[56] the affects upon the size, equipment and operational capability of the armed forces are likely to be offset only by further collaboration in the defence field. The question remains, however, over what form this collaboration is likely to take.

Barring significant domestic and international changes and given the uncertainties in Europe, it seems likely that any major institutional innovations in the defence field are likely, if at all, in the longer rather than the shorter term. In the more immediate future Britain can perhaps be expected to "muddle through", attempting both to increase the area of collaboration, especially in terms of weapons procurement, with other European states and, at the same time, encourage continued American interest in European defence in the context of the Atlantic Alliance. From the British viewpoint, the ideal would seem to be a twin-pillared Atlantic security framework, similar to that envisaged in President Kennedy's Grand Design, with Britain acting as the bridge between Europe and the United States.

Notes

1. See Phillip Darby, *British Defence Policy East of Suez 1947-68* (London: Oxford University Press, 1973), pp. 16-21, and pp. 135-42.
2. This was particularly the case over Singapore in the years before the Lancaster House Conference in April 1956 and also over Kenya a few years later. See Darby, ibid., p. 193.
3. See C.H. Bartlett, *The Long Retreat: A Short History of British Defence Policy 1945-1970* (London: Macmillan, 1972), p.xi.
4. See Harold and Margaret Sprout, "Retreat from World Power: Processes and Consequences of Readjustment", *World Politics*, 1963.
5. See Andrew J. Pierre, *Nuclear Politics : The British experiment with an Independent Strategic Force 1939-1970* (London: Oxford University Press, 1972), p. 71. See also H.C. Deb., Col. 239 (5 March 1946).
6. Pierre, ibid., p. 71.
7. One of the main proponents of this idea was Lord Alanbrooke. See Bartlett, op. cit., p. 11; *The Economist*, 8 February 1947 and 27 March 1948; *Royal United Service Institution Journal* (RUSIJ), 1947, pp. 182-6.
8. See R. Osgood, *NATO : The Entangling Alliance* (London: The University of Chicago Press, 1962).
9. The fifty-year Brussels Pact of mutual collective assistance against any aggressor was signed on 17 March 1948 by Britain, France, the Netherlands and Luxemburg.
10. For the inter-war debate see M. Howard, *The Continental Commitment* (London: Temple Smith, 1972), pp. 96-120. See also Bartlett, op. cit., pp. 20-21.
11. The Lisbon goals involved an attempt to build up a force of 96 divisions in Europe by 1954. See Osgood, op. cit., p. 87.
12. See S. Robinson, *The Global Strategy Paper of 1952*,(Unpublished M.Sc. (Econ.) thesis, University of Wales, 1974).
13. Cmnd. 3540, *Statement on the Defence Estimates*: 1968. Cmnd. 3701, *Supplementary Statement on Defence Policy*: 1968.
14. C. Barnett, *Britain and Her Army 1509-1970* (London: Pelican, 1974), p. 479.
15. See R.L. Clutterbuck, *The Long, Long War* (New York: Praeger, 1966).
16. See G. Blaxland, *The Regiments Depart* (London: Kimber, 1971) pp. 375-410.
17. See D. Rees, *Korea: The Limited War* (London: Macmillan, 1964).
18. J. Howarth, *The Kuwait Operation* (Unpublished M.Sc.(Econ.) thesis, University of Wales, 1972).
19. See A.J. Barker, *Suez : the Seven Day War* (London: Faber and Faber, 1964).
20. This was true of Suez and perhaps of the Aden operations as well.

21. For the extensive responsibilities of Indian troops for Empire defence see Darby, op. cit., p. 2.

22. Sir Anthony Eden, *Full Circle* (London: Cassell, 1960), p. 370-5. The reductions were made following the re-examination of Britain's long-term needs undertaken by Sir Anthony Eden, Lord Salisbury, Mr. Macmillan, Mr. Selwyn Lloyd, Sir Walter Monckton and Mr. Butler in the summer of 1956.

23. Cmnd. 124, *Defence: Outline of Future Policy:* 1957.

24. M. Howard, *Central Organization for Defence* (London: RUSI, 1970), p. 9.

25. The operations included Brunei, Borneo, Aden and the East African Mutinies.

26. See Patrick Gordon Walker, *The Cabinet* (London: Fontana, 1970), p. 124-34.

27. Charles Douglas-Home, "Concentration of Strength", *The Times,* 23 January 1968.

28. Or to cut commitments quickly enough.

29. See Darby, op. cit., p. 168-72.

30. Cmnd. 124, op. cit.

31. Darby, op. cit., p. 68.

32. See Pierre, op. cit., p. 101-11.

33. Ibid., p. 275-82.

34. The term 'total war' is used here to refer to a conflict on a global scale in which the combatants use all of their resources to achieve victory. Total War and Global War are sometimes used synonymously. See Darby, op. cit., p. 76.

35. Cmnd. 9075, *Statement on Defence*½ 1954.

36. See Cdr. W.J. Crowe, *The Policy Roots of the Modern British Royal Navy, 1946-63* (Unpublished Ph.D. dissertation, Princeton University, 1965).

37. The concept of "Broken-backed Warfare" implies that in a nuclear conflict, the initial exchange might not be decisive and war might continue at a lower level of intensity for some time afterwards. The concept implies the necessity for making provision for continuing operations after the initial exchange, particularly at sea. See Darby, op. cit., p. 47.

38. Field-Marshal Montgomery, *Memoirs* (London: Collins, 1958), pp. 487-97.

39. Eden, op. cit., p. 375.

40. Cmnd. 476, *Central Organization of Defence*: 1958.

41. See L.W. Martin, "The Market for Strategic Ideas in Britain: The Sandys Era", *American Political Science Review*, 56/1, March, 1962, pp. 23-41.

42. Cmnd. 1936, *Statement on Defence*: 1963.

43. Cmnd. 3203, *Statement on the Defence Estimates*: 1967.

44. Cmnd. 4290, *Statement on the Defence Estimates:* 1970.

45. Cmnd. 4641, *Government Organization for Defence Procurement and Civil Aerospace.*

46. See L.W. Martin, "The Long Recessional", *Adelphi*, No. 61 (London: ISS, 1969).

47. For an analysis of the implications of membership of the EEC on British defence policy see J. Baylis, "The Defence Implications of British membership of the EEC", *The Royal Air Forces Quarterly*, Spring 1974, and J.C. Garnett, "European Security and an Enlarged Community, in *The Defence of Western Europe* (London: Macmillan, 1974).

48. The main achievement of the Eurogroup so far has been the production of the three-part European Defence Improvement Programme (EDIP) consisting of a special five-year contribution to NATO infrastructure funds, a programme for improvements to national forces not previously planned, and mutual assistance in the provision of transport aircraft to Turkey by Germany. In 1972 also, Britain joined the multilateral organization FINABEL, in which Army Chiefs of Staff of seven Western European countries meet to discuss possibilities for harmonizing tactics, logistics and training. See Cmnd. 5231, *Statement on the Defence Estimates*: 1973.

49. See D. Greenwood, *Budgeting for Defence* (London: RUSI, 1972).
50. See S.W.B. Menaul, "Britain in Europe: The Defence Aspect," *Defence*, Vol. 2, No. 9., September 1971, p. 29.
51. See W. Schutze, *European Defence Co-operation and NATO* (Paris: The Atlantic Institute, 1970).
52. For a discussion of this see Garnett, op. cit.
53. MRV stands for Multiple Re-entry Vehicle as opposed to MIRV which stands for Multiple Independently targetable Re-entry Vehicle.
54. See *The Twelfth Report from the Expenditure Committee: Nuclear Weapons Programme* (London: HMSO, 1973).
55. See I. Smart, "Future Conditional: The Prospect for Anglo-French Nuclear Co-operation", *Adelphi* No. 78 (London, ISS, 1971).
56. The Labour Government initiated a review of defence policy when they came to power in February 1974 designed to be the "most comprehensive ever undertaken in peacetime". The 1974 Labour manifesto pledged to reduce defence expenditure and subsequent statements by the Secretary of State for Defence, Roy Mason, would suggest the Government is attempting to bring defence spending into line with other NATO countries. See *The Economist*, 20-24 May 1974.

FRENCH DEFENCE POLICY

John Baylis

Speaking at a press conference in October 1966, President de Gaulle highlighted the contrast which had existed in French foreign and defence fields for much of the post-war period between the changes and detours of policies and the essential consistency of the central objectives governing them.[1] Although French policies in the Fourth and Fifth Republics had been constantly adjusted to meet the exigencies of domestic and international circumstances, de Gaulle argued that the major goals of policy-makers had remained the constant search for the independence and sovereignty of France, and the re-establishment of the *grandeur* of the nation. Policies may have been in a continual state of flux but French motivation had remained unchanged.

Although the President was undoubtedly correct in this view, what he failed to tell his audience was that the consistent search for greatness and independence had been (and still largley remains) the source of a fundamental dilemma for French policy-makers for much of the period since 1945. On the one hand, French statesmen have framed their policies in the light of the aspirations and indeed the illusion of "grandeur"[2] only to be confronted, on the other hand, with the stark reality of the declining importance and shrinking resources at the disposal of their nation. In such circumstances it is perhaps not surprising that the achievements of French foreign and defence policy in practice have not always been as great as might have been expected from the exalted visions of statesmen like de Gaulle.

Foreign and Defence Policy

In France for much of the post-war period the relationship between foreign and defence policies has been a particularly close one.[3] For leaders of the Fourth Republic until 1958 and more particularly, the Fifth Republic since 1958, defence policy has been seen as one of, if not the, most important instrument to achieve the objectives of French foreign policy. Military forces have been envisaged by successive French governments not only as a means of re-establishing France's prestige and status in Europe and the world as a whole, but also increasingly as a symbol of the nation's independence of both allies and enemies alike.

Nowhere has this been more true than in the development of nuclear weapons in France. Even before France's first atomic explosion in

1960, supporters of the military nuclear programme in both the Fourth and the Fifth Republics saw nuclear weapons as an important instrument both to enhance the nation's political status and her military capability. There was, however, a major difference in interpretation between the two Republics on the role that nuclear weapons were designed to perform. For the leaders of the Fourth Republic, atomic weapons were seen as providing support for French policy within the existing framework of the North Atlantic Treaty Organization. It was envisaged that nuclear weapons could provide a base for a more independent national policy and that they could enhance France's standing and prestige but in both cases this was to be within the Atlantic Alliance. For de Gaulle, however, the development of atomic armaments were designed primarily to support "his independent foreign policies which sought to change the European and international system and France's role in it".[4] The *force de frappe* was seen as a tool which could be used to pursue the President's broader foreign policy objectives which were much "bolder and more grandly conceived than those of French leaders before 1958".[5] These bolder objectives are summarized by Wilfred L. Kohl as being

> the restoration of French grandeur through the achievement of a global role for France and — so far as possible — coequal status with the United States and Great Britain; the subordination of West Germany to France and the preservation of French leadership in Western Europe; reunification of the two halves of the European continent in a loose association of states 'from the Atlantic to the Urals', and an independent role for this 'European' Europe in world politics.[6]

To General de Gaulle, nuclear weapons were more important from a diplomatic than a strategic angle. Such weapons were seen as a "jeton de presence" among the superpowers of the world.[7] They were a *force de persuasion* which would enable the voice of france to be heard and which would secure a seat for France at the bargaining table with the other Great Powers.[8] The identification of France with other members of the select nuclear club concealed the enormous disparity between the members in terms of military strength while at the same time emphasizing the qualitative superiority of France over other non-nuclear states which justified her presence in the negotiations in which the major problems of mankind were discussed.

The policy of re-establishing France to her "rightful" position in international affairs also involved the search for equality of status within the Atlantic Alliance with the other two nuclear powers, the United States and Great Britain. To gain such equality, de Gaulle, like the later leaders of the Fourth Republic, realized that France required a nuclear capability similar to that of the Anglo-Saxon states. To achieve this objective the French President (again like his predecessors) was not averse to entering into collaboration with the United States.[9] Consequently with the amendment to the McMahon Act in 1958 which gave preferential treatment to Great Britain, the authorities in Paris sought similar treatment for France. De Gaulle, however, was to find that nuclear sharing was something that the American Government was only prepared to countenance with its closest of allies, Great Britain. On a number of occasions when the prospects of co-operation seemed good, American Congressional opposition prevented agreement. In July 1958 after John Foster Dulles' visit to Paris, a promise was given of American help in the building of a submarine reactor. The offer, however, had to be withdrawn after objections from the Joint Congressional Committee on Atomic Energy. Again in 1959 negotiations between French and American firms to produce a French Intermediate Range Ballistic Missile were cut short by an agreement between the State and Defence Departments to prohibit all co-operation between the firms involved. Similarly in 1962 when Secretary of Defence Robert McNamara and General Maxwell Taylor, Chairman of the Joint Chiefs of Staff, recommended a sharing of atomic information with France after discussions with Pierre Messmer, the French Minister of the Armed Forces, the recommendation was not taken up by the American Government.

The disappointment and resentment caused by these American responses served to reinforce de Gaulle's view that France should push ahead with her own nuclear programme. The failure to get American assistance, particularly in light of the preferential treatment given to Britain served likewise to confirm the French view of Anglo-Saxon predominance within the alliance and in so doing strengthened the determination and conviction of Charles de Gaulle to create a national nuclear force which would have as one of its primary purposes the freeing of France from strategic dependence on the United States.[10]

The French nuclear programme also held an important place in French relations with Germany and the determination of both Fourth and Fifth Republican governments to avoid subordination to the new West German state. The question of the military uses of nuclear power was first raised in the French Cabinet on 26 December 1954 at a time when questions of German rearmament loomed large in political circles in France. Mendès-France, who brought the issue to the Cabinet and who at the same time made the decision to launch a secret programme of studies and preparations for a prototype of a nuclear weapon, did so because of his fear of domination by a rearmed Germany within the Western Alliance.

From this period on "the theme of keeping ahead of Germany runs like a thread through subsequent debates on foreign and defence policies"[11] in France. This is well illustrated by the discussions which took place over the establishment of EURATOM. During the negotiations the French insisted on modifying a clause in a draft of the treaty which would have required her to renounce the fabrication of atomic weapons. France could thereby develop a military nuclear capability while the same right was denied to the German Government.[12] The leaders of the Fourth Republic therefore, and later the Fifth Republic, have shown themselves willing to accept partnership with Germany provided that France was the senior member. The best way to achieve this superiority was seen to be through the development of a national nuclear force, the creation of which was denied to Germany.

French partnership with Germany which was symbolized by the French-German treaty of January 1963 together with the possession of a national nuclear force was also the basis of de Gaulle's long-range pan-European design. From 1960, de Gaulle increasingly began to develop his ideal of a "European *entente* from the Atlantic to the Urals", which would enable Europe to solve "its problems peacefully, particularly that of Germany, including reunification, and to attain, inasmuch as it is the main hearth of civilization, a material and human development worthy of its resources and its capacities."[13] To de Gaulle, France was the only European power capable of taking the initiative to achieve the grand design of reuniting the two halves of Europe to enable the Continent to play a major role in world affairs independent of the two superpowers, America and Russia. In the short term before an all-European settlement could be achieved, however, France would be responsible for taking the co-ordination of West European states a stage further. In 1959 therefore, the French President put forward a new initiative in the form of the Fouchet Plan designed to achieve increased West European political co-operation that would have "started Europe along the path toward European confederation."[14] From de Gaulle's point of view, support for a political union of Western European states represented an attempt not only to unify Europe but also to co-ordinate European and more particularly German, foreign and defence policies under the leadership of France and to "achieve a consensus on a more independent European stance in security matters".[15] Again the focal point of this objective was the French nuclear force. As part of his plan, the General argued for the establishment of a European defence arrangement which would be built around the nucleus of the French atomic force. The rather vague implication of this proposal was that French nuclear forces would be placed at the disposal of Western Europe when West European political integration reached a sufficient level. The lack of an indication of French willingness to share control of her nuclear force, however, led to the breakdown of these Fouchet discussions in 1962. France's partners soon realized that de Gaulle's proposals were directed more at enhancing the French position in Western Europe than at developing a new role for Europe in a revised international system.

Despite the failure of the Fouchet Plan, the national nuclear force was again at the heart of a new French initiative in the mid-1960s once again to break away from the *status quo* in Europe represented by the two alliance systems dominated by the Soviet Union and the United States. On this occasion the *force de frappe* served to underpin French withdrawal from the NATO military command in 1966. Once again this move was aimed at replacing the western defence system based on the Atlantic Alliance by a new security framework which would embrace the European continent as a whole. This time the withdrawal from the military structure of NATO was synchronized with a policy of *rapprochement* with the Soviet Union and East European states. The Soviet Government, however, was unreceptive to the new French initiative and in 1968 with the Russian invasion of Czechoslovakia and growing domestic problems at home, de Gaulle began, to a certain extent, to modify the independent line implicit in the policies adopted in 1966.

In both the Fouchet Plan and the design in the mid-sixties for a pan-European security arrangement, the French possession of a nuclear capability was of critical importance. The Force Nucléaire Stratégique (FNS) was perceived as an instrument designed principally to serve the Gaullist policy of re-establishing France as a Great Power in Western Europe and on the international stage as well as securing the independence of the nation from domination by the United States. The pursuit of such a policy, however, involved a fundamental dilemma for French leaders. With the limited resources available to the French leaders, France was not able to play the world role envisaged by those like de Gaulle. Only an independent united Europe could rival the other two superpowers on the same terms. To gain the power base needed to play the role she aspired to, therefore, France would have had to pool her resources with the other European allies and allow herself to become integrated into a unified European political union. In so doing France could then perhaps have been part of a great independent bloc. But in the process the nation would also have lost its independence and also sovereignty so highly valued by French leaders, particularly in the military field. Given her limited national power base, therefore, it was unlikely that France could be both 'great' and 'independent'. Nevertheless the attempt to have it both ways has been very much a characteristic of French foreign and defence policies.

National Control and Defence Integration

The second World War provided contradictory lessons as far as French policy-makers in the post-war period were concerned. On the one hand French liberation by the allies emphasized the efficacy of defence alliances and the need for France to co-operate closely in the military fields with other states if renewed threats to her security materialized. On the other hand the experience of the first part of the century, as well as other events in the Second World War, suggested an alternative interpretation. As Wolf Mendl points out,

> Neither the alliance system before World War I nor the attempt
> to construct a system of collective security between the wars,
> saved France from great suffering and a feeling that she had
> been used as an advance pawn and as a source of manpower in
> terms of the peripheral strategy of the Anglo-American powers.[16]

Such a perception of past experience led naturally to the feeling that in
the last resort France would have to provide for her own security herself. French interests were unlikely to coincide exactly with those of
her allies and in the vital sphere of defence she must retain as great a
degree of self-sufficiency and independence as possible.

The contradiction between these two attitudes has remained at the
heart of French policies towards alliances since 1945. Initially in 1946
the new Premier, Charles de Gaulle, attempted to strengthen French
security *vis-à-vis* Germany and at the same time to re-establish French
independence of Britain and the United States by signing a treaty with
the Soviet Union. Such a demonstration of independence, however,
was short-lived. Increasingly, as relations between the West and Russia
deteriorated, French political, economic and military weakness forced
her to depend more on the Anglo-Saxon states. In 1947 the Dunkirk
Treaty was signed with Great Britain against the possibility of future
German aggression. Similarly in 1948, France joined the Brussels Pact
which, although directed mainly at the Soviet Union, was also, largely
on French initiative, designed once again to forestall potential German
aggressive moves.[17]

With this increased emphasis, however, in French defence policy on
co-operation with allies (an emphasis taken an important stage further
with the signing of the NATO Treaty in April 1949), the defence planners in France increasingly had to face the problem of determining the
degree of integration with allies in the defence field which would give
her the security she needed but which would not be deterimental to the
continuation of national sovereignty and control over defence policy.
The situation was made more complicated for French leaders when the
deterioration of the international situation caused by the Berlin Blockade and the Korean War led the American Government to put pressure
on its allies to accept West German rearmament to reinforce the western
defence effort. Continuing suspicions of Germany caused the French
Government to put forward the so-called Pleven Plan which called for the
creation of a European Defence Community (EDC) in which German
forces would be allowed to form part of a European Army but would
not be under the control of the German Government. For the integra-
tionists in France in particular, the EDC would serve the cause of
European unity and also would enhance French security against
Germany and Russia. From the beginning, however, the plan was

severely criticized by those who saw it as a threat to national sovereignty and on 30 August 1954 the Treaty, which had been put forward by a French Government, was rejected by the French National Assembly. Instead a compromise was accepted on the basis of the British-sponsored Paris Agreements whereby the Western European Union (WEU) was extended to include Germany and Italy. Britain also agreed to station troops permanently on the Continent, in part at least to alleviate French apprehensions of German rearmament.

Although towards the end of the Fourth Republic increasing criticisms were made in France of dependence on the United States in the defence field, particularly after the American refusal to help France in Indo-China prior to Dien Bien Phu and the active hostility at the time of Suez, Fourth Republican governments nevertheless sought to enhance France's political status and military role within the existing framework of the North Atlantic Alliance. The creation of the Fifth Republic under de Gaulle in 1958, however, led to a new twist in French attitudes towards the question of integration or self-sufficiency in the defence field. The fundamental importance of French sovereignty and the need to enhance France's status caused the new President to question the structure of NATO and American domination of the organization. De Gaulle's criticisms came to rest on two important arguments. On the one hand he believed that the launching of the Soviet Sputnik in October 1957 had greatly downgraded the credibility of the American guarantee to Europe. The Soviet capability of attacking the American homeland suggested to de Gaulle that it was increasingly unlikely that an American President would risk the devastation of the United States to save Europe. On the other hand, he also saw the risk which events in the Middle East and the Formosa Straits Crisis had demonstrated, that France might be dragged into a war by the United States. A conflict between the United States and the Soviet Union over which the French Government had no control would almost certainly, de Gaulle argued, escalate into a war in which France was involved regardless of the fact that her vital interests might not be at stake.

The French President's dissatisfaction with the existing structure of NATO led him to send his famous secret memorandum to President Eisenhower and Prime Minister Macmillan in September 1958. In his note to the two leaders, de Gaulle suggested the creation of a new tripartite organization consisting of Britain, France and the United States which would take 'joint decisions' on all global questions affecting their security interests. 'France', de Gaulle argued, 'was ready to resume its historic role in world affairs' alongside the other Great Powers.[18] He also threatened that France's subsequent co-operation in NATO would depend on the acceptance of his demands for the tripartite organization.

A certain amount of evidence exists to suggest that de Gaulle's directorate proposal was a tactical ploy on his part which, once rejected by Great Britain and the United States, could then be used to justify his subsequent actions in progressively reducing France's participation in NATO.[19] Whether or not the General had a detailed blueprint for action is difficult to establish. He does, however, point out in his memoirs that he did not expect a favourable response to his proposal and that the memorandum was the key to his plan for a step-by-step disengagement from NATO, "an objective already clearly formulated in 1958".[20]

Subsequent French policies towards NATO would also seem to reinforce this view. In December 1958, following what he considered to be the unstatisfactory response by the United States to his proposals, de Gaulle announced his unwillingness to integrate French tactical aircraft into a European air defence command.[21] This was followed in March 1959 by the withdrawal of French naval units which had previously been committed to NATO's Mediterranean command. The most far-reaching attack so far against the organization, however, was delivered by the President in a speech at the Ecole Militaire on 3 November 1959 when he refused the NATO tenet of 'integration' and emphasized his sacred principle of national defence. "It is necessary", he argued, "that the defence of France be French. . . the concept of war or even of a battle in which France would no longer be herself and would not act on her own accord, following her own goals, such a concept cannot be admitted." France could combine her defence with that of other countries and associate her strategy with others, but integration could not be accepted: "each country must play its own part."[22]

The ideas expressed in this speech in 1959 have remained at the core of French defence policy ever since. In 1966, with the perception of a much-reduced Soviet threat, de Gaulle considered it opportune to take his policy to its logical conclusion and withdraw from the military structure of NATO. The subsequent movement towards neutralism designed to emphasize French independence in foreign policy, however, had to be curtailed to a certain extent due to the combination of domestic and international events of 1968-69. The Soviet invasion of Czechoslovakia in 1968 and the domestic and monetary crisis of 1969 caused de Gaulle to temper his aspirations and in part to reappraise his attitudes towards French relations with the other NATO members. Just before the General left office there were signs that France was once again interested in closer joint nuclear and military co-operation within the Alliance. The high water mark of French interest in further co-operation came in March 1969 in a lecture given by the French Chief of Staff, General Michel Fourquet at the Institute of Higher Defence Studies.[23] In his speech General Fourquet argued that the task of containing an enemy attack short of resorting to tactical or strategic nuclear weapons could be accomplished more effectively and efficiently through alliance action rather than through discrete attempts by the several states themselves. The implication of what Fourquet was saying seemed to be that given her limited resources France could only defend herself particularly at the conventional level through a much greater degree of co-operation with her allies than had been characteristic of French defence policy since 1966.

Since General Fourquet delivered his lecture in 1969, however, despite the change in emphasis recommended by the Chief of Staff, more recent writings on French defence policy seem to suggest that there has been to a certain extent another cooling off in French interest in greater alliance co-operation in military affairs.[24] Greater domestic and international stability has allowed the Pompidou and d'Estaing governments to pursue what is still largely an independent foreign and defence policy.[25]

The Relationship between Conventional and Nuclear Forces

A problem closely related to the debate between defence integration or national control and one equally affected by the central dilemma facing policy-makers has been that of the relative balance between conventional and nuclear forces in French defence policy thinking.

For most of the Fourth Republic operations overseas and NATO commitments focused attention on the importance of essentially conventional forces. France's colonial wars and pressure from the United States for rearmament in the early 1950s to counter the large Soviet armies in Eastern Europe meant that the limited resources available were spent in particular on attempting to provide the conventional manpower and equipment so badly needed. The Army, as it had in the past, remained the most important of the three Services. The great debate in French defence circles in this period concentrated on whether the nation's interests would be best served by a mass army of citizen soldiers or a highly trained professional force. The debate was resolved during this period, as it had been traditionally, in favour of a citizen army. Despite the development of an atomic energy programme in France from 1946,[26] little thought was given to the production of nuclear weapons until the mid-fifties. In the first seven years after the war the only interest which French defence planners had in atomic weapons was in the protection which would be needed against such devices on the field of battle. For this purpose the structure and tactics of the army were adapted to the defence against an enemy employing such weapons. Concentration was therefore centred on the need for light divisions, battlegroups and the easy dispersion of forces and little attention was given to how French forces themselves would utilize atomic armaments.

Despite this emphasis, however, in the defence policies of the governments of the Fourth Republic on conventional forces, the continuing desire to re-establish France to what was considered to be her rightful position in the world in large part contributed to a growing campaign throughout the 1950s, in particular by a small group within the

Commissariat a l'Energie Atomique (CEA) for the development of French nuclear weapons. The main emphasis of the CEA from its inception by de Gaulle in 1946 was to create a nuclear establishment for essentially peaceful purposes. Increasingly from 1954, however, pressure from a small group of dedicated administrator-technocrats, politicians and military officers in the CEA pushed successive governments to produce nuclear weapons.[27] Partly due to the pressure of this group the question of a French nuclear programme for military purposes was first raised at Cabinet level on 26 December 1954 when an inter-ministerial committee was covened by Premier Mendès-France to study the question of the military applications of atomic energy. With the rather inconclusive results of the Committee, pressure on the government was increased, especially after the humiliations of Indo-China and the Suez affair, by public campaigns, particularly by men like Colonel Ailleret and General Ely.

Colonel Charles Ailleret, who held the post of *commandant des armes spéciales,* conducted a number of studies on atomic weapons with a small group of officers from 1952 onwards. During the 1950s Ailleret was to become one of the major military protagonists for nuclear weapons. He conducted his campaign in numerous articles arguing his case not from firm notions of nuclear strategy but rather on the basis of a narrow view of their military advantages as the most modern weapons.[28] His main contention was that atomic weapons were both cheaper than conventional explosives and also far more effective. Although he had no clear thesis about their strategic and political uses, he did anticipate de Gaulle's later views in his recognition that nuclear weapons would allow France "to assert herself with much more weight in alliances."[29]

Another influential advocate of French nuclear development was General Paul Ely who returned to France in 1956 from Indo-China to become *chef d'état – major-général des armées.*[30] In this capacity he established a committee to study nuclear weapons and their strategic implications. On the basis of these studies General Ely was the first to advocate the idea of a *force de frappe* (strike force) which was to become so famous under de Gaulle. To Ely, however, the notion of a *force de frappe* was a broad military concept which would include both conventional and nuclear forces. In an article he published in 1957 he argued that France should have the capability to operate anywhere in the world to meet different kinds of threats at different kinds of level.[31] To achieve this "flexible response", Ely argued that France required a spectrum of forces (including atomic weapons) to meet varying kinds of conflict. As far as he was concerned, however, such a force had to be placed "fully within the framework of NATO."[32]

The gathering momentum of these pressures on successive governments to initiate a military nuclear programme finally led to the decision by the Defence Minister, Bourgès-Manoury, to create a nuclear force in the spring of 1957. This was followed by the announcement in April 1958 by Premier Felix Gaillard that 1960 had been set as the target date for the first French atomic test. The decision therefore to create a nuclear force was taken by a government of the Fourth Republic. With the Algerian crisis, however, it was left to the leaders of the Fifth Republic to execute the policy laid down by their predecessors. On assuming power de Gaulle immediately accelerated the atomic weapons programme and in 1959 unveiled his plans for a *force de frappe* which he envisaged as an "advanced instrument representing an enormous potential of massive destruction capable of instant use anywhere on the globe without preliminary mobilization."[33]

Despite the relatively greater emphasis, however, on nuclear technology in the first years of the Fifth Republic, the continuation of the Algerian conflict meant that French defence policy had to retain a balance between conventional and nuclear forces. Reflecting this need the Minister of National Defence declared in 1958 that the possession of of nuclear weapons and defence against subversion had equal priority. Thus in his first five year plan (*loi-programme*) for defence, between 1960 and 1965, de Gaulle attempted a complete reorganization of national defence which would secure the necessary balance between conventional and nuclear forces.[34] The French Armed Forces were organized in three tiers: the "Force Nucléaire Stratégique" (FNS); the "Forces d'Intervention", which were renamed the "Forces de Manoeuvre" in 1964; and the "Defense Operationnelle du Territoire" (DOT). According to the first *loi-programme,* the Forces de Manoeuvre were designed for the defence of French frontiers, for NATO operations and also for the defence of the French Community and French interests overseas. It was envisaged that they would consist of five mechanized divisions and one light division ("d'intervention outre mer") together with the necessary naval and air forces. The DOT on the other hand were to consist of 100 regiments to be used essentially for internal defence.

With the end of the Algerian War and the increasing economic strains facing France, the attempt to create such a wide spectrum of military forces became more difficult. De Gaulle's dilemma was that to re-establish herself as a world power France had to possess both the conventional forces to intervene overseas and the atomic forces to gain membership of the nuclear club. Economic realities, however, dictated that France could not have both, at least on the ambitious scale laid down in 1960. In such circumstances, de Gaulle had little doubt that French objectives of independence and *grandeur* could best be served through the continuation of the nuclear programme, even if this meant scaling down conventional forces.

Although therefore the Government claimed with some justice that its defence plans in 1960[35] were an attempt to achieve a balance between conventional and nuclear forces, by the start of the second *loi-*

programme in 1965 a growing imbalance was in fact clearly emerging. This second five-year plan envisaged only three fully armoured divisions equipped with AMX tanks and two equipped with 'materials moins recent' for the 'Forces de Manoeuvre' by the end of the decade. It also reduced the proposed size of the DOT forces from 100 regiments to 25 regiments and 1 alpine brigade. In terms of resource allocation the declining importance of conventional forces was clearly demonstrated by the significant reduction in spending on conventional equipment.. Under the second *loi-programme* 377 million francs disappeared from the army estimates. There was also a projected reduction of manpower in the armed forces from 1,009,000 in January 1963 to the goal of 700,000 during the late sixties. The ground forces in particular were to be cut back and national service was gradually to become more selective, thus reflecting the radical change from a mass citizen army to a highly trained professional force.[36]

It had now become obvious that the FNS was very much the central feature of French defence policy and that other elements would be sacrificed if necessary to retain its position. From 1965 onwards conventional forces in French defence policy therefore were viewed increasingly in the role of support for, and defence of, the FNS. In his study of French defence policy, Mendl argues that "after 1970 the principal mission of the navy will be to protect the nuclear submarines; air defence will cover the strategic nuclear force; the "Forces de Manoeuvre" and the forces of the interior will defend the SSBS."[37]

Strategic Thinking in France

The changing balance between conventional and nuclear forces is both a reflection of, and reflected in, the constant adjustments which have taken place in French strategic thinking in the post-war period.[38] For much of the Fourth Republic the focus of the strategic debate centred on the two preoccupations of European defence and counter-insurgent campaigns overseas. In the European theatre, French conventional forces were seen as playing their part in an overall allied strategy. French forces, like those of her allies, were designed to identify Soviet aggression and delay Soviet advances into Western Europe. During the 'pause' resulting from conventional operations it was hoped that time would be gained both for negotiations to take place and for the decisions to be made, if necessary, to use nuclear weapons.

Besides these European operations, French forces were also seen as having the important role overseas of countering insurgent activity in her colonies. The perceived importance and the continuing necessity during the 1940s and 1950s of fighting subversive campaigns led to the development in French defence circles of what became known as *la Guerre Revolutionnaire* doctrine.[39] The experiences both of Indo-China and Algeria led to a growing interest amongst strategic planners in the writings of Mao Tse-tung and the attempt to produce a coherent theory of counter-revolutionary warfare to defeat France's enemies. To many political and military leaders in France the main threat to French, and indeed Western security, emanated from the indirect strategy adopted by the Communist states in Africa, Asia and Latin America. The belief in the global significance of the campaign in Algeria, in particular, led to priority being given in French defence policy in the last years of the Fourth Republic and the early years of the Fifth Republic to the concentration of military resources on countering this perceived threat. *Guerre Revolutionnaire* therefore in some ways became the dominant theme in French strategic thinking during this period.[40]

Growing disillusionment, however, with the American guarantee to Western Europe and alliance strategy together with the humiliations emanating from the failures of French counter-revolutionary operations led to a gradual reappraisal of strategic thinking.[41] The conventional and counter-revolutionary elements of French strategy began to give way to a new strand in politico-military thinking as the French military nuclear programme gathered momentum from the mid-fifties onwards. Defence planners increasingly emphasized the revolutionary impact of nuclear weapons in introducing a new dimension into warfare. The focus of attention gradually moved away from the need to provide large conventional forces capable of fighting in the European theatre and subversive campaigns overseas. Instead greater stress was laid on the importance of preventing wars from breaking out. Nuclear deterrence rather than conventional and unconventional defence now gradually emerged to hold the centre of the strategic stage in France.

Although French literature on strategic matters was overshadowed to a large extent, both in terms of 'breadth and sophistication' by the American writings on the subject, a number of books and articles on the French nuclear force began to appear from 1963-4 onwards. Pierre Gallois and André Beaufre in particular entered the strategic debate with various works which provided theoretical justification for the national nuclear deterrent.

In his writings General Gallois argued that the establishment of a 'balance of terror' between the superpowers meant that the credibility of the US guarantee to defend Europe had been greatly reduced.[41] It was therefore axiomatic that middle powers, such as France, should not rely on military alliances and should possess their own nuclear forces to enhance their national security. To Gallois nuclear proliferation was inevitable, and indeed desirable, since the greater the number of states possessing nuclear weapons, the greater the degree of international stability through deterrence. In contrast to Gallois' rather extreme and dogmatic analysis, André Beaufre's writings have a subtlety and sophistication which has put him in the front rank of strategic thinkers.[42] In order to avoid the danger of international instability which national nuclear forces may create, Beaufre, unlike Gallois, argued that alliances were necessary. To General Beaufre the decision to use nuclear forces must remain in national hands, but they must be 'co-ordinated' within some form of alliance framework.

Similar but not identical views were put forward by another leading French writer on nuclear strategy, Raymond Aron.[43] Like Beaufre, Aron expressed his opposition to the Anglo-Saxon monopoly of nuclear weapons and the utility of French nuclear weapons. Aron, however, was opposed to the notion of a strictly national deterrent and argued instead for some form of European nuclear force. For Aron, as for General Stehlin, a former air force chief of staff, the nationalistic framework in which de Gaulle developed his *force de frappe* was something to regret.[44] To both it would have been far preferable had the President taken steps to promote a European deterrent with French nuclear armaments as the nucleus of the force.

Although not as extreme, de Gaulle's views however, in many ways had more in common with Gallois than with either Beaufre or Aron. In 1964 de Gaulle spelled out the concept of 'proportional deterrence' which has remained in large part at the centre of French strategic doctrine ever since. The General maintained that it was not necessary to match the nuclear capabilities of the United States and USSR for he argued, '. . . once reaching a certain nuclear capability . . . the proportion of respective means has no absolute value.'[45] What was important was to have the capability to survive an enemy first strike and to inflict an unacceptable degree of damage on an aggressor by way of retaliation. 'The deterrent exists', de Gaulle said, "provided that one has the means to wound the possible aggressor mortally, that one is very determined to do it and that the aggressor is convinced of it."[46]

In the early days of the development of the French nuclear force, nuclear strategy was based essentially on the notion of massive retaliation. Once serious aggression by an opponent had been identified the instantaneous and total use of France's national nuclear force would follow against the adversary's cities. With the development of tactical nuclear weapons, French strategic doctrine underwent a slight modification. It was felt that conventional forces backed by the threatened, or actual use, of tactical nuclear weapons might cause the enemy to pause and consider the consequences of his actions. Despite the delay, however, between the identification of aggression and the use of strategic weapons, it was thought that the pause could only be of a limited duration. France would then be forced to reply with her whole nuclear arsenal.

In essence French strategic thinking was to remain largely predicated on this modified concept of massive retaliation until the changes introduced by General Fourquet in March 1969.[47] In his speech at the Institute of Higher National Defence Studies, the new French Chief of Staff of the Armed Forces went out of his way specifically to reject not only the 'all or nothing' doctrine of massive retaliation but also the idea of meeting aggression at all levels with the appropriate force implicit in the American doctrine of flexible response. Fourquet argued instead for a strategy of "graduated deterrence" designed to raise the threshold of nuclear response higher than that of massive retaliation but not as high as that of flexible response.[48] The Chief of Staff saw graduated deterrence as a way of overcoming the 'suicide or surrender' choice of massive retaliation and retaining the element of deterrence which he considered had been downgraded in the doctrine of flexible response. Conventional and tactical nuclear weapons were seen as increasing the number of options available to decision-makers and the threat or even the actual use of the latter would act as a potent deterrent to further escalation. According to General Fourquet's analysis, France's limited conventional forces would be used to test the enemy's intentions. If the test proved positive in the sense that a major threat was identified, French tactical nuclear weapons would then be used both to slow down the enemy's advance and to communicate the seriousness of the French government's resolve to fight a nuclear war if necessary. In so doing it was hoped that time would be bought both for the enemy to reconsider the implications of his aggression and also for the decision to use the nation's strategic nuclear forces should it become necessary.

General Fourquet's address also significantly modified French strategic doctrine in another way. During the mid-1960s the movement for greater independence in French defence policy and the attempt to re-establish French status in the world led to the adoption of the strategy of *Tous Azimuths*. According to this doctrine which was introduced largely on the initiative of Fourquet's predecessor, General Ailleret, France was to prepare for attack from any quarter.[49] In an article in December 1967, General Ailleret argued that the threat from Russia had virtually disappeared and that it was difficult to foresee the nature of conflicts which would occur in the future and the coalition of states which might be involved. Because of this uncertainty present alliances were unlikely to be of much value.[50] His conclusion was that France should concentrate on building a complete independent defence system which would include "a significant quantity. . . of megaton ballistic missiles, with a world-wide range." Ailleret argued that such a system would be aimed at all points of the globe rather than directed against any one power in particular. In so doing France would be able "to wield the maximum power afforded by its national resources."[51]

This rather ambitious doctrine, emphasizing French independence and power, however, foundered on the rocks of the Czech invasion and the domestic problems of 1968. The increased anxiety over Soviet intentions and the economic crisis were reflected in Fourquet's implicit abandonment of the concept of *Tous Azimuths*. In his speech Fourquet emphasised the need to meet a potential invasion from the East which would require the co-ordination of allied armies. Although Fourquet reiterated the traditional arguments against integration and the importance of sovereign control of defence, the trend of his argument suggested that he believed that France would have to collaborate with her NATO allies in an emergency. It would seem therefore that the renewed perception of the possibility of a future Soviet threat and the need to reallocate resources away from defence to other areas of domestic society, forced the realization on French defence planners, that the degree of independence inherent in the 'Tous Azimuths' doctrine was over-ambitious. French strategic doctrine had to be brought back more into line with the realities of France's position in the world.

Commitments and Capabilities

The changing balance between conventional and nuclear forces reflected in the evolution of French strategic doctrine has quite naturally had a significant impact on the ability of France to perform her defence commitments.

During the 1940s and 1950s the relative emphasis on conventional forces enabled French governments to use military force in an attempt to re-establish control over parts of their empire lost during the Second World War. Operations were mounted in Syria, Indo-China, Madagascar and later Algeria to reassert French authority. Even the Suez expedition in the autumn of 1956 can be viewed as part of the French colonial campaigns which dominated French defence policy until 1962. Egypt was regarded in France as the primary foreign base supporting the rebels in Algeria. It was hoped that the successful invasion of Suez would secure the two objectives of cutting off supplies to the rebels and humiliating Nasser which would result in a significant moral defeat for the nationalists.

The failure of French military forces in her colonial campaigns and the humiliation which her defeats caused contributed, in large part, to the movement away from reliance on conventional forces to greater emphasis on nuclear weapons in defence policy. As in Britain, Suez in particular contributed to the switch in priorities in favour of atomic weapons. As one commentator has put it, "Militarily, the experience of Suez did not support the rationale of a weak nuclear force, but politically and emotionally it strengthened its appeal, particularly as France was shaken less by the Russian menace than by a sense of being deserted by her American ally."[52]

Despite the gradual downgrading of conventional forces in the 1960s, to maintain the desired pre-eminence of nuclear forces France has not correspondingly reduced the scale of her world-wide commitments to bring them into line with her reduced capabilities. To the contrary the 1972 White Paper speaks in traditionally expansive terms.

To this. . . search for a European balance founded on real commitments defined with precision is added. . . another orientation marked by our effort of co-operation. It is a matter here to support, in case of emergency by military aid, the independence of certain states of Francophone culture. . . and to participate in safeguarding and in restoring peace in the Mediterranean basin.[53]

In contrast to her rather modest capabilities therefore, French aspirations would seem to remain global, based on the continuing vision of France as an independent world power.

In reality the size of her intervention forces suggest that France could not be expected to sustain a lengthy or a large-scale operation abroad. The dilemma can be seen clearly from French overseas operations in the last ten years. Despite the belief that France has a major role to play in Black Africa, the only interventions France has been capable of mounting have been strictly limited ones.[54] In Gabon in 1964, French forces were used in a small 'quick-fix' action to reinstate the deposed government after a surprise *coup d'état*[55] Operations in Chad likewise in the early period of the Pompidou Administration revealed both the limited capability of French conventional forces and the degree of public opposition at home which can be expected in similar operations in the future. As one writer has put it, "Questions persist. . . about France's material capacity to support the role assigned to its military forces."

Conclusion

The priority given to the FNS and the imbalance between French aspirations to perform world-wide commitments and her limited conventional capability remains, and is likely to remain for some time to come, an important characteristic of French defence policy.

Recognition of the need to eradicate some of the main weaknesses of French conventional strength was seen in the third *loi-programme* (1971-75) and in the two military plans that span the decade up to 1985.[56] An examination of French defence planning for this period, initiated by the Pompidou administration, reveals the determination of French defence officials to allocate resources for the improvement of the armed forces in general and in particular the Navy. The new President, Giscard D'Estaing, also promised a reappraisal of France's conventional strength as part of the defence review initiated in the summer of 1974.[57] Much of the modernization promised, however, is designed to improve the quality of conventional forces which support the deterrent force. Increased emphasis is being placed in French defence policy on the need to achieve a greater degree of integration between conventional and nuclear forces while at the same time qualitatively strengthening the deterrent components of the French military establishment. The French ballistic missile submarine fleet, for example, will be expanded to five vessels by 1980[58] and the range of its missiles will be substantially increased. Similar expansion is planned for the Intermediate Range Ballistic Missile force on the Plateau d'Albion in southern France and it is hoped to fit the force with multiple warheads sometime after 1980. Plans also exist for the improvement and expansion of the French tactical nuclear force. In particular, France's battlefield Pluton system became operational in 1974 with the intention eventually of equipping six regiments with the missile mounted on a modified chassis from the AMX-30 tank.[59] Despite the President's professed concern over the state of France's conventional forces, the 1974 Defence Budget, representing in fact an 11 per cent increase on the year before, concentrated attention on the strategic nuclear programme which once again received a disproportionately large share of the available resources.[60]

It would be wrong therefore to conclude from the changes which have occurred in the post-Czechoslovakia period that a major reversal of French defence thinking has taken place. Although a more pragmatic and realistic approach to defence has been adopted particularly when compared with the more 'heady' days of *Tous Azimuths,* the search for *grandeur* and independence still remain important elements in French defence policy. Contemporary strategic doctrine in France still appears to rule out too close a co-operation with allied forces on the grounds that "national control is needed to test the intentions of an aggressor as quickly as possible."[61]

There is no doubt that the political atmosphere between NATO and France has improved a great deal in recent years. Since 1969 and Fourquet's speech, France has adopted a policy of co-operation 'a là carte', or selective co-operation, with NATO countries. France has participated in naval exercises in the Mediterranean and has undertaken talks with NATO on the role of France in a nuclear conflict in Europe. Despite such illustrations of increased co-operation, however, examples of collaboration of this sort are in general strictly limited. Negotiations on France's participation in a reformulated NATO communication system apparently did not progress particularly satisfactorily. France also continues to ignore both the NATO Nuclear Defence Affairs Committee and Nuclear Planning Group as well as the informal meetings of the Eurogroup. Similarly there are still important differences between current French strategic thinking and that of other NATO countries. French strategists tend to feel that the nuclear threshold set by NATO is too high to maintain a credible deterrent posture in Europe.

On the basis of the evidence which exists therefore, one leading authority on French defence policy has maintained that "given the present French attitude, it is difficult to conclude that NATO and

French co-operation on the critical questions of nuclear weapons — or of conventional forces for that matter — have advanced very much beyond the more hostile period of the late 1960s."[62] Such a view would seem to be confirmed by the policies of the new French President, Giscard D'Estaing, which despite the change in style contain many of the hallmarks of traditional French policy. One example of this is the interest being shown in defence circles in France in the establishment of a new West European defence pact based on the West European Union (WEU) concept.[63] The French interest in revitalising the WEU was brought out clearly in a speech made by Foreign Minister Jobert to the WEU Parliamentary Assembly in November 1973.[64] Jobert proposed that the WEU should become the forum for future discussions on Europe's defence arrangements. Again in July 1974 the new French Foreign Minister, Sauvagnargues, in his first speech before the foreign affairs commission of the National Assembly, emphasized the importance of French independence of NATO and by implication his support of the WEU idea. French government officials were also said to be sounding out Common Market partners in August 1974 on the need for a West European Defence Council which would meet regularly and discuss security problems common to all members.[65]

As far as the French are concerned the WEU concept would seem to have a number of distinct advantages. It is an entirely European institution, independent of the USA, and groups together the leading member countries of the Nine. The WEU is seen as a much better forum than the Eurogroup within NATO. In this sense once again the French are taking the lead in attempting to create a European defence organization outside NATO independent of the United States which would form the core of the larger designs of the new French President for European Union. The WEU concept would also ensure another important function in French foreign and defence policy; that of co-ordinating French policies with those of Germany while at the same time retaining French superiority in the military field. The original Protocol establishing the WEU placed a major limitation on West German freedom in military affairs through the German undertaking not to manufacture nuclear weapons.

Contemporary French interest in the WEU concept and the new President's determination to press for European Union by 1980 would seem to confirm the continuing importance in French foreign and defence policy of the notions of independence and greatness. Despite the various modifications forced on French defence planners by the dilemmas created by the incompatability between over-ambitious aspirations and the nation's limited resources,[66] the aim of pursuing these two objectives as far as possible still appears to be an important motivating force in French defence policy. As such, although more pragmatic and realistic than in the mid-sixties, French policy in the defence field is likely to be faced in the future by much the same kind of dilemma as they have faced in the past. The problem is likely to remain for some time to come of how much *grandeur*, and how much independence, in the defence field is compatible with domestic stability and national security? As in the past, the degree to which these two objectives are pursued is likely to be determined both by internal and external events.[67]

The French dilemma, however, runs deeper than this. The problem is not just one of the incompatability between the means available and the objectives sought. There is also a fundamental contradiction between the objectives themselves which is likely to cause increasing problems for French leaders in the future. Although from the French viewpoint the notion of *grandeur* involves in part national independence it also involves the creation of a strong political, economic and particularly military power base. Without such a national power base 'greatness', at least in terms of the other superpowers, would require the pooling of Western European resources as a whole in some form of European Union. The decision of the new President to press for such a European Union by 1980 and a European defence organization, while at the same time increasing expenditure on national defence policy, suggests that sooner or later a more fundamental choice will have to be made between the relative importance of the two objectives. So far, because of the relatively small incremental steps which have been taken towards European integration, successive French governments to a certain extent have been able to obfuscate the difficulties of achieving 'greatness' while at the same time remaining independent. If the more important decisions of European integration are ever made, the French will have to decide whether to lose a large part of their sovereignty in the hope of achieving 'greatness' as part of a European block or to retain their national independence and forgo the opportunity of *grandeur* which membership of a European Union could bring. The only solution from the French point of view may be the projection of their national objectives to the supra-national level; France at the core of a European superstate pursuing policies independent of both the Soviet Union and United States.

Notes

1. "In the world as it is", de Gaulle said, "people sometimes feign surprise over the so-called changes and detours of France's actions. And there are even those who have spoken of Machiavellianism. Well, I believe that while the circumstances are changing around us, in truth there is nothing more constant than France's policy. For this policy, throughout the extremely varied vicissitudes of our times and our world – this policy's essential goal is that France be and remain an independent nation." Quoted by Roy C. Macridis in "French Foreign Policy", in Macridis (ed.), *Foreign Policy in World Politics* (New Jersey: Prentice-Hall, 1967), p. 74.
2. The policy of 'grandeur' was thought of partly in terms of independence but also in terms of the provision of the material foundations not necessarily to match the other superpowers but certainly to rival them.

3. In his study of French military policy Wolf Mendl describes "defence policy as the function of foreign policy". See W. Mendl, *Deterrence and Persuasion: French Nuclear Armament in the Context of National Policy 1945-69* (London: Faber and Faber, 1970), p. 18.

4. W.L. Kohl, *French Nuclear Diplomacy* (Princeton: Princeton University Press, 1971), p. 6.

5. Ibid., p. 6.

6. Ibid., pp. 6-7.

7. *Notes et Etudes Documentaires,* No. 3343 (6 December 1966) The English translation is in *Survival,* January 1968, pp. 12-16.

8. W. Mendl, op. cit.

9. Mendl argues that "the possibility of American assistance was continually evoked in the years right up to and immediately after the first atomic explosion." Ibid., p. 57.

10. The United States had also entered into agreements with Canada, West Germany, the Netherlands, Turkey and Greece providing them with some nuclear information regarding the training of personnel and the stockpiling of nuclear explosives in these countries. A similar treaty was not signed with the French until 1961.

11. Mendl, op. cit., p. 33.

12. Ibid., pp. 31-5.

13. Kohl, op. cit., p. 133.

14. Ibid., p. 268.

15. Ibid.

16. Mendl, op. cit., p. 70.

17. As Mendl says, 'Throughout the period since the end of the war, one might well ask, "Whom were the French watching on the Rhine — the Russians or the Germans?" Ibid., p. 35.

18. See D. Schoenbrum, *The Three Lives of Charles de Gaulle,* (New York: Atheneum, 1965), pp. 295-300.

19. For the debate about the different interpretations of de Gaulle's Tripartite Proposal see Kohl, op. cit., pp. 74-81.

20. De Gaulle, *Memoires d'espoir: Le Renouveau, 1958-62* (Paris: Plon, 1970), pp. 214-15.

21. Although the French subsequently encouraged the belief that the US did not reply to the 1958 memorandum, Eisenhower did in fact respond on 20 October 1958. See footnote 51 in Kohl, op. cit., p. 73.

22. Charles de Gaulle, speech at Centre des Hautes Etudes Militaires, 3 November 1959, p. 1.

23. "Emploi des differents systèmes de forces dans le cadre de la strategic de dissuasion," *Revue de défense nationale,* May 1969, pp. 757-67; a translation of the article appears in *Survival,* July 1969, pp. 206-11.

24. See Kolodziej, op. cit., p. 30. This is seen particularly in French attitudes towards MBFR and ESC. See Kolodziej, "French Military Doctrine", in F.B. Horton, A.C. Rogerson and E.L. Warner Ed., *Comparative Defense Policy* (Johns Hopkins University Press Baltimore, 1974).

25. See *The Financial Times,* 18 January 1973.

26. The nuclear programme was initiated by an ordinance issued by the Provisional Government establishing the Commissariat à l'Energie Atomique (CEA) on 18 October 1945. French scientists such as Henri Becquerel had played an important role in early atomic research prior to 1900.

27. For a discussion of the effectiveness of this pressure group see Kohl, op. cit., p. 7.

28. For a discussion of Ailleret's role in the campaign for nuclear weapons see Kohl, ibid., pp. 21-2, 30-32.

29. Ailleret, *L'Aventure atomique francaise* (Paris: Grasset, 1968), p. 114. Quoted in Kohl, Ibid., p. 31.

30. Kohl, ibid., pp. 44-7.

31. General Ely, 'Notre Politique militaire,' *Revue de défense nationale,* July 1957, pp. 1040-47.
32. Ibid.
33. General Lavand, quoted in *Le Monde,* 18 August 1960.
34. There was, however, an increased emphasis on nuclear weapons in the *loi-programme* and the new policy had to survive two censure motions in the National Assembly before coming into effect.
35. For a criticism of the balance of conventional forces and nuclear weapons even in 1960 see Bosquet's article in *L'Express,* 25 February 1960.
36. The National Service Law of 9 July 1965 broke the institution of universal military service which had lasted since the "Great Revolution".
37. Mendl, "French Defence Policy", *Survival,* April 1968. Mendl also quotes a Gaullist deputy, M. Jean-Paul Palewski who in the debate on the military budget for 1968 claimed that "by 1980 the number of squadrons, including transport aircraft, at the disposal of the air force will equal those of the Swiss air force today."
38. For an excellent analysis of French strategic thinking see Kolodziej, op. cit.
39. See P. Paret, *French Revolutionary Warfare* (London: Pall Mall Press, 1964).
40. Mendl argues that "from 1954 onwards soldiers and politicians preached the new doctrine of war in which the West, conceived in terms of civilization, defended itself in a constant struggle against the forces of world communism." op. cit., p. 101.
41. See especially the two essays by Gallois in *Pour contre la force de frappe* (Paris: Editions John Didier, 1963) entitled "Chaque puissance nucléaire a deux visages" and "Pierrelatte a ses raisons." See also "The Raison d'Etre of French Defence Policy", *International Affairs,* October 1963, pp. 497-510, and Kohl, op. cit., p. 172.
42. See Beaufre's *Deterrence and Strategy* (London: Faber, 1965) and *Introduction to Strategy* (London: Faber 1965). See also *Nato and Europe* (New York: Knopf, 1966).
43. Many of Aron's articles about the French force and NATO were written for *Le Figaro.* See, for example, "A l'ombre de l'apocalypse nucléaire", 17 August 1966 and "Force nucléaire nationale et Alliance atlantique." See also Kohl, op. cit., p. 175.
44. See General Stehlin's "The Evolution of Western Defence", *Foreign Affairs,* October 1963, pp. 70-83, and "French thoughts on the Alliance", NATO's *Fifteen Nations* (August-September 1964).
45. Press Conference, 23 July 1964. Speeches and Press Conferences No. 208 (France: Ambassade de France), p. 9. See also Gallois, *Balance of Terror* (Boston: Houghton Mifflin Co., 1961).
46. Ibid.
47. See *Survival,* July 1969.
48. See Kohl, op. cit., pp. 162-4 and pp. 265-6.
49. See Ailleret, "Défense 'dirigée' ou défense 'tous azimuts' ", *Revue de défense nationale,* December 1967, pp. 1923-32. The English translation appeared in *Survival,* February 1968, pp. 38-43.
50. Ailleret did not quite go as far as Gallois and argue that all alliances were obsolete, however. See Gallois, op. cit.
51. Ailleret, "Défense 'dirigée' ou défense 'tous azimuts' ", op. cit.
52. Mendl, op. cit., p. 106.
53. *French White Paper on National Defence, 1972* (Ambassade de France, Service de Presse et d'Information).
54. France has a series of Bilateral Security Accords with a number of Black African States.
55. The problems of such 'quick-fix' actions are dealt with in Kolodziej's chapter, op. cit.

56. Kolodziej, ibid., p. 45. Kolodziej maintains that this is true not only of France's conventional capability but also of her nuclear forces as well which are likely to remain in the foreseeable future both small and vulnerable.

57. See Bellini, *French Defence Policy* (London: Royal United Services Institute for Defence Studies, 1974), pp. 56-67.

58. See *The Financial Times*, 8 August 1974.

59. The *Redoubtable* was the first French nuclear submarine which went into service in 1971. The *Terrible* and *Foudroyant*, went into service in 1972 and 1974 respectively. It is hoped that the *Indomptable* and *Tonnant* will be in service before 1980.

60. See Bellini, op. cit.

61. See *The Times*, 10 June 1974.

62. Kolodziej, op. cit., pp. 30-31.

63. See *Evening Standard*, 19 August 1974.

64. *Le Monde*, 21 June 1973.

65. *Evening Standard*, op. cit.

66. In his book, Wolf Mendl highlights the economic implications of French defence policy particularly in terms of the proportion (10%) of scientific manpower absorbed by defence and the detrimental effects on educational and technological progress. *Survival*, op. cit.

67. The 1972 White Paper in particular reveals the recognition of the causal inter-relation of these two environments.

GLOSSARY

ACTIVE DEFENCE usually refers to the interception of an attack by the deployment and use of defensive missiles or airplanes.

ASSURED DESTRUCTION CAPABILITY involves the ability to inflict an unacceptable degree of damage upon an aggressor, even after absorbing a surprise first strike.

AREA DEFENCE refers to the capability of defending valued property over a fairly widespread geographical area.

BALANCE OF TERROR refers to an equilibrium between states based on the possession by each side of weapon systems which allow them to cause unacceptable damage to their opponent(s).

BRINKMANSHIP usually refers to the use of a diplomatic strategy which aims at forcing an opponent to reach a settlement by deliberately creating the risk of nuclear war.

CONTROLLED RESPONSE involves the reply to an enemy attack which is deliberately limited in order to try to persuade an opponent to adopt similar limits and so avoid escalation to a higher level of military activity.

COUNTERFORCE CAPABILITY involves the ability to destroy a sufficient proportion of an enemy's nuclear forces to make the latter's retaliation acceptable.

COUNTERFORCE STRATEGY refers to the targetting of the enemy's retaliatory forces and general military forces, rather than of his population centres.

COUNTERVALUE CAPABILITY involves the ability to destroy an opponent's economic and human resources by attacking his cities.

COUNTERVALUE STRATEGY refers to the targetting of an enemy's cities to hold them as "hostages" in order to deter an attack on one's homeland.

DAMAGE LIMITATION involves the attempt to minimize injury and damage which a nuclear attack might cause if deterrence were to fail.

DETERRENCE involves the adoption of various measures designed to limit one's opponents' freedom of choice among certain policies by raising the cost of some of them to an unacceptable level.

(a) ACTIVE DETERRENCE involves a specific threat to prevent a particular action by an adversary.

(b) EXTENDED DETERRENCE refers to a declared intention to retaliate if a specified third party is attacked.

(c) MINIMUM DETERRENCE involves the attempt to deter an attack through the reliance on a small retaliatory force capable of destroying a small number of an opponent's cities.

ESCALATION is a strategy involving a threat or use of increased violence in the context of Soviet/American confrontation; it is designed to demonstrate commitment by threatening an adversary with the possibility of all-out war.

FAIL-SAFE is a procedure adopted in the United States whereby nuclear delivery vehicles can proceed to their targets only if specific orders to do so are received at a certain time in their flight.

FIRST STRIKE CAPABILITY refers to the possession of a strategic nuclear force which can be launched against an opponent before he initiates an attack but which is vulnerable to enemy destruction.

FLEXIBLE RESPONSE refers to the ability to respond to aggression at the appropriate level through the possession of a wide spectrum of conventional and nuclear forces.

FLEXIBLE ESCALATION refers to the limited ability to respond to aggression at the conventional level and the threat to escalate the conflict by the use of tactical nuclear weapons if and when the conventional defence is overwhelmed.

MASSIVE RETALIATION refers to the strategy adopted by the United States in 1954 which involved the declared intention of responding to any aggression at whatever level by an all-out nuclear attack on the aggressor's homeland.

PASSIVE DEFENCE involves the attempt to absorb an enemy attack by removing targets from offensive reach or protecting them *in situ* against the effects of nuclear explosions.

PRE-EMPTIVE STRIKE involves the launching of a nuclear attack in anticipation of an opponent's decision to resort to nuclear war.

SECOND STRIKE CAPABILITY refers to the possession of an invulnerable nuclear force capable of retaliating against an aggressor even after a surprise first strike.

STRATEGIC NUCLEAR PARITY refers to a relationship of rough equality between opposing nuclear forces, measured in terms of the number of launch vehicles, warheads or megatonnage.

STRATEGIC NUCLEAR SUFFICIENCY is a term used by American security planners to refer to a situation in which the United States possesses the capability to (a) maintain an adequate retaliatory force to deter a surprise attack on US strategic forces; (b) provide no incentive for the Soviet Union to strike the US first in a crisis and (c) prevent the Soviet Union from gaining the ability to cause considerably greater urban/industrial destruction than the United States could inflict on the USSR in a nuclear war.[1]

1. For a far more detailed description of the "jargon" and technical language of strategic studies see E. Luttwak, *A Dictionary of Modern War* (London: Allen Lane, The Penguin Press, 1971); I. Smart, "Advanced Strategic Missiles: A Short Guide", *Adelphi Papers*, No. 63, December 1969; and Kintner and Pfaltzgraff, *SALT: implications for Arms Control in the 1970s* (University of Pittsburgh Press, 1973), pp. 423-9 Urs Schwartz and Laszlo Hadik, *Strategic terminology: a trilingual glossary,* (New York: Praeger, 1966).

ABBREVIATIONS

AAM	air-to-air missile		ICBM	intercontinental ballistic missile
ABM	anti-ballistic missile		IRBM	intermediate-range ballistic missile
ADM	atomic demolition mine			
AEW	airborne early warning		KT	kiloton
AMF	Allied Mobile Force		MAD	Mutual Assured Destruction
ANZAM	Australia, New Zealand, and Malaya		MARV	Manoeuverable Re-entry Vehicle
ANF	Atlantic Nuclear Force		MBFR	mutual balanced force reductions
ARVN	Army of (South) Vietnam			
ASEAN	Association of South-East Asian Nations		MIRV	multiple independently targetable re-entry vehicle
ASM	air-to-surface missiles		MLF	Multilateral Force
ASROC	anti-submarine rocket		MRBM	medium-range ballistic missile
ASW	anti-submarine warfare			
BAOR	British Army of the Rhine		MRCA	multiple role combat aircraft
BMD	ballistic missile defence		MRV	multiple re-entry vehicle
CENTO	Central Treaty Organization		MT	megaton
CEA	Commissariat a l'Energie Atomique		NATO	North Atlantic Treaty Organization
CEP	circular error probable		NLF	National Liberation Front (of South Vietnam)
COMECON	Council for Mutual Economic Aid		NPT	Non-Proliferation Treaty
CPSU	Communist Party of the Soviet Union		OTH	over-the-horizon-radar
			PLA	People's Liberation Army
CVA	attack aircraft carrier		RV	re-entry vehicle
CVAN	nuclear-power attack carrier		SAC	Strategic Air Command
DOT	Defense Operationnelle du Territoire		SALT	Strategic Arms Limitation Talks
ECM	electronic counter-measures		SEATO	South-East Asia Treaty Organization
EDC	European Defence Community		SLBM	submarine-launched ballistic missile
EEC	European Economic Community		SRAM	short-range attack missile
ESC	European Security Conference		SSBN	nuclear-powered, missile-firing submarine
FBS	forward-based nuclear delivery systems		STOL	short take-off and landing
ENS	Force Nucleaire Stratégique		TNT	Tri-nitro-toluene
FOBS	fractional orbital bombard-ment system		ULMS	undersea long-range missile system
GCD	general and complete disarmament		VLF	very low frequency
GVN	government of (South) Vietnam		VTOL	vertical take-off and landing
IAEA	International Atomic Energy Agency		WEU	Western European Union

INDEX